RADIANT

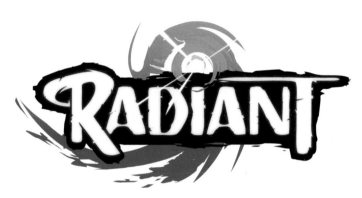

TONY VALENTE

CONTENTS

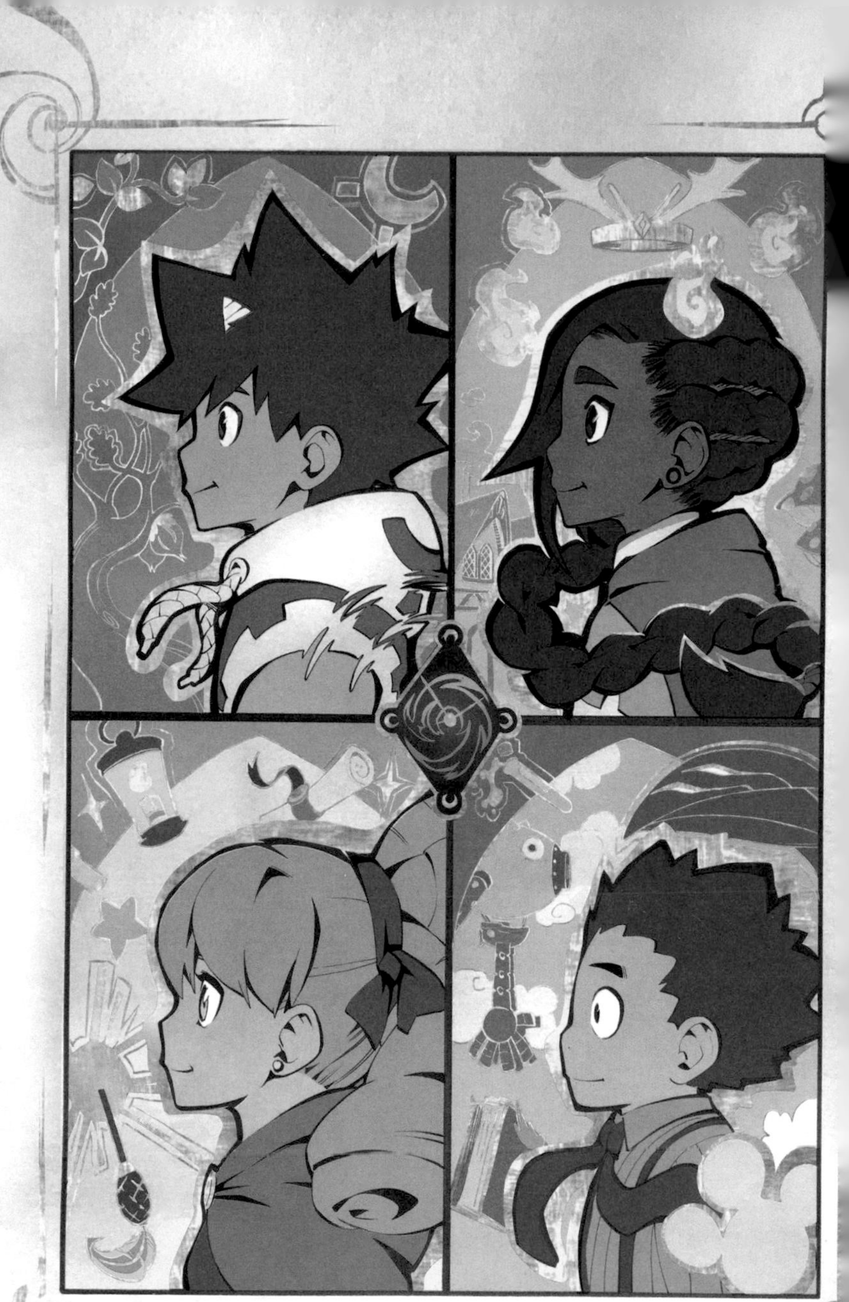

Summary of the previous volume:

While trying to protect the people of Bôme against the Domitors' sudden attack, our band of friends is once again split up! Mélie has suffered a personality change and has joined up with the Domitors, Doc is still stuck in the Inquisitor Academy, and Ocoho has had to team up with Lupa and Diabal to help her rescue Mélie. Seth, meanwhile, is also in a serious predicament with no aces left up his sleeve, imprisoned as he is by the Inquisition in their most heavily guarded tower, with a troupe of Nemeses booked on his skin and his powers gradually being siphoned out of him. Dragunov, however, is convinced Seth is innocent. Trying to reason with Torque to deal with the Inquisition's incessant pursuit of Infected, he ends up admitting to having killed Konrad, which Torque regards an absolute act of treason! In a fit of rage, Torque introduces Dragunov to his sword...

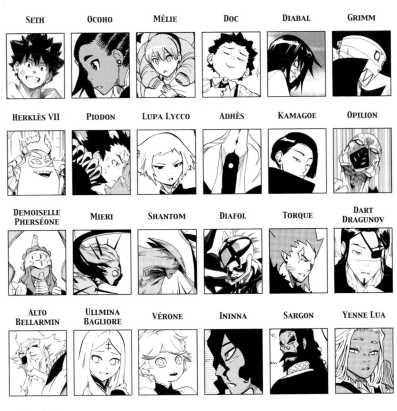

Seth

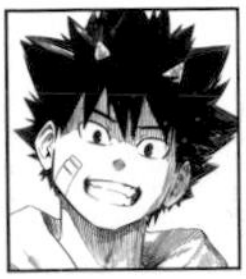

Ocoho

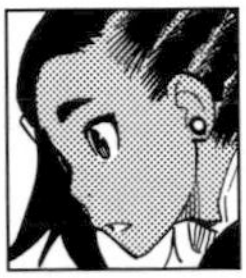

Mélie

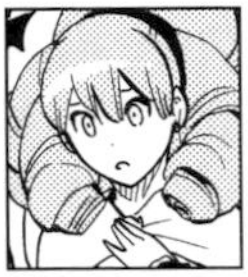

Doc

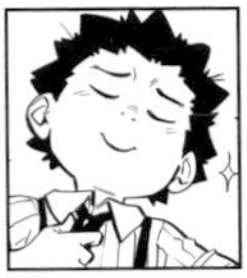

Diabal

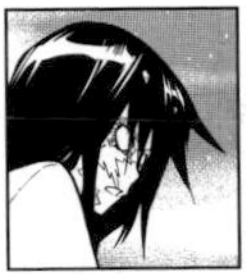

Grimm

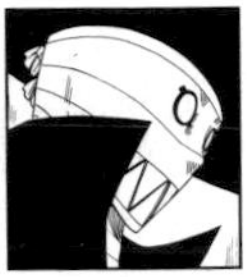

Herklès VII

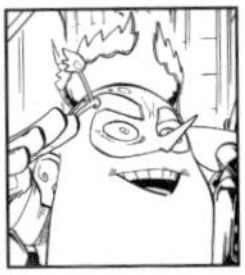

Piodon

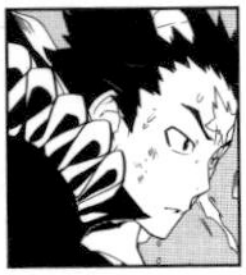

Lupa Lycco

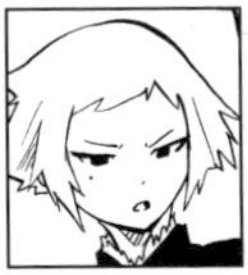

Adhès

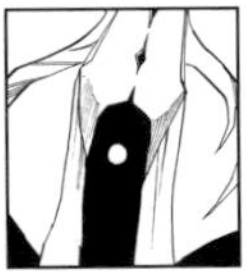

Kamagoe

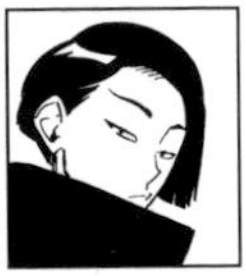

Opilion

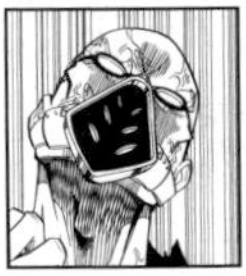

Demoiselle Pherséone

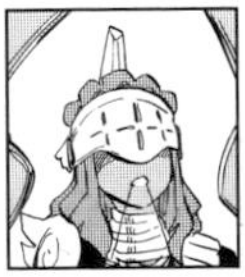

Mieri

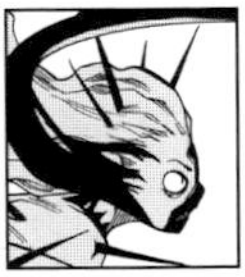

Shantom

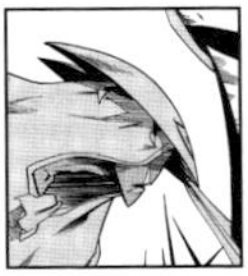

Diafol

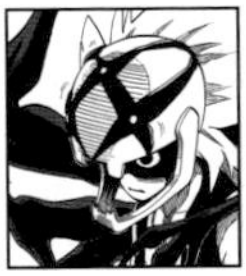

Torque

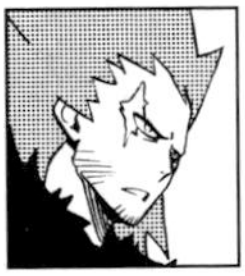

Dart Dragunov

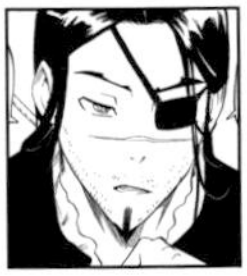

Alto Bellarmin

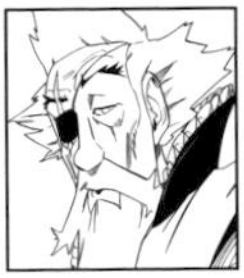

Ullmina Bagliore

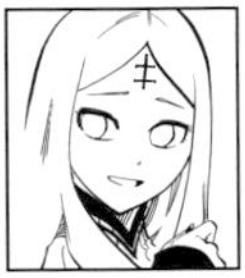

Vérone

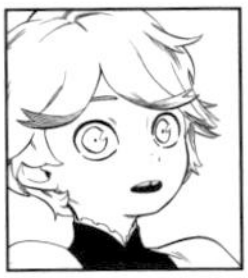

Ininna

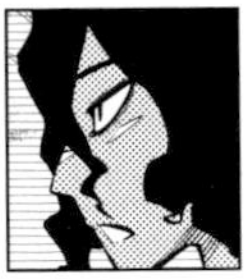

Sargon

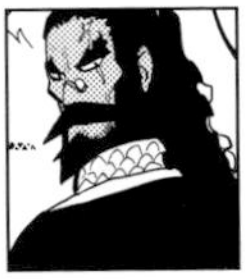

Yenne Lua

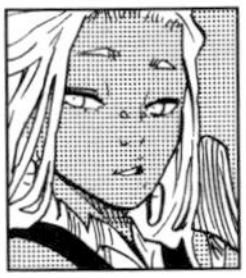

Enga Lua

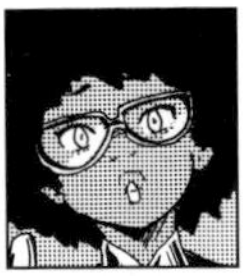

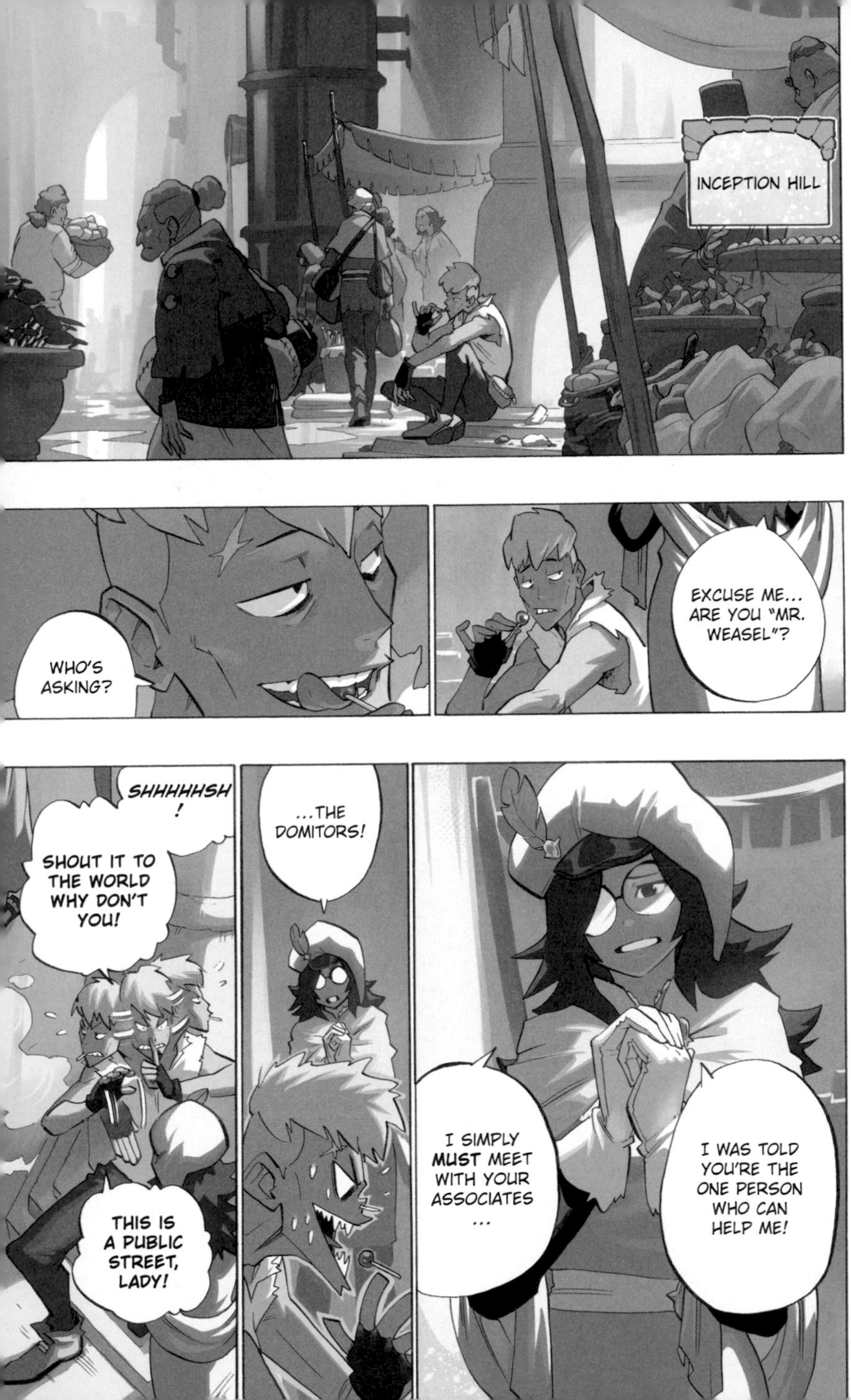
INCEPTION HILL
EXCUSE ME... ARE YOU "MR. WEASEL"?
WHO'S ASKING?
I WAS TOLD YOU'RE THE ONE PERSON WHO CAN HELP ME!
I SIMPLY **MUST** MEET WITH YOUR ASSOCIATES ...
...THE DOMITORS!
SHHHHHSH!
SHOUT IT TO THE WORLD WHY DON'T YOU!
THIS IS A PUBLIC STREET, LADY!

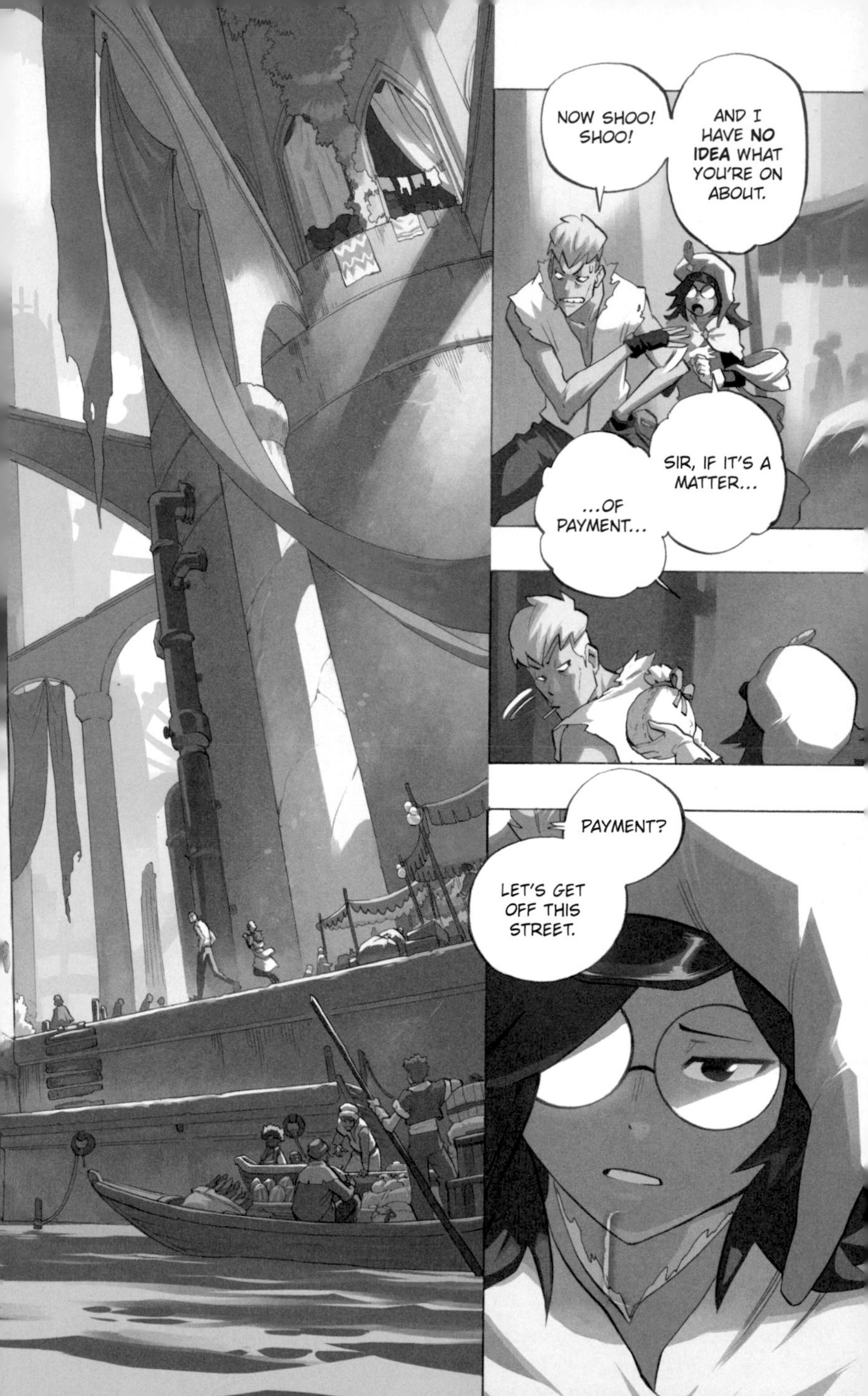
AND I HAVE **NO IDEA** WHAT YOU'RE ON ABOUT.
NOW SHOO! SHOO!
SIR, IF IT'S A MATTER...
...OF PAYMENT...
PAYMENT?
LET'S GET OFF THIS STREET.

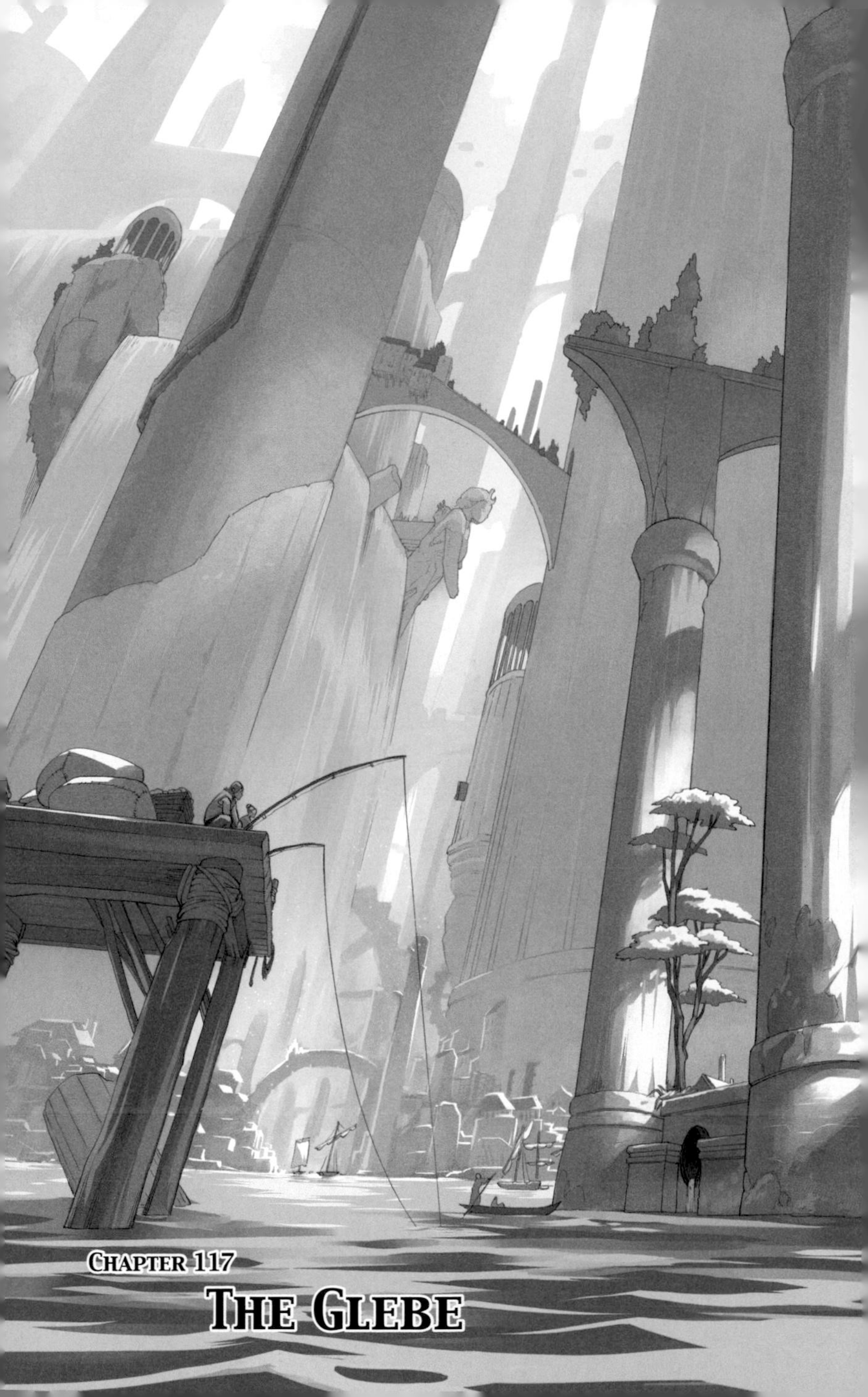
CHAPTER 117
THE GLEBE

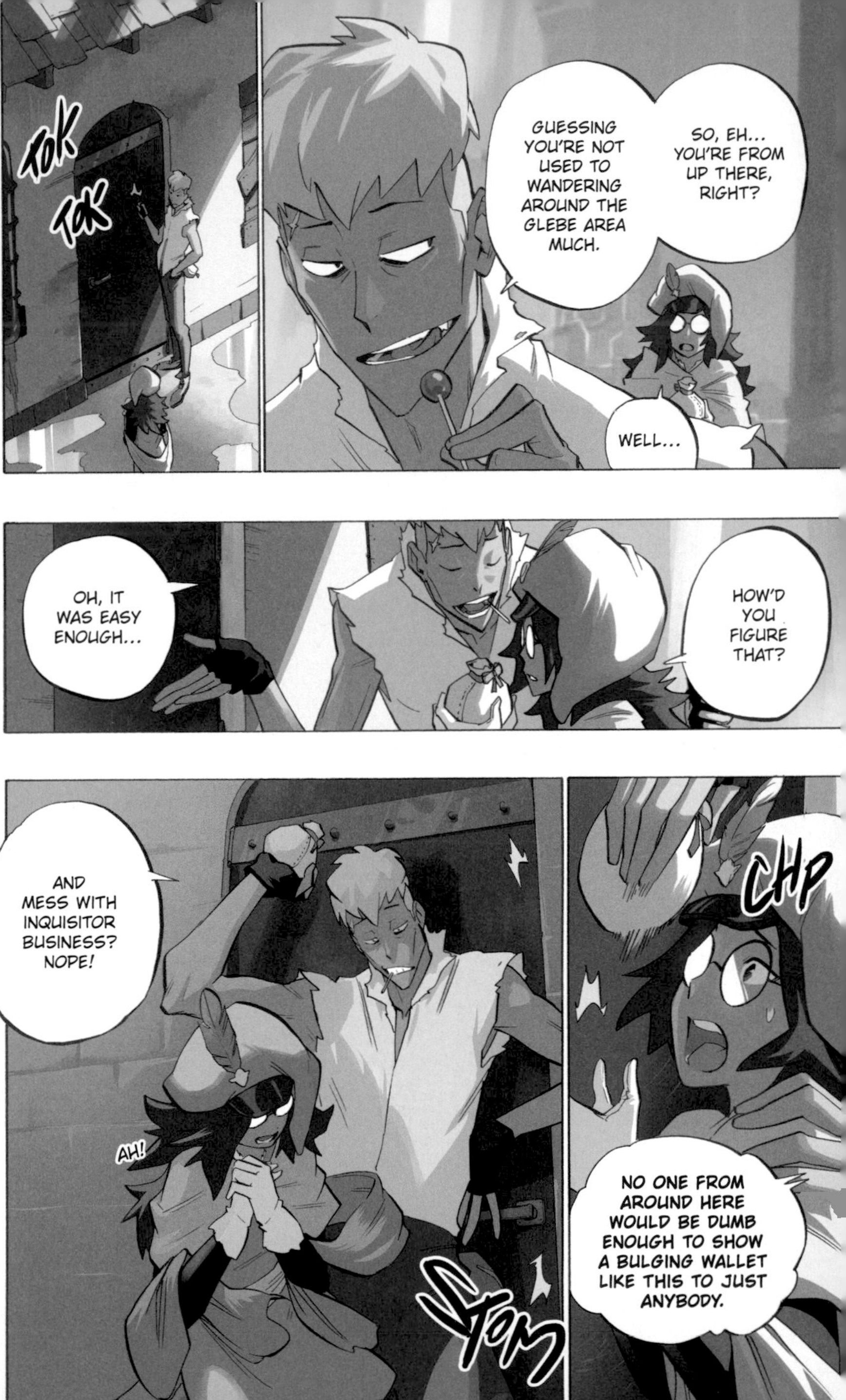
SO, EH... YOU'RE FROM UP THERE, RIGHT?
GUESSING YOU'RE NOT USED TO WANDERING AROUND THE GLEBE AREA MUCH.
WELL...
TOK TOK
HOW'D YOU FIGURE THAT?
OH, IT WAS EASY ENOUGH...
CHP
NO ONE FROM AROUND HERE WOULD BE DUMB ENOUGH TO SHOW A BULGING WALLET LIKE THIS TO JUST ANYBODY.
AND MESS WITH INQUISITOR BUSINESS? NOPE!
AH!
STOM

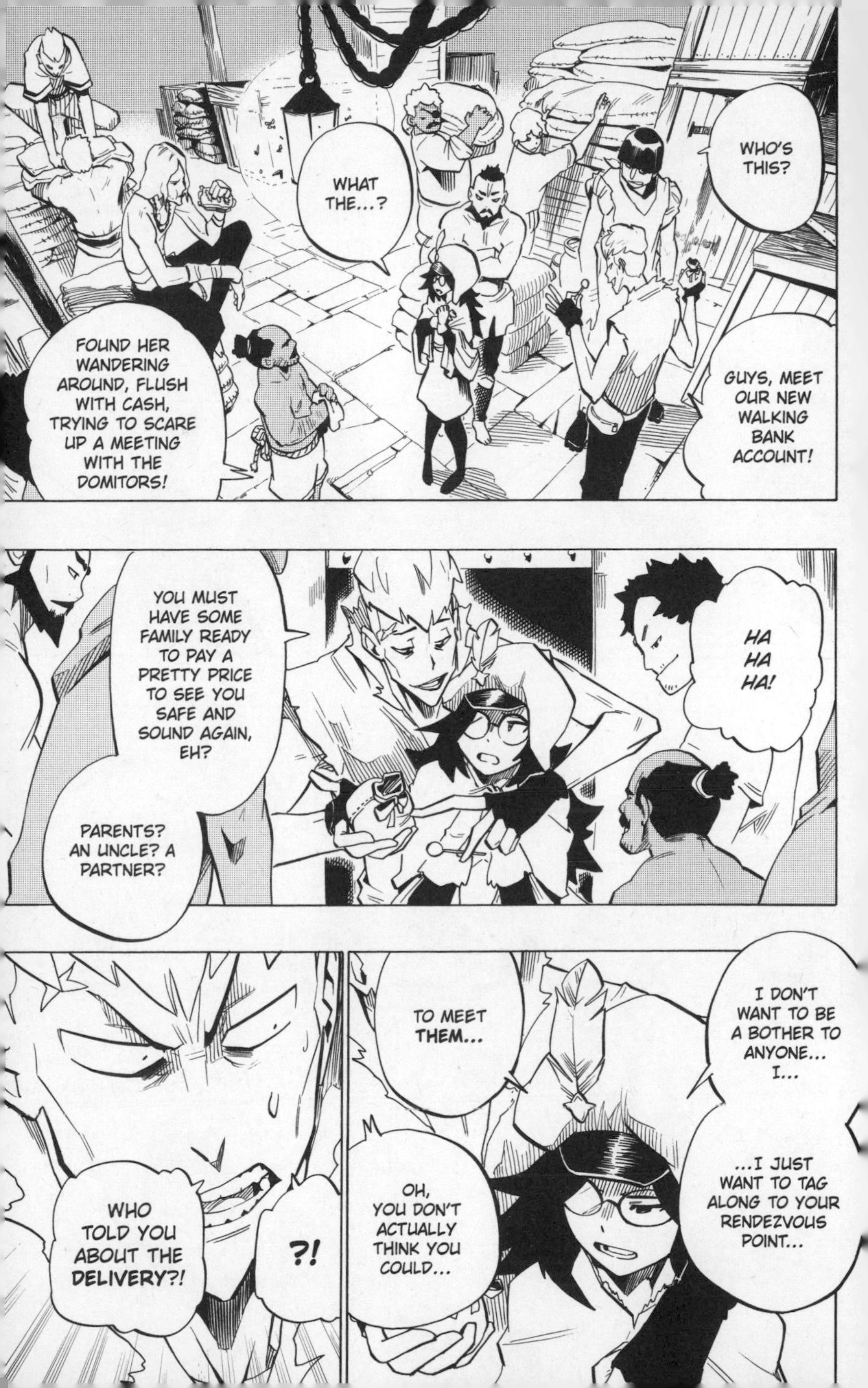
WHO'S THIS?
WHAT THE...?
GUYS, MEET OUR NEW WALKING BANK ACCOUNT!
FOUND HER WANDERING AROUND, FLUSH WITH CASH, TRYING TO SCARE UP A MEETING WITH THE DOMITORS!
HA HA HA!
YOU MUST HAVE SOME FAMILY READY TO PAY A PRETTY PRICE TO SEE YOU SAFE AND SOUND AGAIN, EH?
PARENTS? AN UNCLE? A PARTNER?
I DON'T WANT TO BE A BOTHER TO ANYONE... I...
...I JUST WANT TO TAG ALONG TO YOUR RENDEZVOUS POINT...
TO MEET THEM...
OH, YOU DON'T ACTUALLY THINK YOU COULD...
?!
WHO TOLD YOU ABOUT THE DELIVERY?!

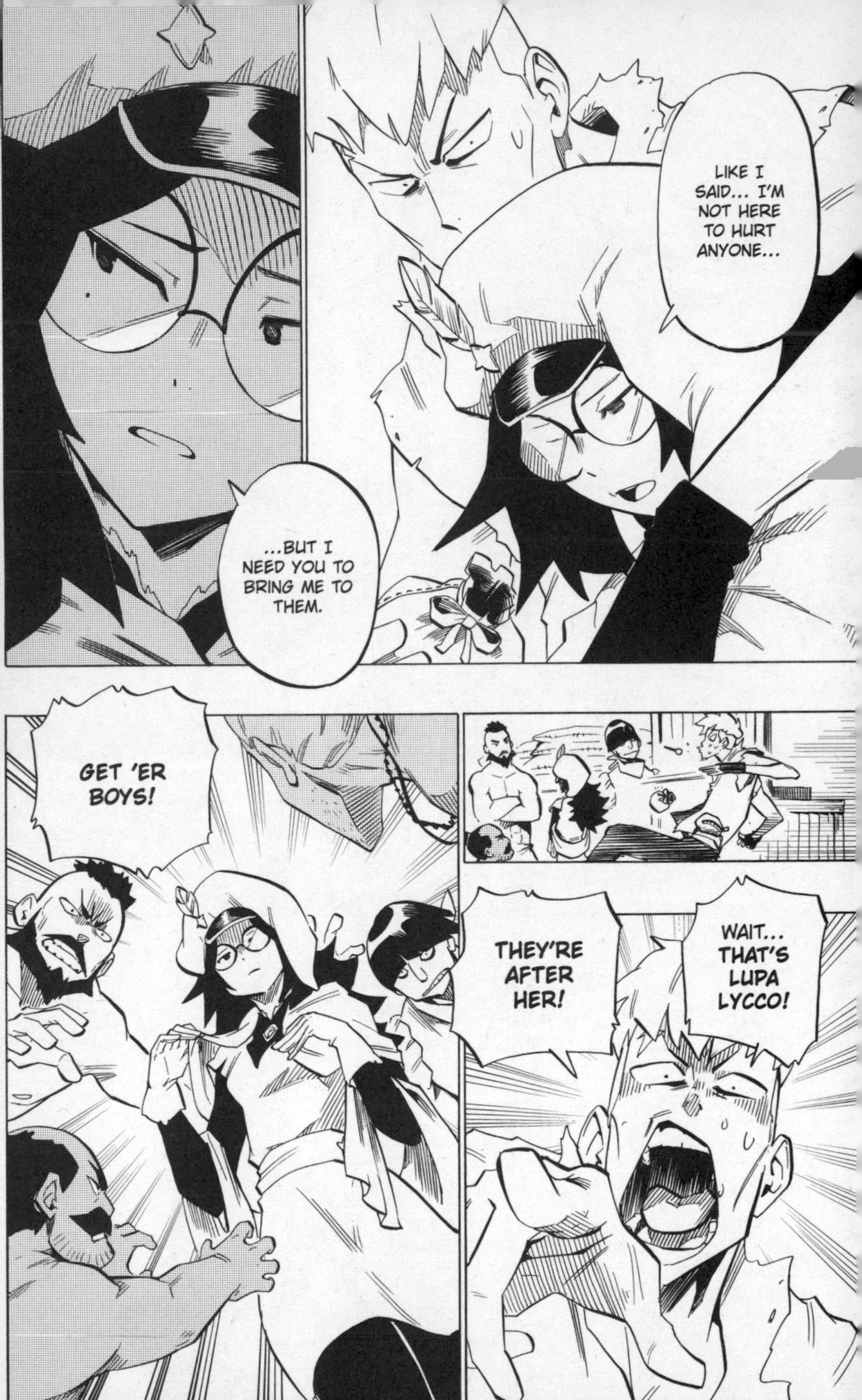
LIKE I SAID... I'M NOT HERE TO HURT ANYONE...
...BUT I NEED YOU TO BRING ME TO THEM.
WAIT... THAT'S LUPA LYCCO!
THEY'RE AFTER HER!
GET 'ER BOYS!

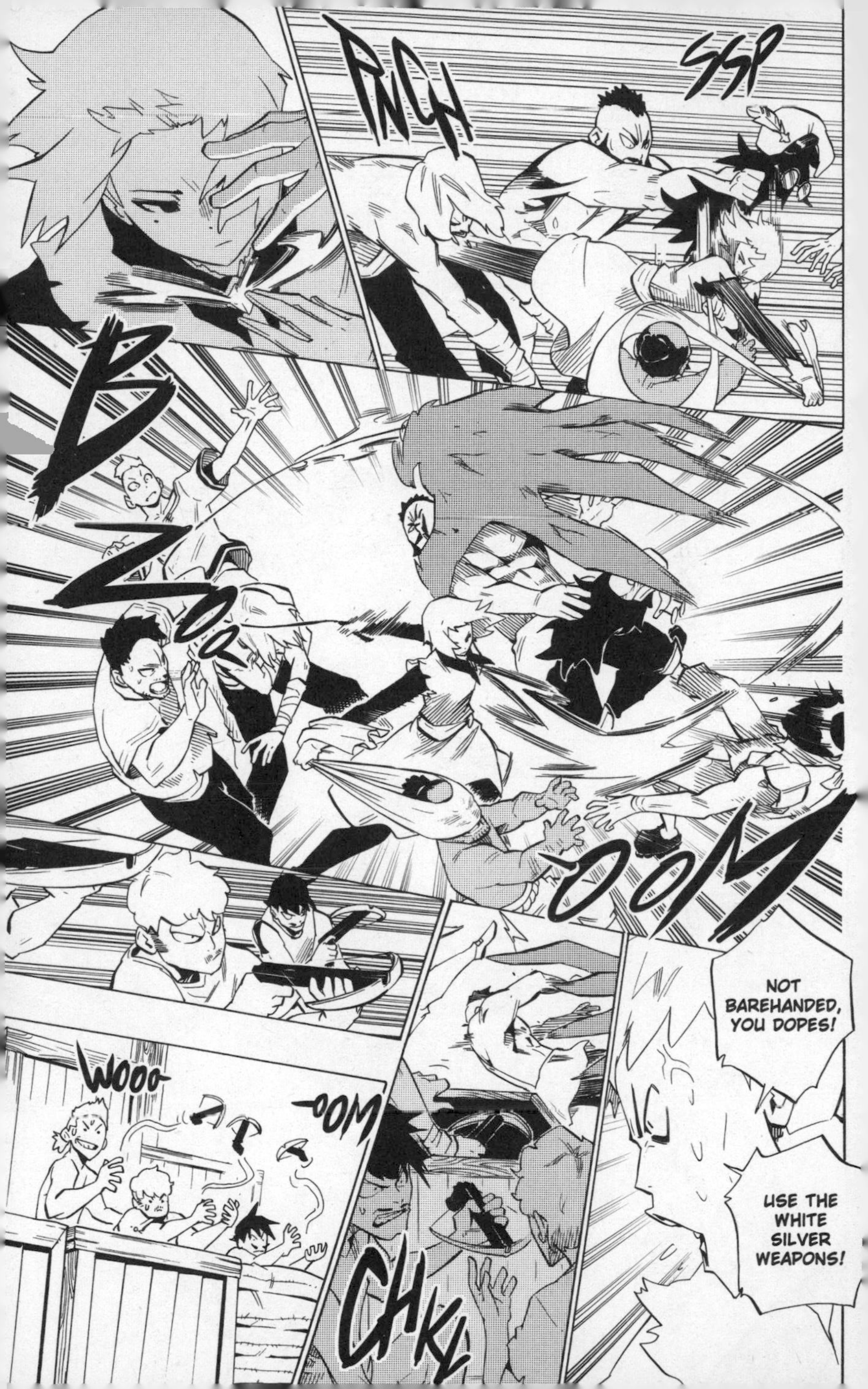
SSIP
PNCH
B
ZOOOOOM
NOT BAREHANDED, YOU DOPES!
USE THE WHITE SILVER WEAPONS!
CHK
WOOO
-OOM

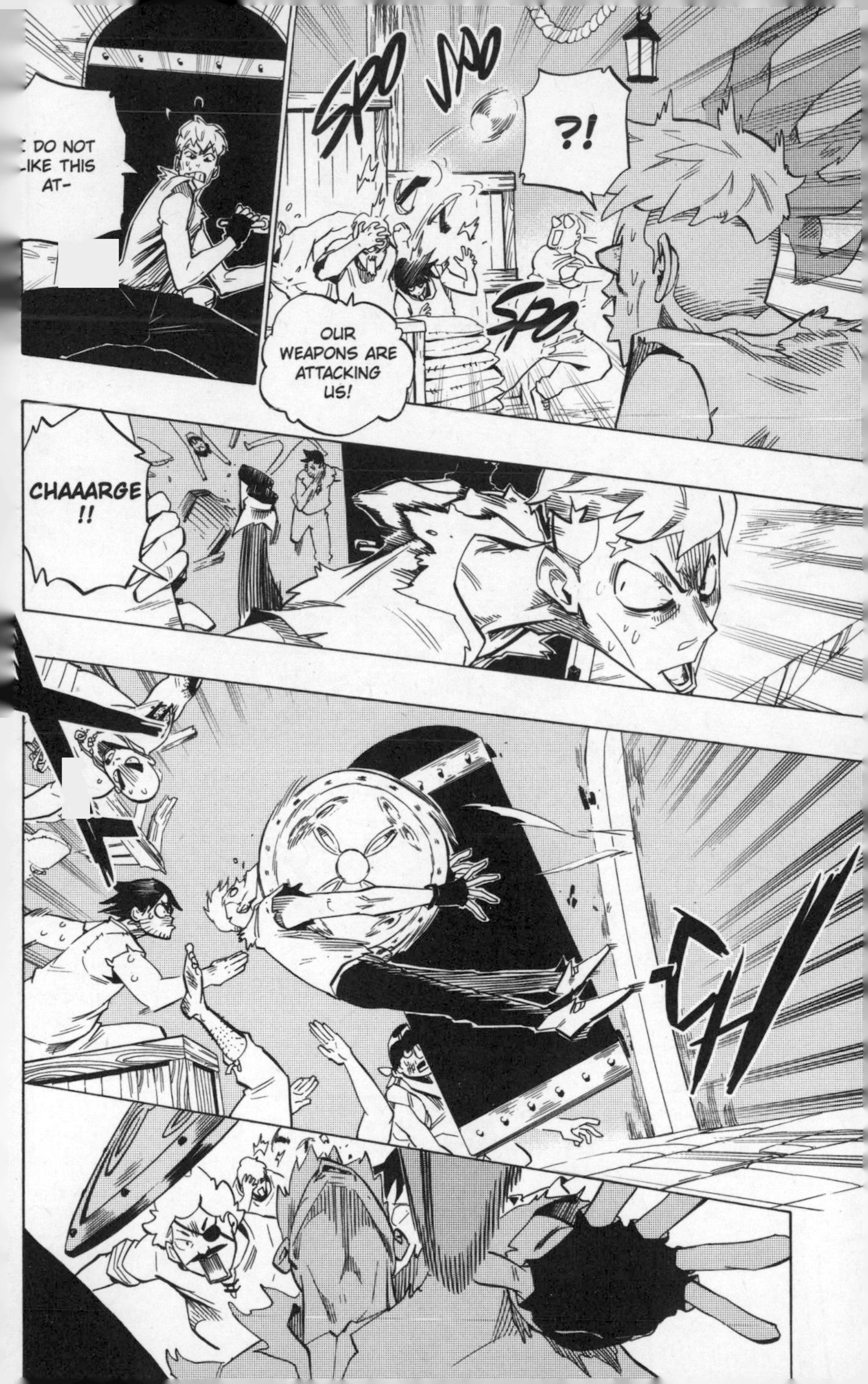
SPO SPO
?!
SPO
OUR WEAPONS ARE ATTACKING US!
DO NOT LIKE THIS AT-
CHAAARGE!!
CH

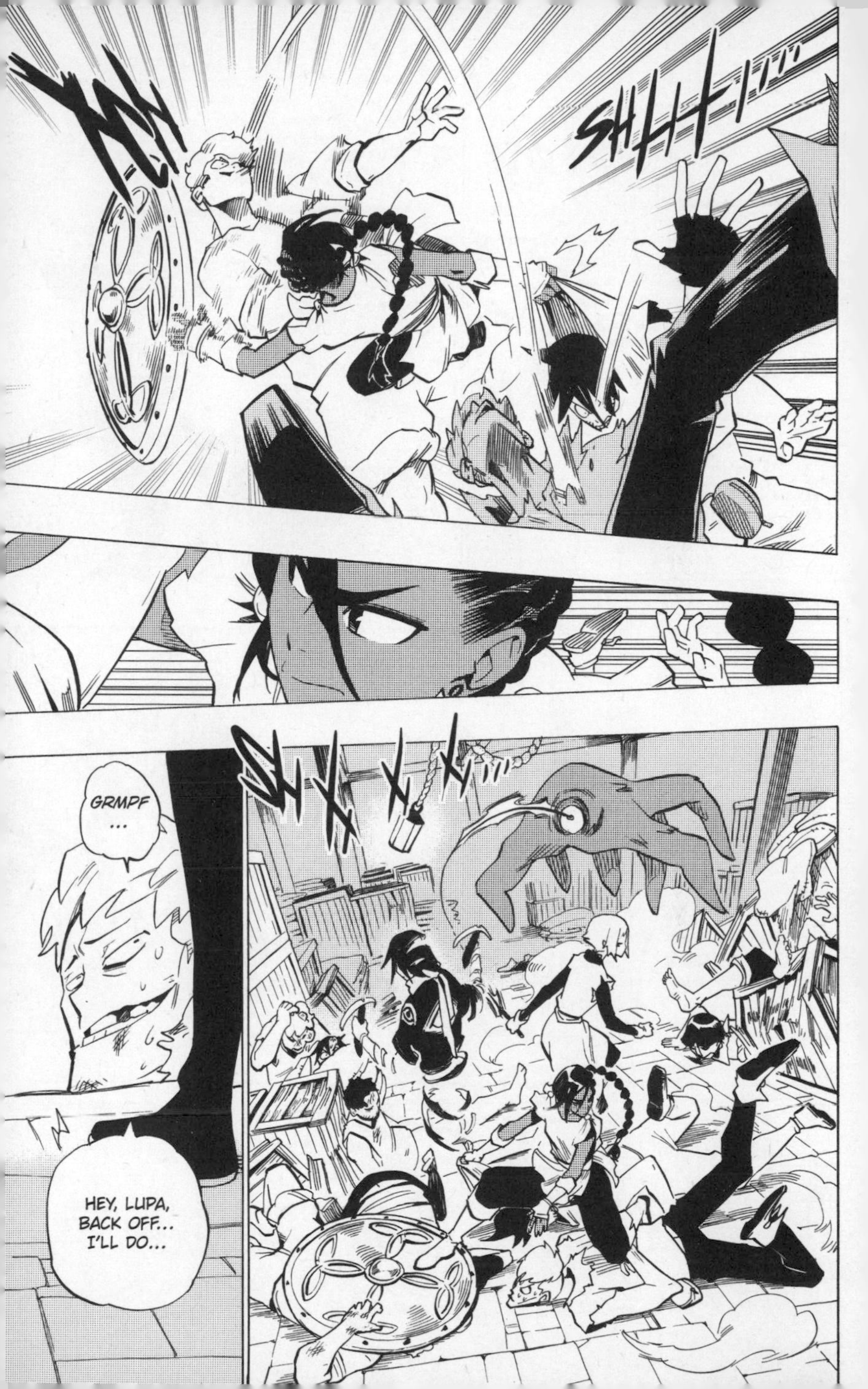
SHHHH...
SHHHH...
GRMPF ...
HEY, LUPA, BACK OFF... I'LL DO...

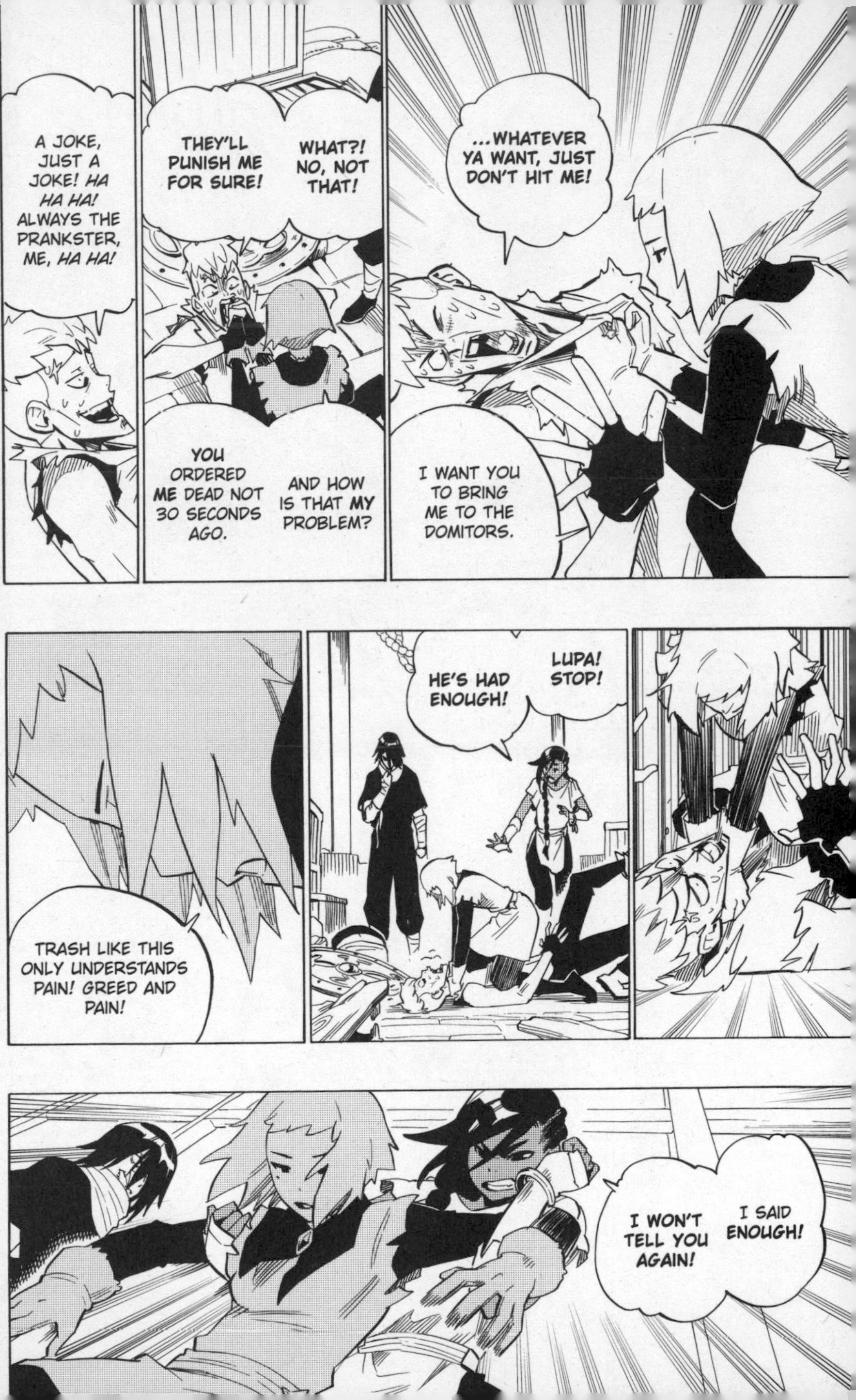
...WHATEVER YA WANT, JUST DON'T HIT ME!
I WANT YOU TO BRING ME TO THE DOMITORS.
WHAT?! NO, NOT THAT!
THEY'LL PUNISH ME FOR SURE!
AND HOW IS THAT MY PROBLEM?
YOU ORDERED ME DEAD NOT 30 SECONDS AGO.
A JOKE, JUST A JOKE! HA HA HA! ALWAYS THE PRANKSTER, ME, HA HA!
LUPA! STOP!
HE'S HAD ENOUGH!
TRASH LIKE THIS ONLY UNDERSTANDS PAIN! GREED AND PAIN!
I SAID ENOUGH!
I WON'T TELL YOU AGAIN!

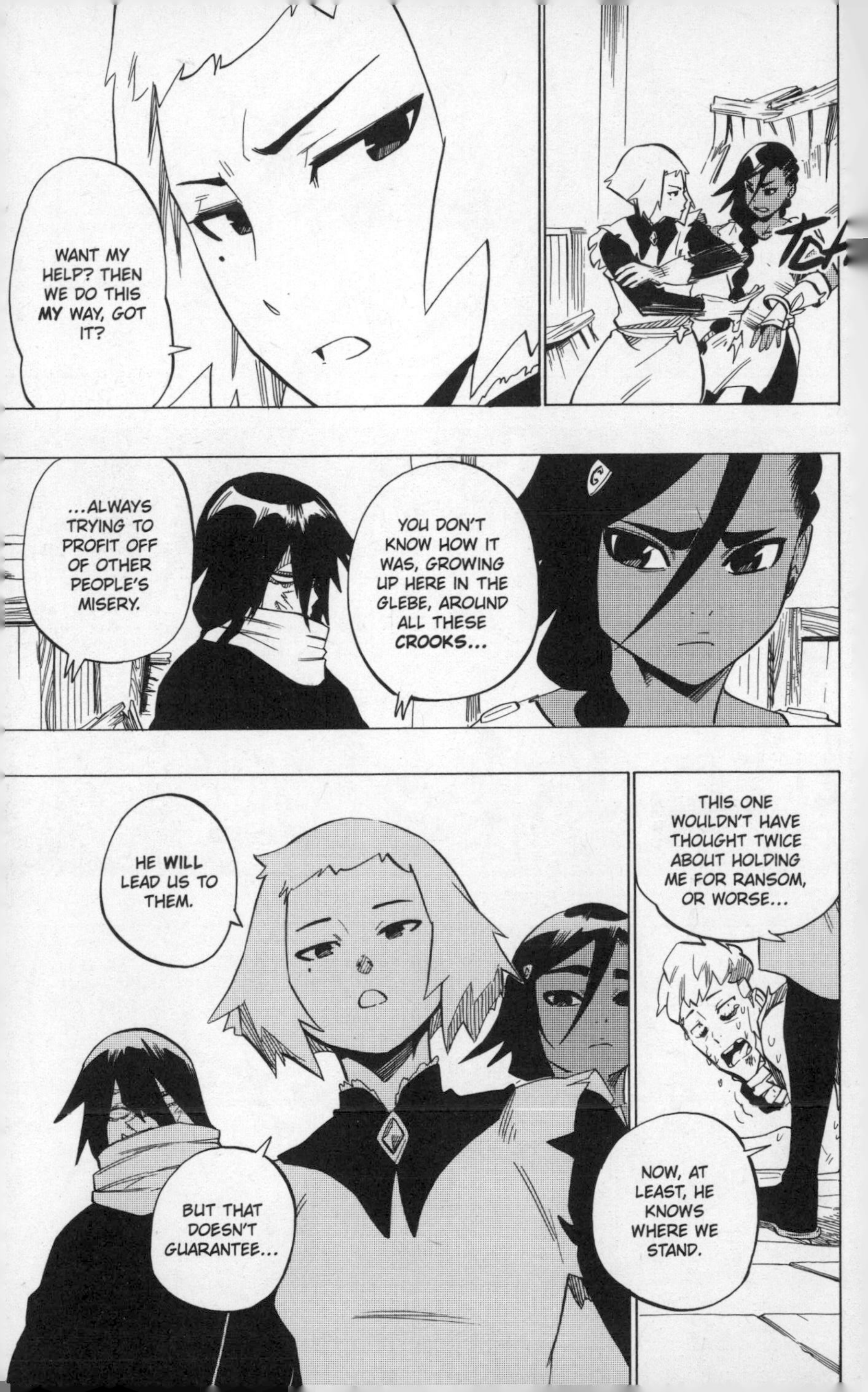
TCH
WANT MY HELP? THEN WE DO THIS MY WAY, GOT IT?
YOU DON'T KNOW HOW IT WAS, GROWING UP HERE IN THE GLEBE, AROUND ALL THESE CROOKS...
...ALWAYS TRYING TO PROFIT OFF OF OTHER PEOPLE'S MISERY.
THIS ONE WOULDN'T HAVE THOUGHT TWICE ABOUT HOLDING ME FOR RANSOM, OR WORSE...
NOW, AT LEAST, HE KNOWS WHERE WE STAND.
HE WILL LEAD US TO THEM.
BUT THAT DOESN'T GUARANTEE...

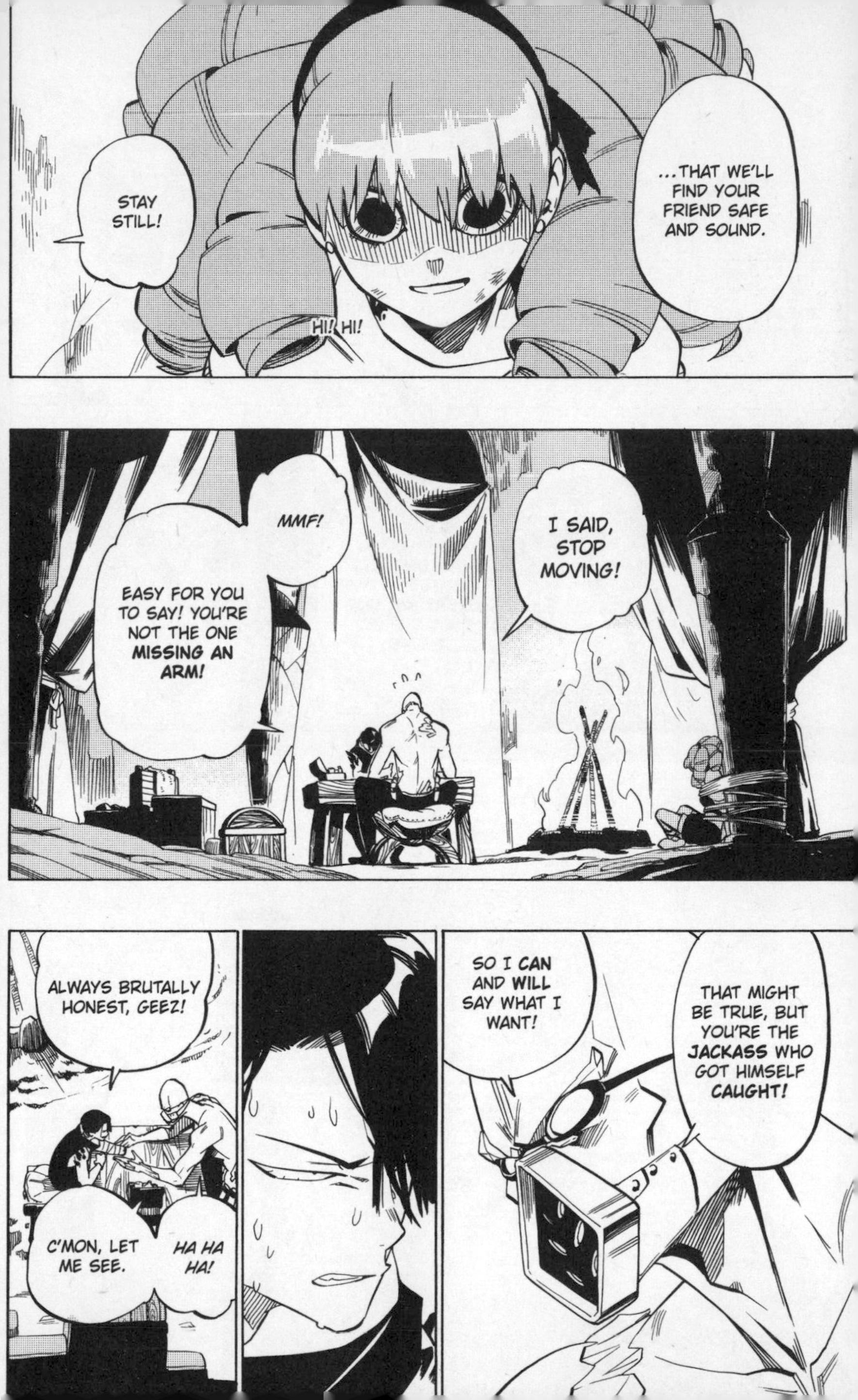
...THAT WE'LL FIND YOUR FRIEND SAFE AND SOUND.
STAY STILL!
HI! HI!
I SAID, STOP MOVING!
MMF!
EASY FOR YOU TO SAY! YOU'RE NOT THE ONE MISSING AN ARM!
THAT MIGHT BE TRUE, BUT YOU'RE THE JACKASS WHO GOT HIMSELF CAUGHT!
SO I CAN AND WILL SAY WHAT I WANT!
ALWAYS BRUTALLY HONEST, GEEZ!
HA HA HA HA!
C'MON, LET ME SEE.

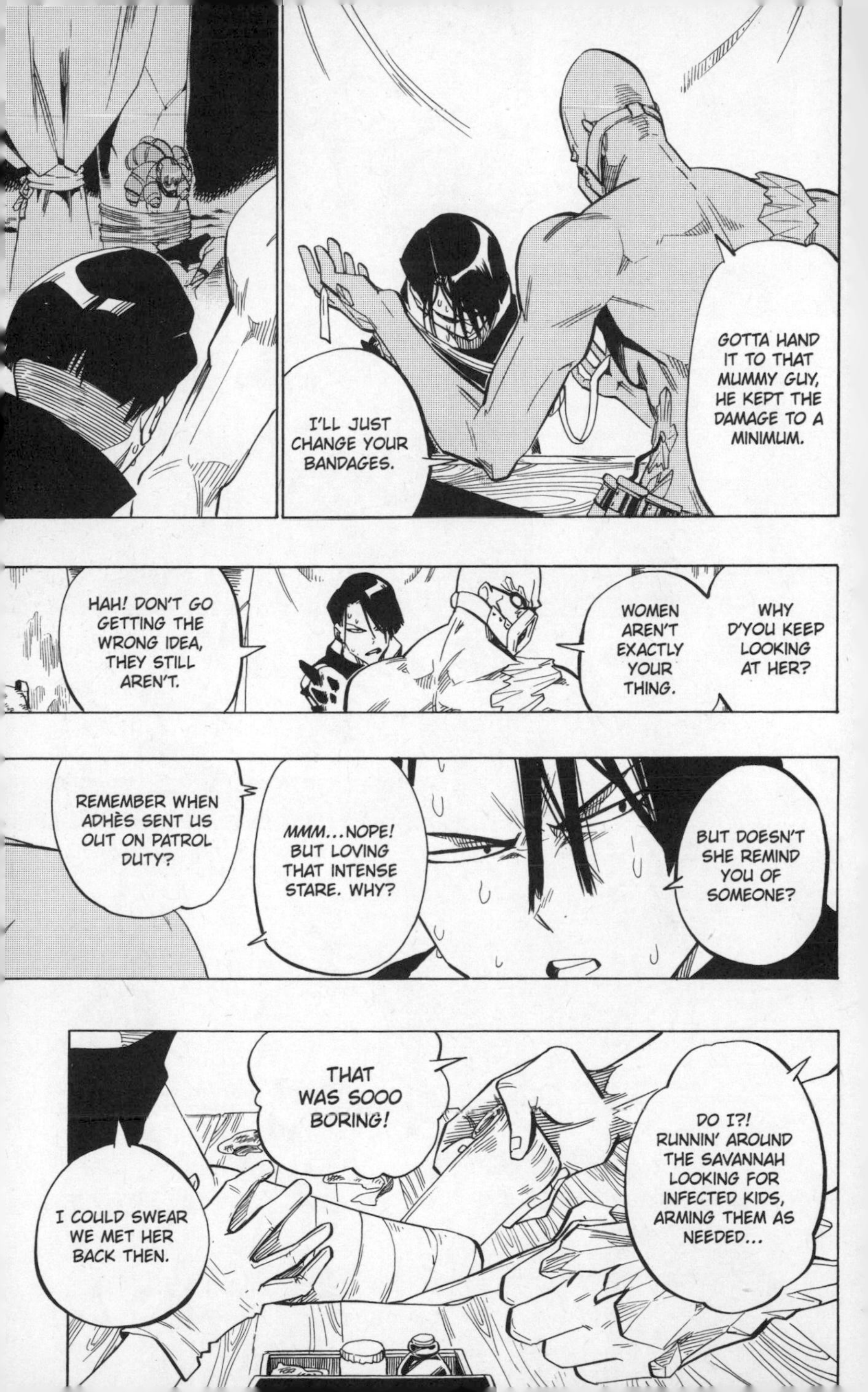
GOTTA HAND IT TO THAT MUMMY GUY, HE KEPT THE DAMAGE TO A MINIMUM.
I'LL JUST CHANGE YOUR BANDAGES.
WHY D'YOU KEEP LOOKING AT HER?
WOMEN AREN'T EXACTLY YOUR THING.
HAH! DON'T GO GETTING THE WRONG IDEA, THEY STILL AREN'T.
BUT DOESN'T SHE REMIND YOU OF SOMEONE?
MMM...NOPE! BUT LOVING THAT INTENSE STARE. WHY?
REMEMBER WHEN ADHÈS SENT US OUT ON PATROL DUTY?
DO I?! RUNNIN' AROUND THE SAVANNAH LOOKING FOR INFECTED KIDS, ARMING THEM AS NEEDED...
THAT WAS SOOO BORING!
I COULD SWEAR WE MET HER BACK THEN.

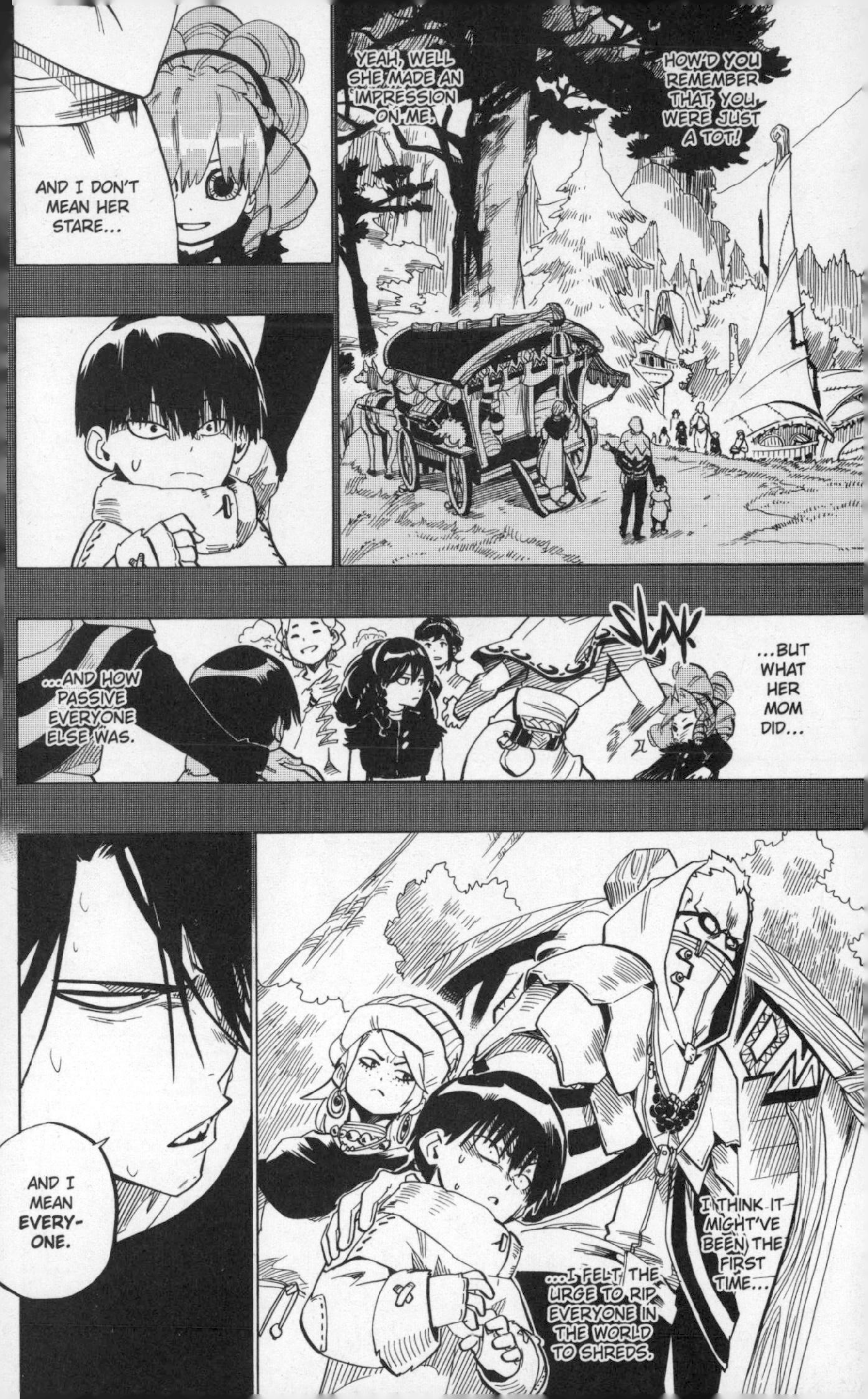
HOW'D YOU REMEMBER THAT, YOU WERE JUST A TOT!
YEAH, WELL SHE MADE AN IMPRESSION ON ME.
AND I DON'T MEAN HER STARE...
...BUT WHAT HER MOM DID...
SLAK
...AND HOW PASSIVE EVERYONE ELSE WAS.
I THINK IT MIGHT'VE BEEN THE FIRST TIME...
...I FELT THE URGE TO RIP EVERYONE IN THE WORLD TO SHREDS.
AND I MEAN EVERY-ONE.

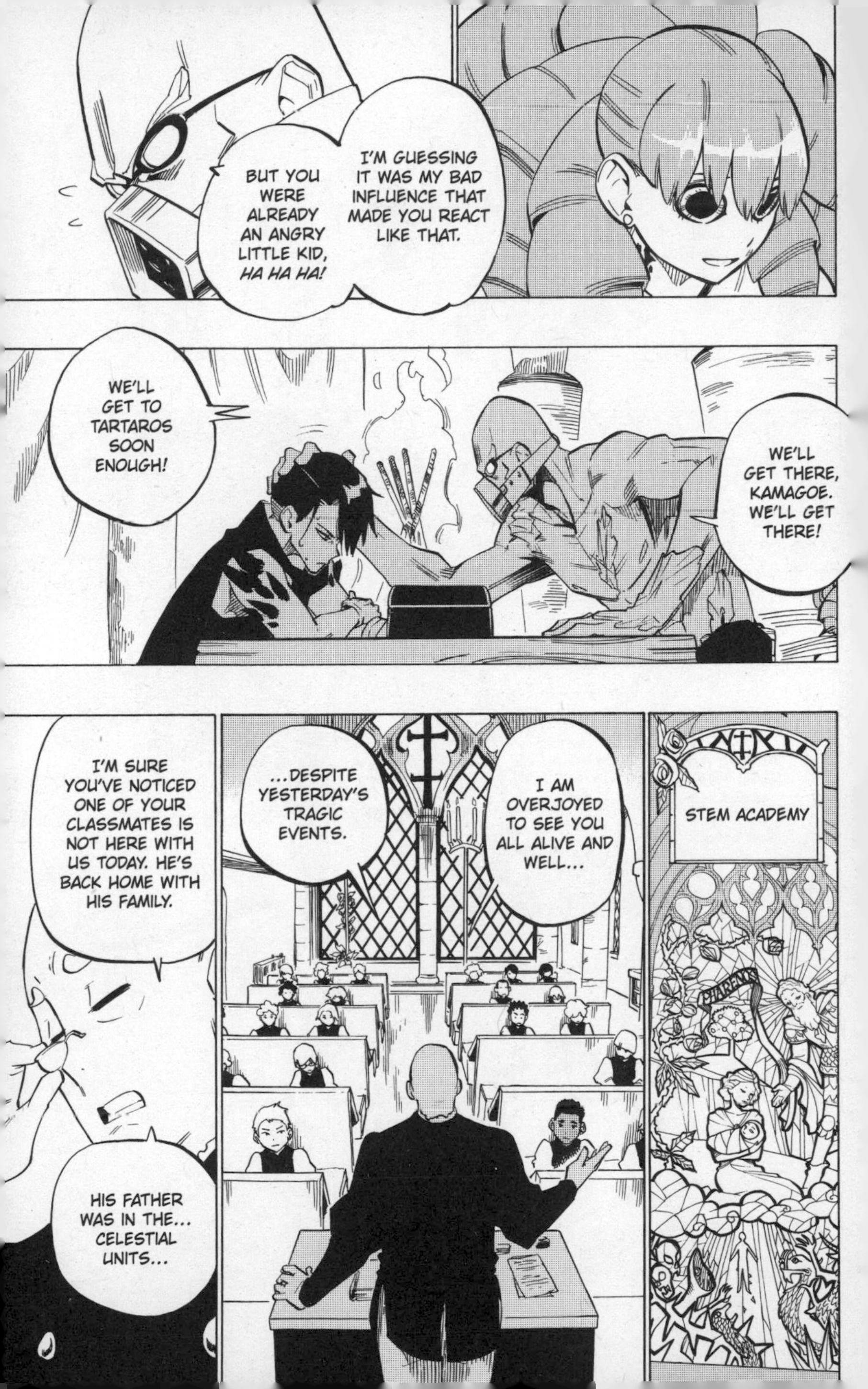
I'M GUESSING IT WAS MY BAD INFLUENCE THAT MADE YOU REACT LIKE THAT.
BUT YOU WERE ALREADY AN ANGRY LITTLE KID, *HA HA HA!*
WE'LL GET THERE, KAMAGOE. WE'LL GET THERE!
WE'LL GET TO TARTAROS SOON ENOUGH!
STEM ACADEMY
I AM OVERJOYED TO SEE YOU ALL ALIVE AND WELL...
...DESPITE YESTERDAY'S TRAGIC EVENTS.
I'M SURE YOU'VE NOTICED ONE OF YOUR CLASSMATES IS NOT HERE WITH US TODAY. HE'S BACK HOME WITH HIS FAMILY.
HIS FATHER WAS IN THE... CELESTIAL UNITS...

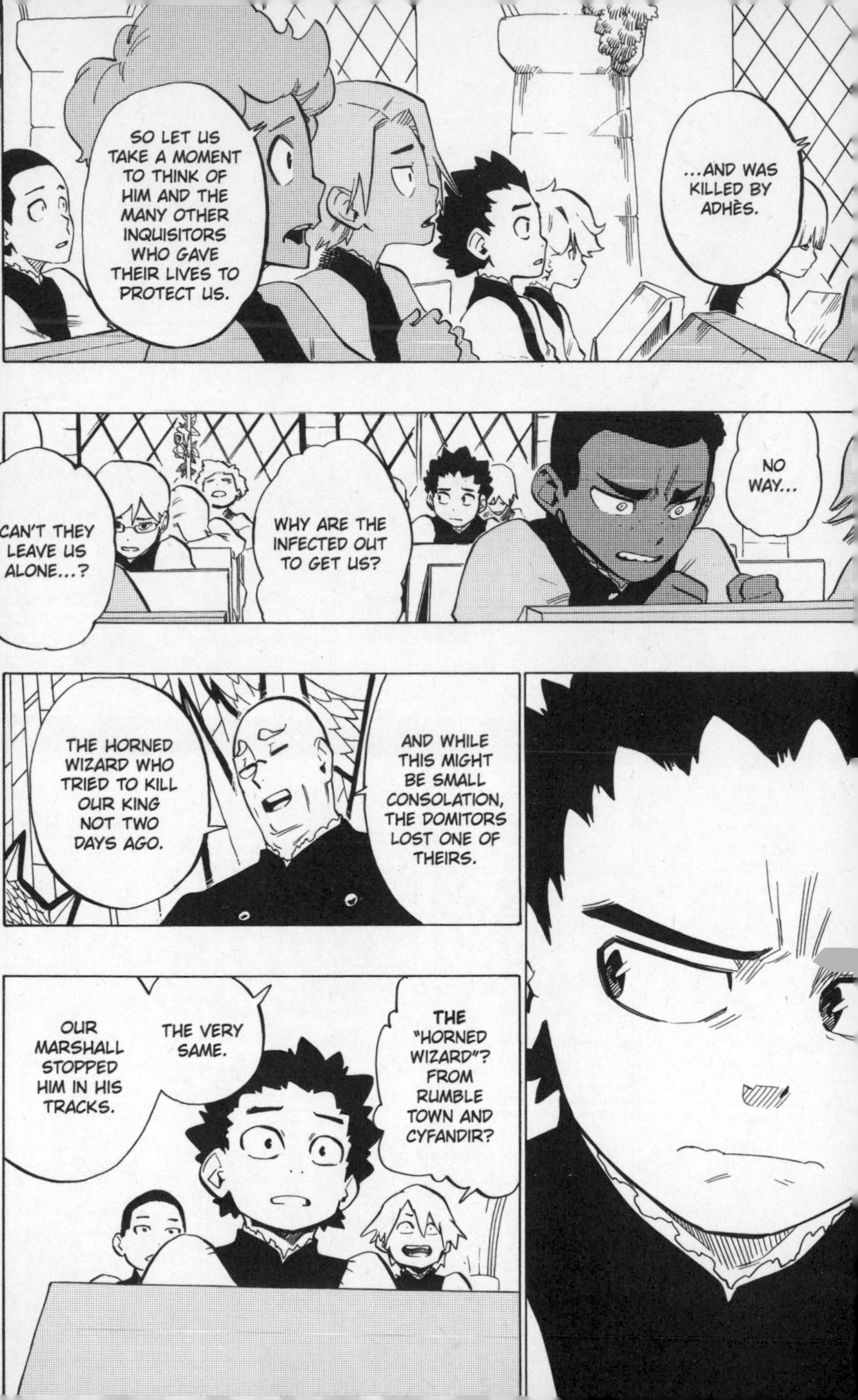
...AND WAS KILLED BY ADHÈS.
SO LET US TAKE A MOMENT TO THINK OF HIM AND THE MANY OTHER INQUISITORS WHO GAVE THEIR LIVES TO PROTECT US.
NO WAY...
WHY ARE THE INFECTED OUT TO GET US?
CAN'T THEY LEAVE US ALONE...?
AND WHILE THIS MIGHT BE SMALL CONSOLATION, THE DOMITORS LOST ONE OF THEIRS.
THE HORNED WIZARD WHO TRIED TO KILL OUR KING NOT TWO DAYS AGO.
THE "HORNED WIZARD"? FROM RUMBLE TOWN AND CYFANDIR?
THE VERY SAME.
OUR MARSHALL STOPPED HIM IN HIS TRACKS.

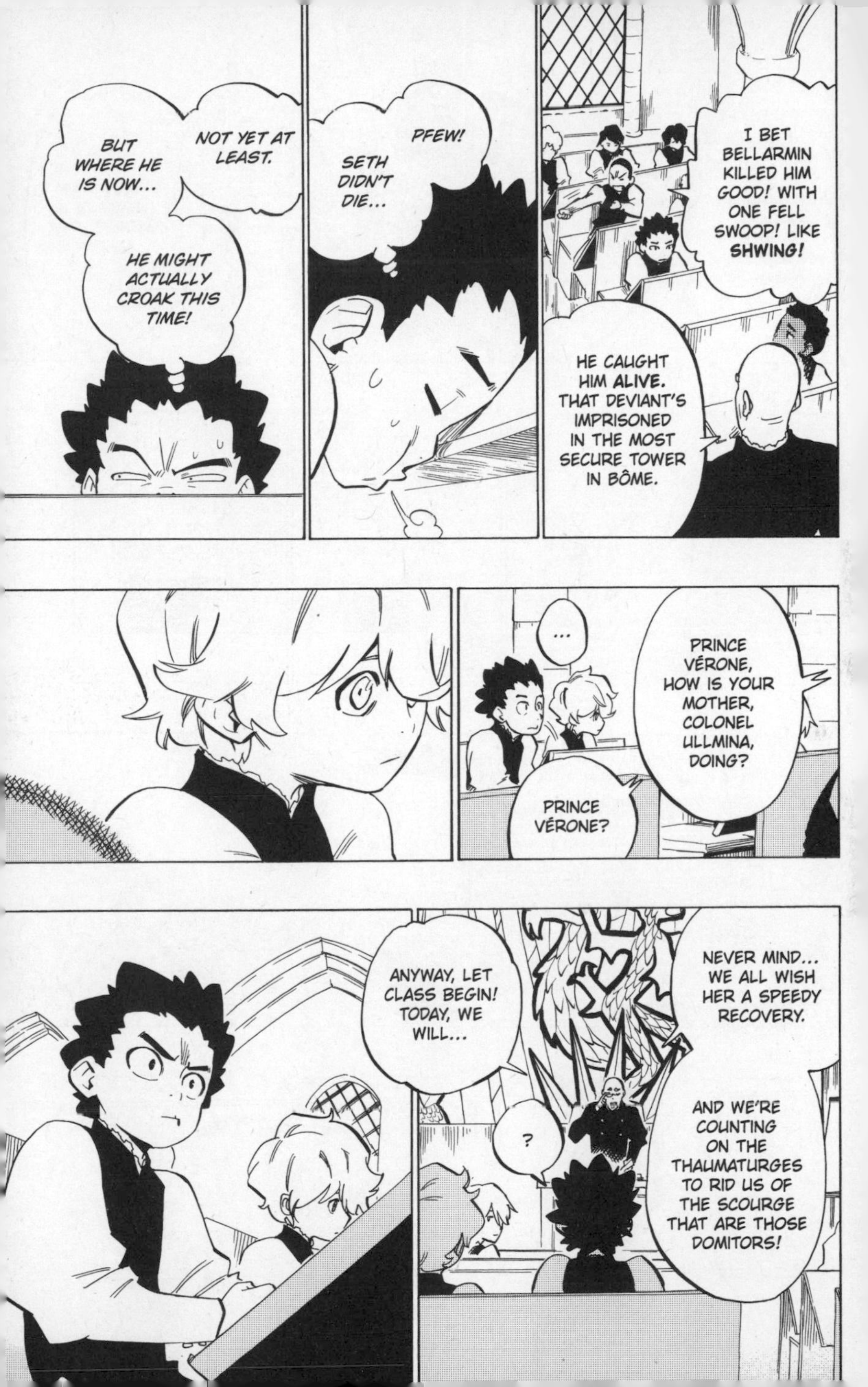
I BET BELLARMIN KILLED HIM GOOD! WITH ONE FELL SWOOP! LIKE SHWING!
HE CAUGHT HIM ALIVE. THAT DEVIANT'S IMPRISONED IN THE MOST SECURE TOWER IN BÔME.
PFEW!
SETH DIDN'T DIE...
NOT YET AT LEAST.
BUT WHERE HE IS NOW...
HE MIGHT ACTUALLY CROAK THIS TIME!
PRINCE VÉRONE, HOW IS YOUR MOTHER, COLONEL ULLMINA, DOING?
...
PRINCE VÉRONE?
NEVER MIND... WE ALL WISH HER A SPEEDY RECOVERY.
AND WE'RE COUNTING ON THE THAUMATURGES TO RID US OF THE SCOURGE THAT ARE THOSE DOMITORS!
ANYWAY, LET CLASS BEGIN! TODAY, WE WILL...
?

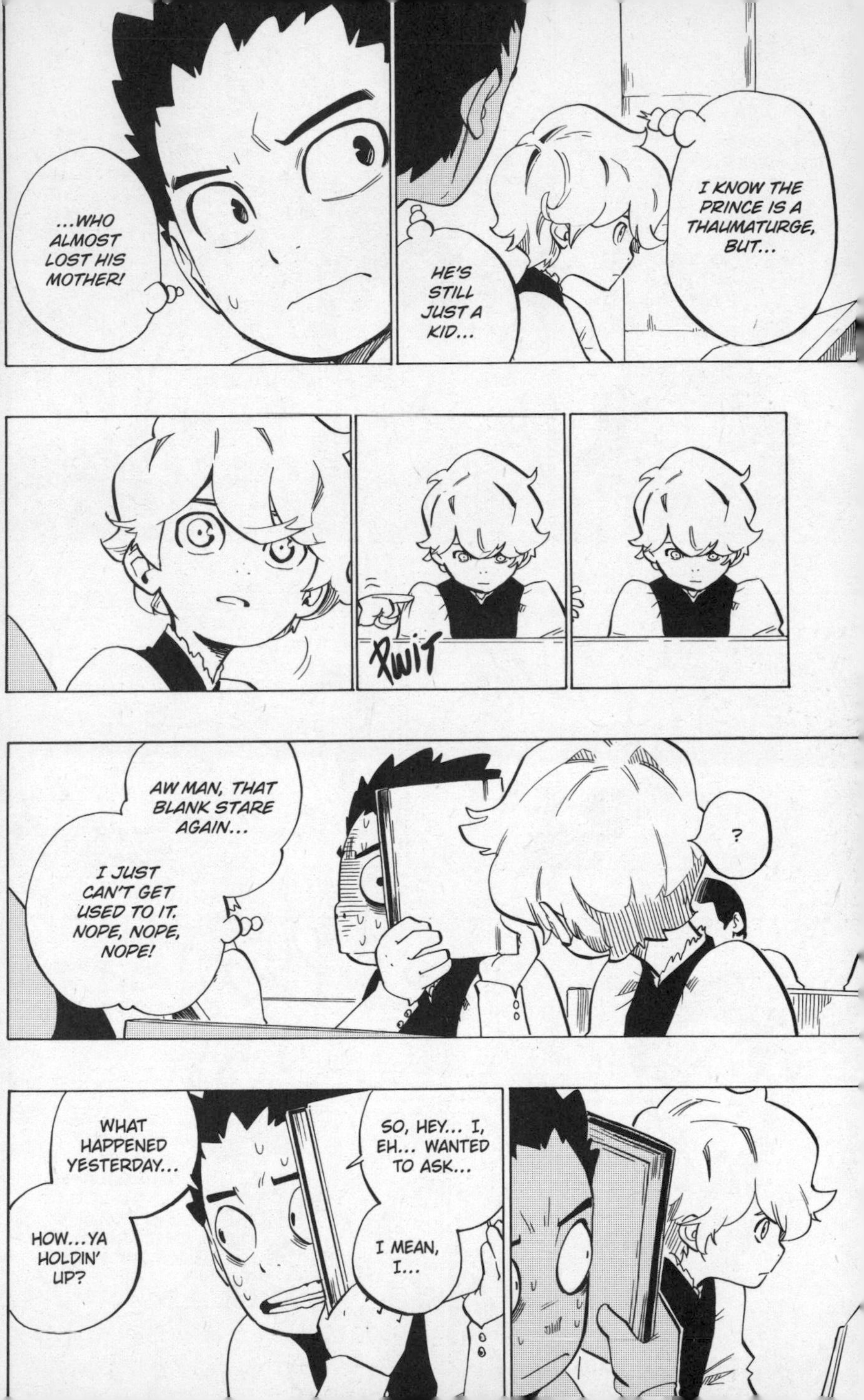
I KNOW THE PRINCE IS A THAUMATURGE, BUT...
HE'S STILL JUST A KID...
...WHO ALMOST LOST HIS MOTHER!
PWIT
?
AW MAN, THAT BLANK STARE AGAIN...
I JUST CAN'T GET USED TO IT. NOPE, NOPE, NOPE!
SO, HEY... I, EH... WANTED TO ASK...
I MEAN, I...
WHAT HAPPENED YESTERDAY...
HOW...YA HOLDIN' UP?

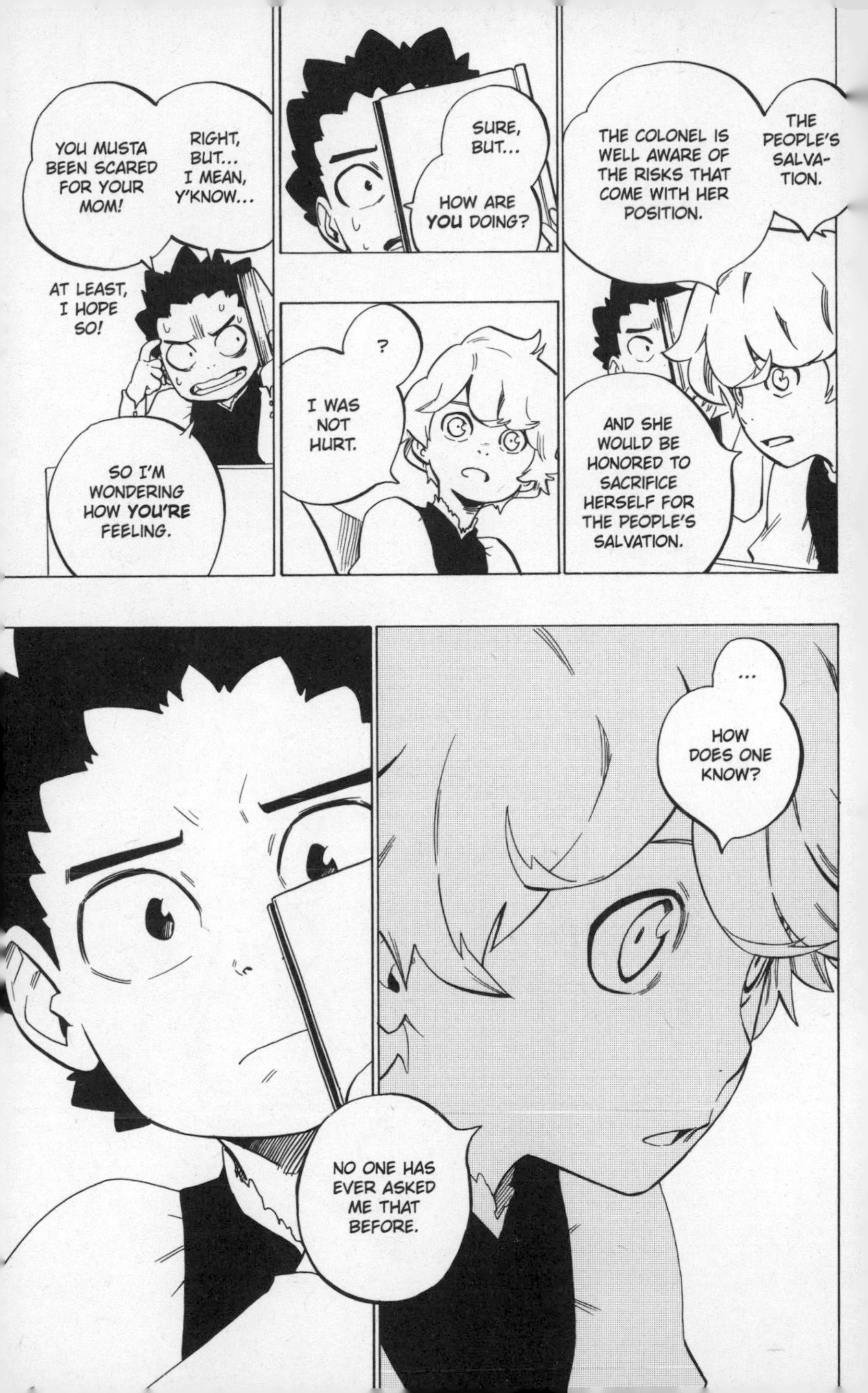
THE PEOPLE'S SALVATION.
THE COLONEL IS WELL AWARE OF THE RISKS THAT COME WITH HER POSITION.
AND SHE WOULD BE HONORED TO SACRIFICE HERSELF FOR THE PEOPLE'S SALVATION.
SURE, BUT... HOW ARE YOU DOING?
?
I WAS NOT HURT.
RIGHT, BUT... I MEAN, Y'KNOW...
YOU MUSTA BEEN SCARED FOR YOUR MOM!
AT LEAST, I HOPE SO!
SO I'M WONDERING HOW YOU'RE FEELING.
...
HOW DOES ONE KNOW?
NO ONE HAS EVER ASKED ME THAT BEFORE.

LUPA'S FAVORITE
DISGUISE
ACCESSORY...

HIDES HER
TRADEMARK MOLE.

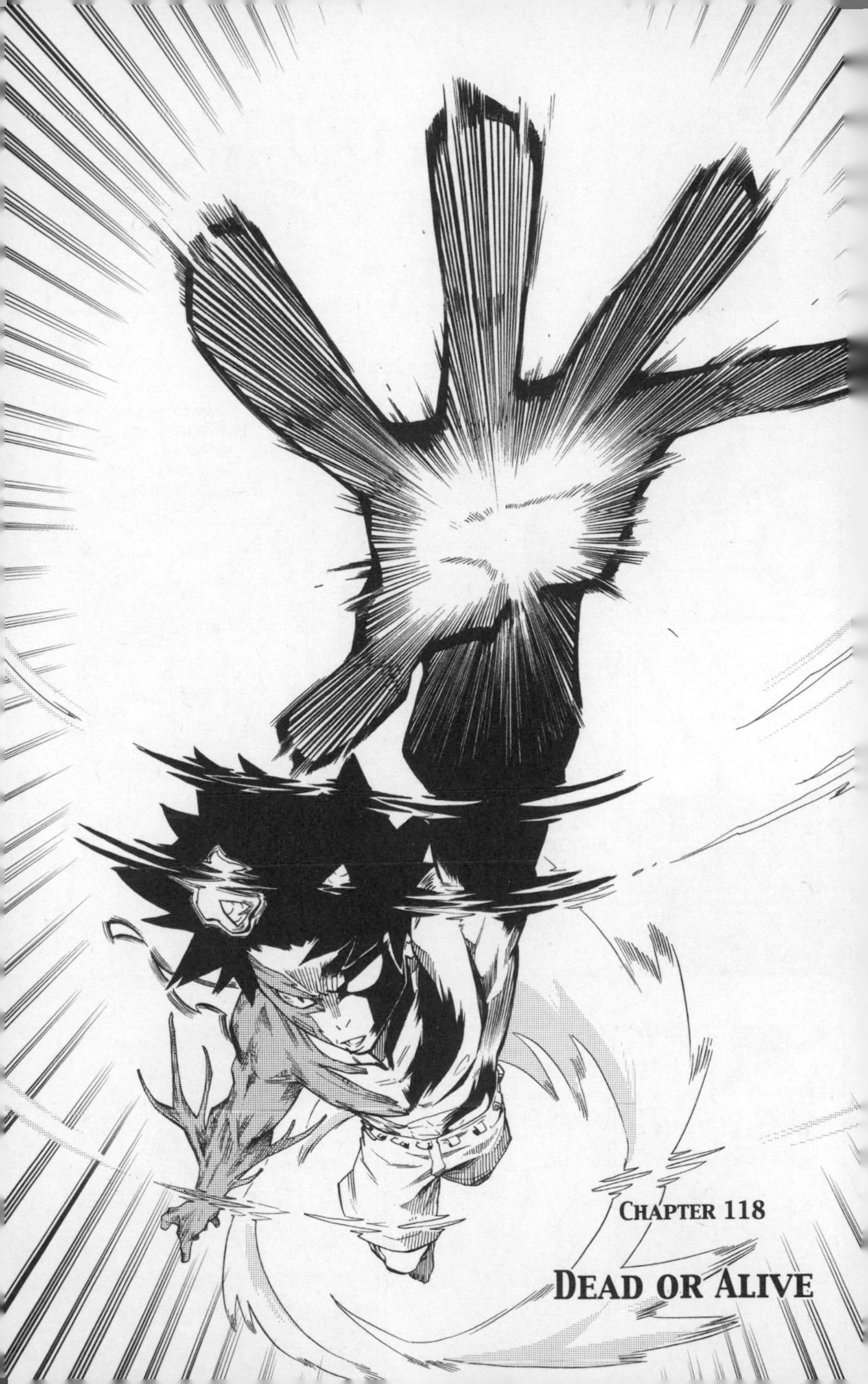

Chapter 118

Dead or Alive

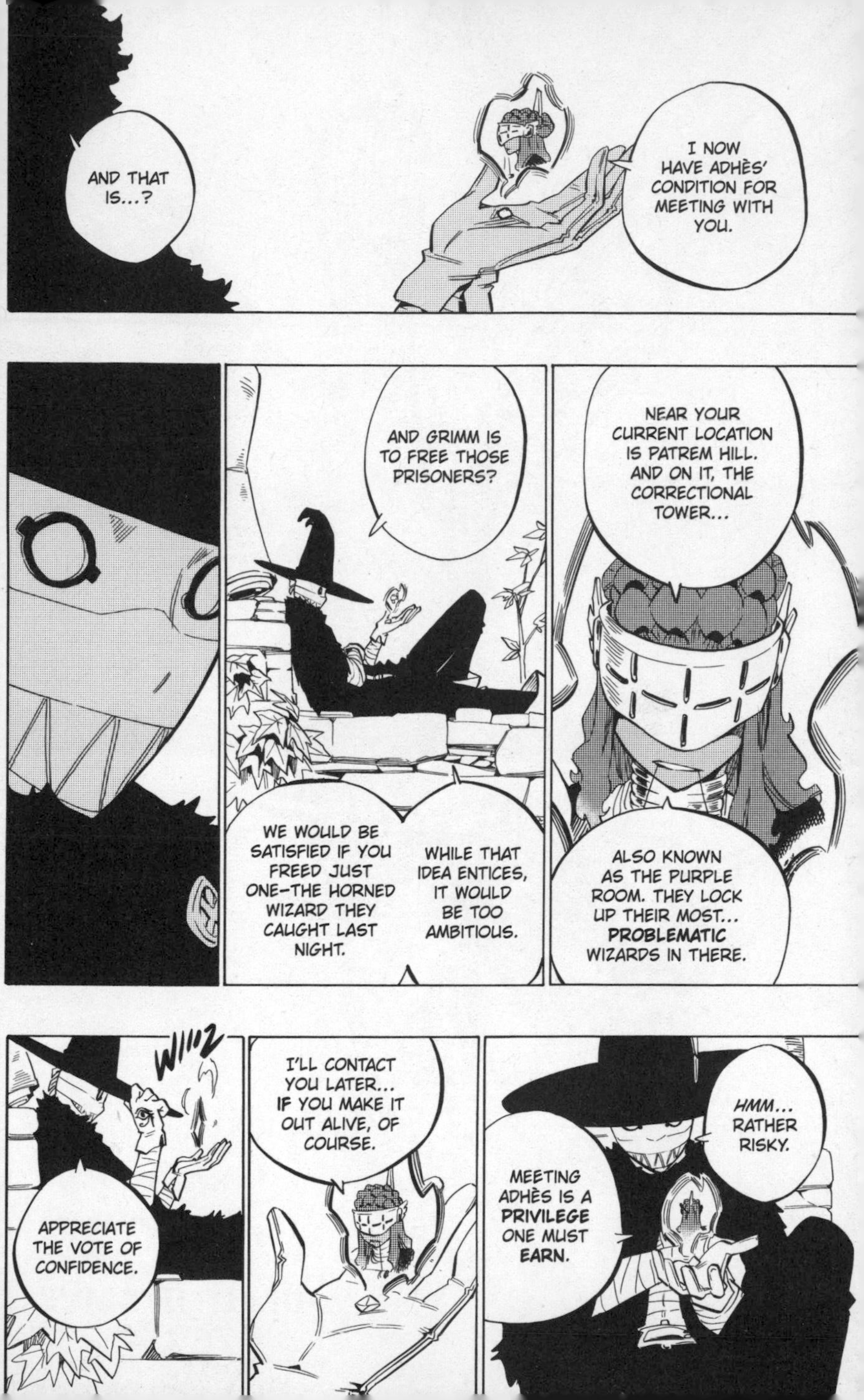
I NOW HAVE ADHÈS' CONDITION FOR MEETING WITH YOU.
AND THAT IS...?
NEAR YOUR CURRENT LOCATION IS PATREM HILL. AND ON IT, THE CORRECTIONAL TOWER...
ALSO KNOWN AS THE PURPLE ROOM. THEY LOCK UP THEIR MOST... **PROBLEMATIC** WIZARDS IN THERE.
AND GRIMM IS TO FREE THOSE PRISONERS?
WHILE THAT IDEA ENTICES, IT WOULD BE TOO AMBITIOUS.
WE WOULD BE SATISFIED IF YOU FREED JUST ONE—THE HORNED WIZARD THEY CAUGHT LAST NIGHT.
HMM... RATHER RISKY.
MEETING ADHÈS IS A **PRIVILEGE** ONE MUST **EARN.**
I'LL CONTACT YOU LATER... **IF YOU MAKE IT OUT ALIVE,** OF COURSE.
APPRECIATE THE VOTE OF CONFIDENCE.

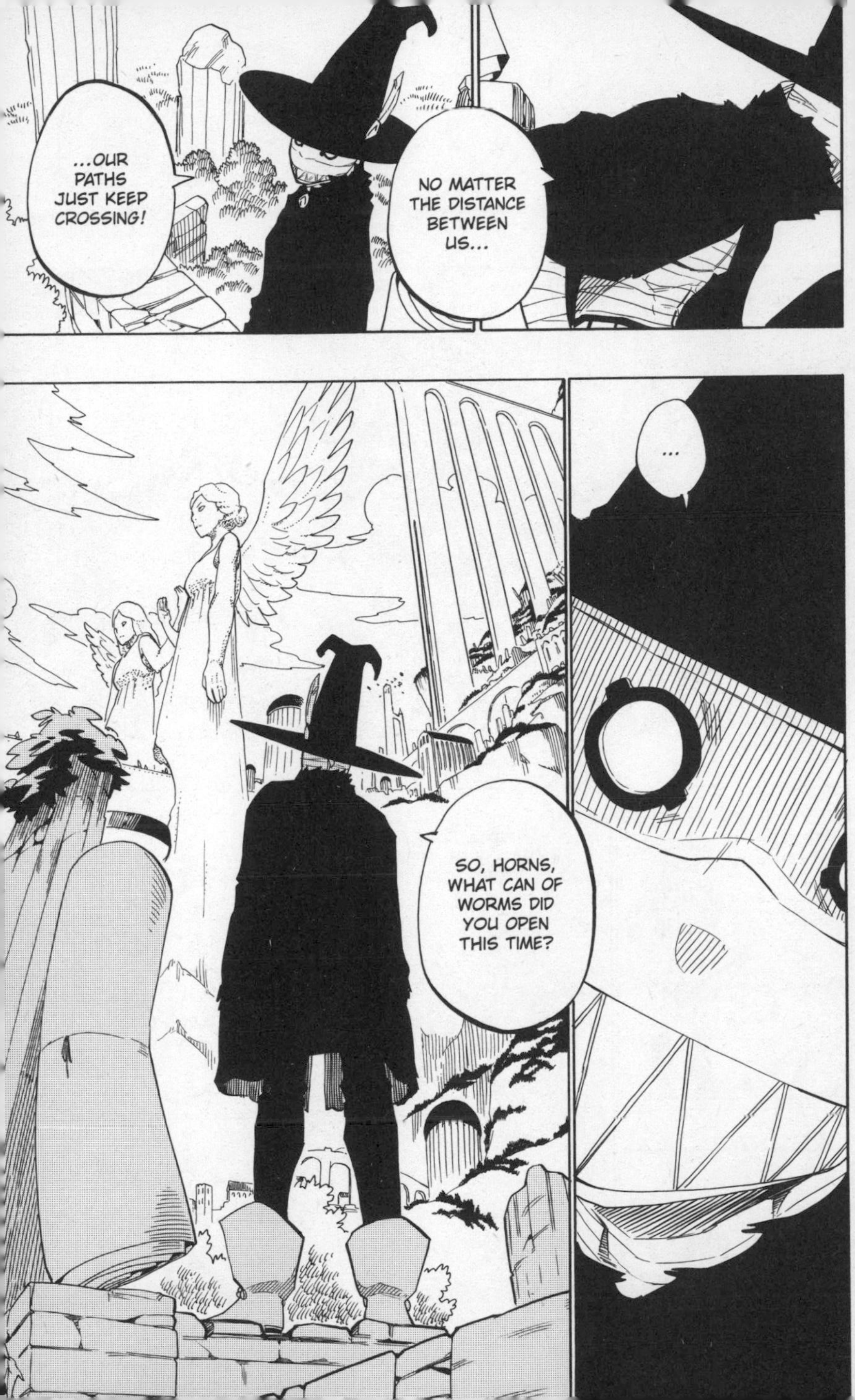
NO MATTER THE DISTANCE BETWEEN US...
...OUR PATHS JUST KEEP CROSSING!
...
SO, HORNS, WHAT CAN OF WORMS DID YOU OPEN THIS TIME?

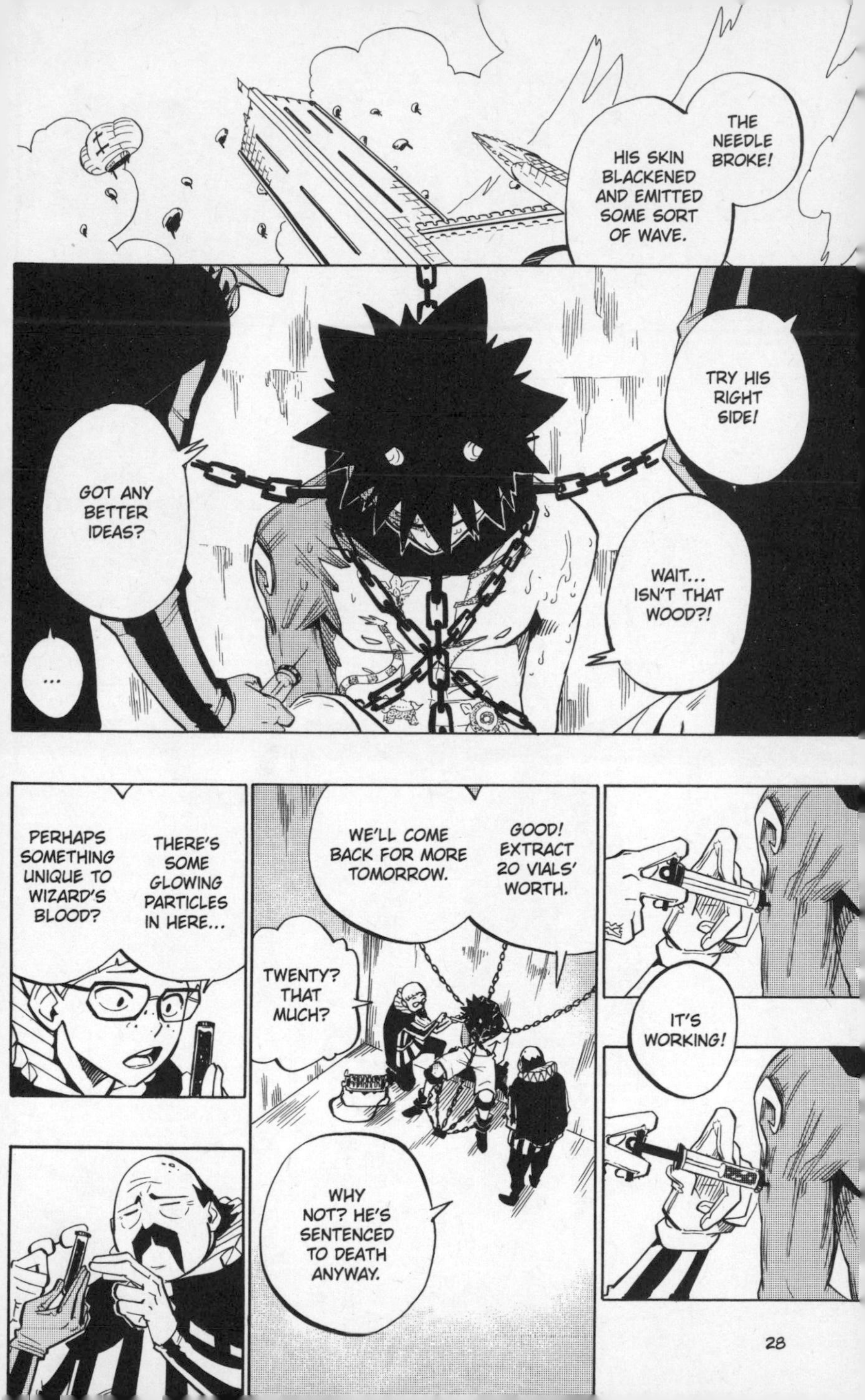
THE NEEDLE BROKE!
HIS SKIN BLACKENED AND EMITTED SOME SORT OF WAVE.
TRY HIS RIGHT SIDE!
GOT ANY BETTER IDEAS?
WAIT... ISN'T THAT WOOD?!
...
IT'S WORKING!
GOOD! EXTRACT 20 VIALS' WORTH.
WE'LL COME BACK FOR MORE TOMORROW.
TWENTY? THAT MUCH?
WHY NOT? HE'S SENTENCED TO DEATH ANYWAY.
THERE'S SOME GLOWING PARTICLES IN HERE...
PERHAPS SOMETHING UNIQUE TO WIZARD'S BLOOD?

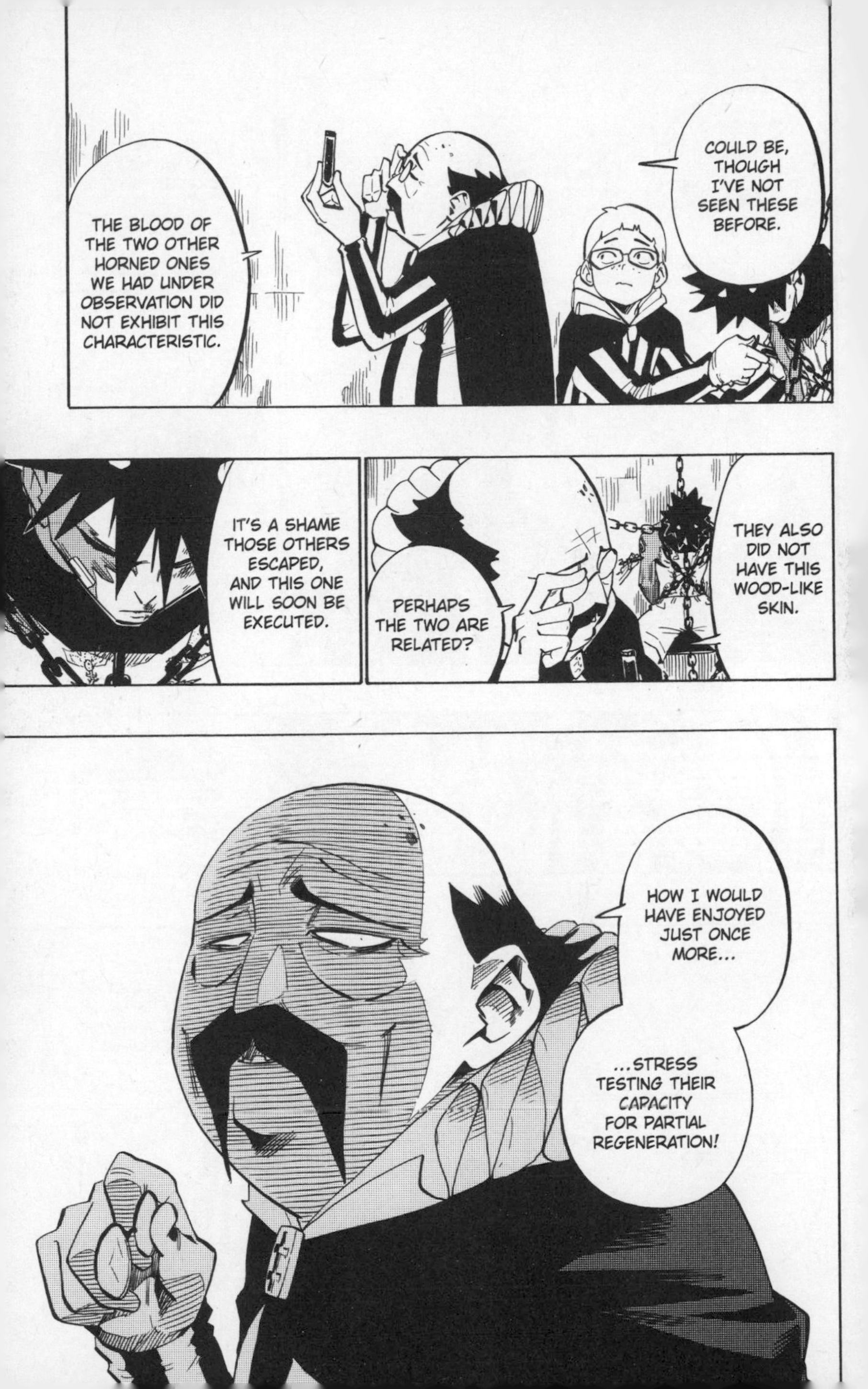
COULD BE, THOUGH I'VE NOT SEEN THESE BEFORE.
THE BLOOD OF THE TWO OTHER HORNED ONES WE HAD UNDER OBSERVATION DID NOT EXHIBIT THIS CHARACTERISTIC.
THEY ALSO DID NOT HAVE THIS WOOD-LIKE SKIN.
PERHAPS THE TWO ARE RELATED?
IT'S A SHAME THOSE OTHERS ESCAPED, AND THIS ONE WILL SOON BE EXECUTED.
HOW I WOULD HAVE ENJOYED JUST ONCE MORE...
...STRESS TESTING THEIR CAPACITY FOR PARTIAL REGENERATION!

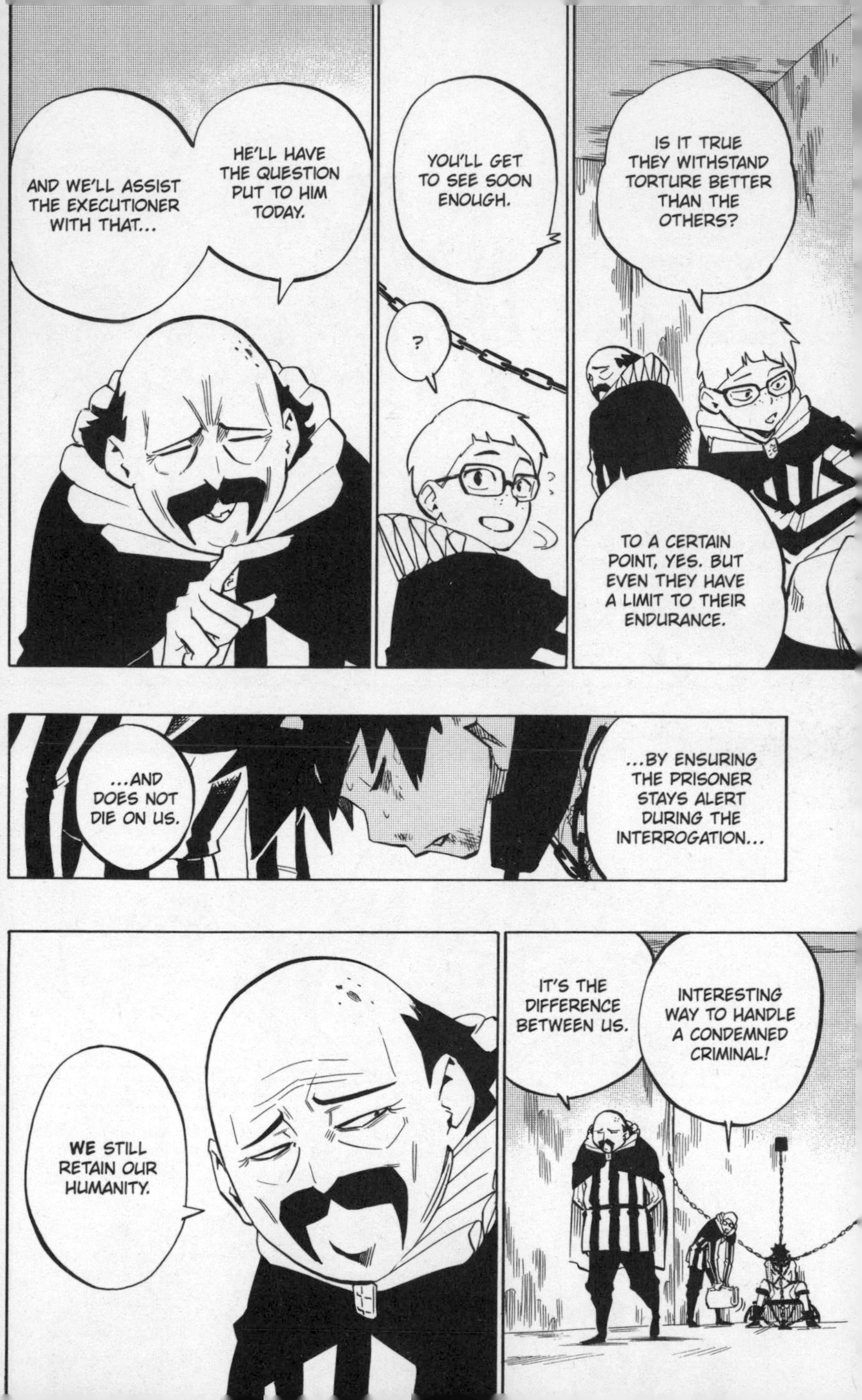
IS IT TRUE THEY WITHSTAND TORTURE BETTER THAN THE OTHERS?
TO A CERTAIN POINT, YES. BUT EVEN THEY HAVE A LIMIT TO THEIR ENDURANCE.
YOU'LL GET TO SEE SOON ENOUGH.
?
HE'LL HAVE THE QUESTION PUT TO HIM TODAY.
AND WE'LL ASSIST THE EXECUTIONER WITH THAT...
...BY ENSURING THE PRISONER STAYS ALERT DURING THE INTERROGATION...
...AND DOES NOT DIE ON US.
INTERESTING WAY TO HANDLE A CONDEMNED CRIMINAL!
IT'S THE DIFFERENCE BETWEEN US.
WE STILL RETAIN OUR HUMANITY.

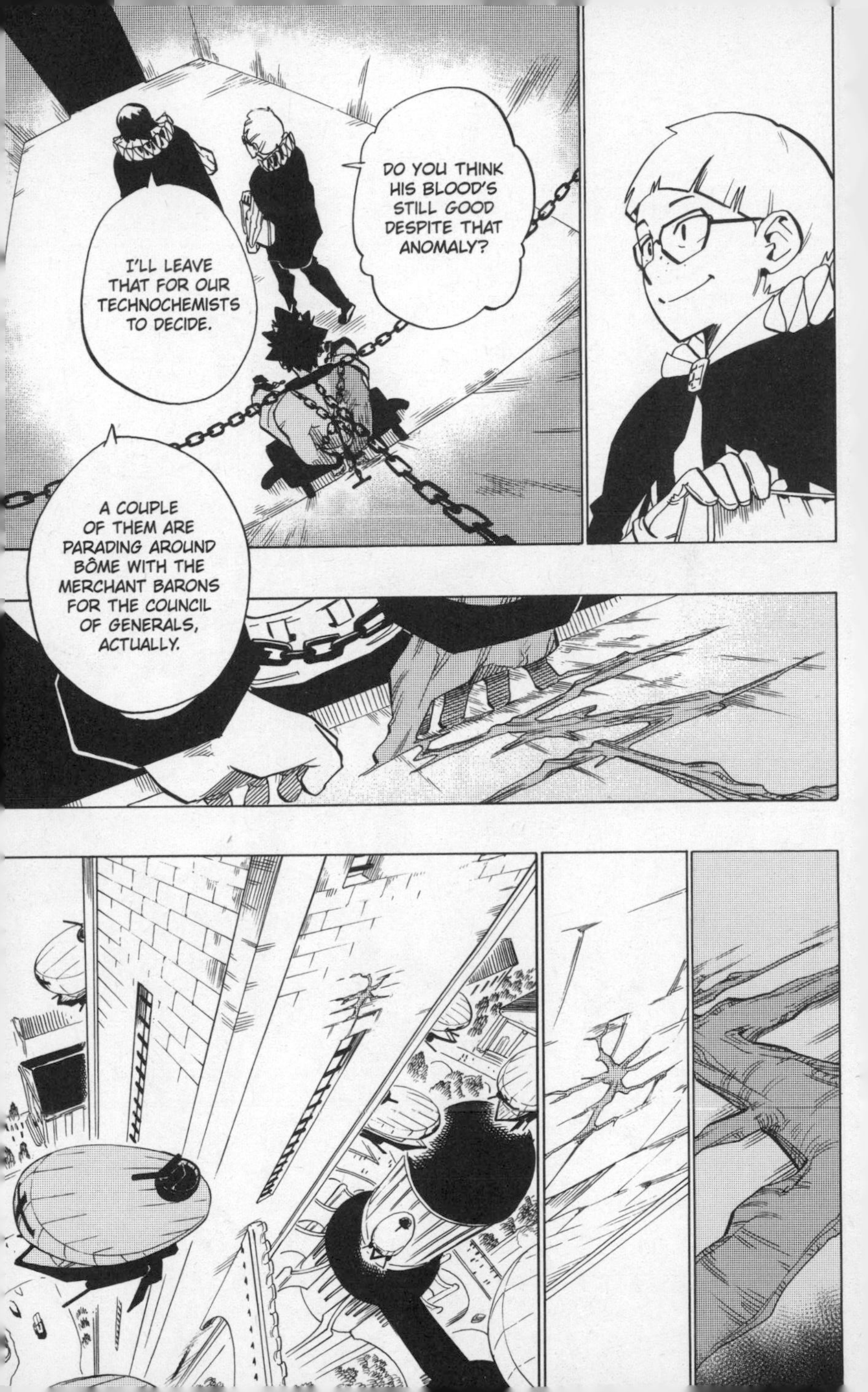
DO YOU THINK HIS BLOOD'S STILL GOOD DESPITE THAT ANOMALY?
I'LL LEAVE THAT FOR OUR TECHNOCHEMISTS TO DECIDE.
A COUPLE OF THEM ARE PARADING AROUND BÔME WITH THE MERCHANT BARONS FOR THE COUNCIL OF GENERALS, ACTUALLY.

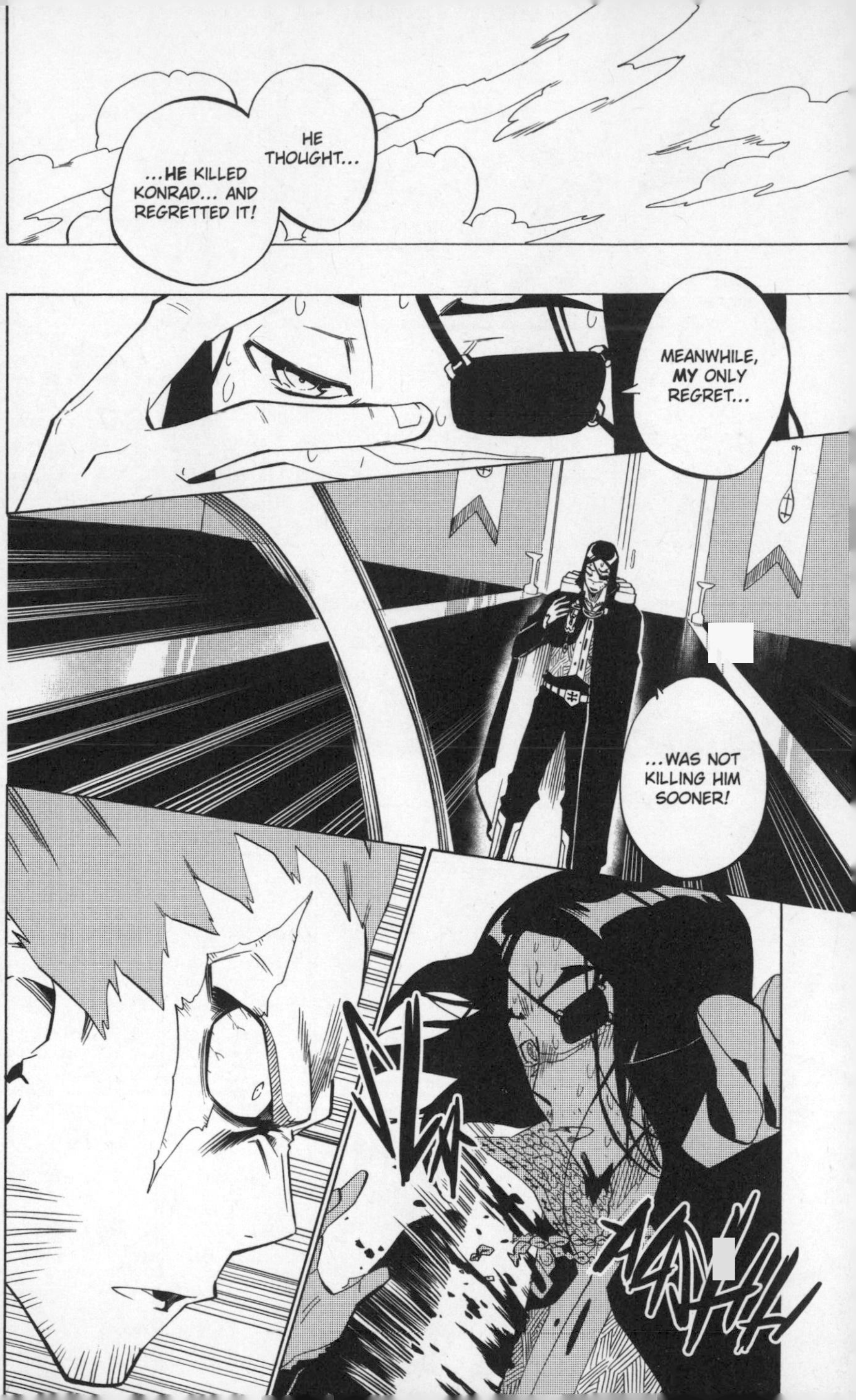
HE THOUGHT...
...HE KILLED KONRAD... AND REGRETTED IT!
MEANWHILE, MY ONLY REGRET...
...WAS NOT KILLING HIM SOONER!

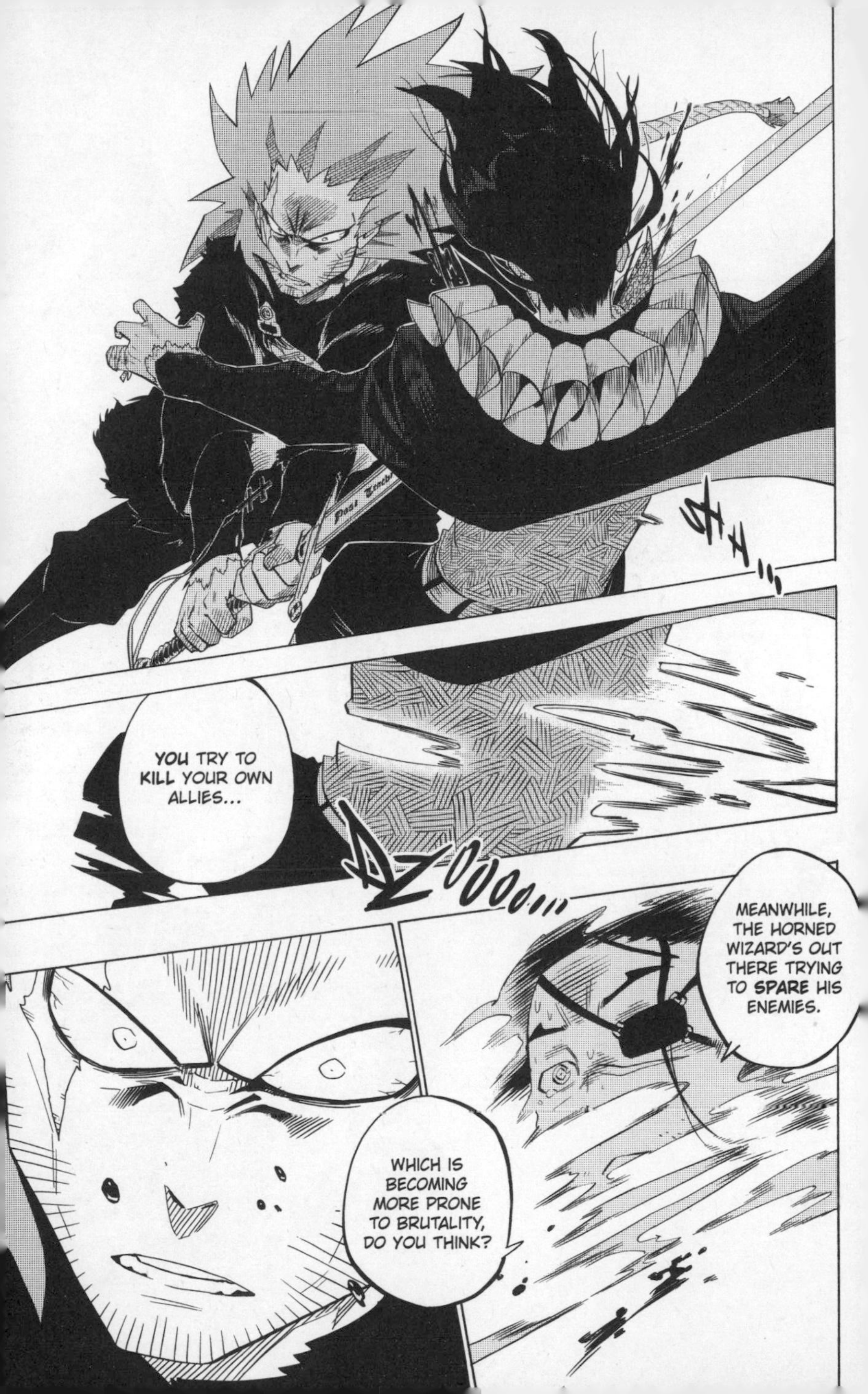
SHH...
YOU TRY TO KILL YOUR OWN ALLIES...
DZOOOO...
MEANWHILE, THE HORNED WIZARD'S OUT THERE TRYING TO SPARE HIS ENEMIES.
WHICH IS BECOMING MORE PRONE TO BRUTALITY, DO YOU THINK?

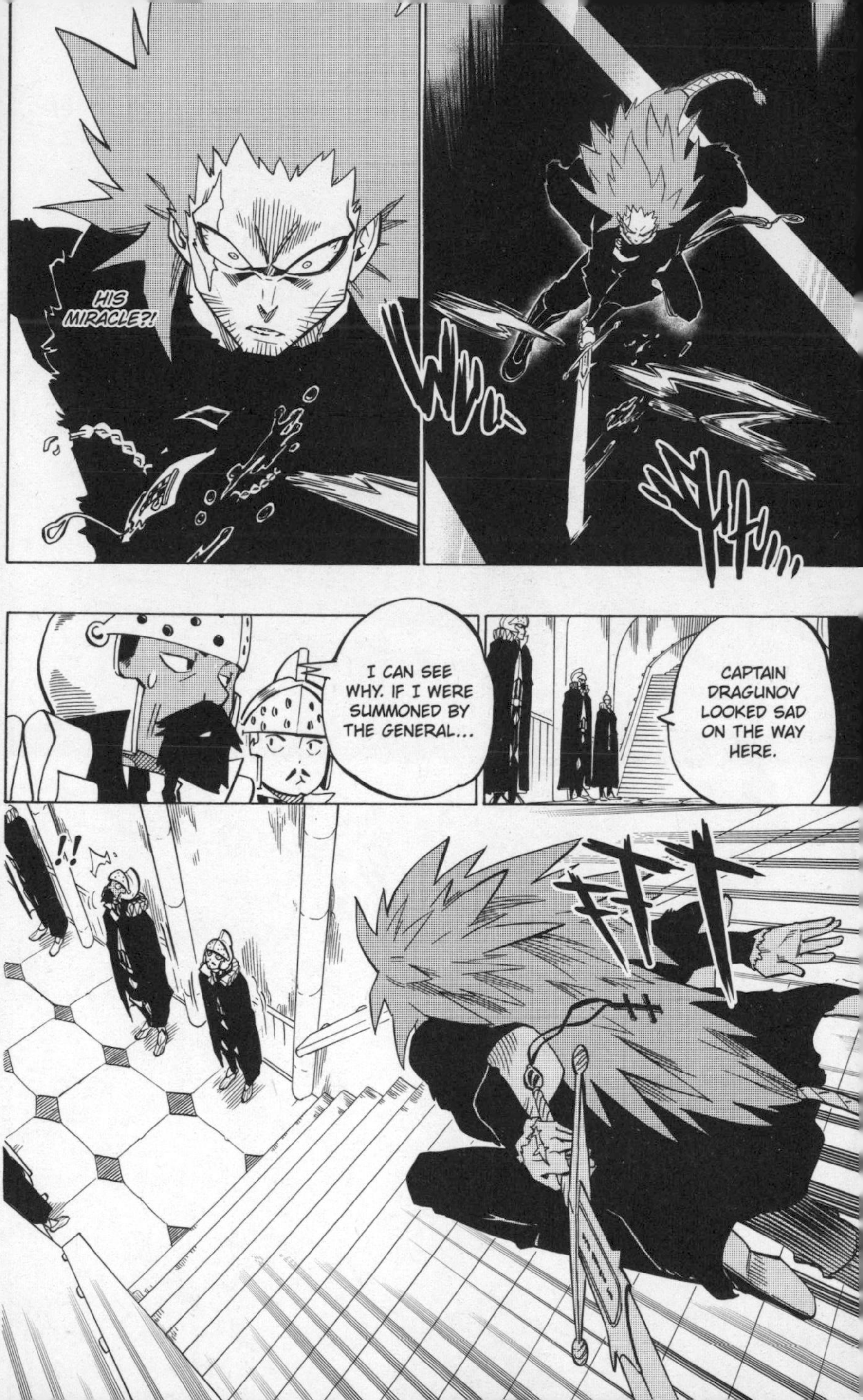
HIS MIRACLE?!
CAPTAIN DRAGUNOV LOOKED SAD ON THE WAY HERE.
I CAN SEE WHY. IF I WERE SUMMONED BY THE GENERAL...
!!

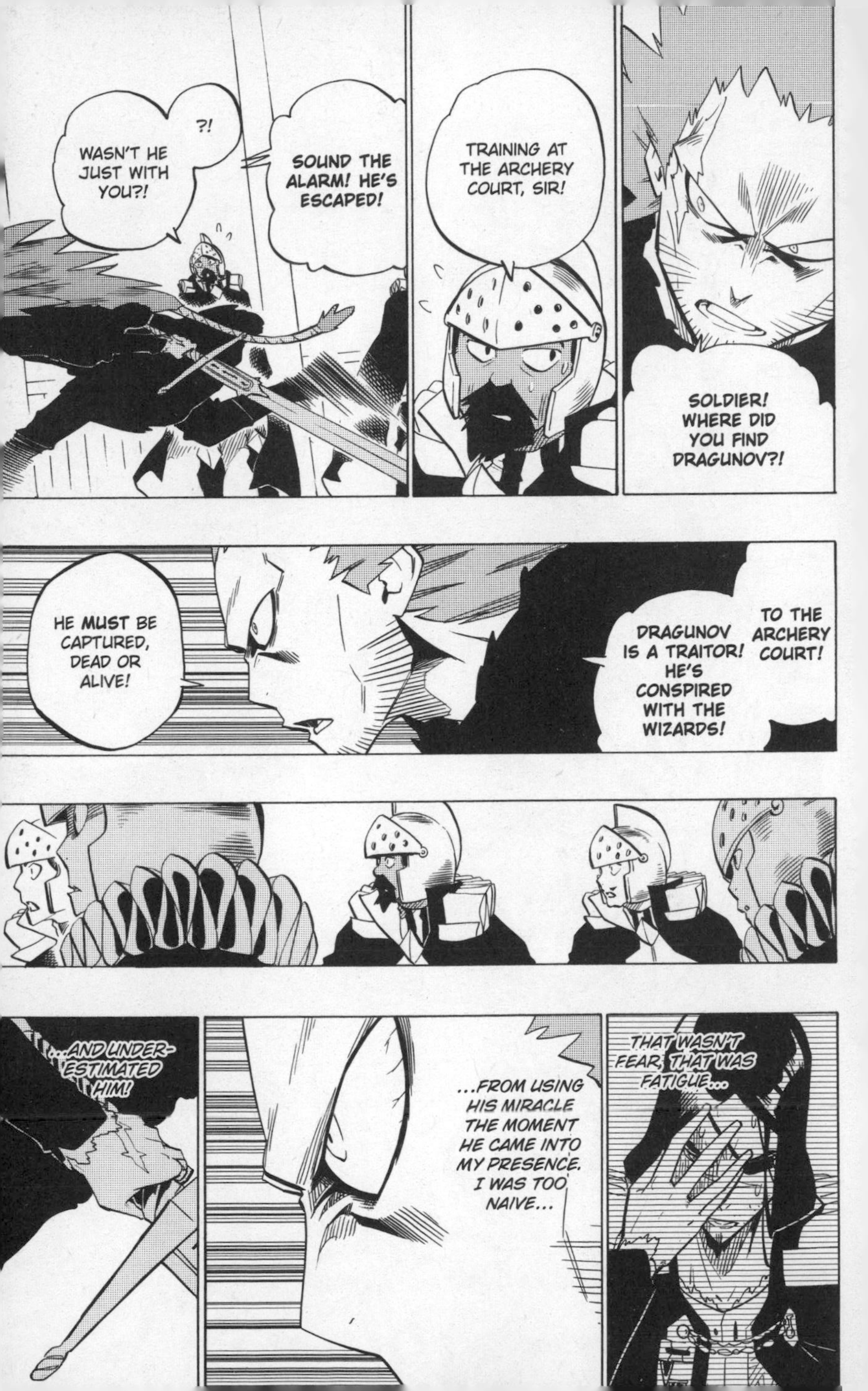
SOLDIER! WHERE DID YOU FIND DRAGUNOV?!
TRAINING AT THE ARCHERY COURT, SIR!
SOUND THE ALARM! HE'S ESCAPED!
?!
WASN'T HE JUST WITH YOU?!
TO THE ARCHERY COURT!
DRAGUNOV IS A TRAITOR! HE'S CONSPIRED WITH THE WIZARDS!
HE MUST BE CAPTURED, DEAD OR ALIVE!
THAT WASN'T FEAR, THAT WAS FATIGUE...
...FROM USING HIS MIRACLE THE MOMENT HE CAME INTO MY PRESENCE. I WAS TOO NAIVE...
...AND UNDER-ESTIMATED HIM!

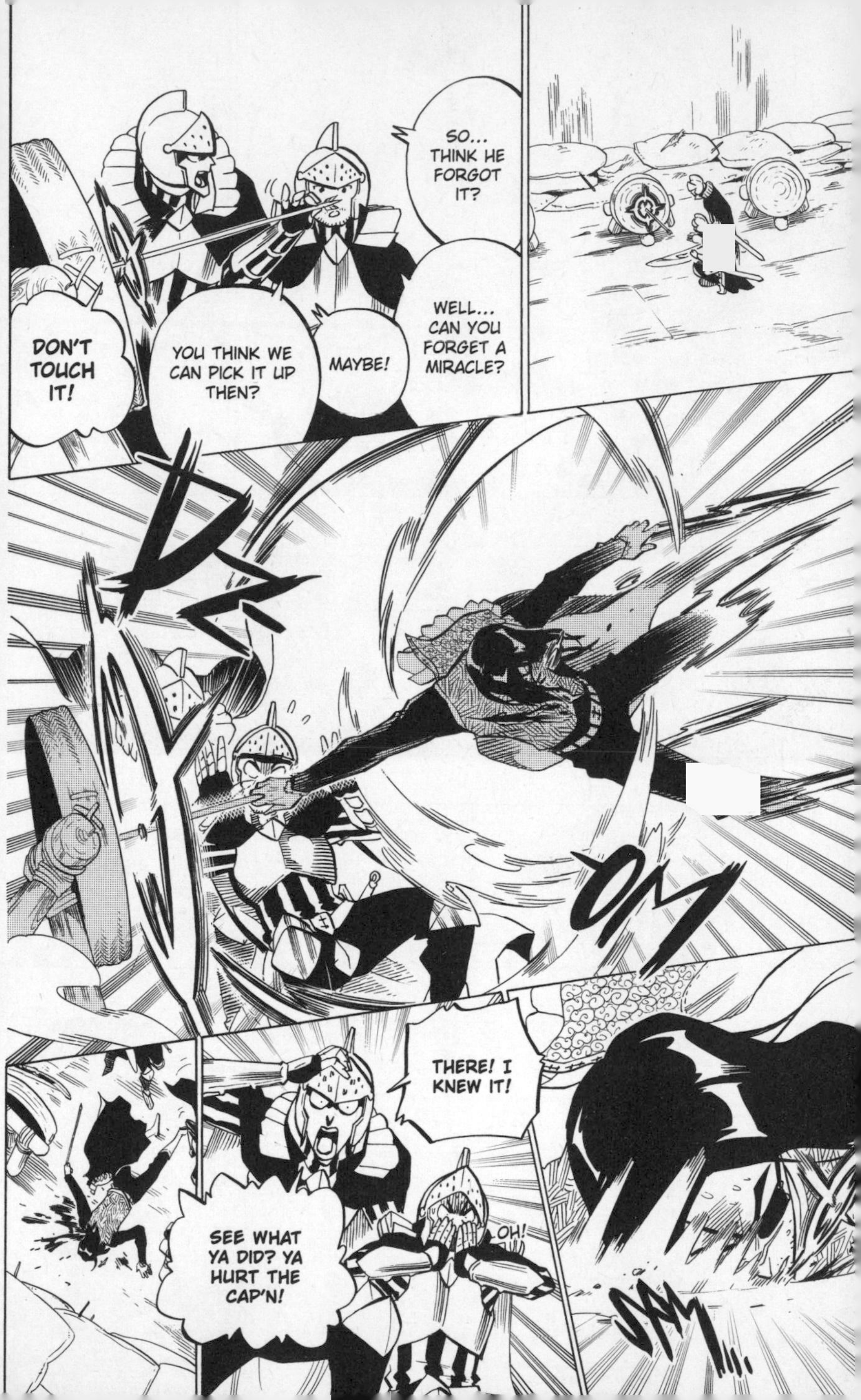
SO... THINK HE FORGOT IT?
WELL... CAN YOU FORGET A MIRACLE?
MAYBE!
YOU THINK WE CAN PICK IT UP THEN?
DON'T TOUCH IT!
THERE! I KNEW IT!
OH!
SEE WHAT YA DID? YA HURT THE CAP'N!

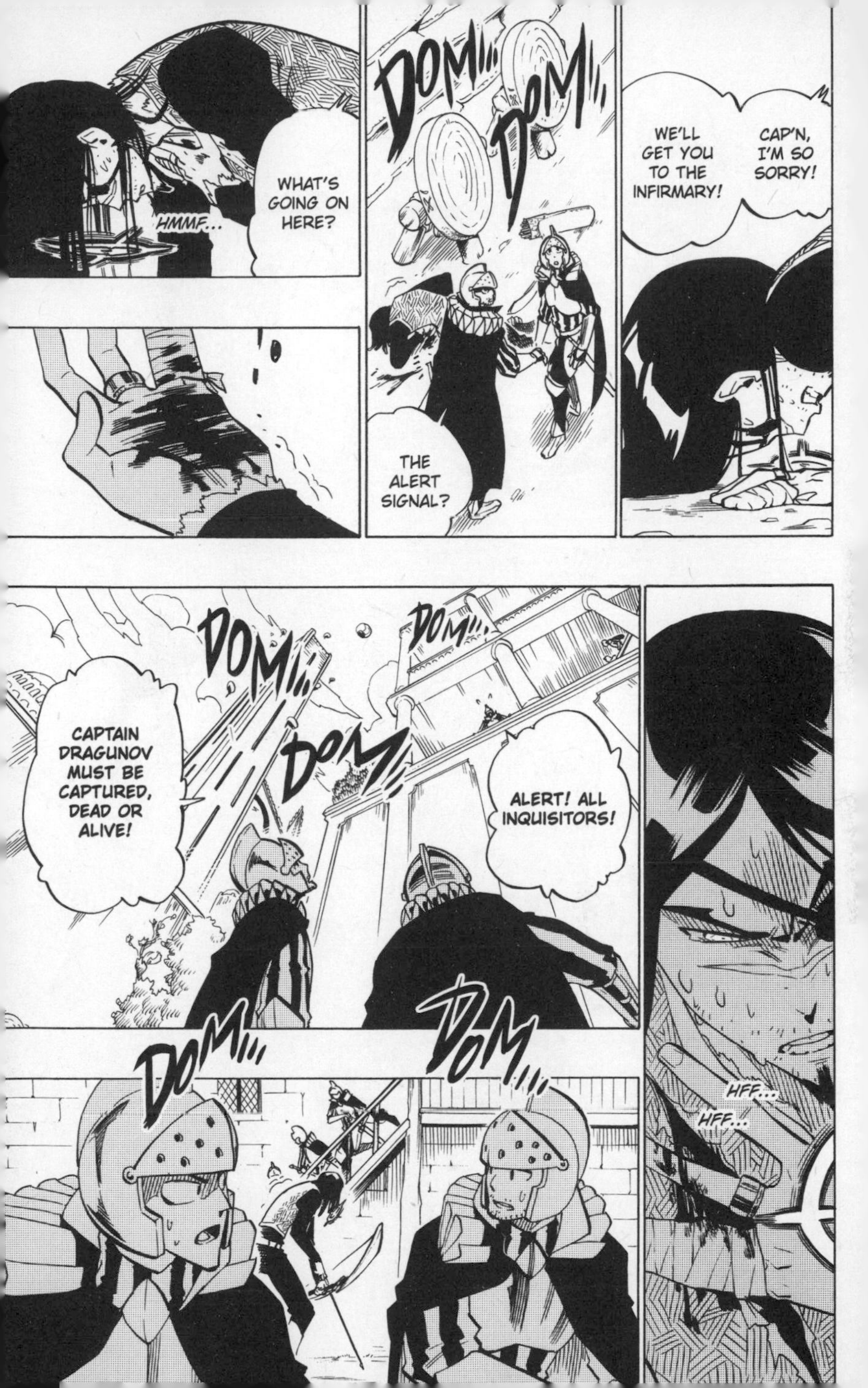
CAP'N, I'M SO SORRY!
WE'LL GET YOU TO THE INFIRMARY!
DOM... DOM...
THE ALERT SIGNAL?
WHAT'S GOING ON HERE?
HMMF...
HFF...
HFF...
DOM...
DOM...
DOM
ALERT! ALL INQUISITORS!
CAPTAIN DRAGUNOV MUST BE CAPTURED, DEAD OR ALIVE!
DOM...
DOM...

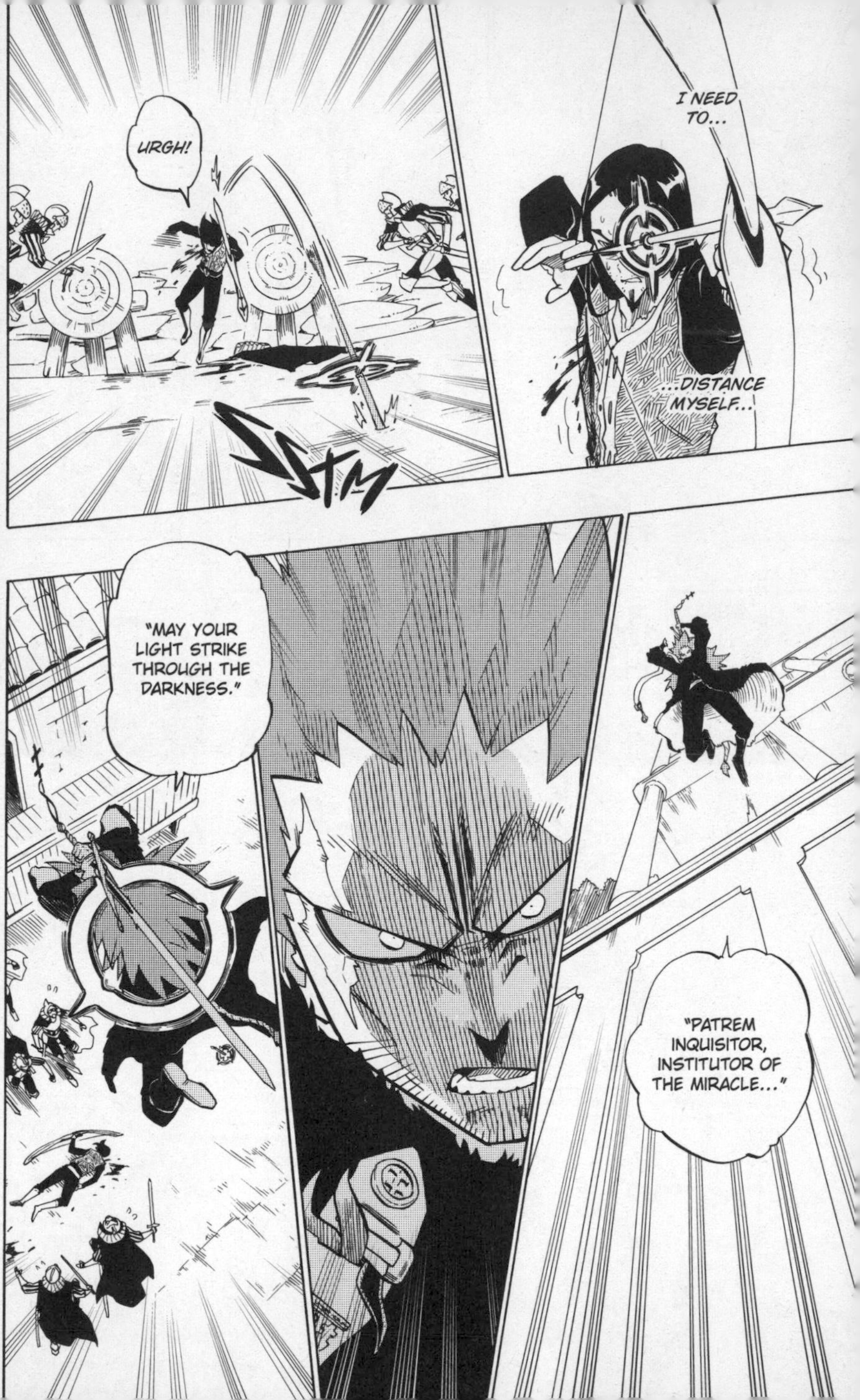
I NEED TO...
...DISTANCE MYSELF...
URGH!
"PATREM INQUISITOR, INSTITUTOR OF THE MIRACLE..."
"MAY YOUR LIGHT STRIKE THROUGH THE DARKNESS."

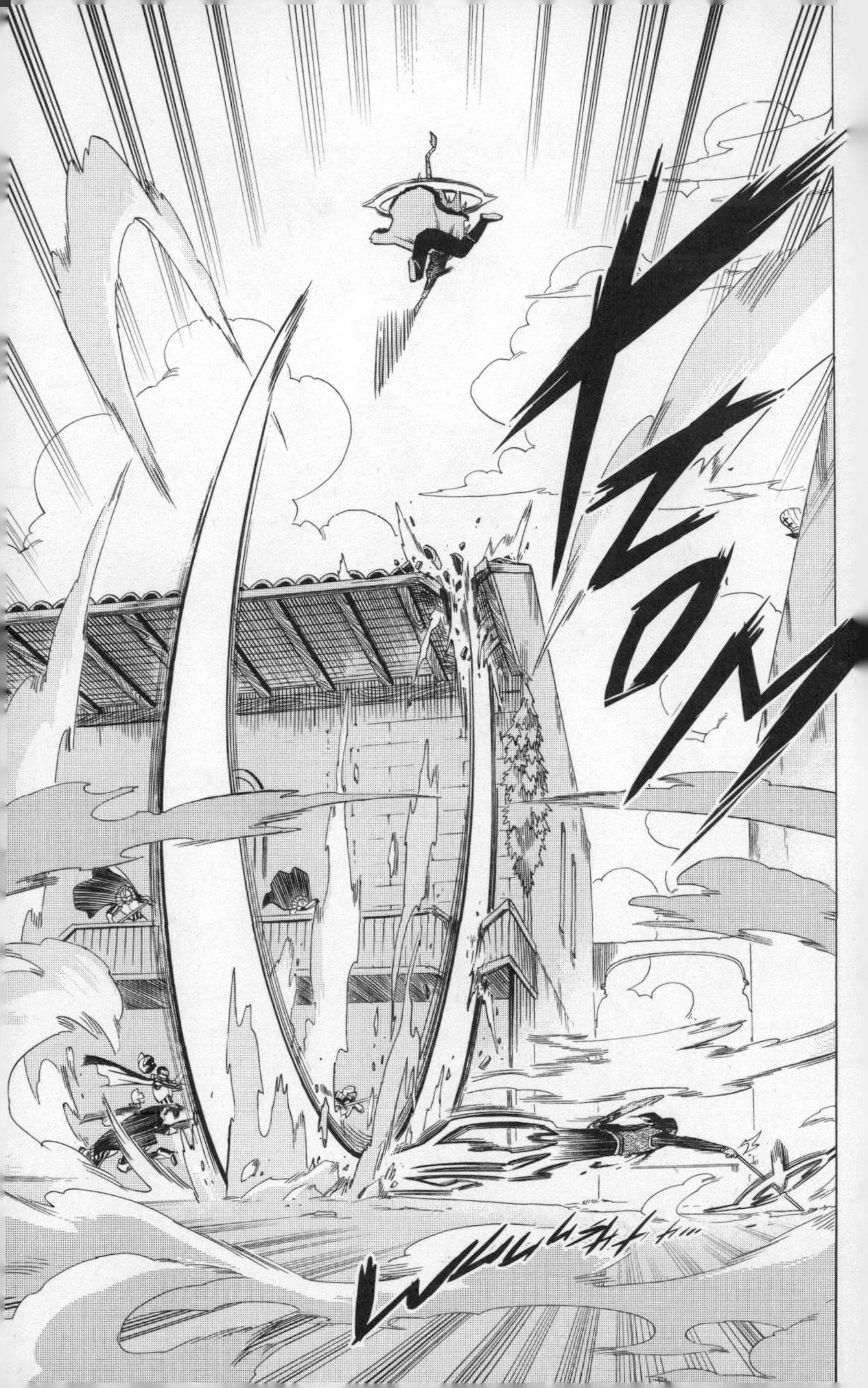

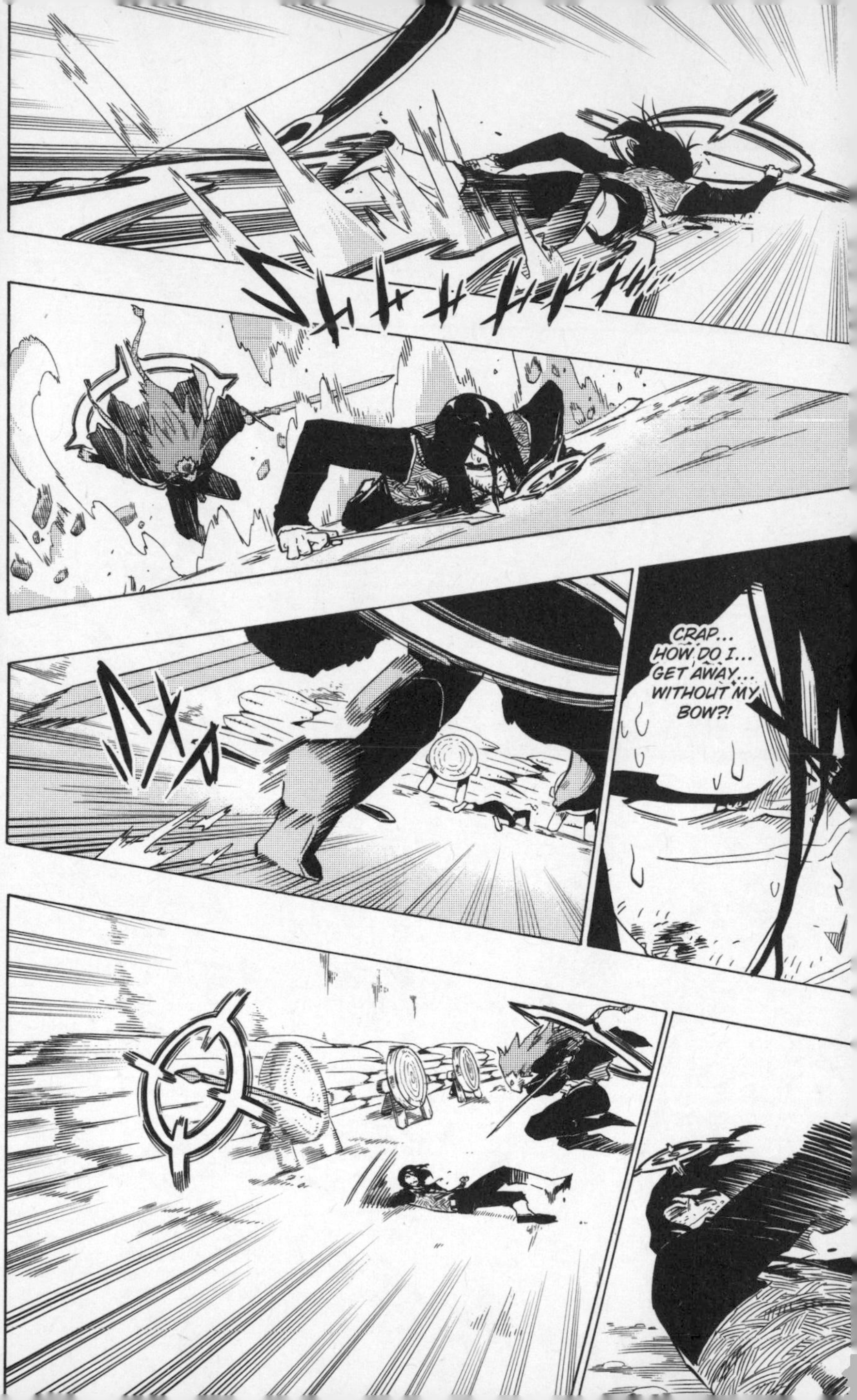
CRAP... HOW DO I... GET AWAY... WITHOUT MY BOW?!

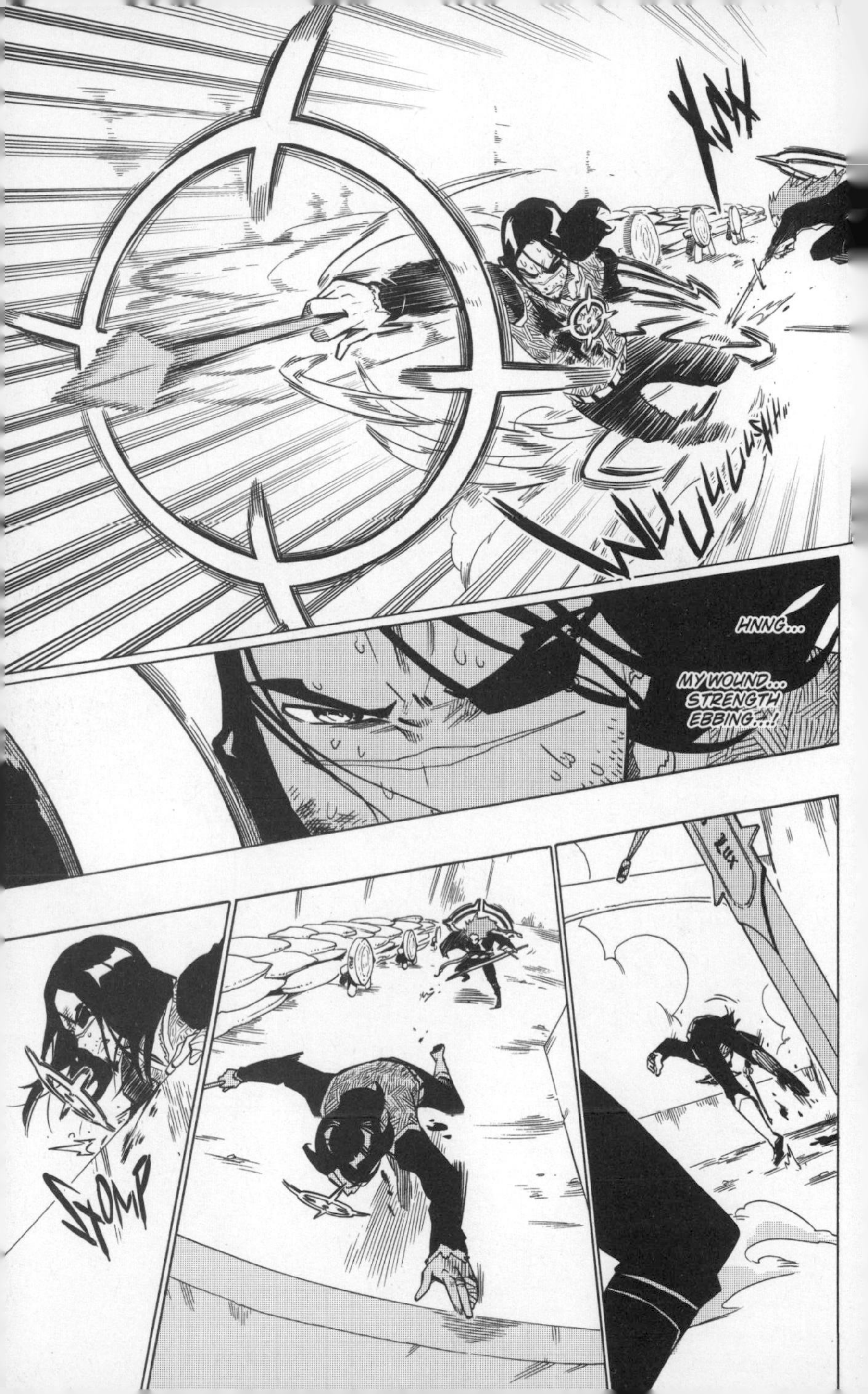

YANK
WUUUUUSHH
HNNG...
MY WOUND... STRENGTH EBBING...!
LUX
STOMP

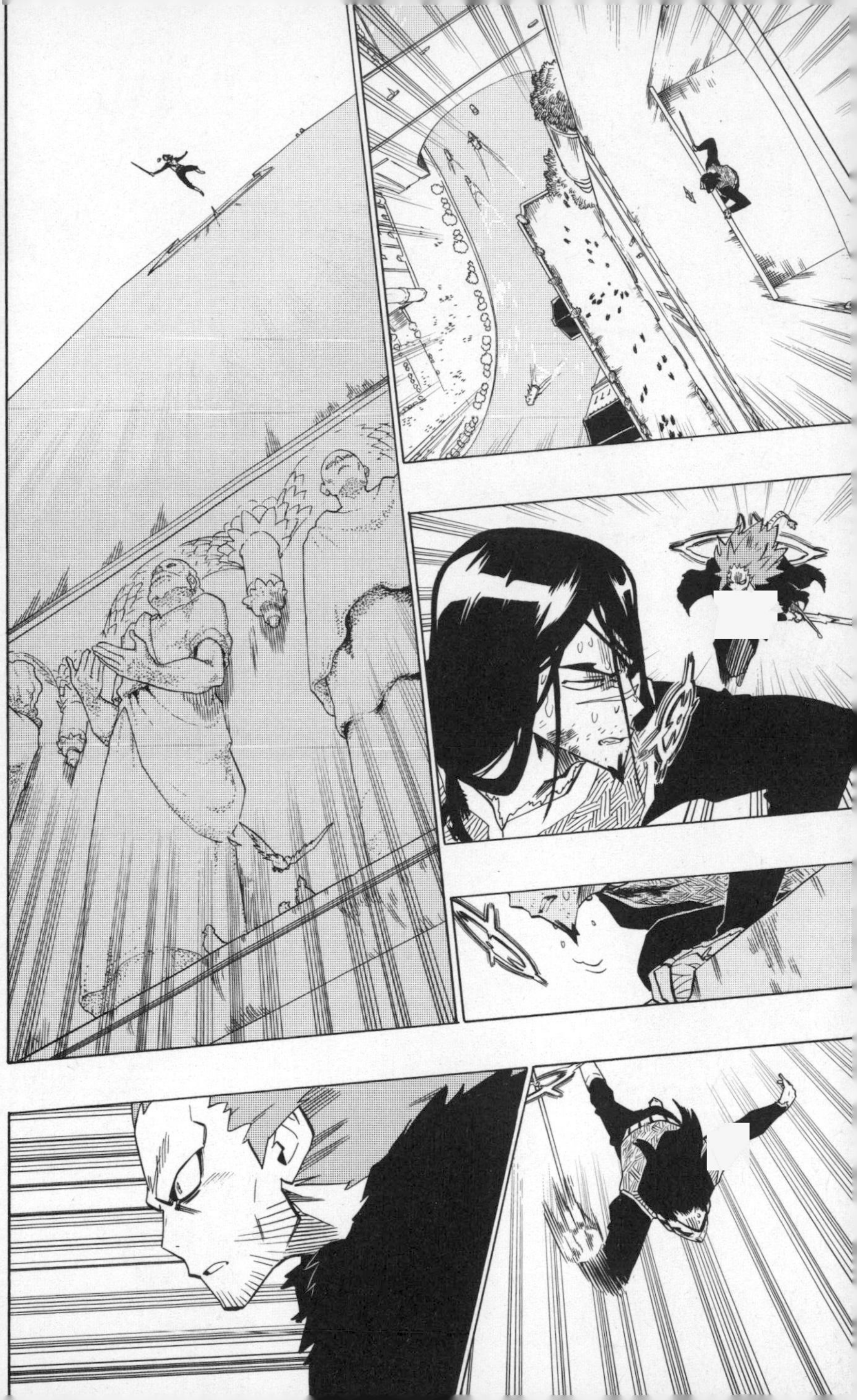

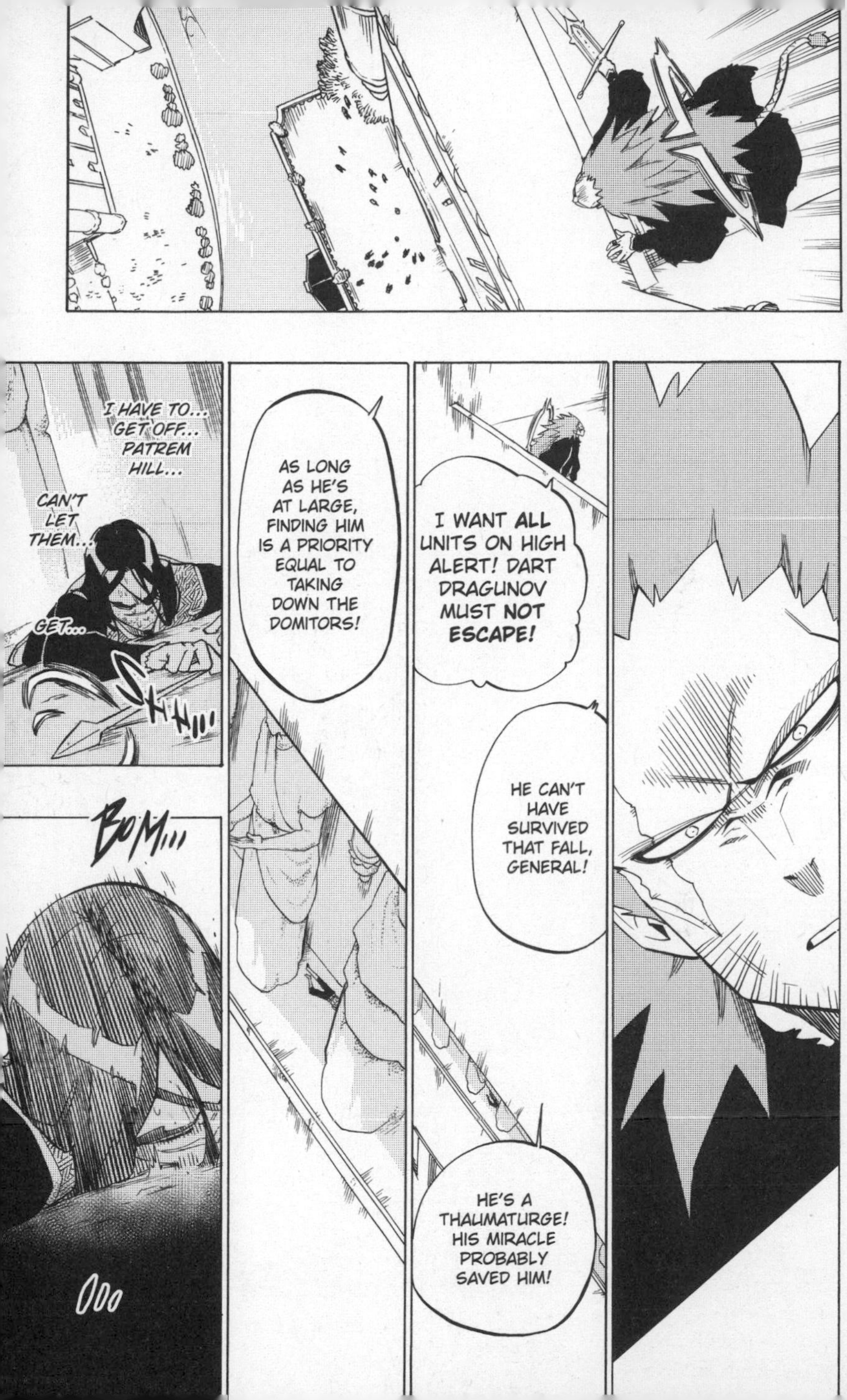
I WANT ALL UNITS ON HIGH ALERT! DART DRAGUNOV MUST NOT ESCAPE!
HE CAN'T HAVE SURVIVED THAT FALL, GENERAL!
HE'S A THAUMATURGE! HIS MIRACLE PROBABLY SAVED HIM!
AS LONG AS HE'S AT LARGE, FINDING HIM IS A PRIORITY EQUAL TO TAKING DOWN THE DOMITORS!
I HAVE TO... GET OFF... PATREM HILL...
CAN'T LET THEM...
GET...
SHH...
BOM...
ooo

MEANWHILE, AT HURLÄ'S...

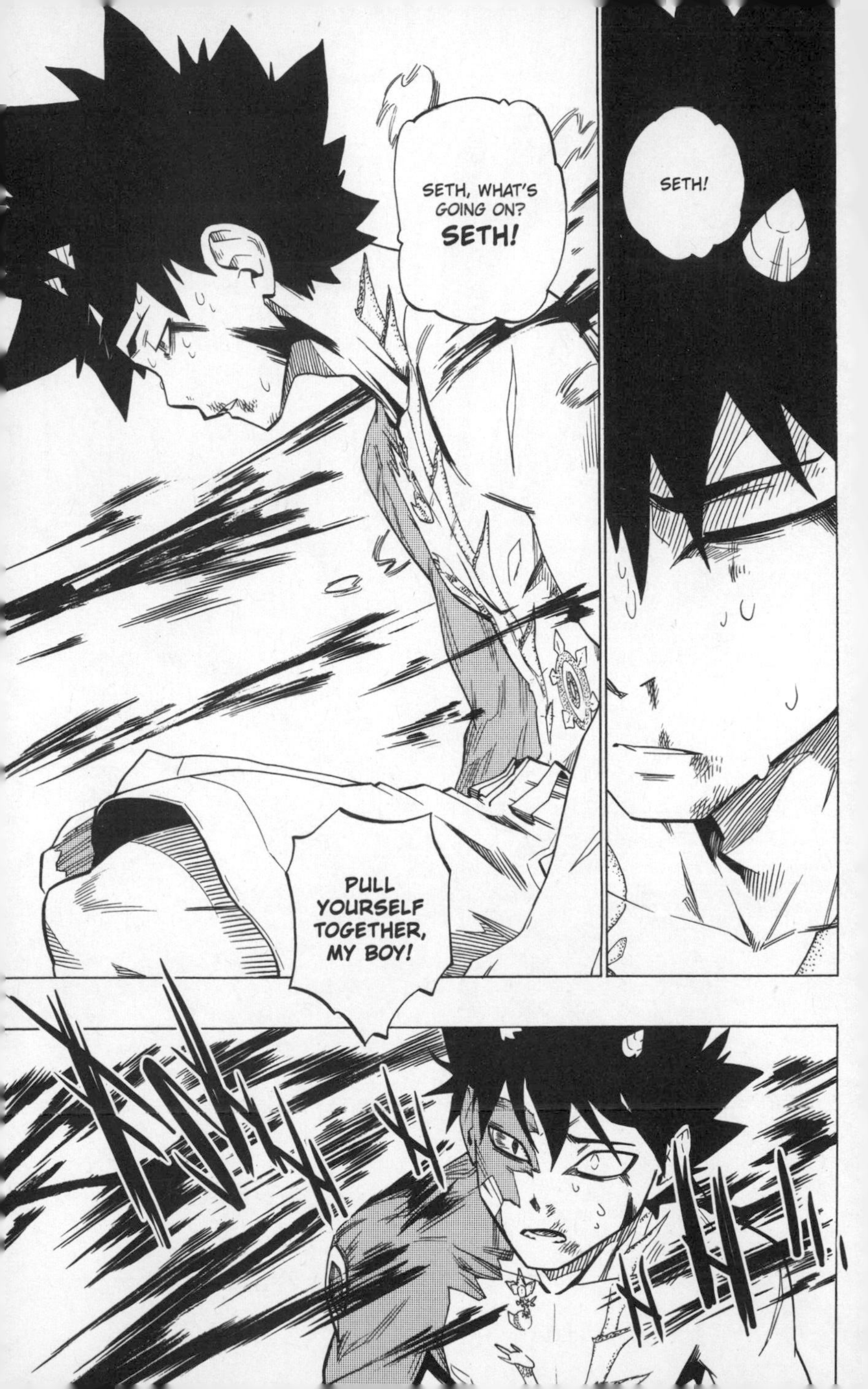
SETH!
SETH, WHAT'S GOING ON? SETH!
PULL YOURSELF TOGETHER, MY BOY!

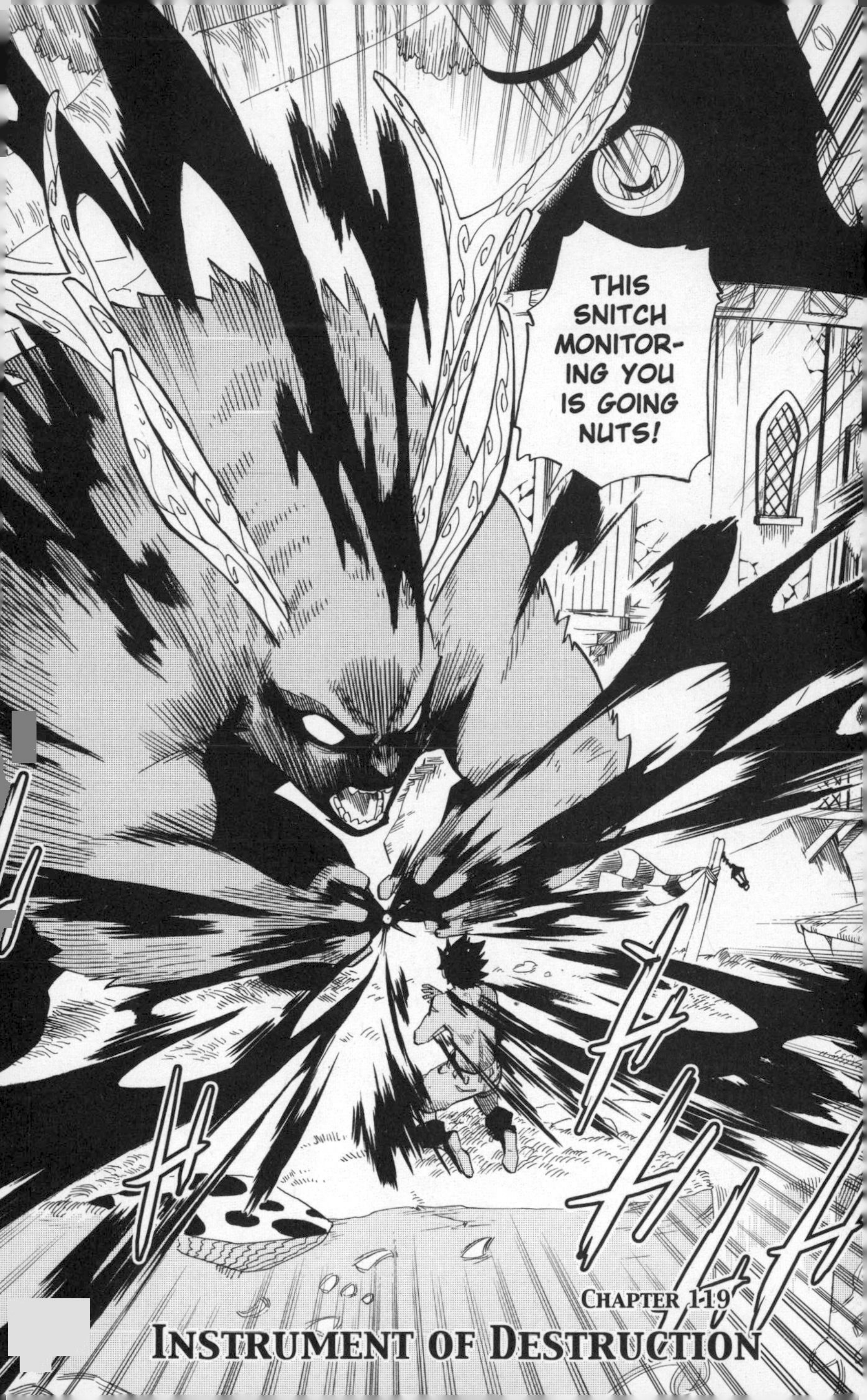
THIS SNITCH MONITORING YOU IS GOING NUTS!

Chapter 119

Instrument of Destruction

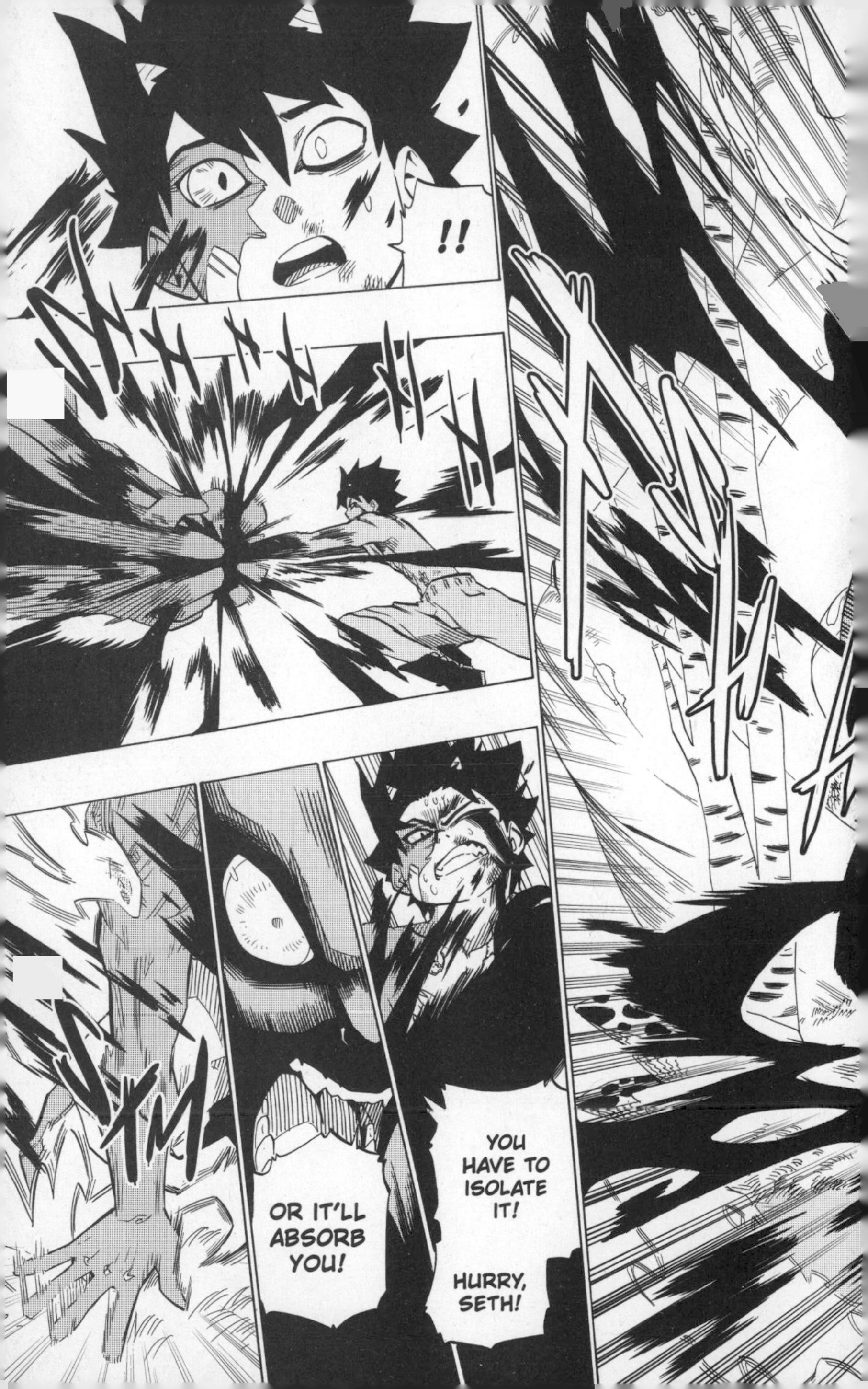
!!
YOU HAVE TO ISOLATE IT!
HURRY, SETH!
OR IT'LL ABSORB YOU!

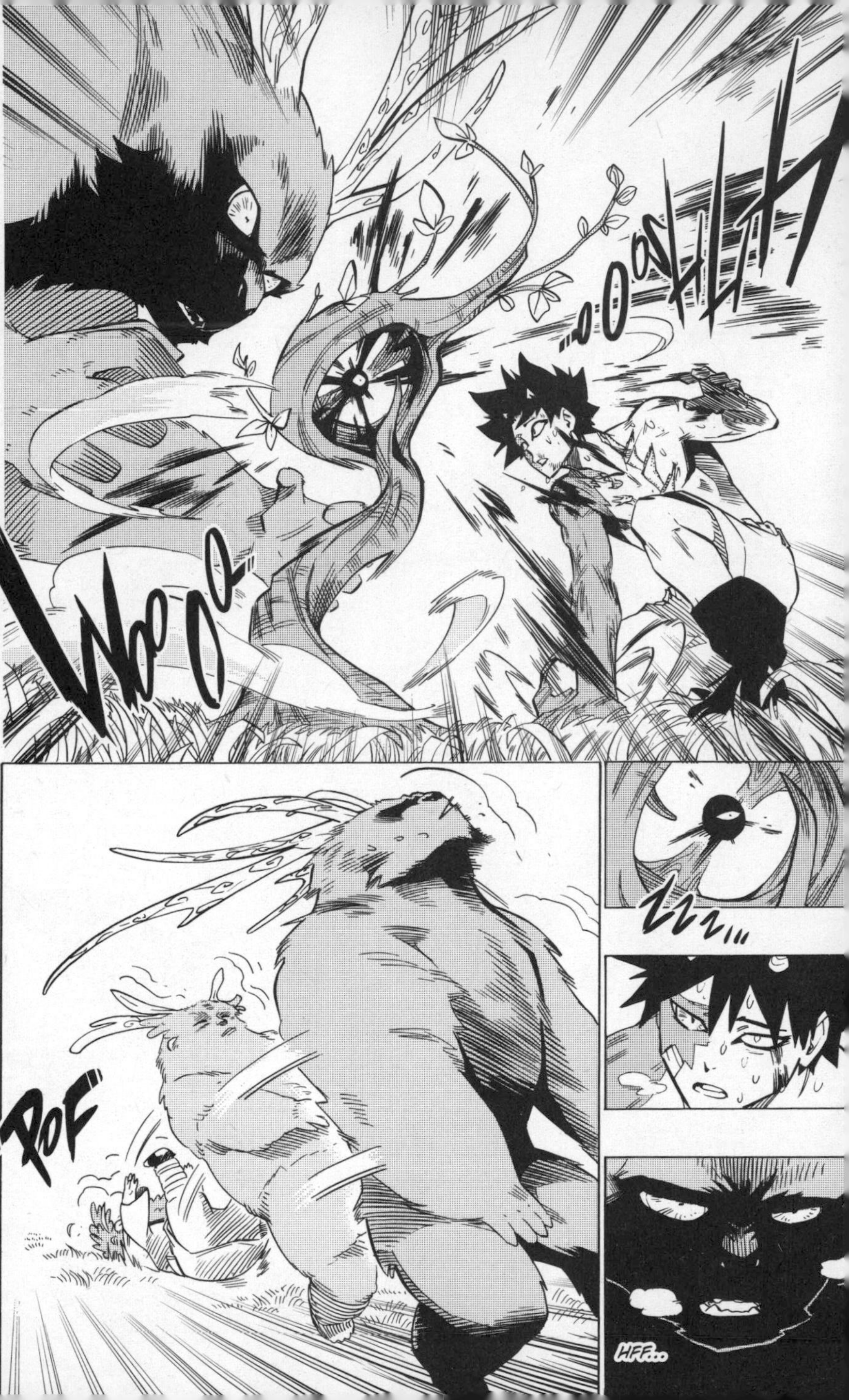
ZZZ...
POF
HFF...

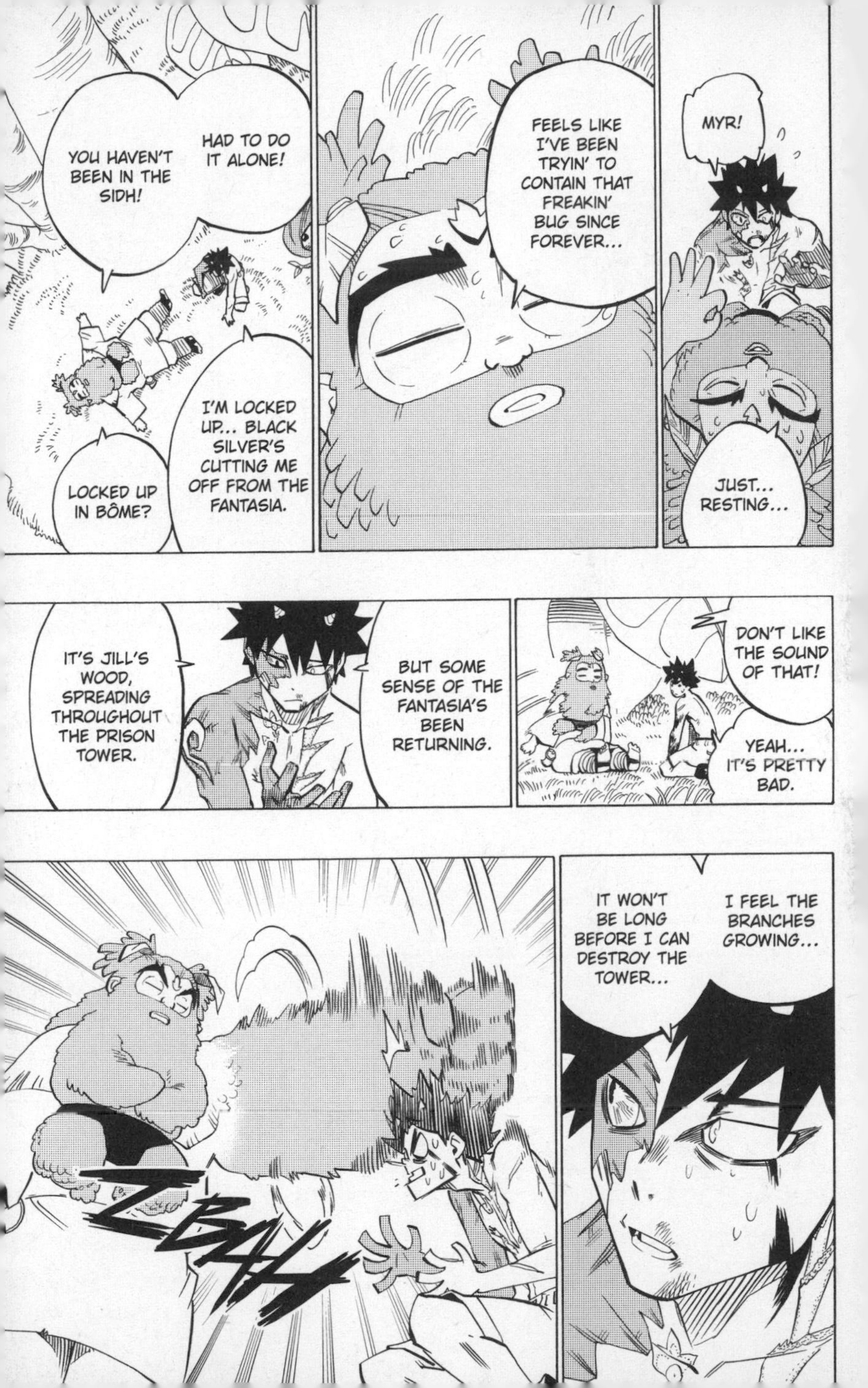
MYR!
JUST... RESTING...
FEELS LIKE I'VE BEEN TRYIN' TO CONTAIN THAT FREAKIN' BUG SINCE FOREVER...
HAD TO DO IT ALONE!
YOU HAVEN'T BEEN IN THE SIDH!
I'M LOCKED UP... BLACK SILVER'S CUTTING ME OFF FROM THE FANTASIA.
LOCKED UP IN BÔME?
DON'T LIKE THE SOUND OF THAT!
YEAH... IT'S PRETTY BAD.
BUT SOME SENSE OF THE FANTASIA'S BEEN RETURNING.
IT'S JILL'S WOOD, SPREADING THROUGHOUT THE PRISON TOWER.
I FEEL THE BRANCHES GROWING...
IT WON'T BE LONG BEFORE I CAN DESTROY THE TOWER...
ZBAH

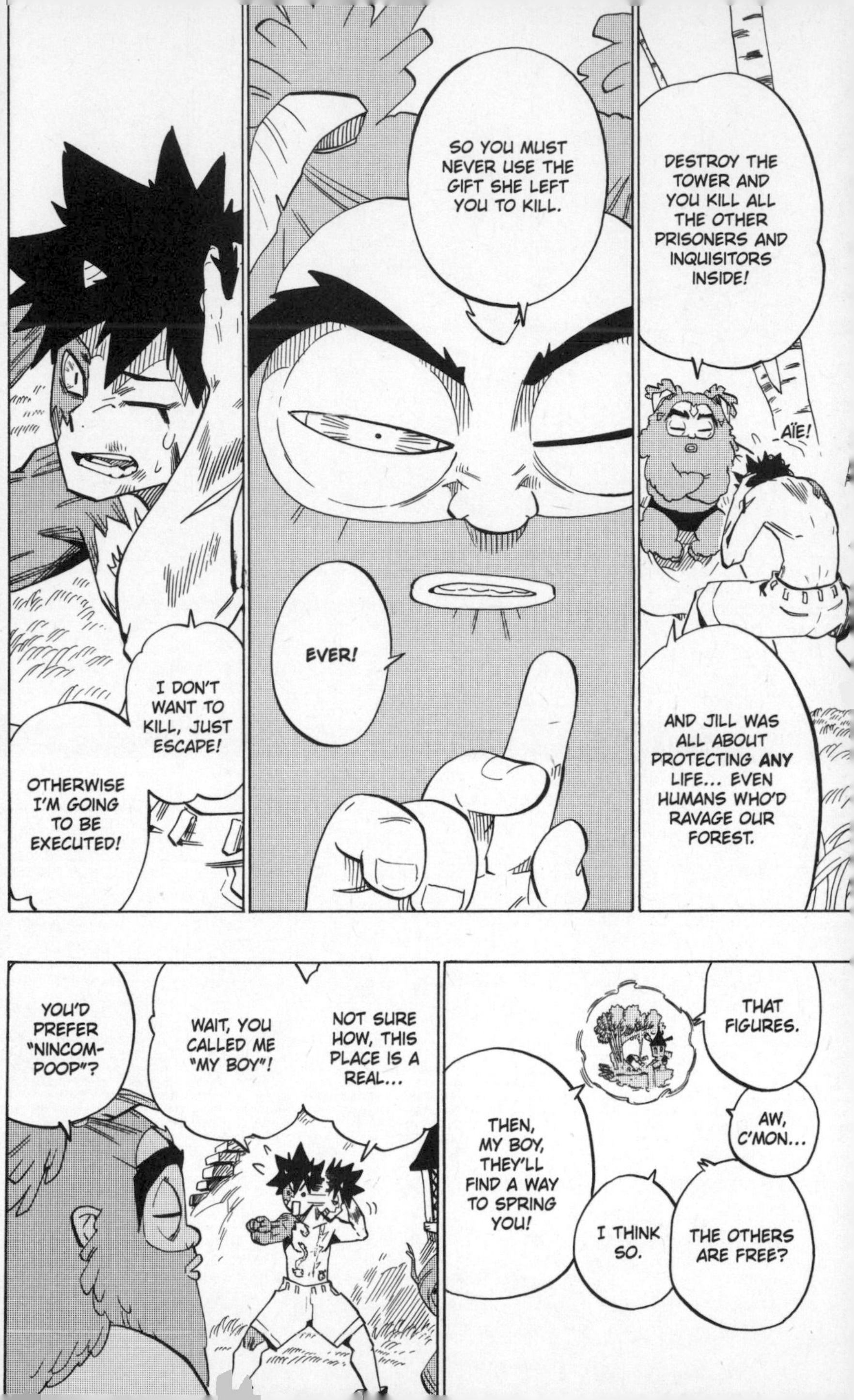
DESTROY THE TOWER AND YOU KILL ALL THE OTHER PRISONERS AND INQUISITORS INSIDE!
AÏE!
AND JILL WAS ALL ABOUT PROTECTING **ANY** LIFE... EVEN HUMANS WHO'D RAVAGE OUR FOREST.
SO YOU MUST NEVER USE THE GIFT SHE LEFT YOU TO KILL.
EVER!
I DON'T WANT TO KILL, JUST ESCAPE!
OTHERWISE I'M GOING TO BE EXECUTED!
THE OTHERS ARE FREE?
I THINK SO.
THEN, MY BOY, THEY'LL FIND A WAY TO SPRING YOU!
AW, C'MON...
THAT FIGURES.
NOT SURE HOW, THIS PLACE IS A REAL...
WAIT, YOU CALLED ME "MY BOY"!
YOU'D PREFER "NINCOM-POOP"?

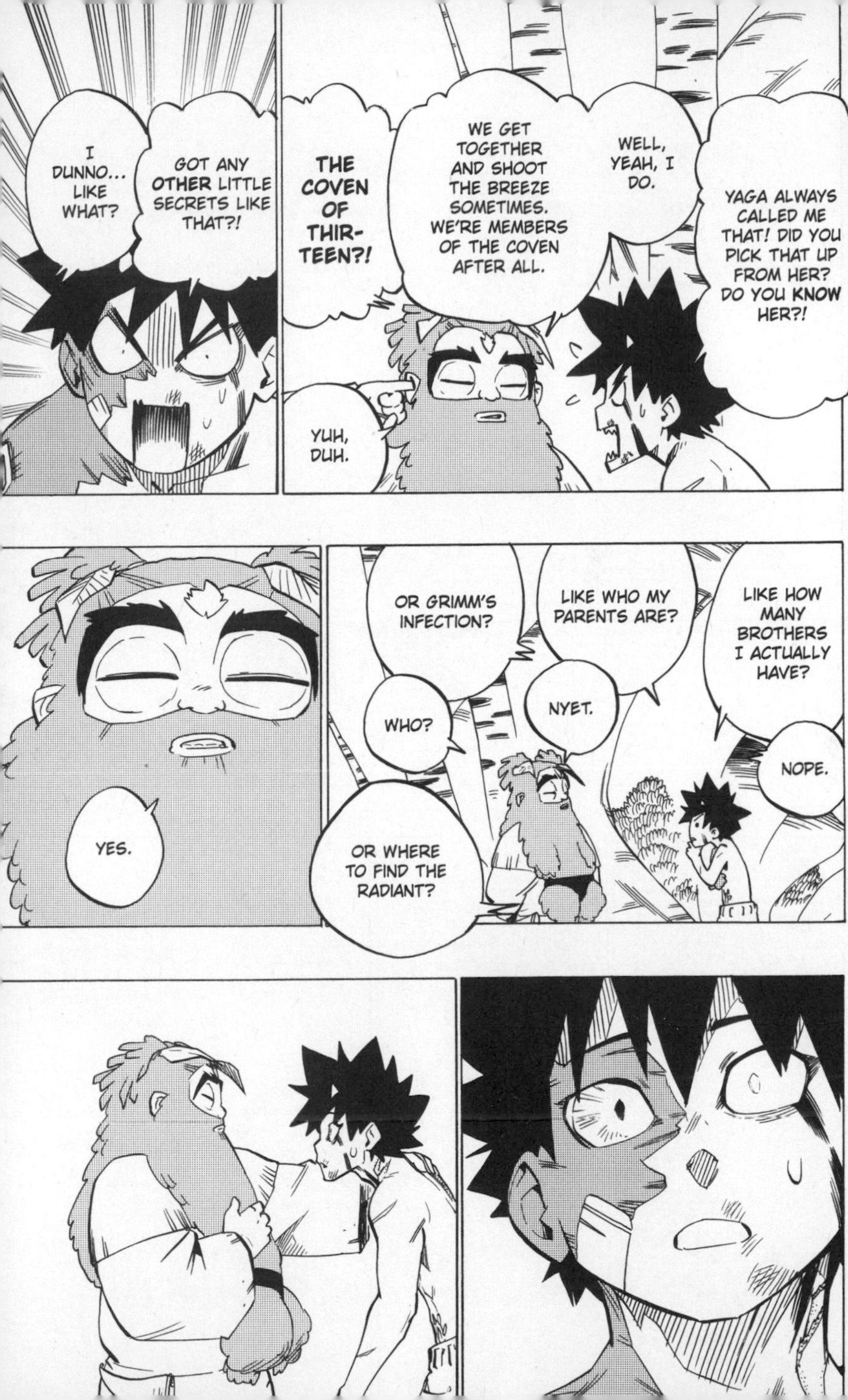
YAGA ALWAYS CALLED ME THAT! DID YOU PICK THAT UP FROM HER? DO YOU KNOW HER?!
WELL, YEAH, I DO.
WE GET TOGETHER AND SHOOT THE BREEZE SOMETIMES. WE'RE MEMBERS OF THE COVEN AFTER ALL.
THE COVEN OF THIR-TEEN?!
YUH, DUH.
GOT ANY OTHER LITTLE SECRETS LIKE THAT?!
I DUNNO... LIKE WHAT?
LIKE HOW MANY BROTHERS I ACTUALLY HAVE?
NOPE.
LIKE WHO MY PARENTS ARE?
NYET.
OR GRIMM'S INFECTION?
WHO?
OR WHERE TO FIND THE RADIANT?
YES.

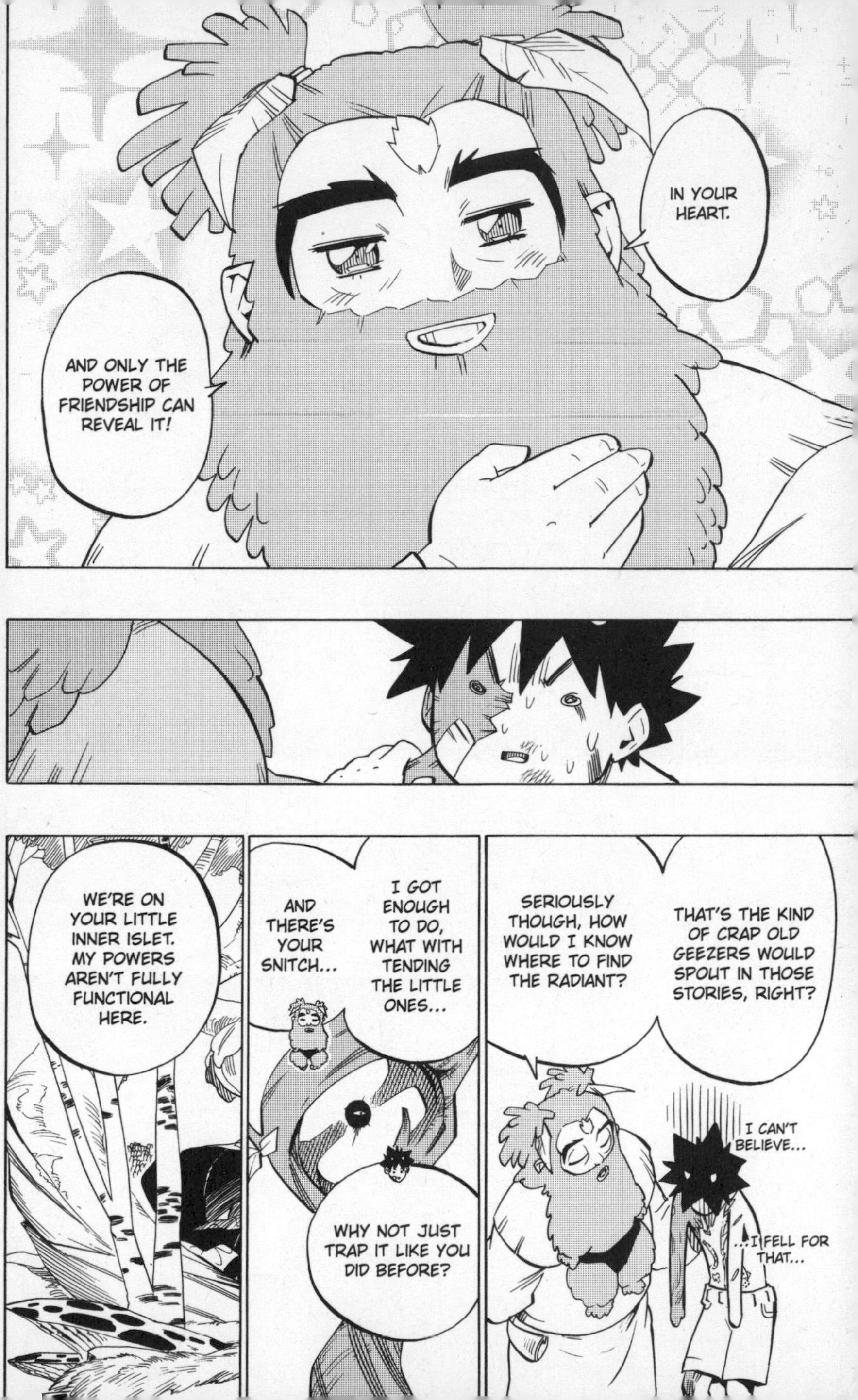
IN YOUR HEART.
AND ONLY THE POWER OF FRIENDSHIP CAN REVEAL IT!
THAT'S THE KIND OF CRAP OLD GEEZERS WOULD SPOUT IN THOSE STORIES, RIGHT?
SERIOUSLY THOUGH, HOW WOULD I KNOW WHERE TO FIND THE RADIANT?
I CAN'T BELIEVE...
...I FELL FOR THAT...
I GOT ENOUGH TO DO, WHAT WITH TENDING THE LITTLE ONES...
AND THERE'S YOUR SNITCH...
WHY NOT JUST TRAP IT LIKE YOU DID BEFORE?
WE'RE ON YOUR LITTLE INNER ISLET. MY POWERS AREN'T FULLY FUNCTIONAL HERE.

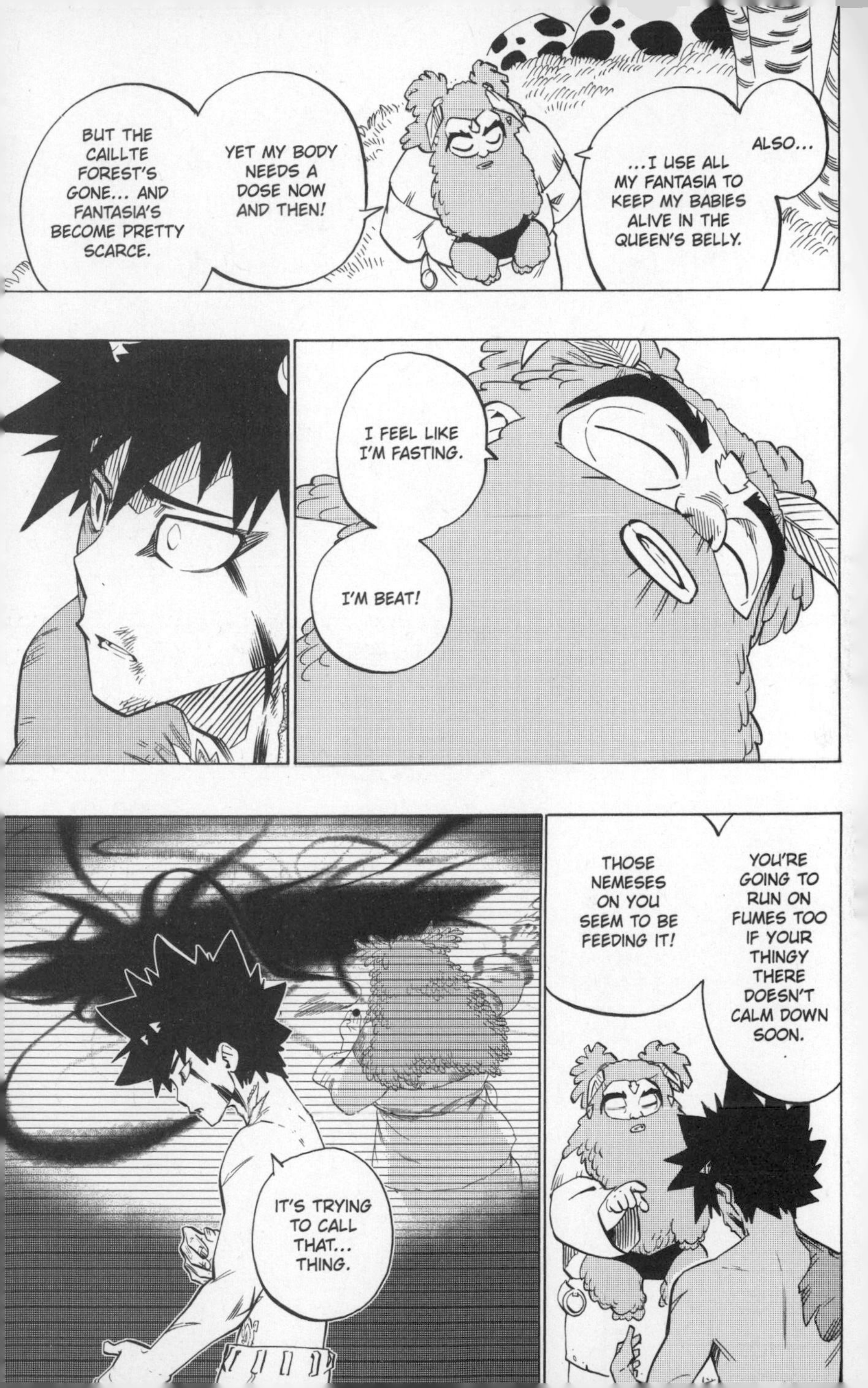
ALSO...
...I USE ALL MY FANTASIA TO KEEP MY BABIES ALIVE IN THE QUEEN'S BELLY.
YET MY BODY NEEDS A DOSE NOW AND THEN!
BUT THE CAILLTE FOREST'S GONE... AND FANTASIA'S BECOME PRETTY SCARCE.
I FEEL LIKE I'M FASTING.
I'M BEAT!
YOU'RE GOING TO RUN ON FUMES TOO IF YOUR THINGY THERE DOESN'T CALM DOWN SOON.
THOSE NEMESES ON YOU SEEM TO BE FEEDING IT!
IT'S TRYING TO CALL THAT... THING.

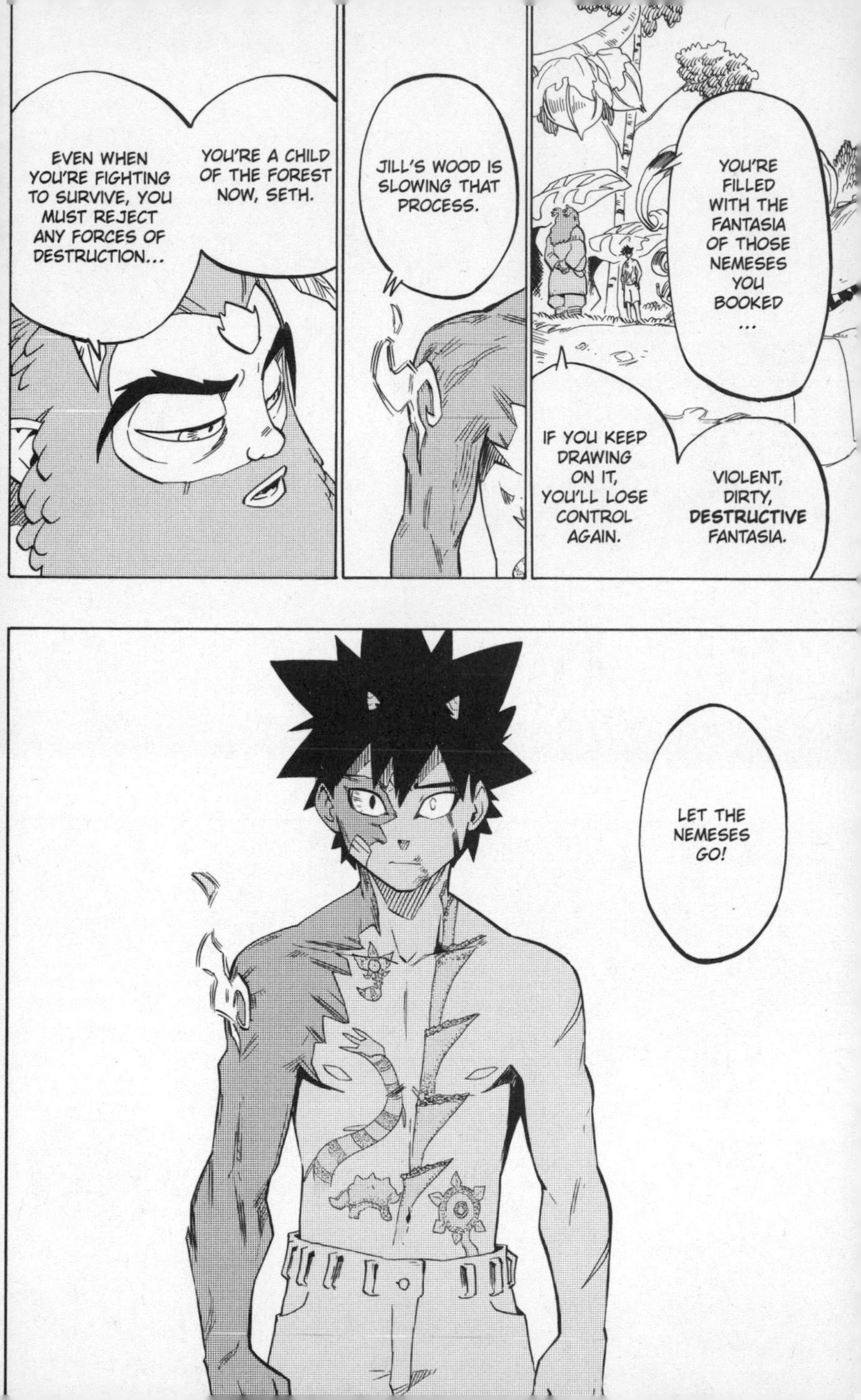
YOU'RE FILLED WITH THE FANTASIA OF THOSE NEMESES YOU BOOKED ...
VIOLENT, DIRTY, **DESTRUCTIVE** FANTASIA.
IF YOU KEEP DRAWING ON IT, YOU'LL LOSE CONTROL AGAIN.
JILL'S WOOD IS SLOWING THAT PROCESS.
YOU'RE A CHILD OF THE FOREST NOW, SETH.
EVEN WHEN YOU'RE FIGHTING TO SURVIVE, YOU MUST REJECT ANY FORCES OF DESTRUCTION...
LET THE NEMESES GO!

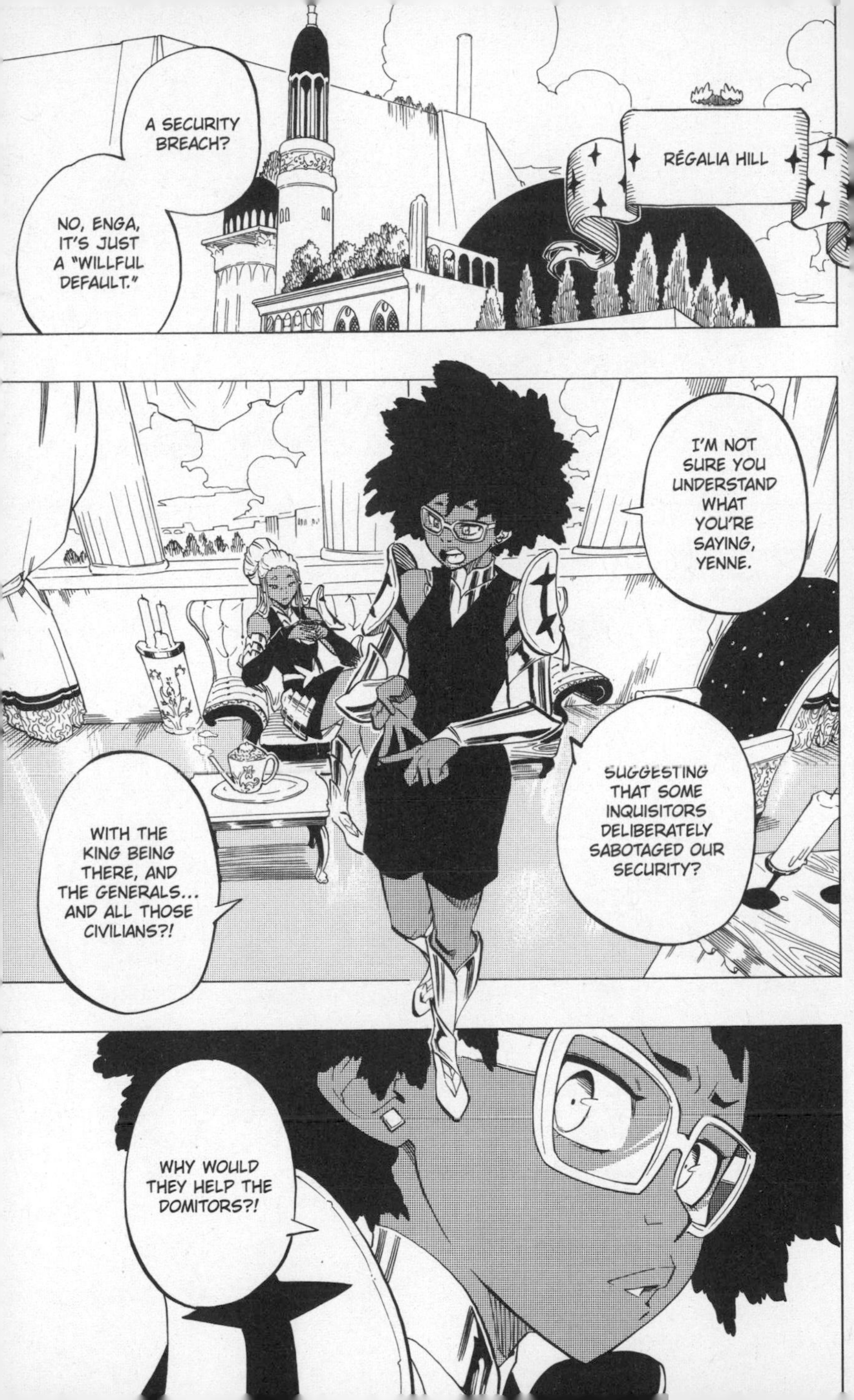
RÉGALIA HILL
A SECURITY BREACH?
NO, ENGA, IT'S JUST A "WILLFUL DEFAULT."
I'M NOT SURE YOU UNDERSTAND WHAT YOU'RE SAYING, YENNE.
SUGGESTING THAT SOME INQUISITORS DELIBERATELY SABOTAGED OUR SECURITY?
WITH THE KING BEING THERE, AND THE GENERALS... AND ALL THOSE CIVILIANS?!
WHY WOULD THEY HELP THE DOMITORS?!

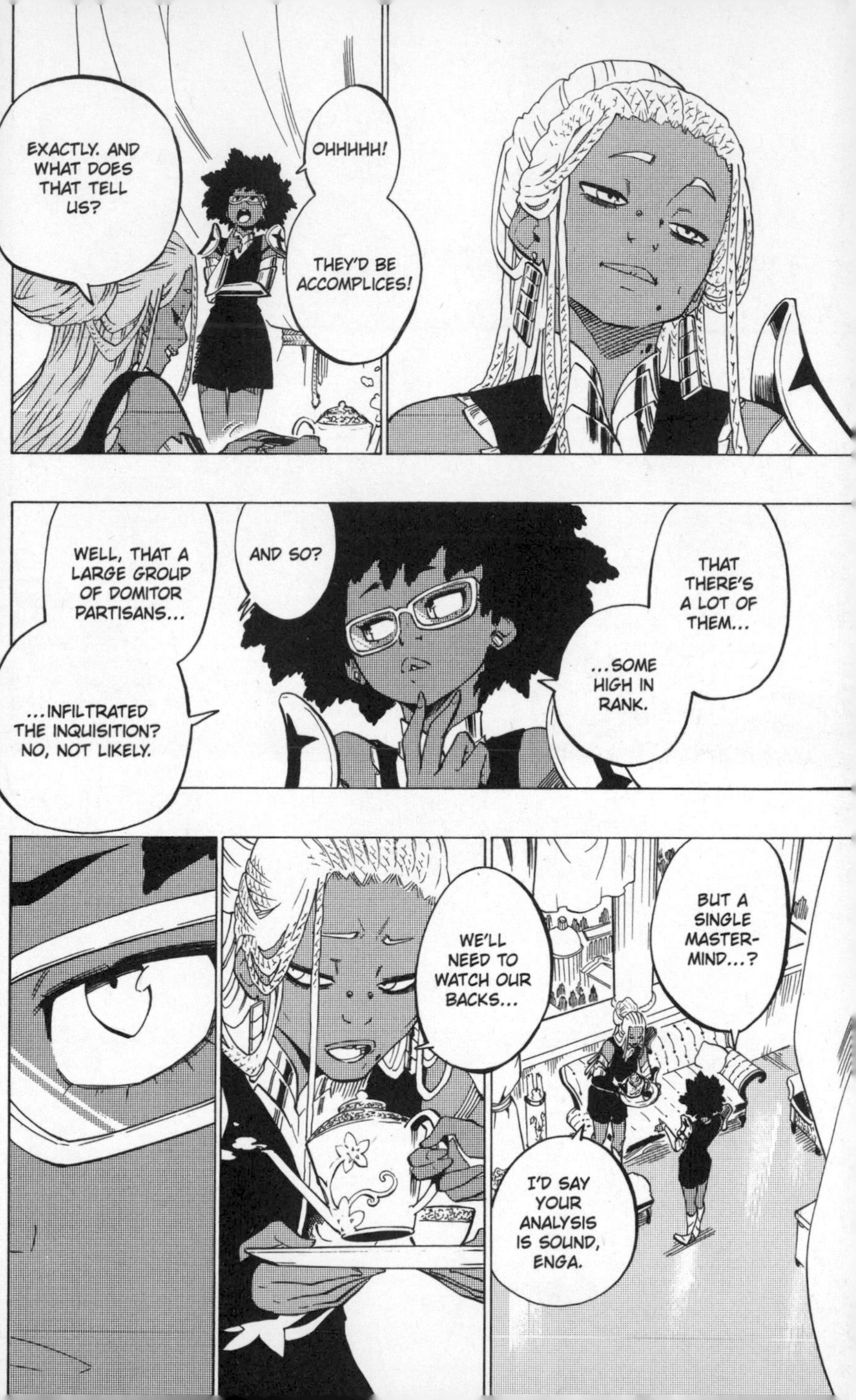
OHHHHH!
THEY'D BE ACCOMPLICES!
EXACTLY. AND WHAT DOES THAT TELL US?
THAT THERE'S A LOT OF THEM...
...SOME HIGH IN RANK.
AND SO?
WELL, THAT A LARGE GROUP OF DOMITOR PARTISANS...
...INFILTRATED THE INQUISITION? NO, NOT LIKELY.
BUT A SINGLE MASTER-MIND...?
I'D SAY YOUR ANALYSIS IS SOUND, ENGA.
WE'LL NEED TO WATCH OUR BACKS...

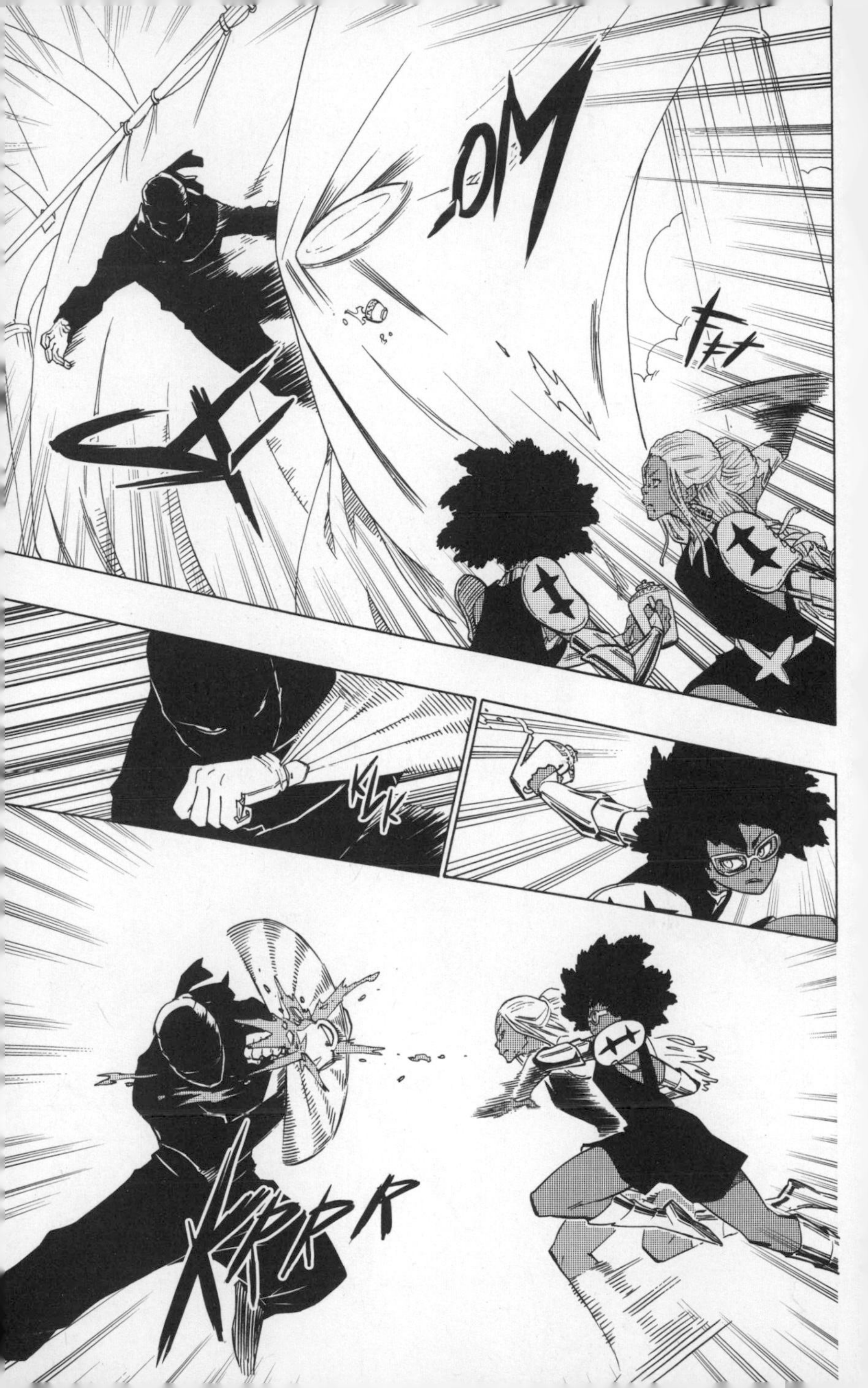

OM
KLK
KRRRR

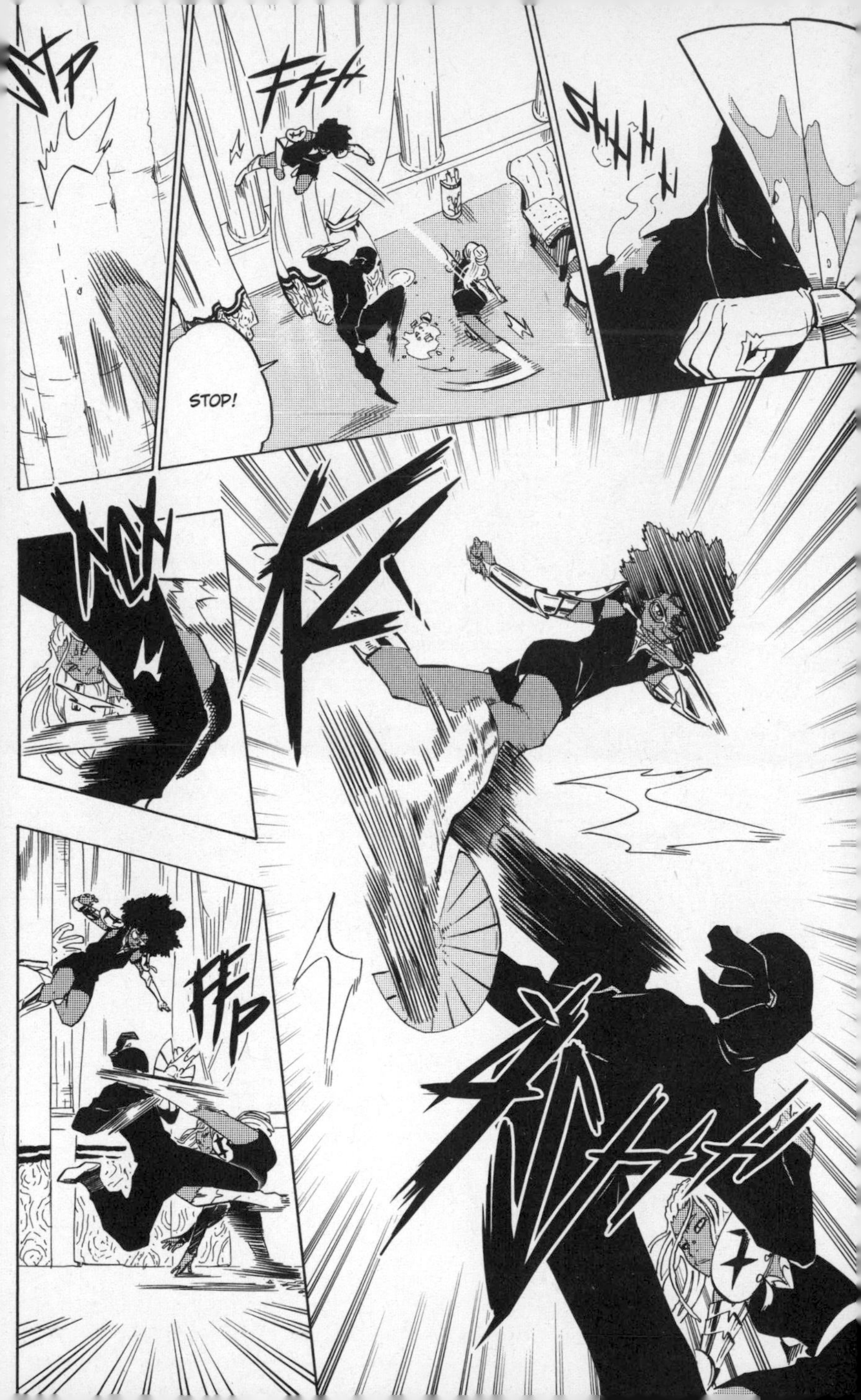
SHHHHHH
FFFF
STOP!
STP
K
THCK
SHHHH
FFP

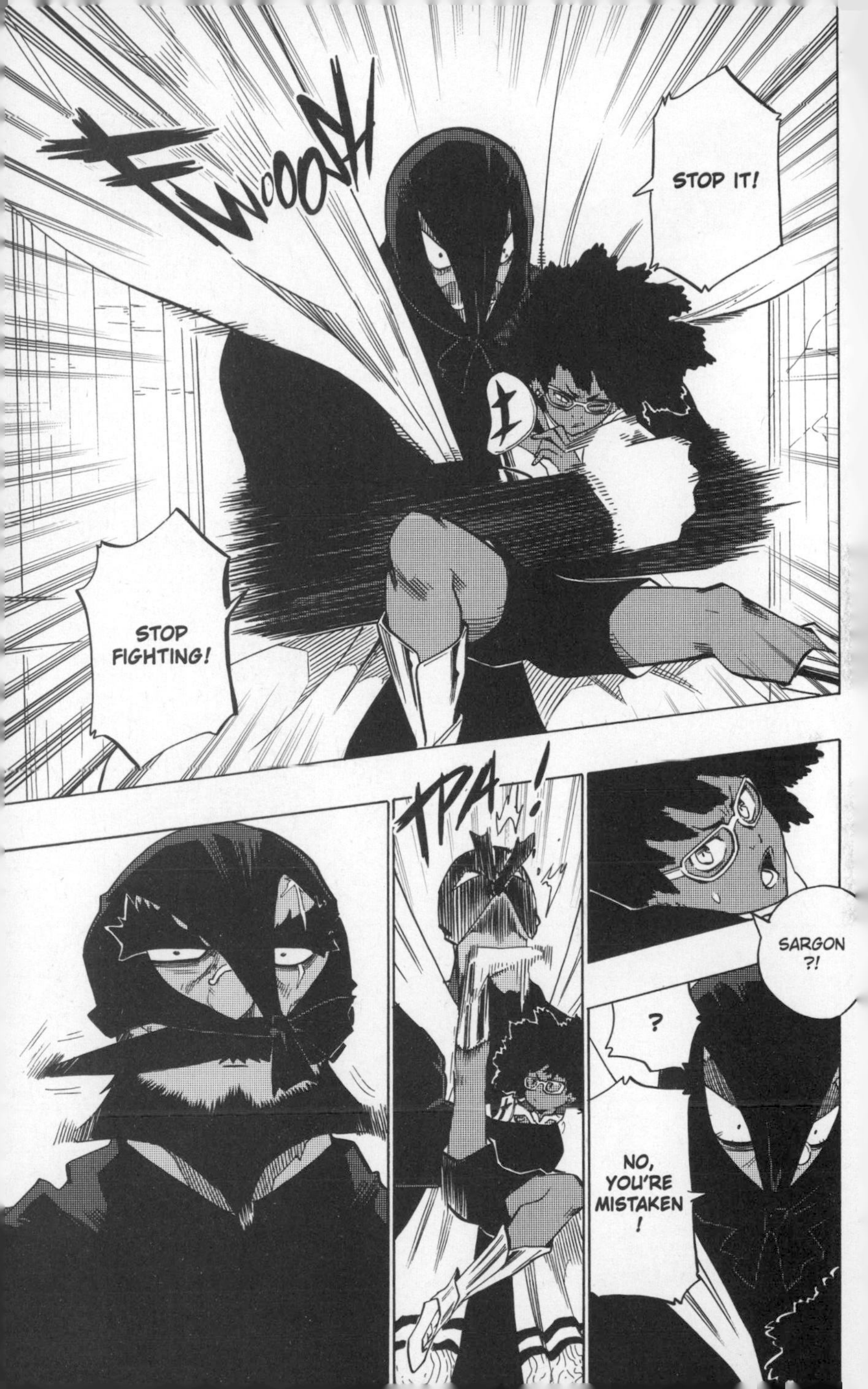
STOP IT!
WOOSH
STOP FIGHTING!
SARGON ?!
?
NO, YOU'RE MISTAKEN !
TPA!

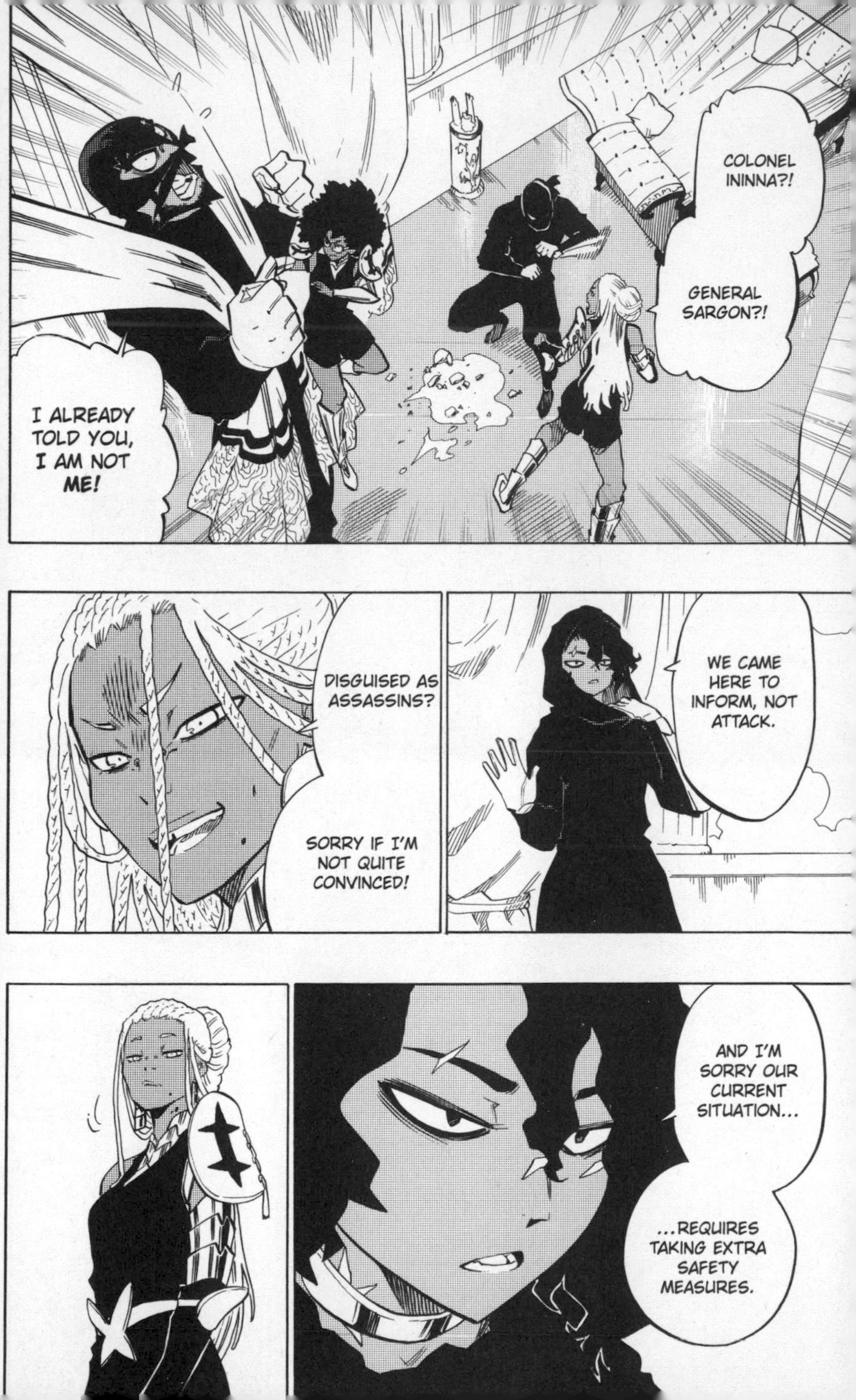
COLONEL ININNA?!
GENERAL SARGON?!
I ALREADY TOLD YOU, I AM NOT ME!
WE CAME HERE TO INFORM, NOT ATTACK.
DISGUISED AS ASSASSINS?
SORRY IF I'M NOT QUITE CONVINCED!
AND I'M SORRY OUR CURRENT SITUATION...
...REQUIRES TAKING EXTRA SAFETY MEASURES.

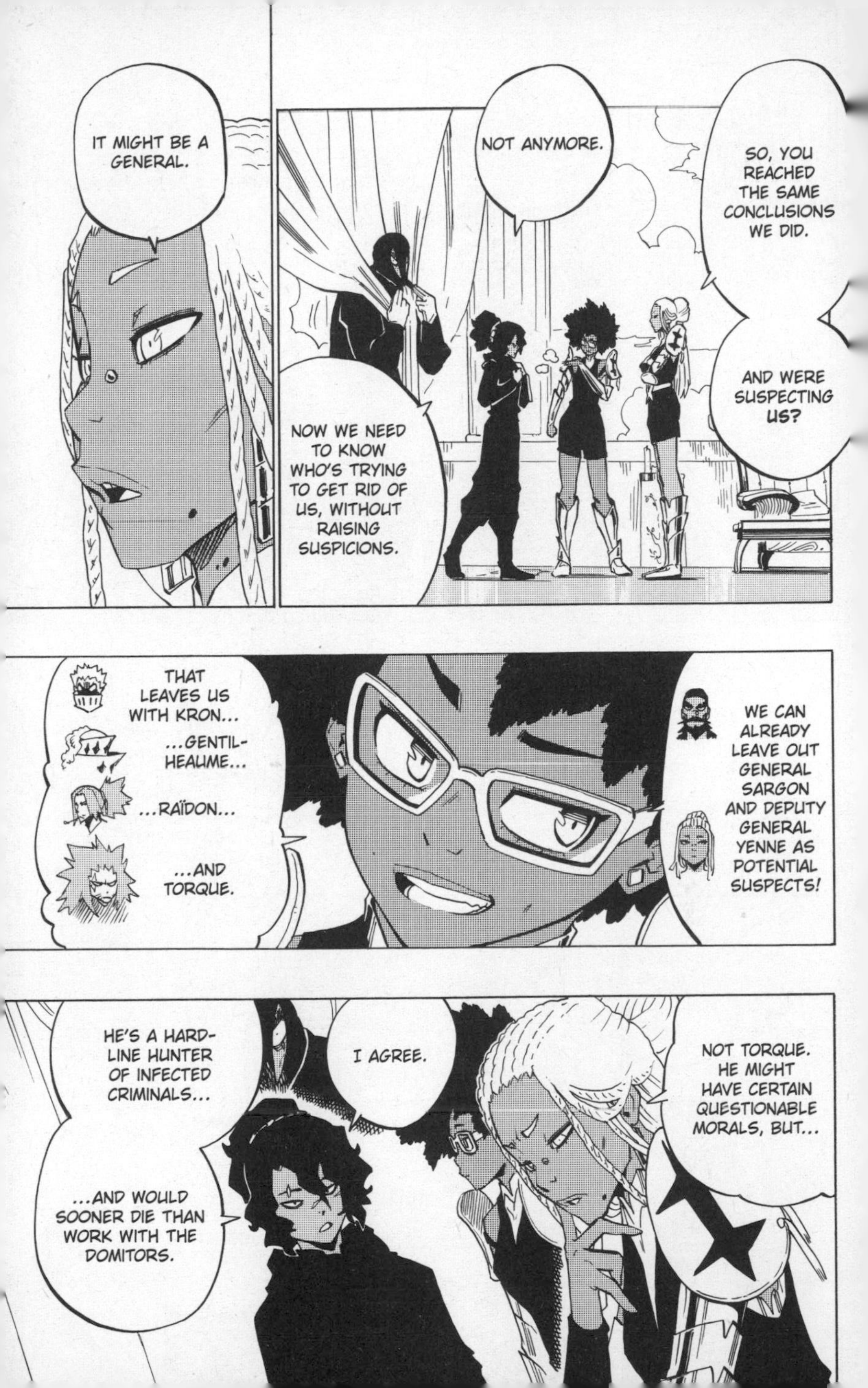
SO, YOU REACHED THE SAME CONCLUSIONS WE DID.
AND WERE SUSPECTING US?
NOT ANYMORE.
NOW WE NEED TO KNOW WHO'S TRYING TO GET RID OF US, WITHOUT RAISING SUSPICIONS.
IT MIGHT BE A GENERAL.
WE CAN ALREADY LEAVE OUT GENERAL SARGON AND DEPUTY GENERAL YENNE AS POTENTIAL SUSPECTS!
THAT LEAVES US WITH KRON...
...GENTIL-HEAUME...
...RAÏDON...
...AND TORQUE.
NOT TORQUE. HE MIGHT HAVE CERTAIN QUESTIONABLE MORALS, BUT...
I AGREE.
HE'S A HARD-LINE HUNTER OF INFECTED CRIMINALS...
...AND WOULD SOONER DIE THAN WORK WITH THE DOMITORS.

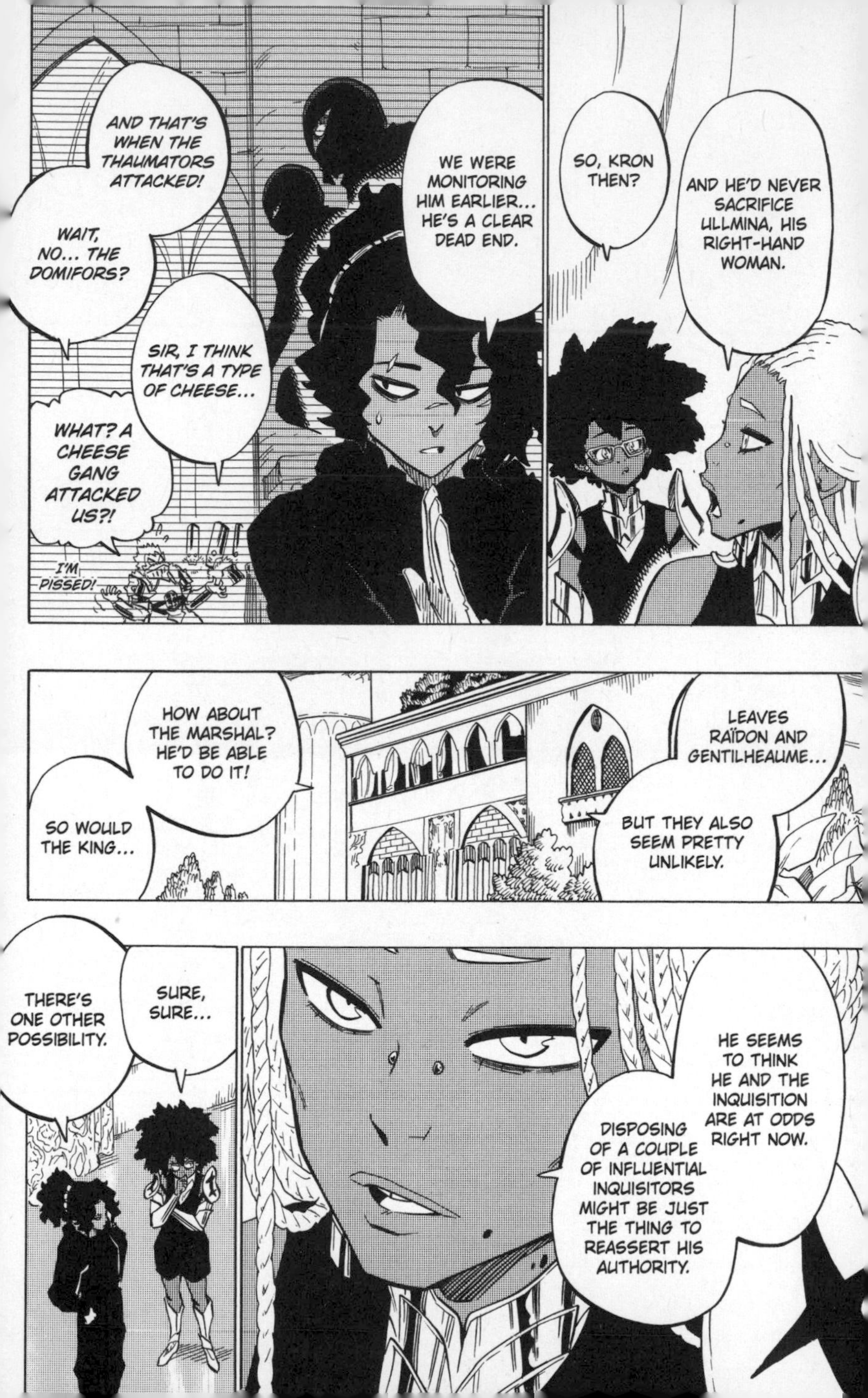
AND THAT'S WHEN THE THAUMATORS ATTACKED!
WAIT, NO... THE DOMIFORS?
SIR, I THINK THAT'S A TYPE OF CHEESE...
WHAT? A CHEESE GANG ATTACKED US?!
I'M PISSED!
WE WERE MONITORING HIM EARLIER... HE'S A CLEAR DEAD END.
SO, KRON THEN?
AND HE'D NEVER SACRIFICE ULLMINA, HIS RIGHT-HAND WOMAN.
HOW ABOUT THE MARSHAL? HE'D BE ABLE TO DO IT!
SO WOULD THE KING...
LEAVES RAÏDON AND GENTILHEAUME...
BUT THEY ALSO SEEM PRETTY UNLIKELY.
THERE'S ONE OTHER POSSIBILITY.
SURE, SURE...
HE SEEMS TO THINK HE AND THE INQUISITION ARE AT ODDS RIGHT NOW.
DISPOSING OF A COUPLE OF INFLUENTIAL INQUISITORS MIGHT BE JUST THE THING TO REASSERT HIS AUTHORITY.

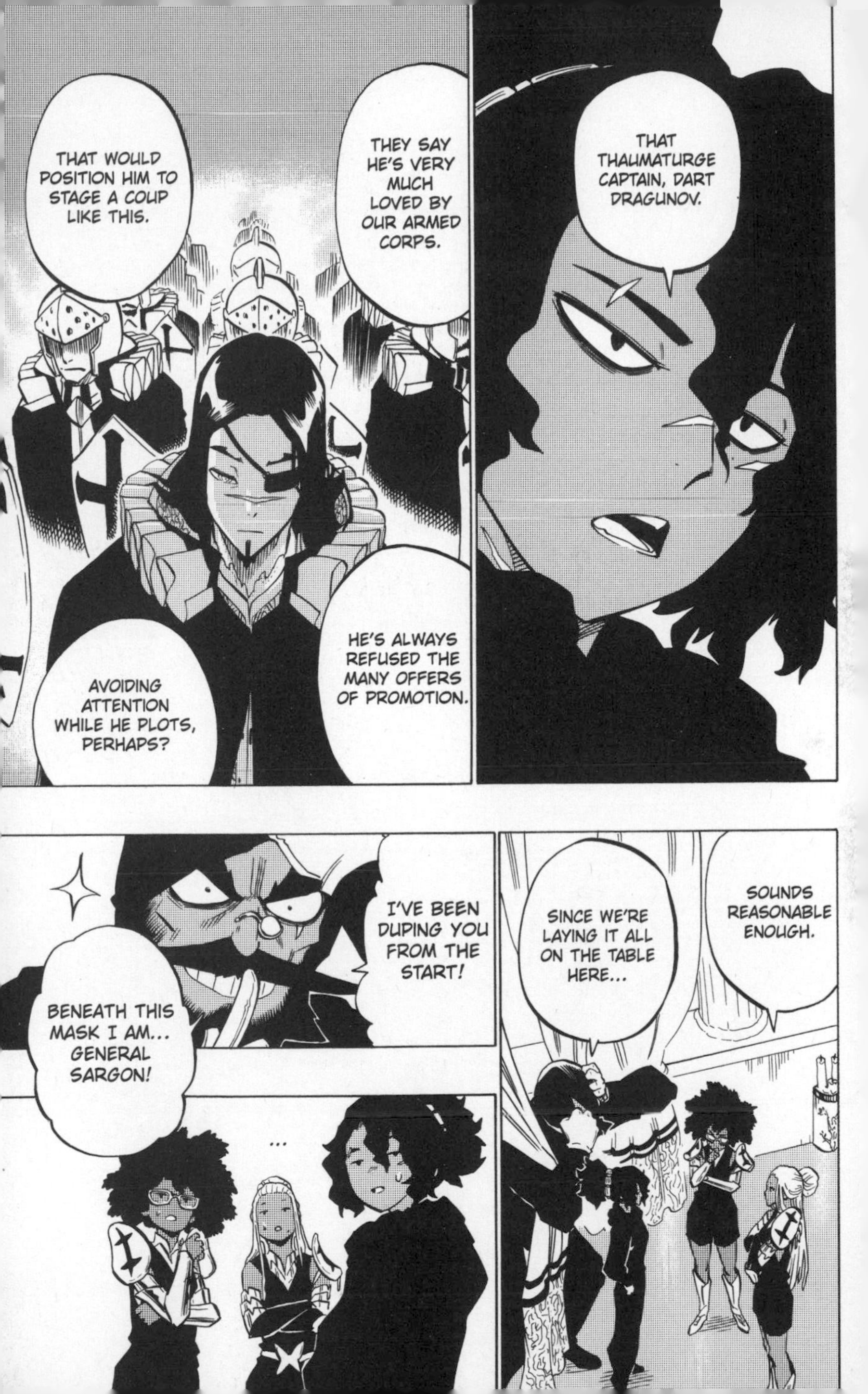
THAT THAUMATURGE CAPTAIN, DART DRAGUNOV.
THEY SAY HE'S VERY MUCH LOVED BY OUR ARMED CORPS.
THAT WOULD POSITION HIM TO STAGE A COUP LIKE THIS.
HE'S ALWAYS REFUSED THE MANY OFFERS OF PROMOTION.
AVOIDING ATTENTION WHILE HE PLOTS, PERHAPS?
SOUNDS REASONABLE ENOUGH.
SINCE WE'RE LAYING IT ALL ON THE TABLE HERE...
I'VE BEEN DUPING YOU FROM THE START!
BENEATH THIS MASK I AM... GENERAL SARGON!
...

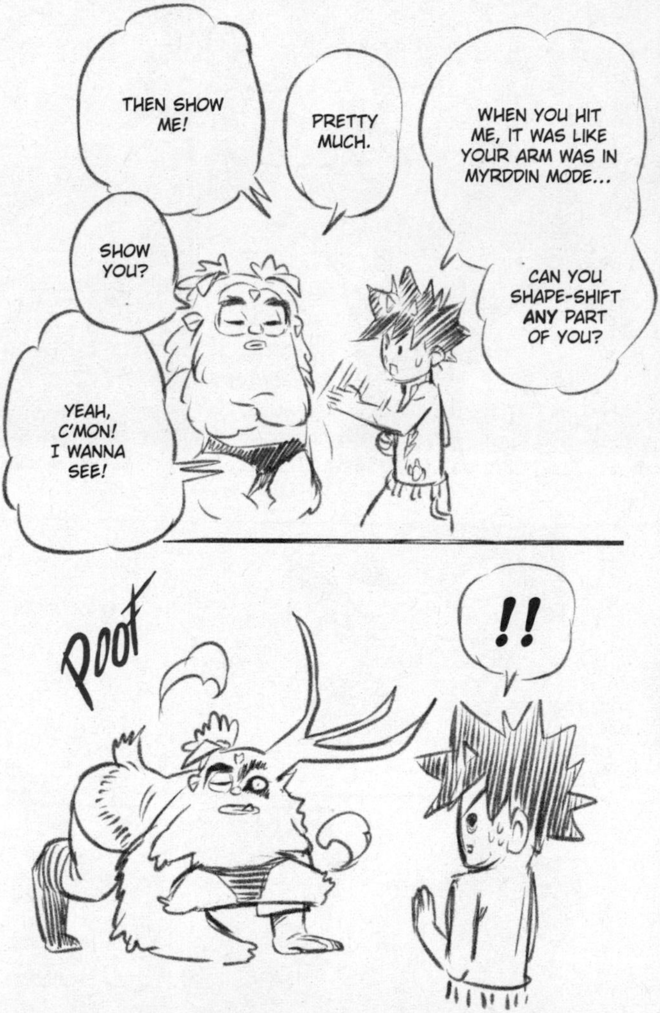
WHEN YOU HIT ME, IT WAS LIKE YOUR ARM WAS IN MYRDDIN MODE...
CAN YOU SHAPE-SHIFT ANY PART OF YOU?
PRETTY MUCH.
THEN SHOW ME!
SHOW YOU?
YEAH, C'MON! I WANNA SEE!
!!
POOF

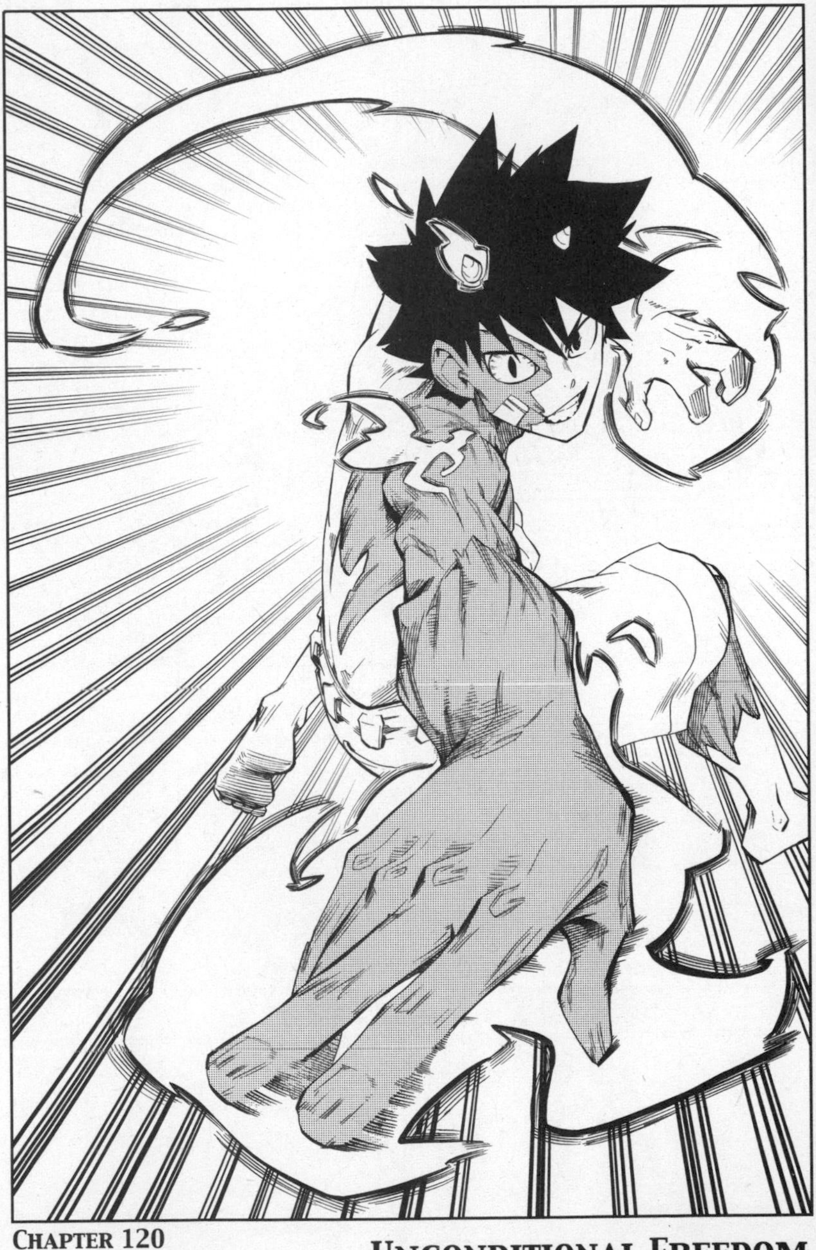

Chapter 120

Unconditional Freedom

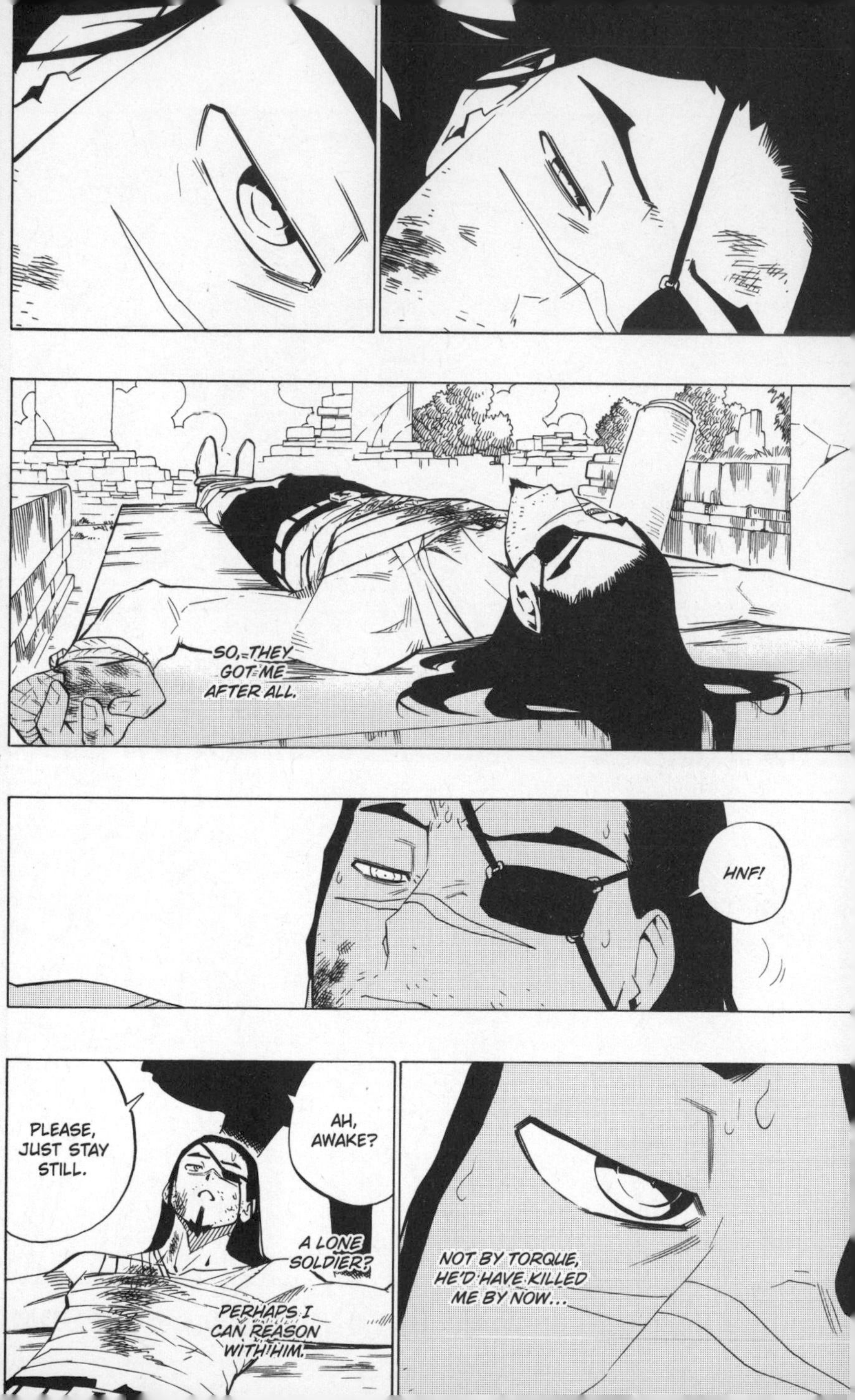
SO, THEY GOT ME AFTER ALL.
HNF!
NOT BY TORQUE, HE'D HAVE KILLED ME BY NOW...
AH, AWAKE?
PLEASE, JUST STAY STILL.
A LONE SOLDIER?
PERHAPS I CAN REASON WITH HIM.

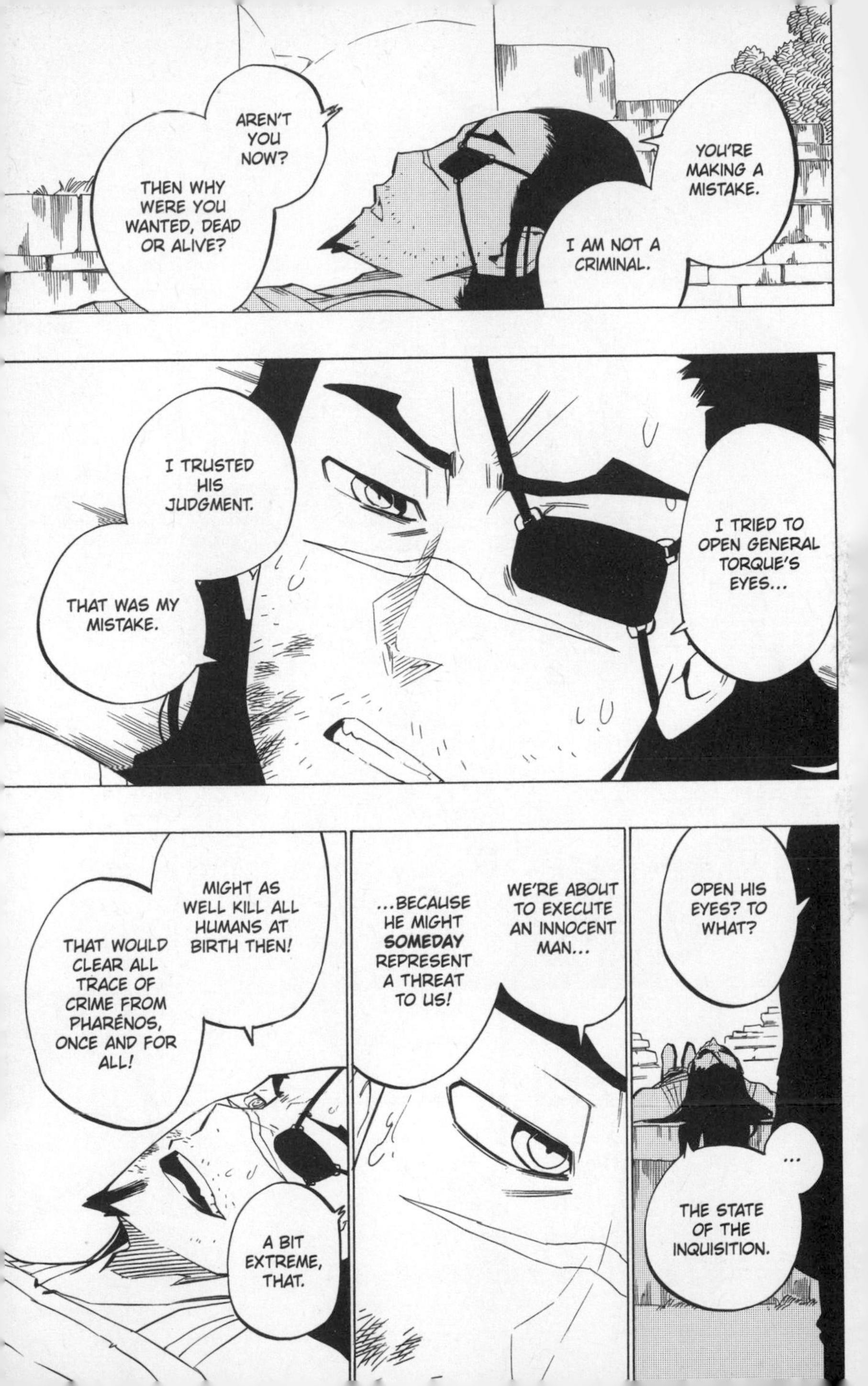
YOU'RE MAKING A MISTAKE.
I AM NOT A CRIMINAL.
AREN'T YOU NOW?
THEN WHY WERE YOU WANTED, DEAD OR ALIVE?
I TRIED TO OPEN GENERAL TORQUE'S EYES...
I TRUSTED HIS JUDGMENT.
THAT WAS MY MISTAKE.
OPEN HIS EYES? TO WHAT?
...
THE STATE OF THE INQUISITION.
WE'RE ABOUT TO EXECUTE AN INNOCENT MAN...
...BECAUSE HE MIGHT **SOMEDAY** REPRESENT A THREAT TO US!
MIGHT AS WELL KILL ALL HUMANS AT BIRTH THEN!
THAT WOULD CLEAR ALL TRACE OF CRIME FROM PHARÉNOS, ONCE AND FOR ALL!
A BIT EXTREME, THAT.

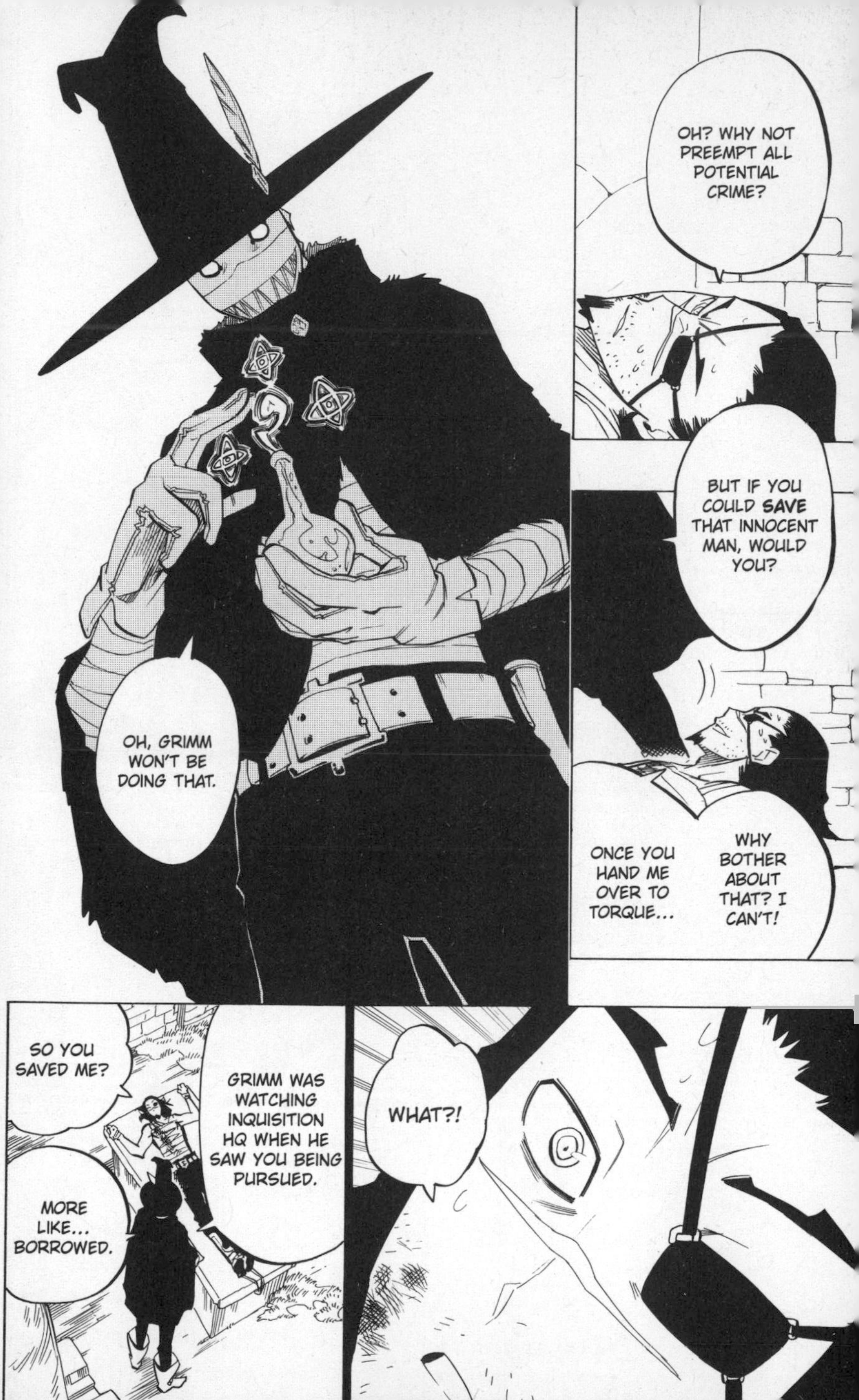
OH? WHY NOT PREEMPT ALL POTENTIAL CRIME?
BUT IF YOU COULD SAVE THAT INNOCENT MAN, WOULD YOU?
WHY BOTHER ABOUT THAT? I CAN'T!
ONCE YOU HAND ME OVER TO TORQUE...
OH, GRIMM WON'T BE DOING THAT.
WHAT?!
GRIMM WAS WATCHING INQUISITION HQ WHEN HE SAW YOU BEING PURSUED.
SO YOU SAVED ME?
MORE LIKE... BORROWED.

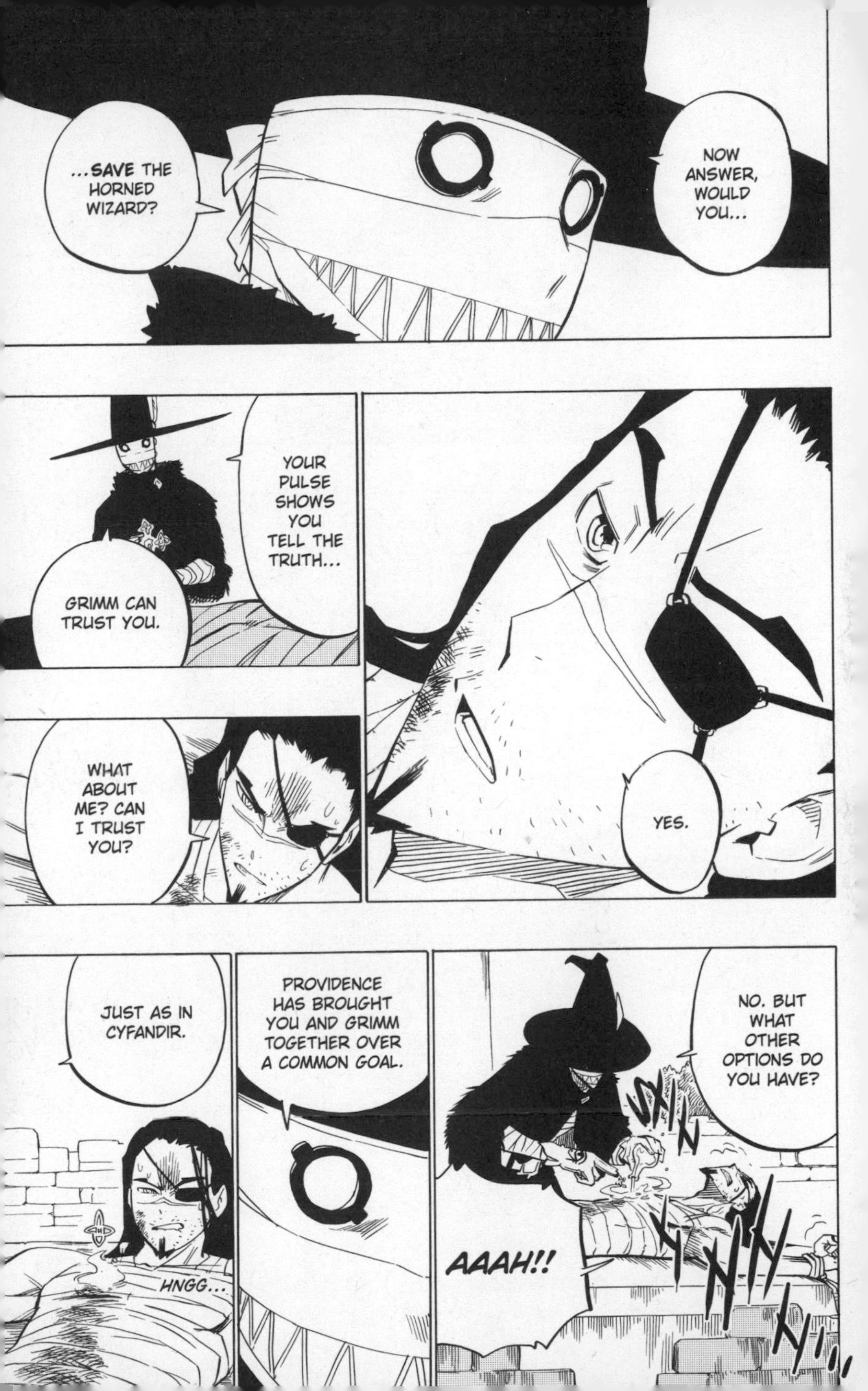
NOW ANSWER, WOULD YOU...
...SAVE THE HORNED WIZARD?
YES.
YOUR PULSE SHOWS YOU TELL THE TRUTH...
GRIMM CAN TRUST YOU.
WHAT ABOUT ME? CAN I TRUST YOU?
NO. BUT WHAT OTHER OPTIONS DO YOU HAVE?
AAAH!!
PROVIDENCE HAS BROUGHT YOU AND GRIMM TOGETHER OVER A COMMON GOAL.
JUST AS IN CYFANDIR.
HNGG...

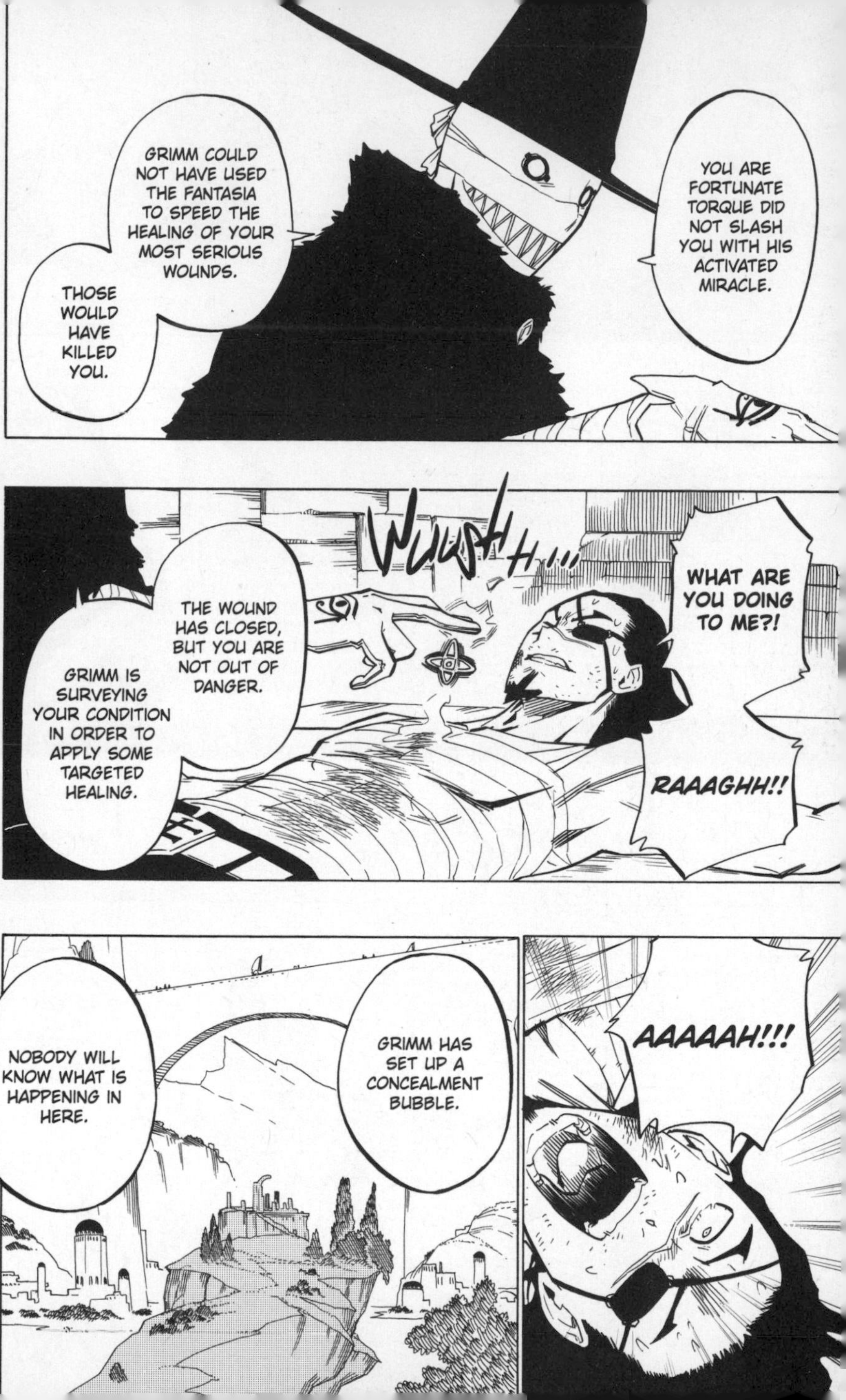
YOU ARE FORTUNATE TORQUE DID NOT SLASH YOU WITH HIS ACTIVATED MIRACLE.
GRIMM COULD NOT HAVE USED THE FANTASIA TO SPEED THE HEALING OF YOUR MOST SERIOUS WOUNDS.
THOSE WOULD HAVE KILLED YOU.
WHAT ARE YOU DOING TO ME?!
RAAAGHH!!
THE WOUND HAS CLOSED, BUT YOU ARE NOT OUT OF DANGER.
GRIMM IS SURVEYING YOUR CONDITION IN ORDER TO APPLY SOME TARGETED HEALING.
AAAAAH!!!
GRIMM HAS SET UP A CONCEALMENT BUBBLE.
NOBODY WILL KNOW WHAT IS HAPPENING IN HERE.

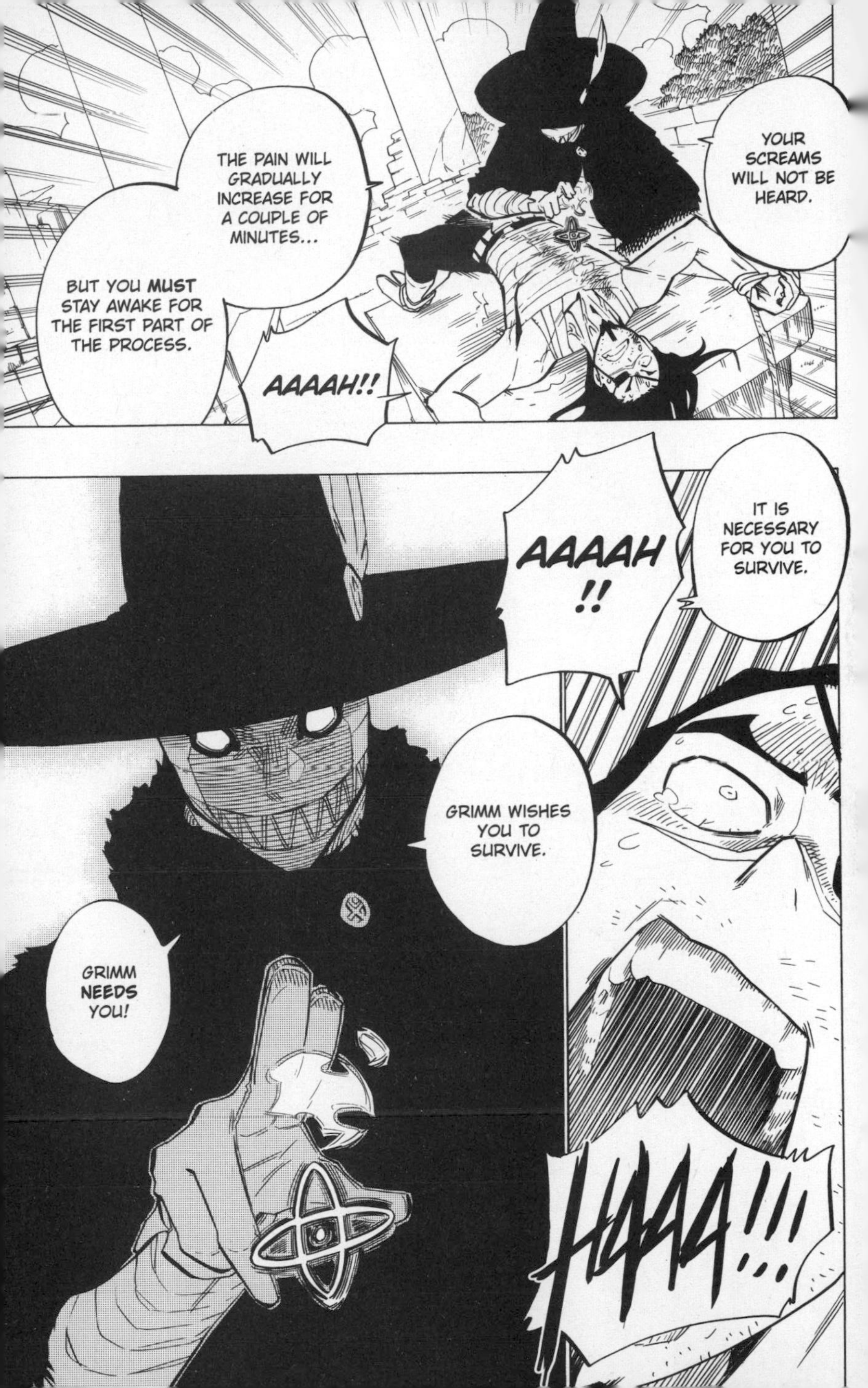
YOUR SCREAMS WILL NOT BE HEARD.
THE PAIN WILL GRADUALLY INCREASE FOR A COUPLE OF MINUTES...
BUT YOU **MUST** STAY AWAKE FOR THE FIRST PART OF THE PROCESS.
AAAAH!!
IT IS NECESSARY FOR YOU TO SURVIVE.
AAAAH !!
GRIMM WISHES YOU TO SURVIVE.
GRIMM NEEDS YOU!
HAAA!!!

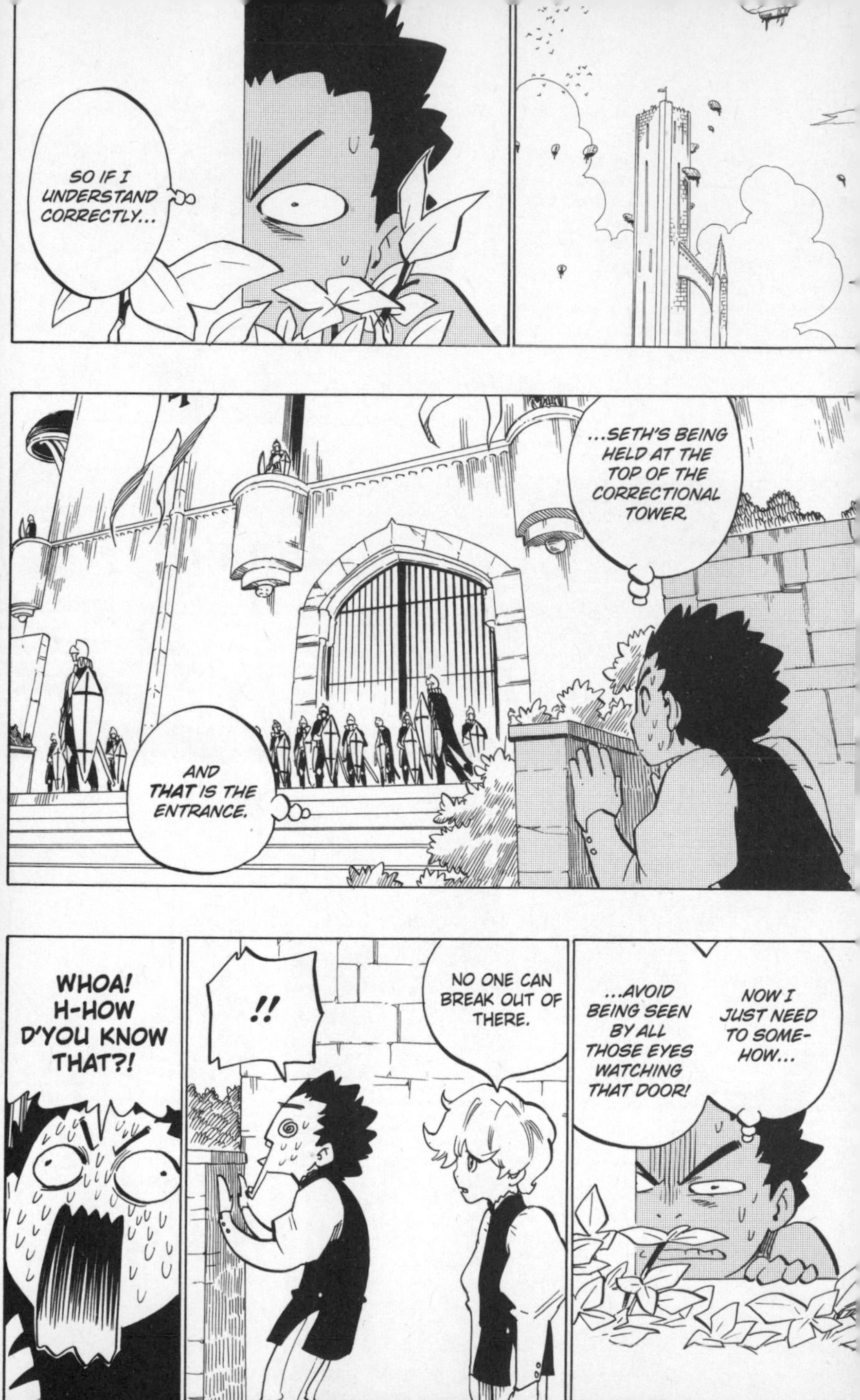
SO IF I UNDERSTAND CORRECTLY...
...SETH'S BEING HELD AT THE TOP OF THE CORRECTIONAL TOWER.
AND THAT IS THE ENTRANCE.
NOW I JUST NEED TO SOME-HOW...
...AVOID BEING SEEN BY ALL THOSE EYES WATCHING THAT DOOR!
NO ONE CAN BREAK OUT OF THERE.
!!
WHOA! H-HOW D'YOU KNOW THAT?!

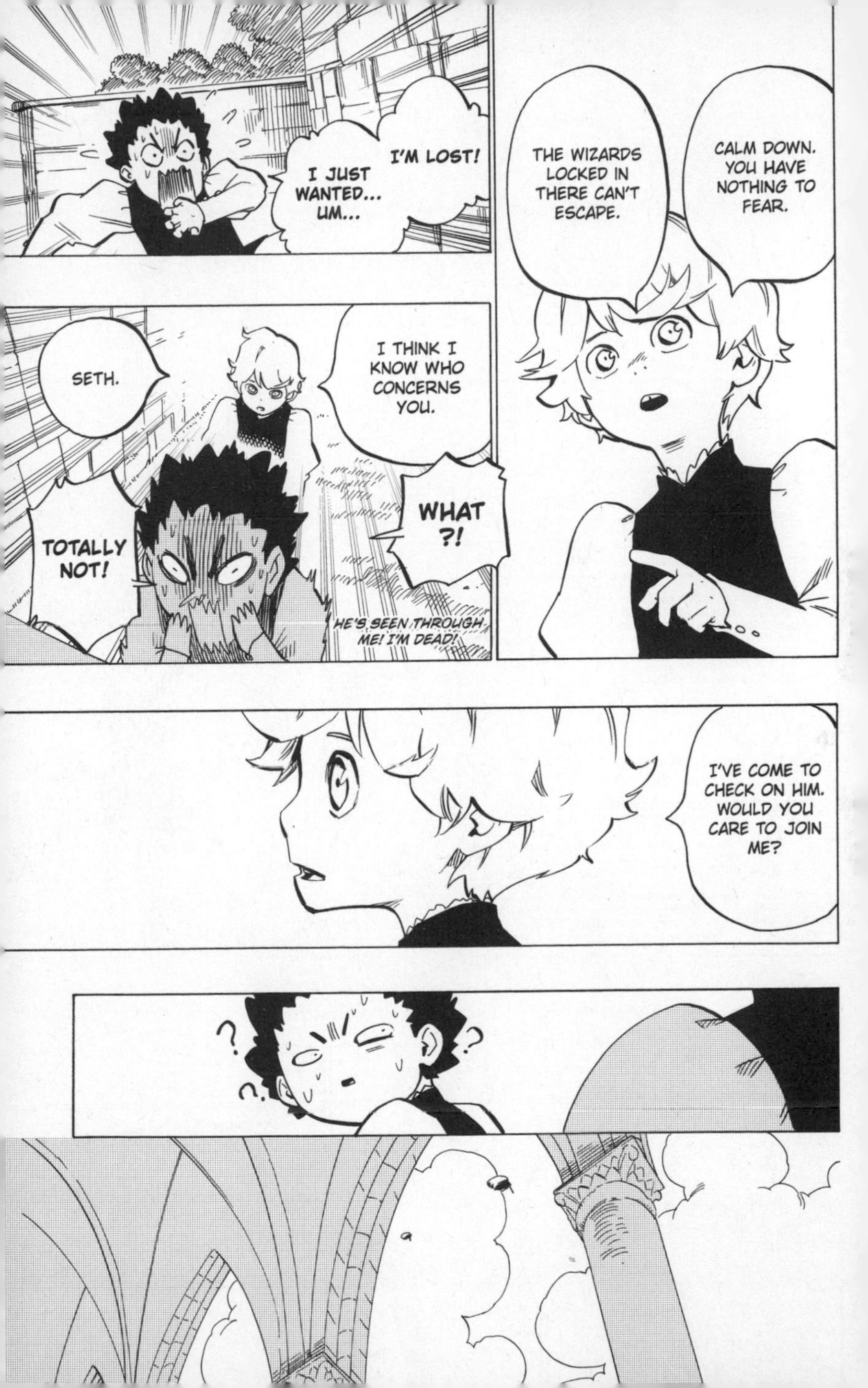
CALM DOWN. YOU HAVE NOTHING TO FEAR.
THE WIZARDS LOCKED IN THERE CAN'T ESCAPE.
I'M LOST!
I JUST WANTED... UM...
I THINK I KNOW WHO CONCERNS YOU.
SETH.
WHAT ?!
TOTALLY NOT!
HE'S SEEN THROUGH ME! I'M DEAD!
I'VE COME TO CHECK ON HIM. WOULD YOU CARE TO JOIN ME?

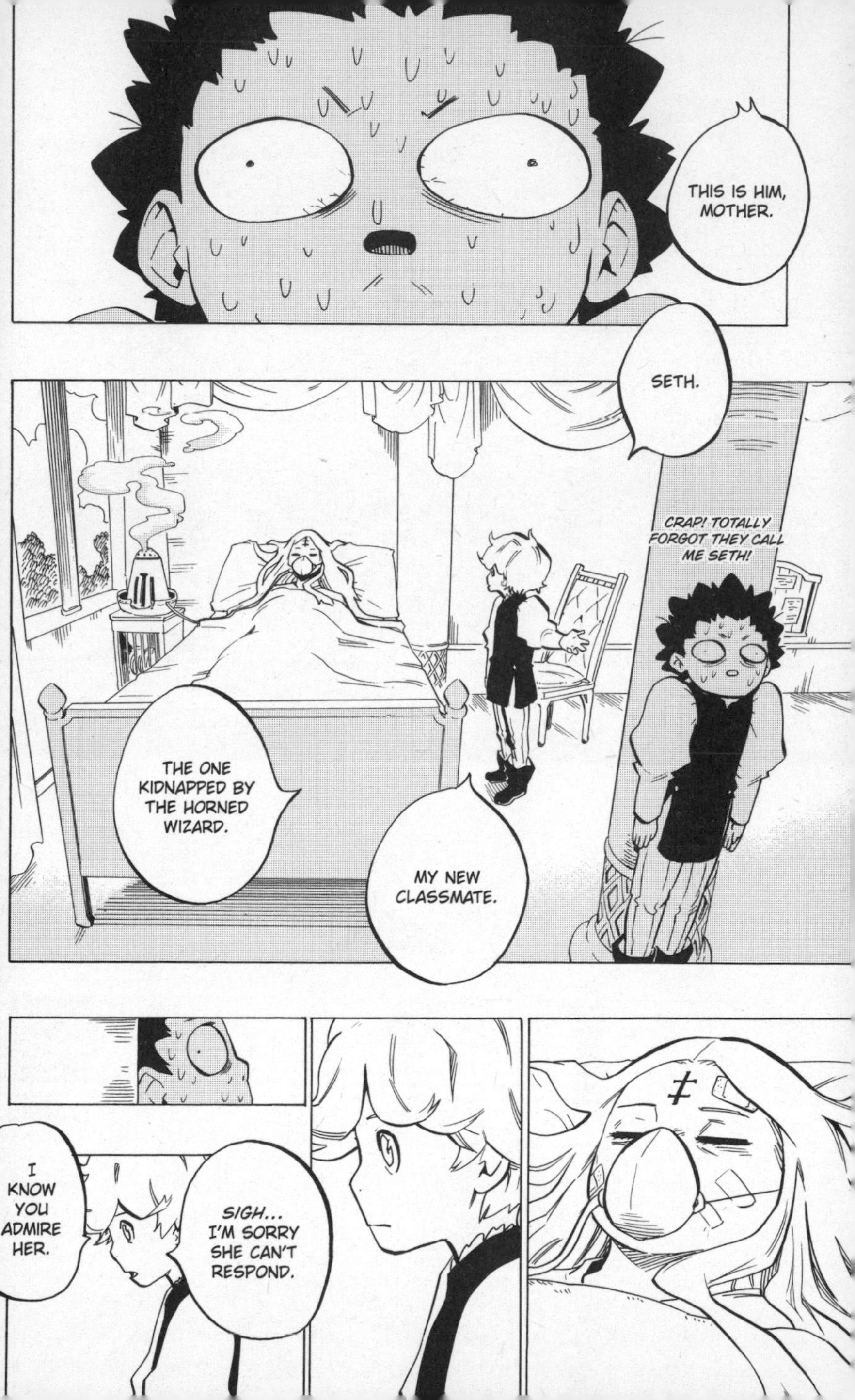
THIS IS HIM, MOTHER.
SETH.
CRAP! TOTALLY FORGOT THEY CALL ME SETH!
MY NEW CLASSMATE.
THE ONE KIDNAPPED BY THE HORNED WIZARD.
SIGH... I'M SORRY SHE CAN'T RESPOND.
I KNOW YOU ADMIRE HER.

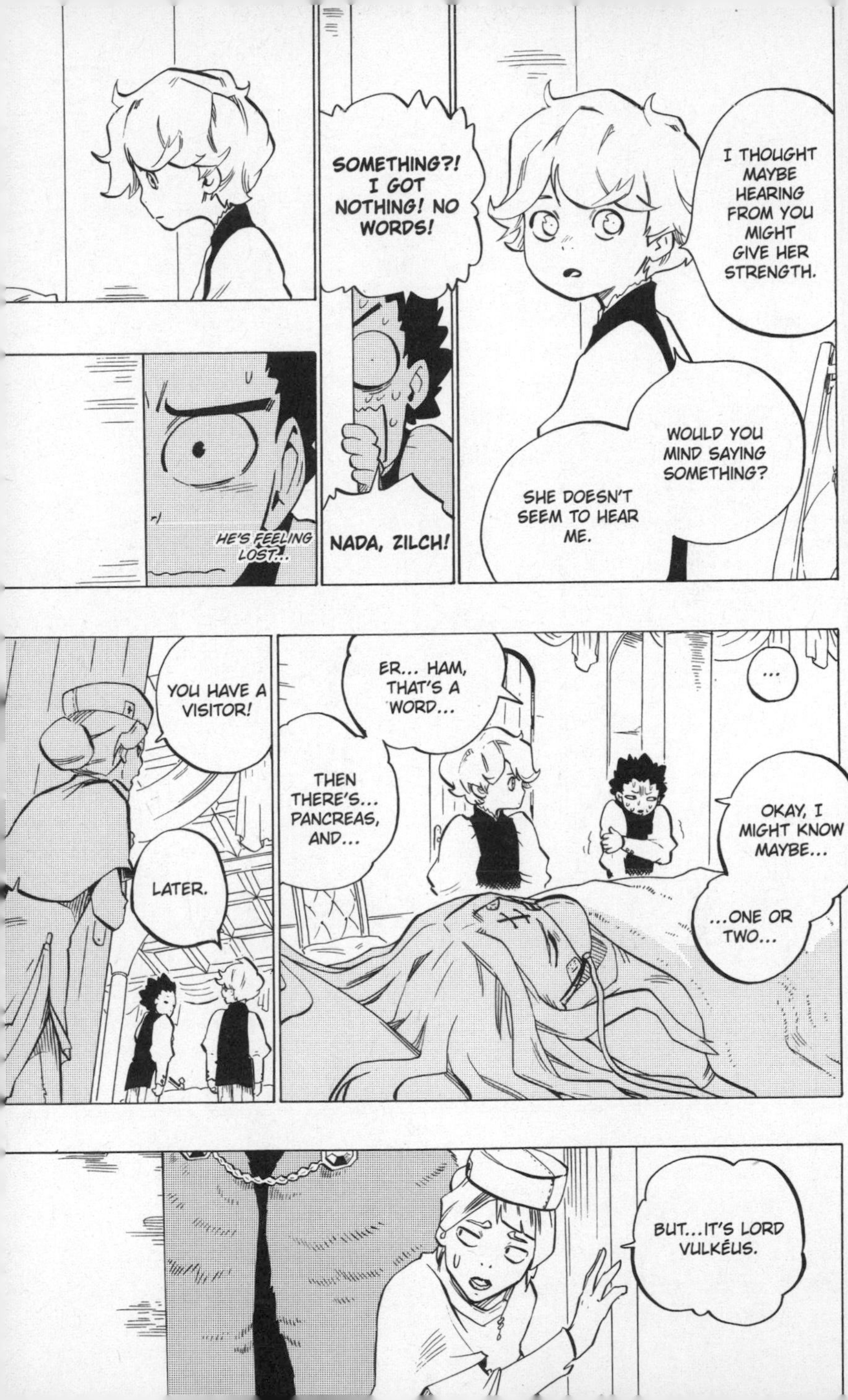
I THOUGHT MAYBE HEARING FROM YOU MIGHT GIVE HER STRENGTH.
WOULD YOU MIND SAYING SOMETHING?
SHE DOESN'T SEEM TO HEAR ME.
SOMETHING?! I GOT NOTHING! NO WORDS!
NADA, ZILCH!
HE'S FEELING LOST...
...
OKAY, I MIGHT KNOW MAYBE...
...ONE OR TWO...
ER... HAM, THAT'S A WORD...
THEN THERE'S... PANCREAS, AND...
YOU HAVE A VISITOR!
LATER.
BUT...IT'S LORD VULKÉUS.

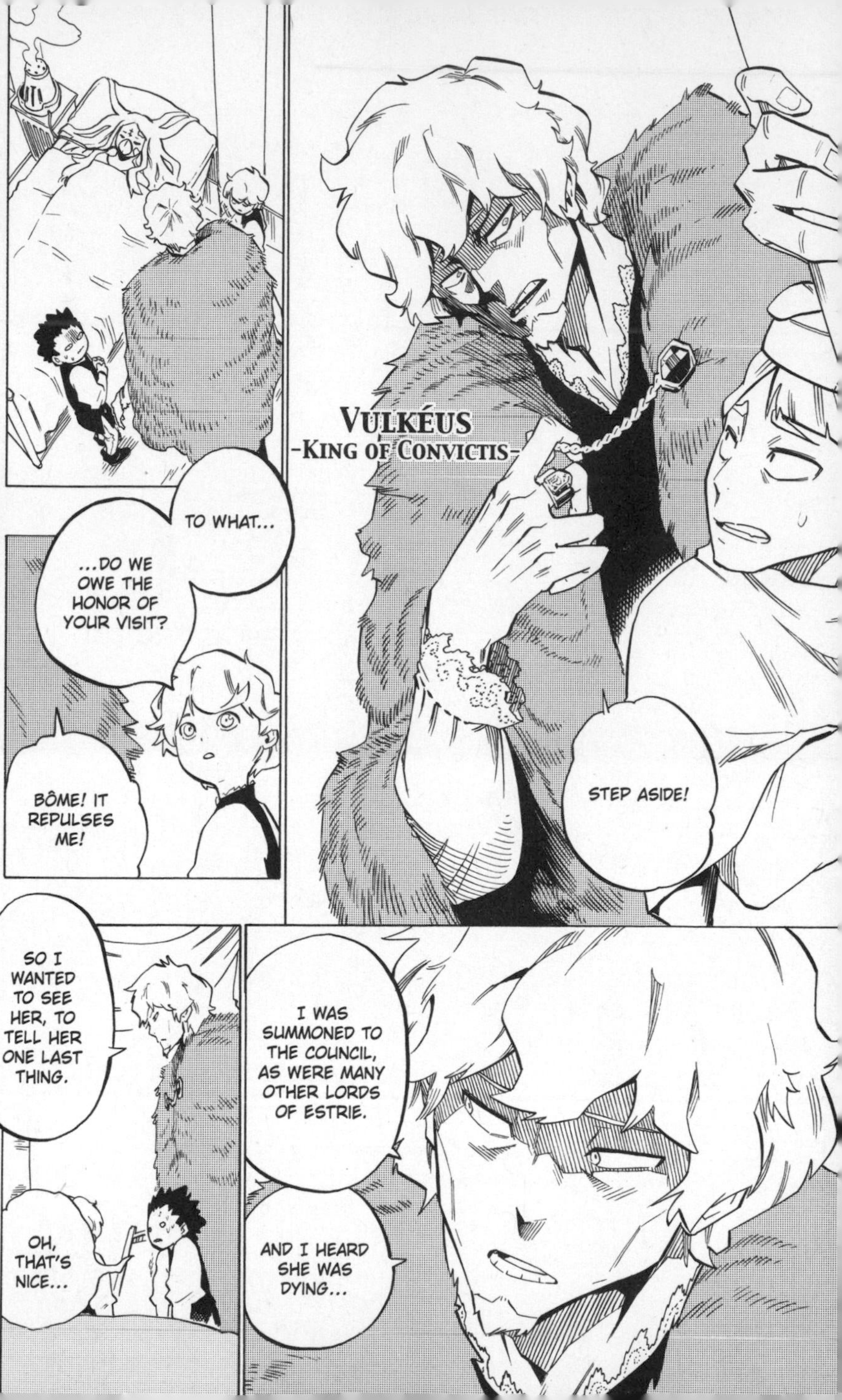
VULKÉUS
-KING OF CONVICTIS-
STEP ASIDE!
TO WHAT...
...DO WE OWE THE HONOR OF YOUR VISIT?
BÔME! IT REPULSES ME!
I WAS SUMMONED TO THE COUNCIL, AS WERE MANY OTHER LORDS OF ESTRIE.
AND I HEARD SHE WAS DYING...
SO I WANTED TO SEE HER, TO TELL HER ONE LAST THING.
OH, THAT'S NICE...

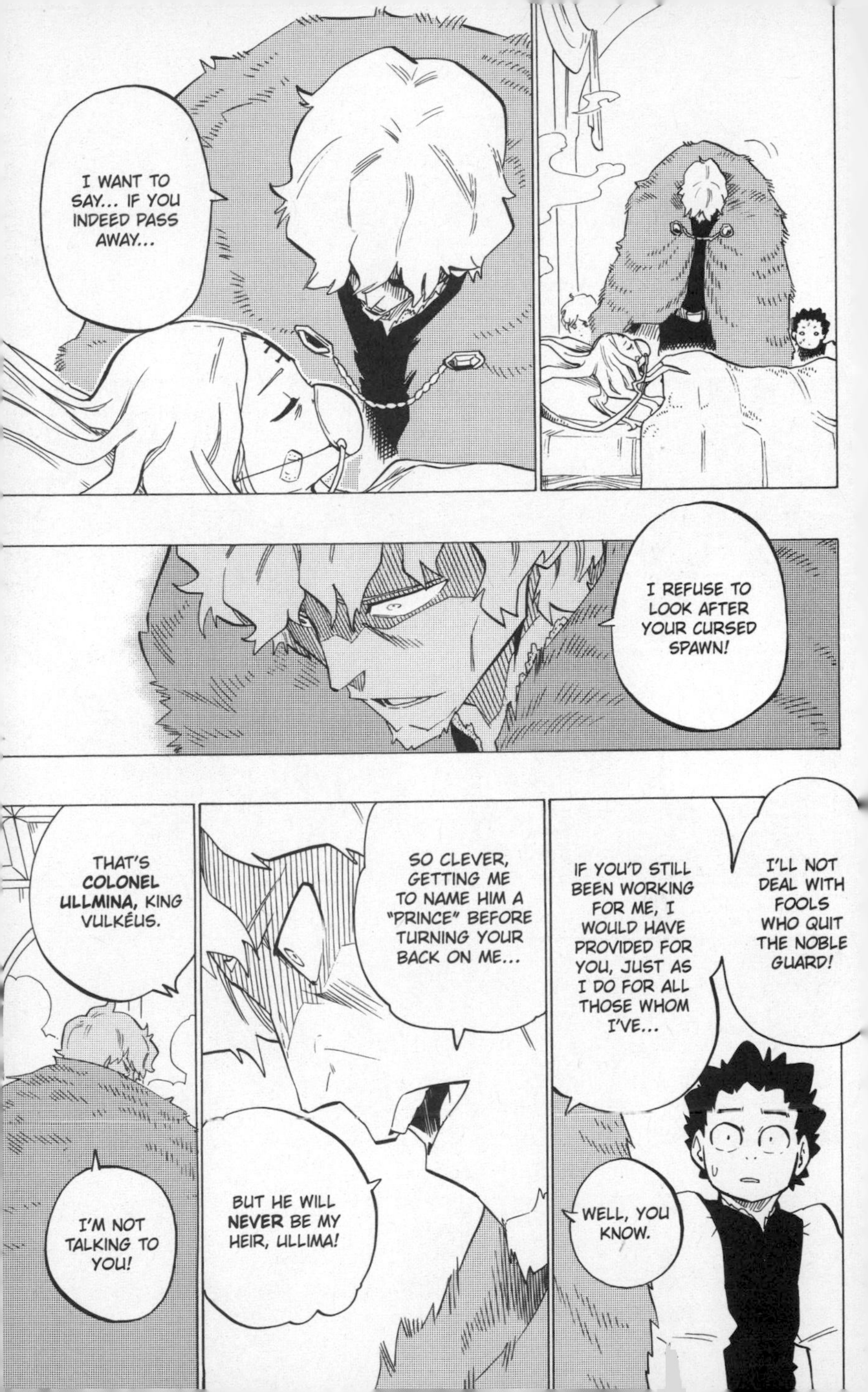
I WANT TO SAY... IF YOU INDEED PASS AWAY...
I REFUSE TO LOOK AFTER YOUR CURSED SPAWN!
I'LL NOT DEAL WITH FOOLS WHO QUIT THE NOBLE GUARD!
IF YOU'D STILL BEEN WORKING FOR ME, I WOULD HAVE PROVIDED FOR YOU, JUST AS I DO FOR ALL THOSE WHOM I'VE...
WELL, YOU KNOW.
SO CLEVER, GETTING ME TO NAME HIM A "PRINCE" BEFORE TURNING YOUR BACK ON ME...
BUT HE WILL **NEVER** BE MY HEIR, ULLIMA!
THAT'S **COLONEL ULLMINA,** KING VULKÉUS.
I'M NOT TALKING TO YOU!

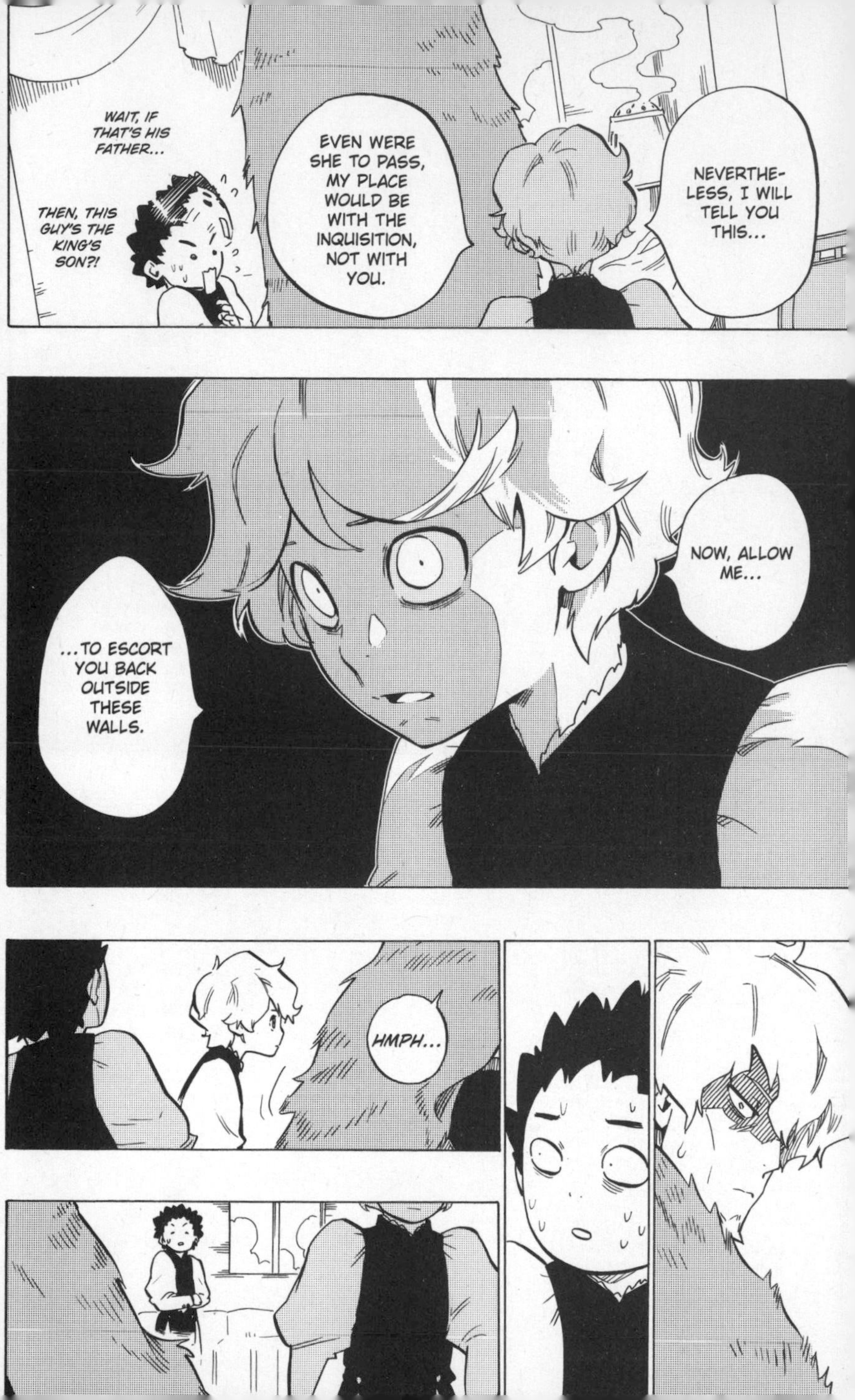
NEVERTHE-LESS, I WILL TELL YOU THIS...
EVEN WERE SHE TO PASS, MY PLACE WOULD BE WITH THE INQUISITION, NOT WITH YOU.
WAIT, IF THAT'S HIS FATHER...
THEN, THIS GUY'S THE KING'S SON?!
NOW, ALLOW ME...
...TO ESCORT YOU BACK OUTSIDE THESE WALLS.
HMPH...

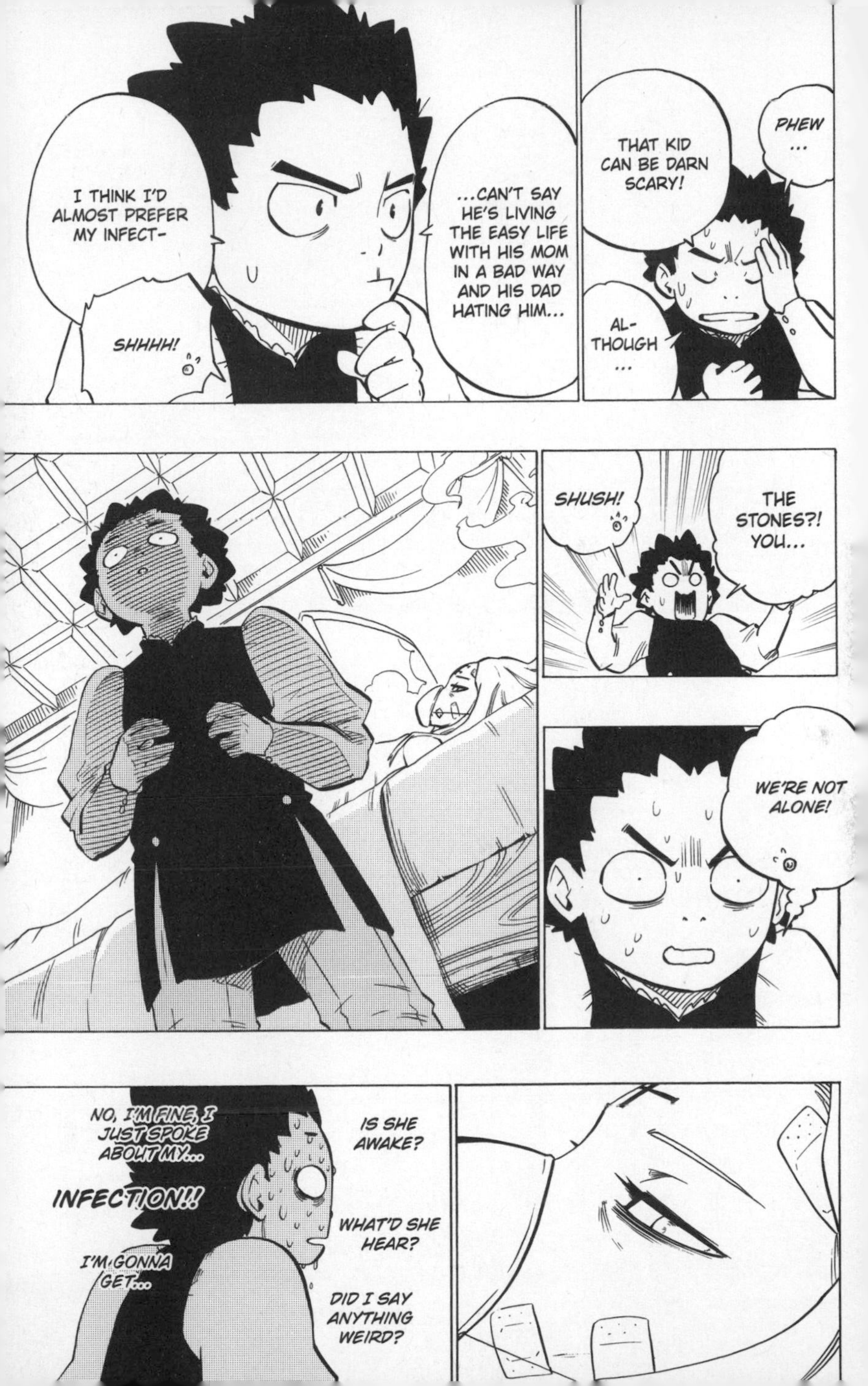
PHEW ...
THAT KID CAN BE DARN SCARY!
AL-THOUGH ...
...CAN'T SAY HE'S LIVING THE EASY LIFE WITH HIS MOM IN A BAD WAY AND HIS DAD HATING HIM...
I THINK I'D ALMOST PREFER MY INFECT-
SHHHH!
THE STONES?! YOU...
SHUSH!
WE'RE NOT ALONE!
IS SHE AWAKE?
WHAT'D SHE HEAR?
DID I SAY ANYTHING WEIRD?
NO, I'M FINE, I JUST SPOKE ABOUT MY...
INFECTION!!
I'M GONNA GET...

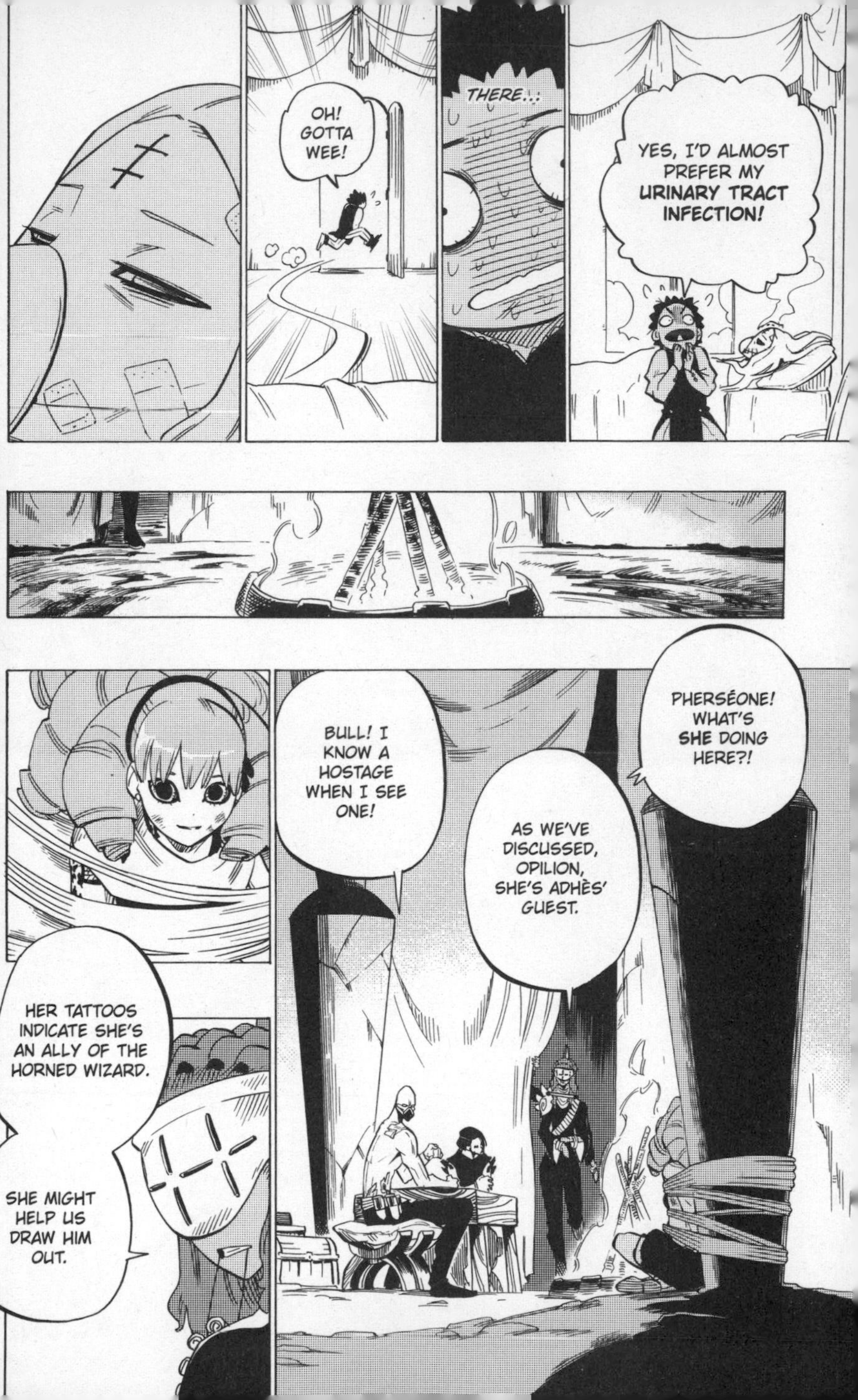
OH! GOTTA WEE!
THERE...
YES, I'D ALMOST PREFER MY URINARY TRACT INFECTION!
PHERSÉONE! WHAT'S SHE DOING HERE?!
AS WE'VE DISCUSSED, OPILION, SHE'S ADHÈS' GUEST.
BULL! I KNOW A HOSTAGE WHEN I SEE ONE!
HER TATTOOS INDICATE SHE'S AN ALLY OF THE HORNED WIZARD.
SHE MIGHT HELP US DRAW HIM OUT.

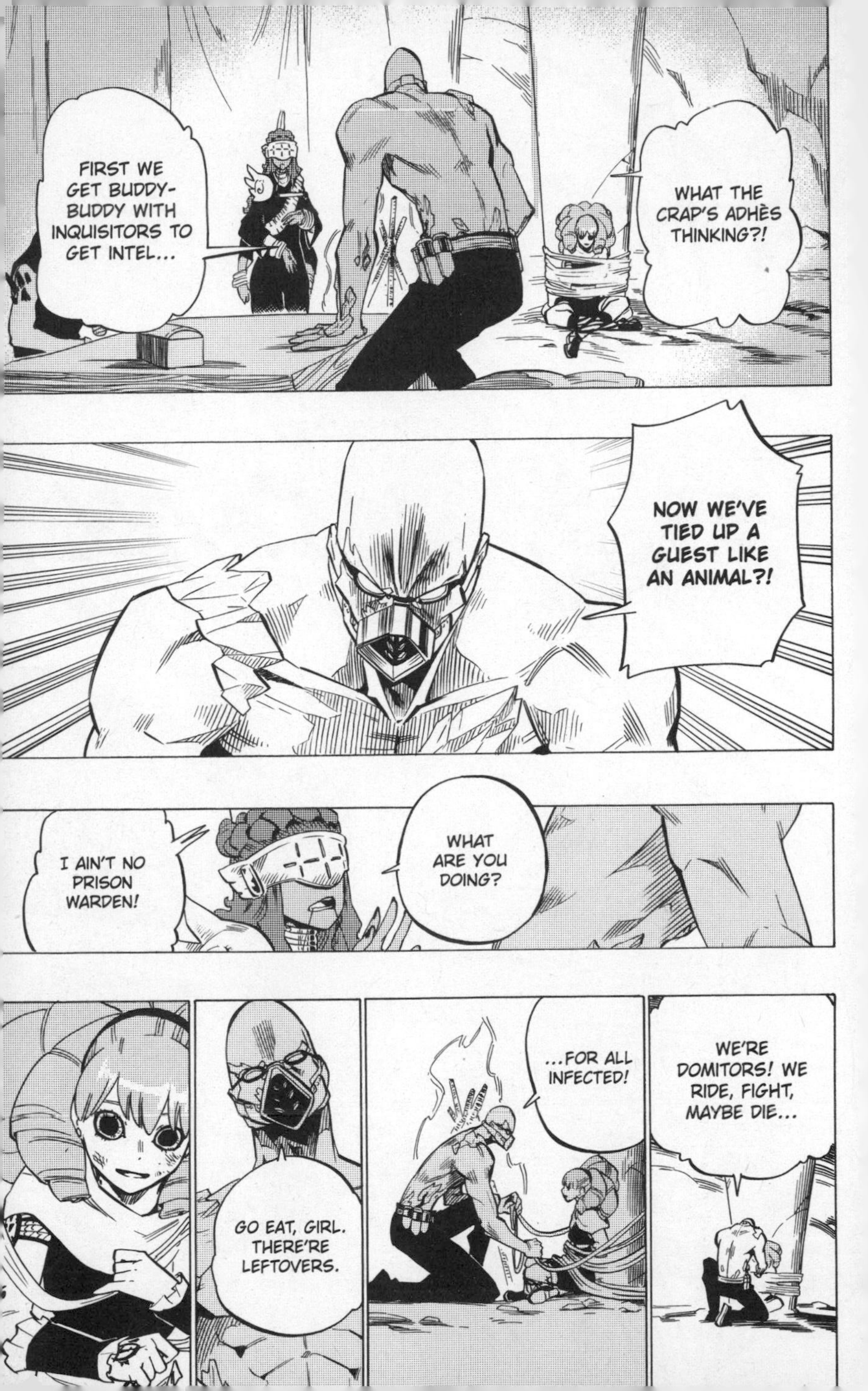
WHAT THE CRAP'S ADHÈS THINKING?!
FIRST WE GET BUDDY-BUDDY WITH INQUISITORS TO GET INTEL...
NOW WE'VE TIED UP A GUEST LIKE AN ANIMAL?!
WHAT ARE YOU DOING?
I AIN'T NO PRISON WARDEN!
WE'RE DOMITORS! WE RIDE, FIGHT, MAYBE DIE...
...FOR ALL INFECTED!
GO EAT, GIRL. THERE'RE LEFTOVERS.

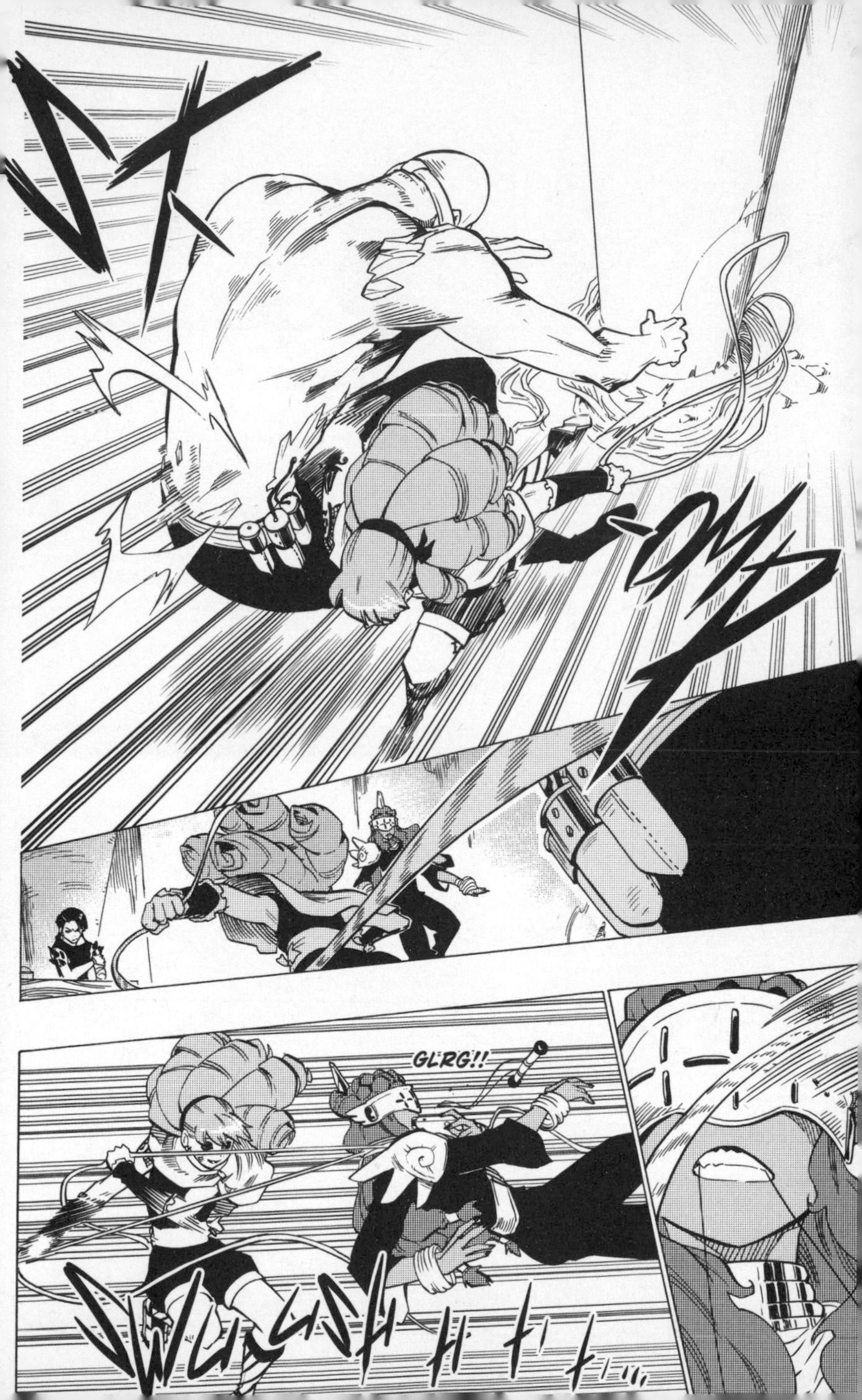
GLRG!!

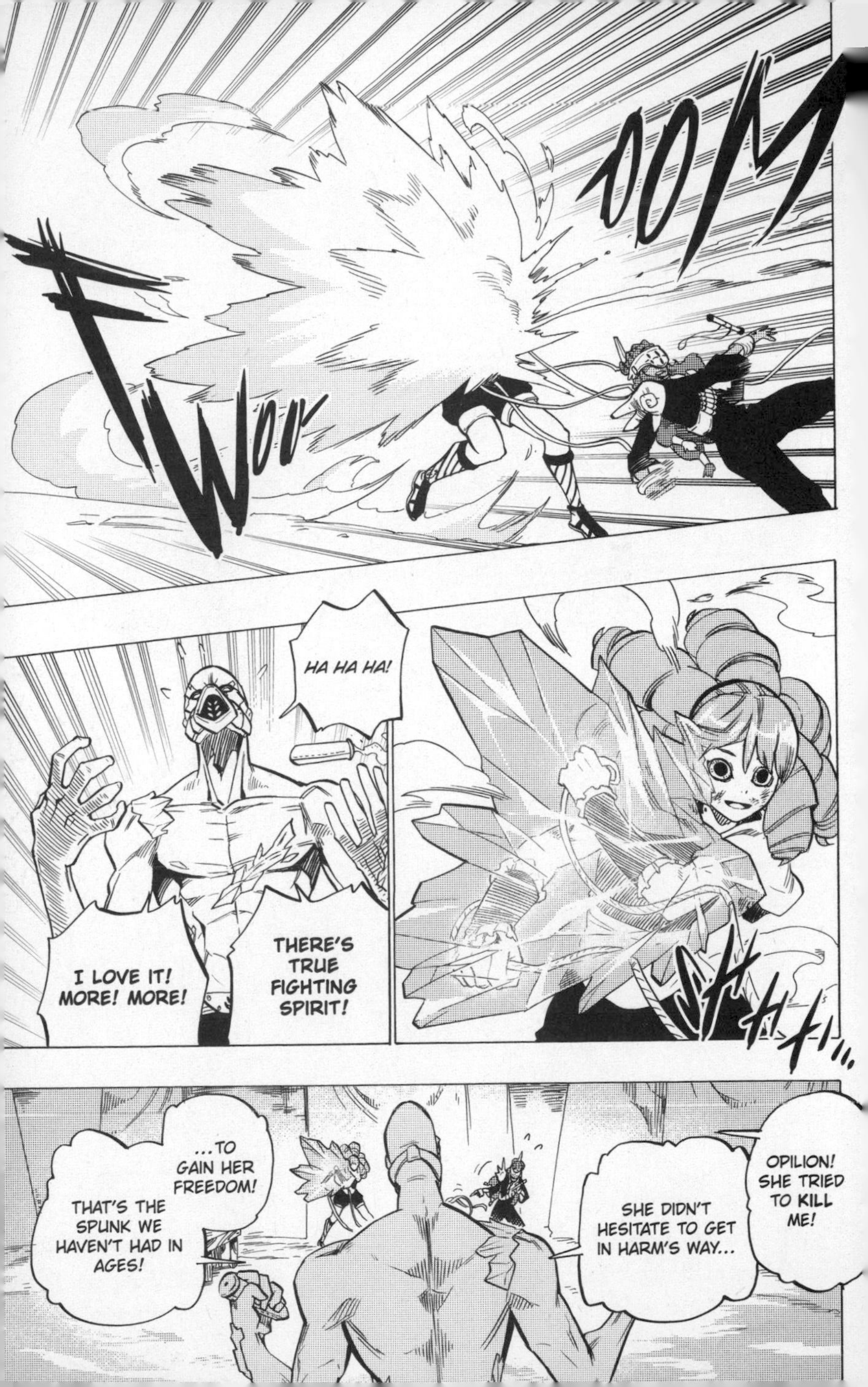
FWOO
OOM
HA HA HA!
THERE'S TRUE FIGHTING SPIRIT!
I LOVE IT! MORE! MORE!
OPILION! SHE TRIED TO KILL ME!
SHE DIDN'T HESITATE TO GET IN HARM'S WAY...
...TO GAIN HER FREEDOM!
THAT'S THE SPUNK WE HAVEN'T HAD IN AGES!

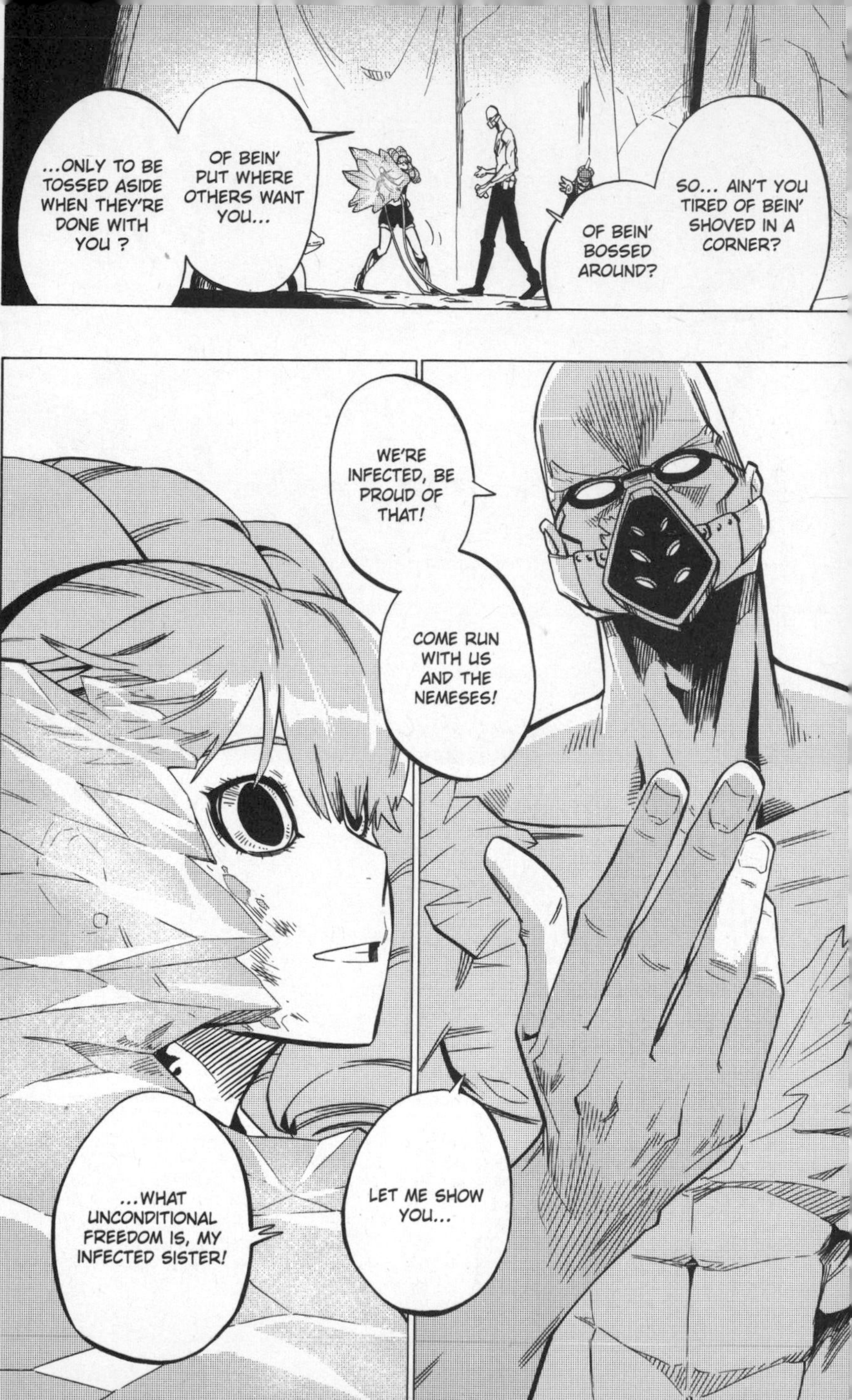
SO... AIN'T YOU TIRED OF BEIN' SHOVED IN A CORNER?
OF BEIN' BOSSED AROUND?
OF BEIN' PUT WHERE OTHERS WANT YOU...
...ONLY TO BE TOSSED ASIDE WHEN THEY'RE DONE WITH YOU ?
WE'RE INFECTED, BE PROUD OF THAT!
COME RUN WITH US AND THE NEMESES!
LET ME SHOW YOU...
...WHAT UNCONDITIONAL FREEDOM IS, MY INFECTED SISTER!

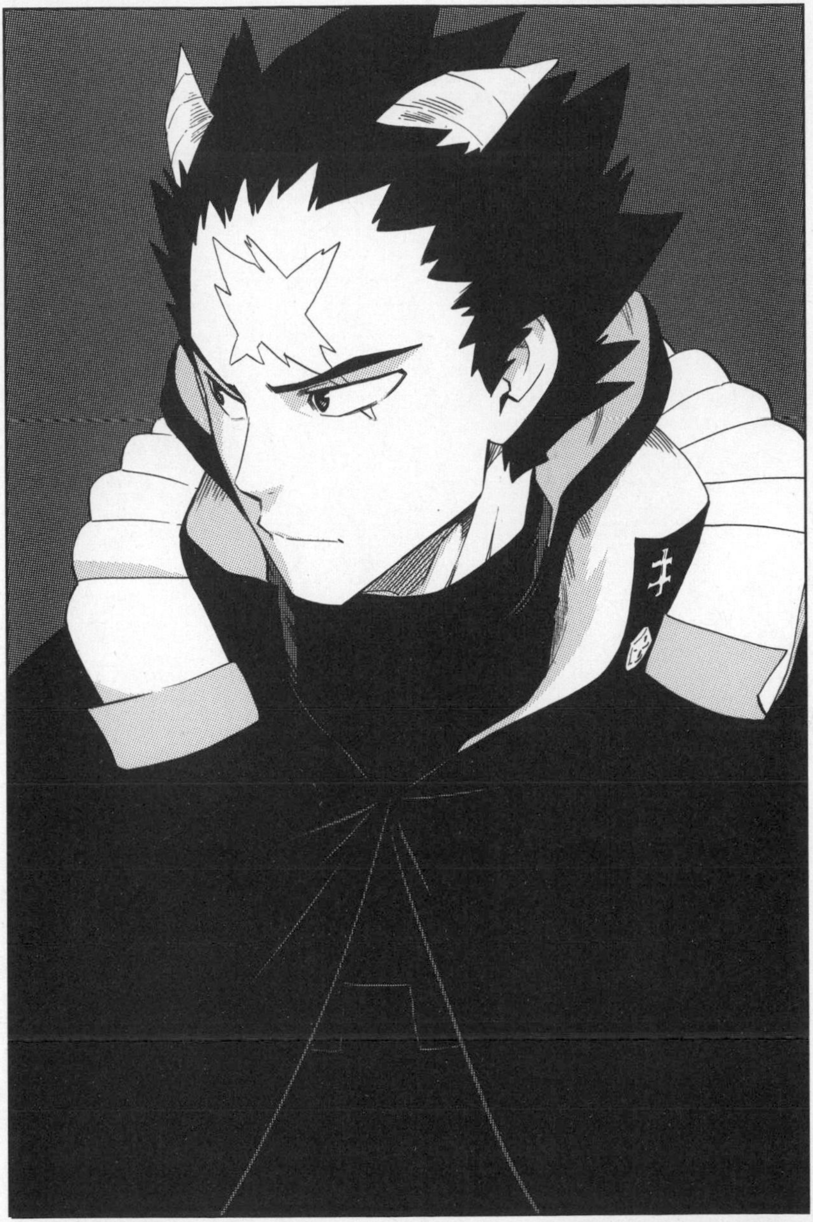

Chapter 121 Appearances

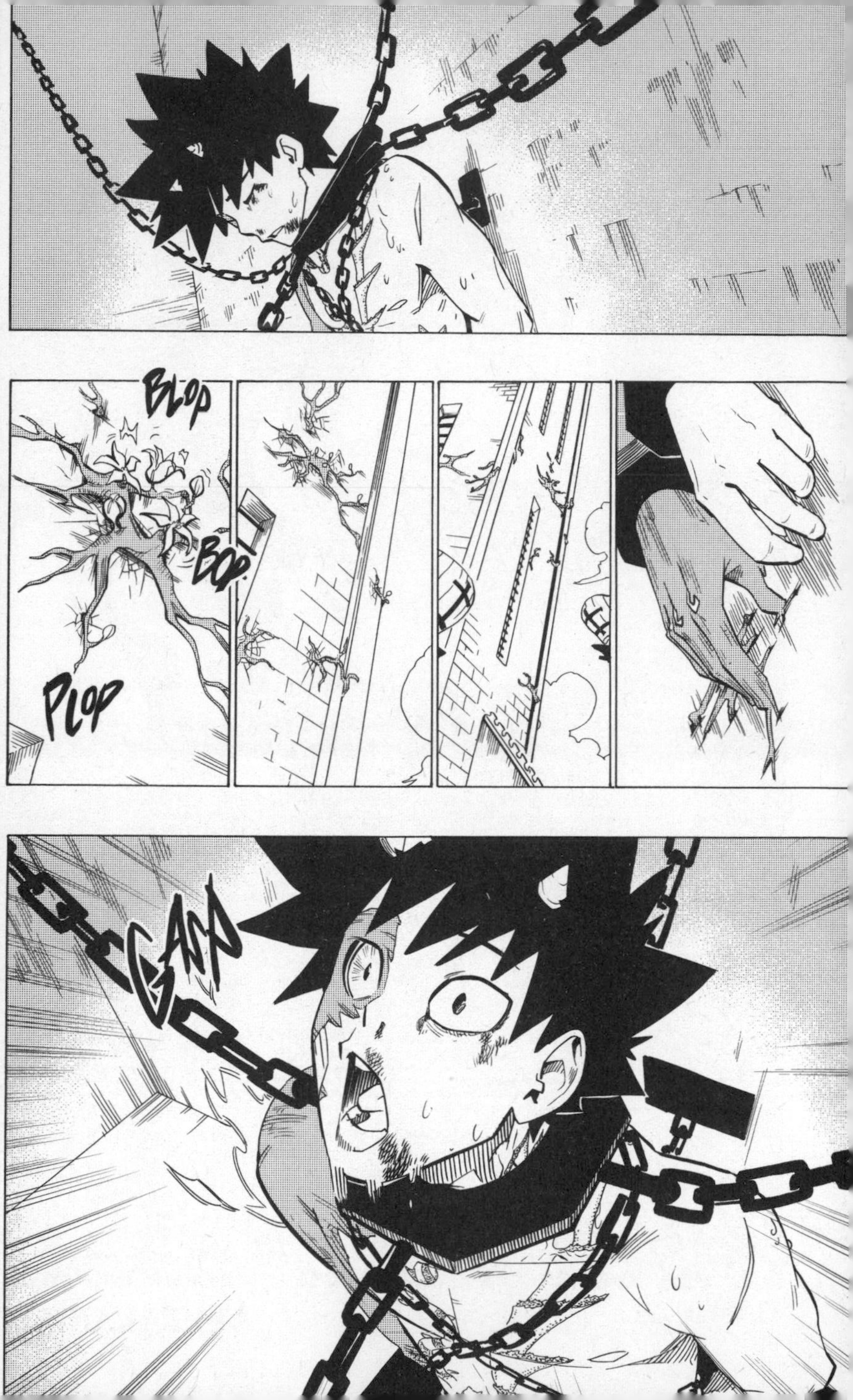
BLOP
BOP!
PLOP
GASP

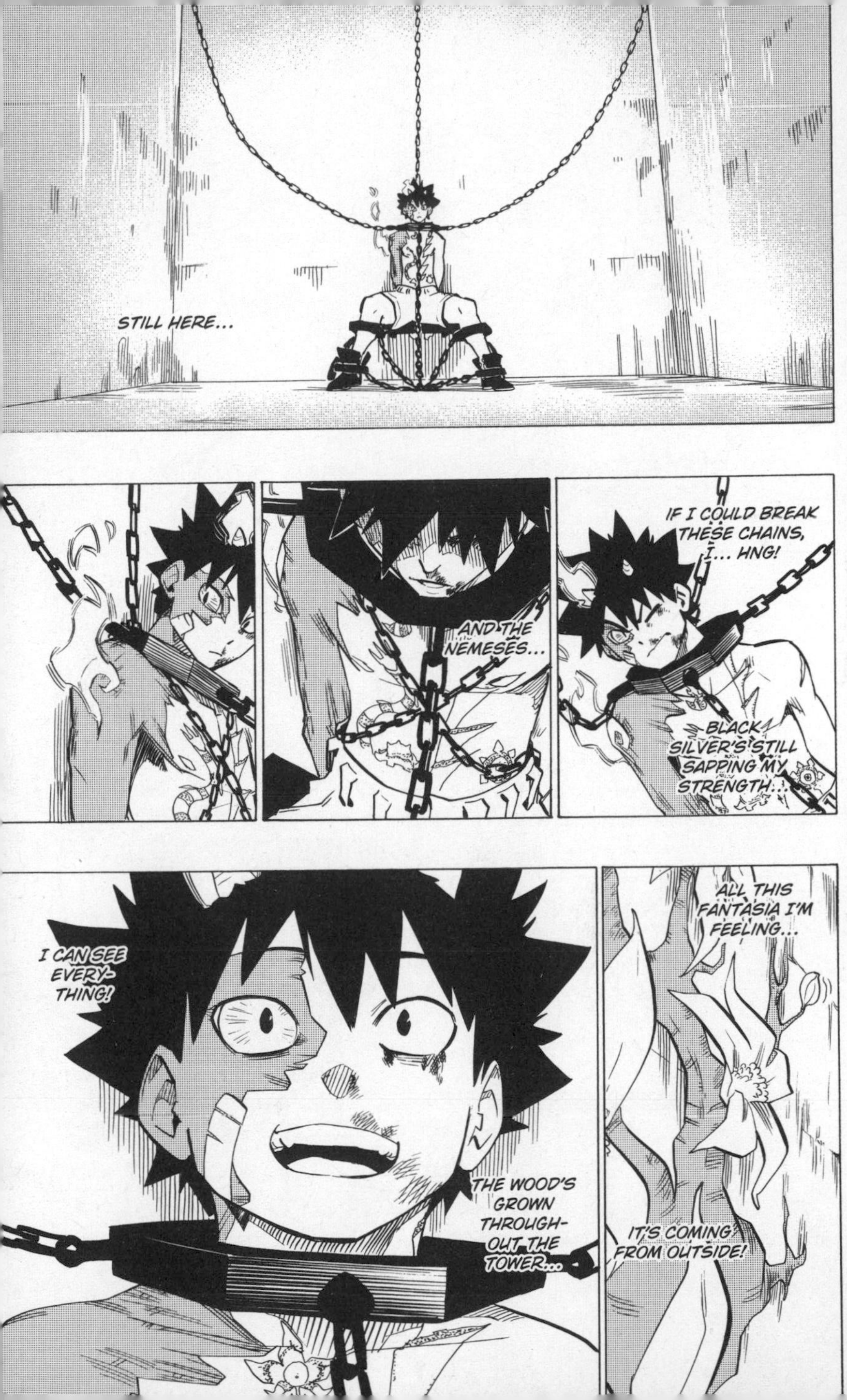
STILL HERE...
IF I COULD BREAK THESE CHAINS, I... HNG!
BLACK SILVER'S STILL SAPPING MY STRENGTH...
AND THE NEMESES...
ALL THIS FANTASIA I'M FEELING...
IT'S COMING FROM OUTSIDE!
THE WOOD'S GROWN THROUGH-OUT THE TOWER...
I CAN SEE EVERY-THING!

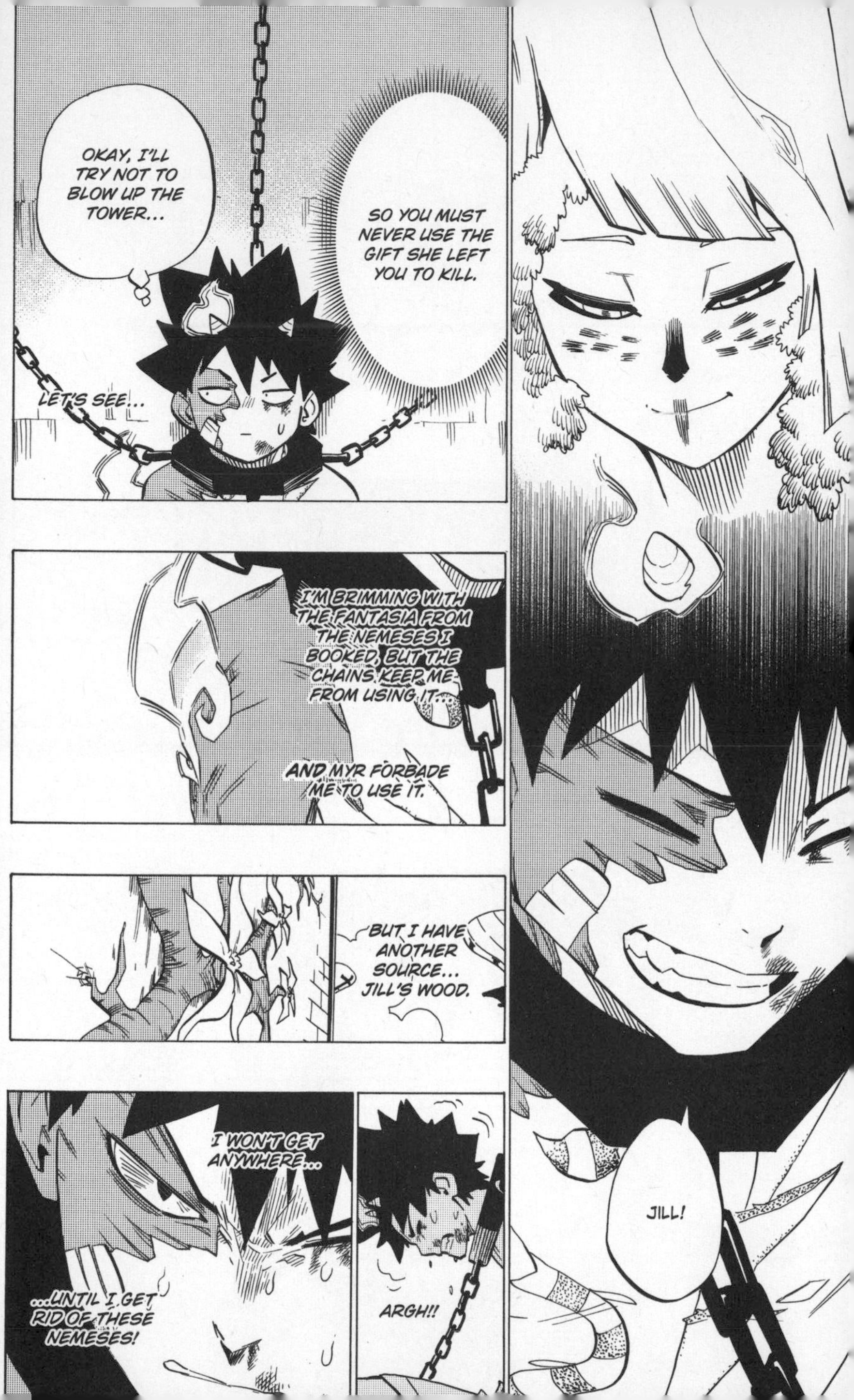
SO YOU MUST NEVER USE THE GIFT SHE LEFT YOU TO KILL.
OKAY, I'LL TRY NOT TO BLOW UP THE TOWER...
LET'S SEE...
I'M BRIMMING WITH THE FANTASIA FROM THE NEMESES I BOOKED, BUT THE CHAINS KEEP ME FROM USING IT...
AND MYR FORBADE ME TO USE IT.
BUT I HAVE ANOTHER SOURCE... JILL'S WOOD.
I WON'T GET ANYWHERE...
...UNTIL I GET RID OF THESE NEMESES!
ARGH!!
JILL!

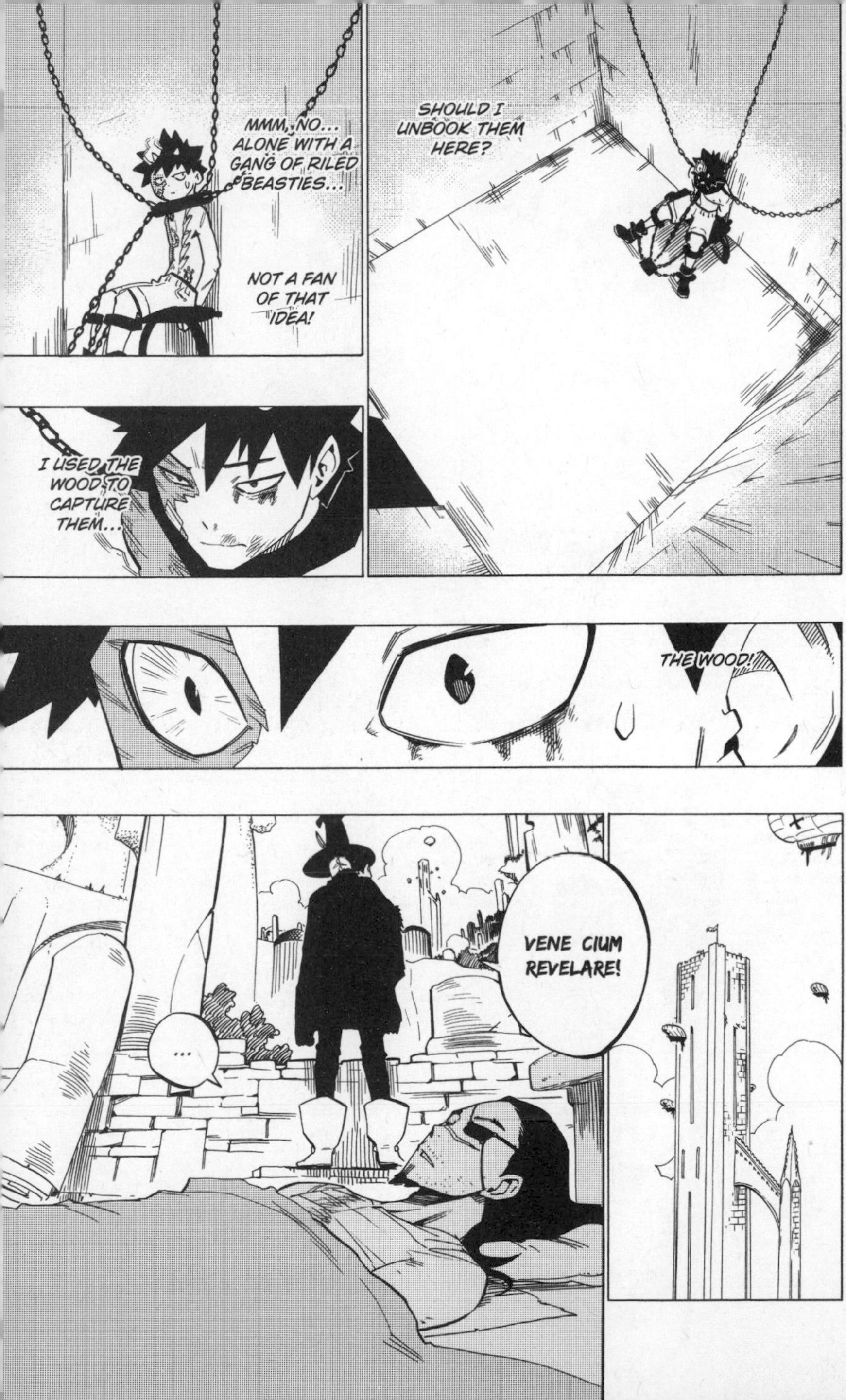
SHOULD I UNBOOK THEM HERE?
MMM, NO... ALONE WITH A GANG OF RILED BEASTIES...
NOT A FAN OF THAT IDEA!
I USED THE WOOD TO CAPTURE THEM...
THE WOOD!
VENE CIUM REVELARE!
...

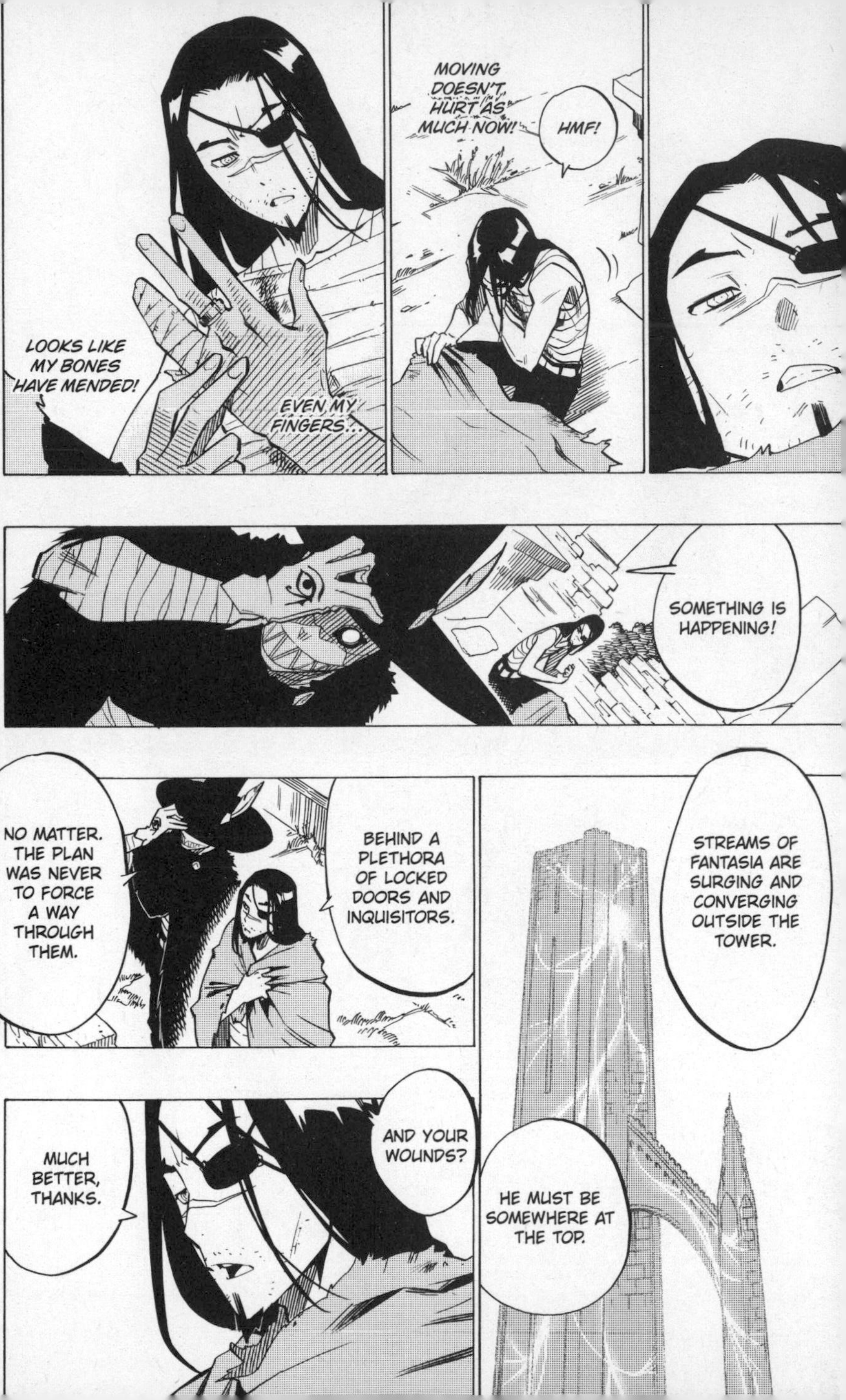
MOVING DOESN'T HURT AS MUCH NOW!
HMF!
LOOKS LIKE MY BONES HAVE MENDED!
EVEN MY FINGERS...
SOMETHING IS HAPPENING!
STREAMS OF FANTASIA ARE SURGING AND CONVERGING OUTSIDE THE TOWER.
HE MUST BE SOMEWHERE AT THE TOP.
BEHIND A PLETHORA OF LOCKED DOORS AND INQUISITORS.
NO MATTER. THE PLAN WAS NEVER TO FORCE A WAY THROUGH THEM.
AND YOUR WOUNDS?
MUCH BETTER, THANKS.

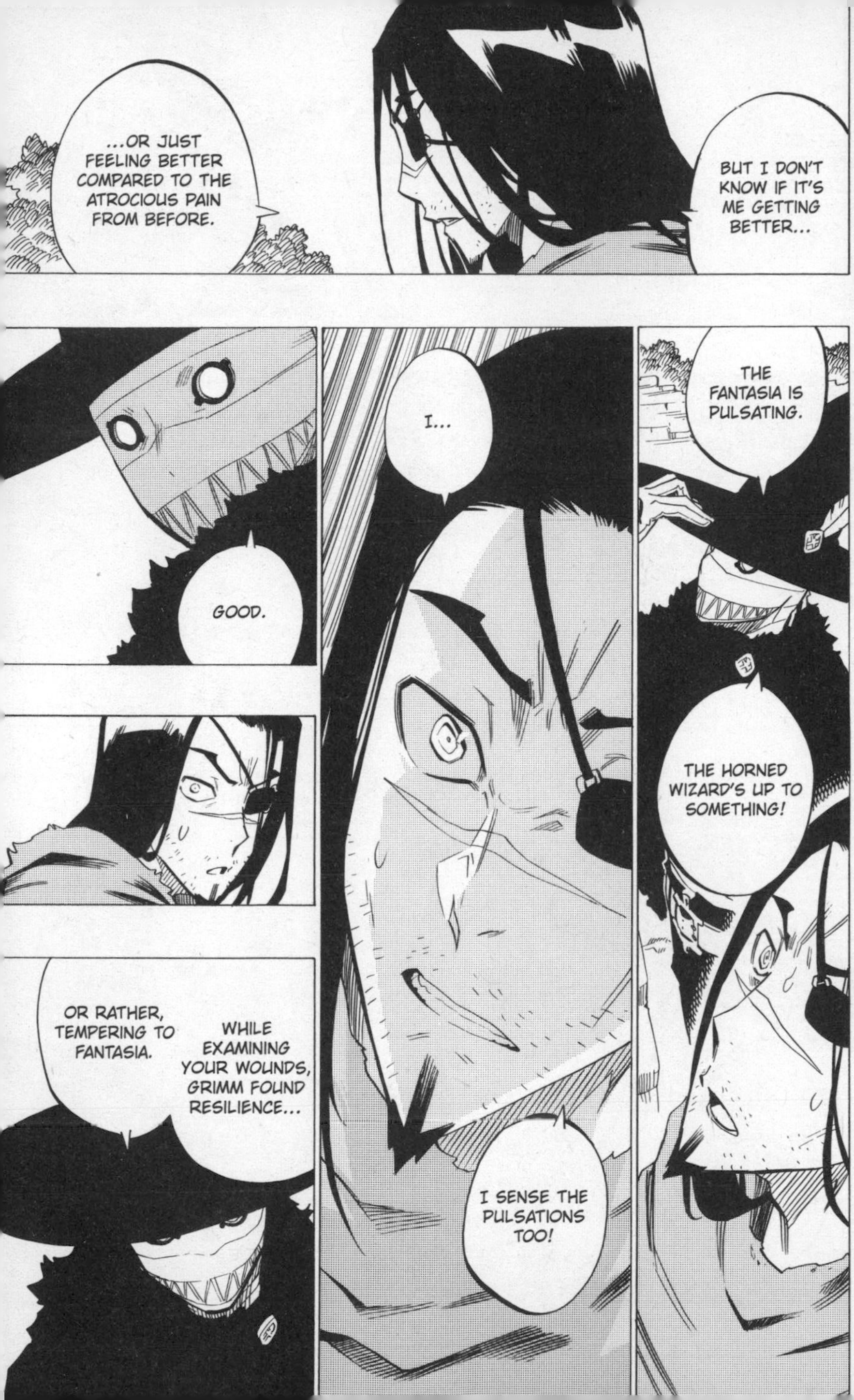
BUT I DON'T KNOW IF IT'S ME GETTING BETTER...
...OR JUST FEELING BETTER COMPARED TO THE ATROCIOUS PAIN FROM BEFORE.
THE FANTASIA IS PULSATING.
THE HORNED WIZARD'S UP TO SOMETHING!
I...
I SENSE THE PULSATIONS TOO!
GOOD.
WHILE EXAMINING YOUR WOUNDS, GRIMM FOUND RESILIENCE...
OR RATHER, TEMPERING TO FANTASIA.

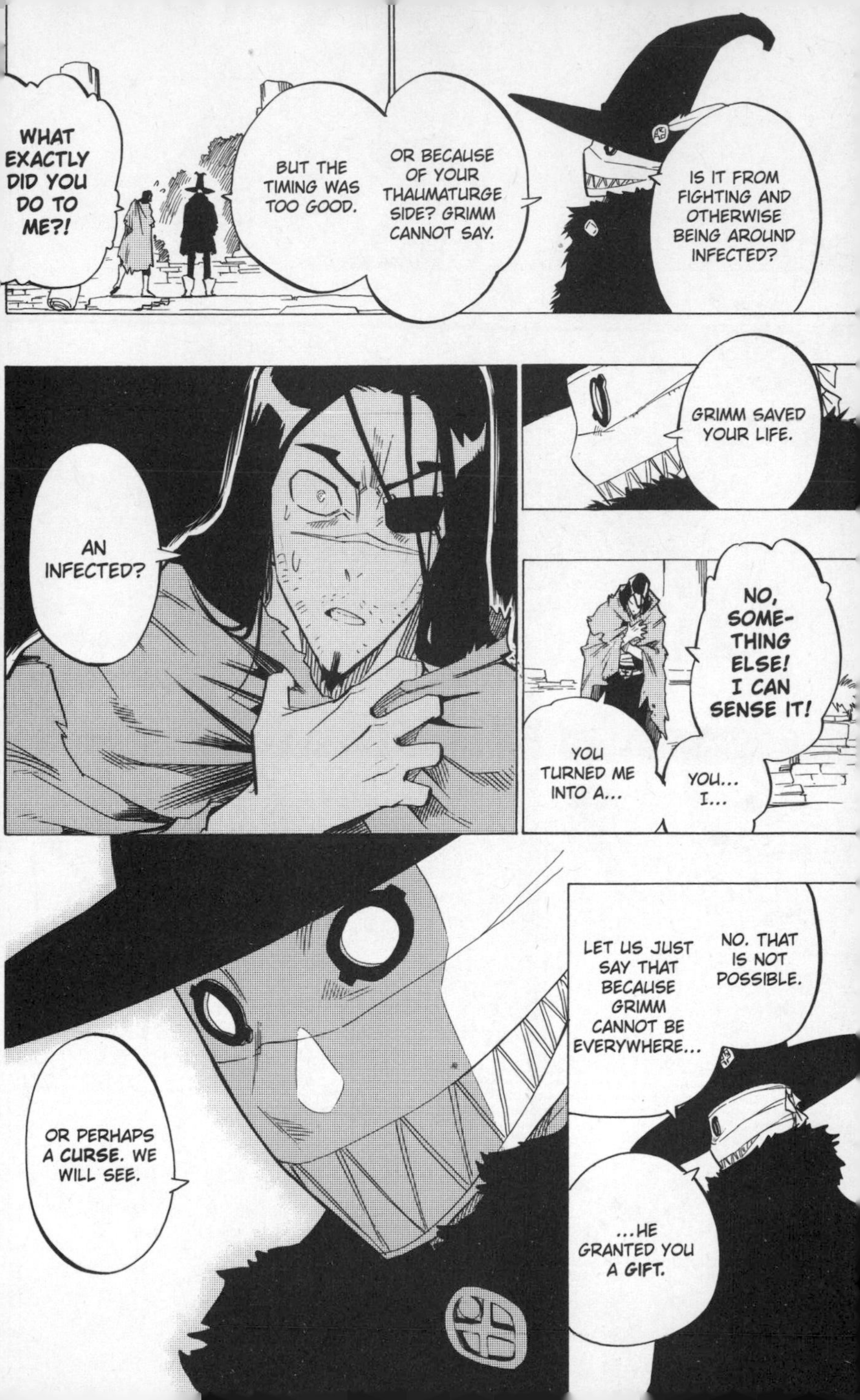
IS IT FROM FIGHTING AND OTHERWISE BEING AROUND INFECTED?
OR BECAUSE OF YOUR THAUMATURGE SIDE? GRIMM CANNOT SAY.
BUT THE TIMING WAS TOO GOOD.
WHAT EXACTLY DID YOU DO TO ME?!
GRIMM SAVED YOUR LIFE.
NO, SOMETHING ELSE! I CAN SENSE IT!
YOU... I...
YOU TURNED ME INTO A...
AN INFECTED?
NO. THAT IS NOT POSSIBLE.
LET US JUST SAY THAT BECAUSE GRIMM CANNOT BE EVERYWHERE...
...HE GRANTED YOU A GIFT.
OR PERHAPS A CURSE. WE WILL SEE.

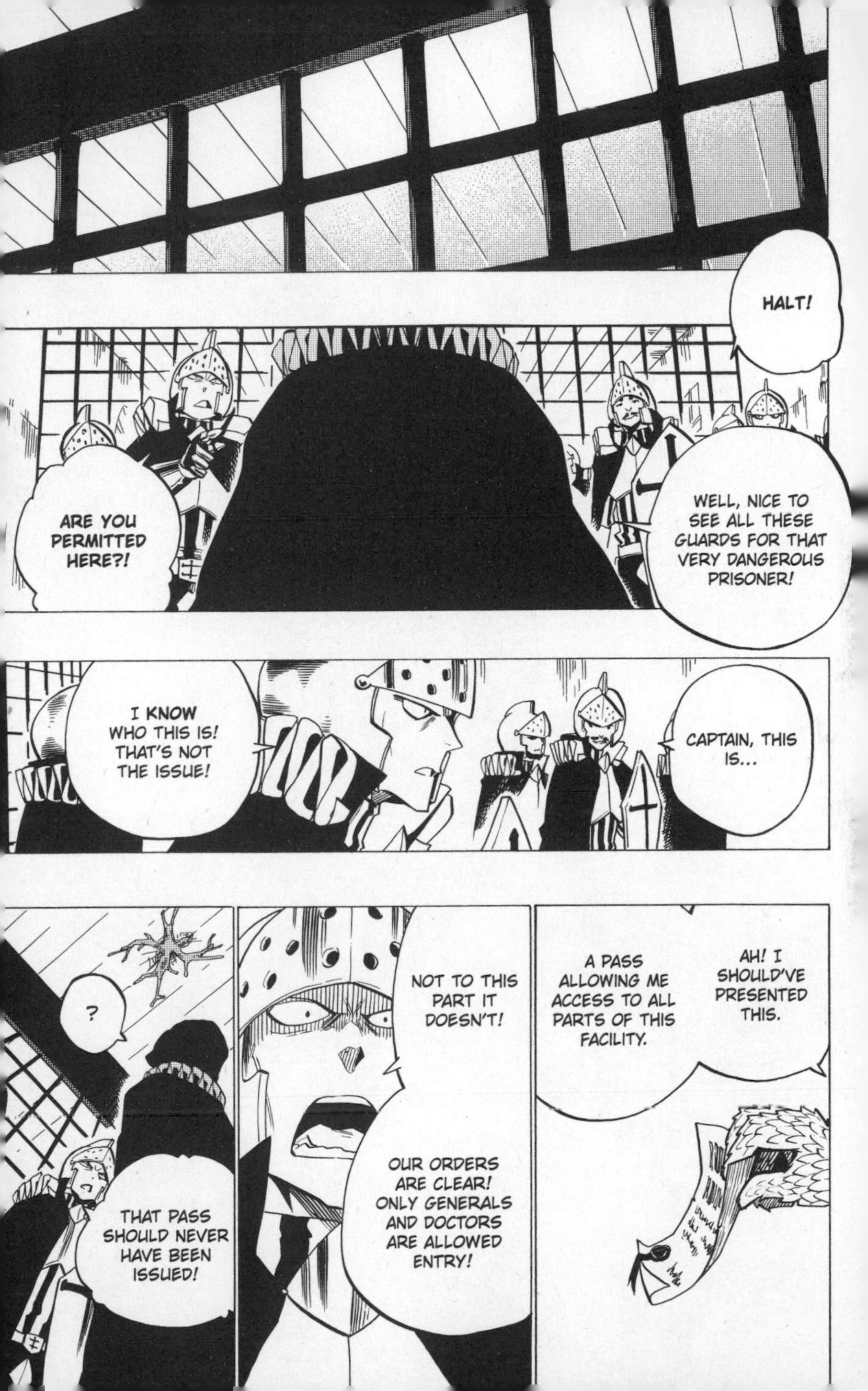
HALT!
WELL, NICE TO SEE ALL THESE GUARDS FOR THAT VERY DANGEROUS PRISONER!
ARE YOU PERMITTED HERE?!
CAPTAIN, THIS IS...
I KNOW WHO THIS IS! THAT'S NOT THE ISSUE!
AH! I SHOULD'VE PRESENTED THIS.
A PASS ALLOWING ME ACCESS TO ALL PARTS OF THIS FACILITY.
NOT TO THIS PART IT DOESN'T!
OUR ORDERS ARE CLEAR! ONLY GENERALS AND DOCTORS ARE ALLOWED ENTRY!
?
THAT PASS SHOULD NEVER HAVE BEEN ISSUED!

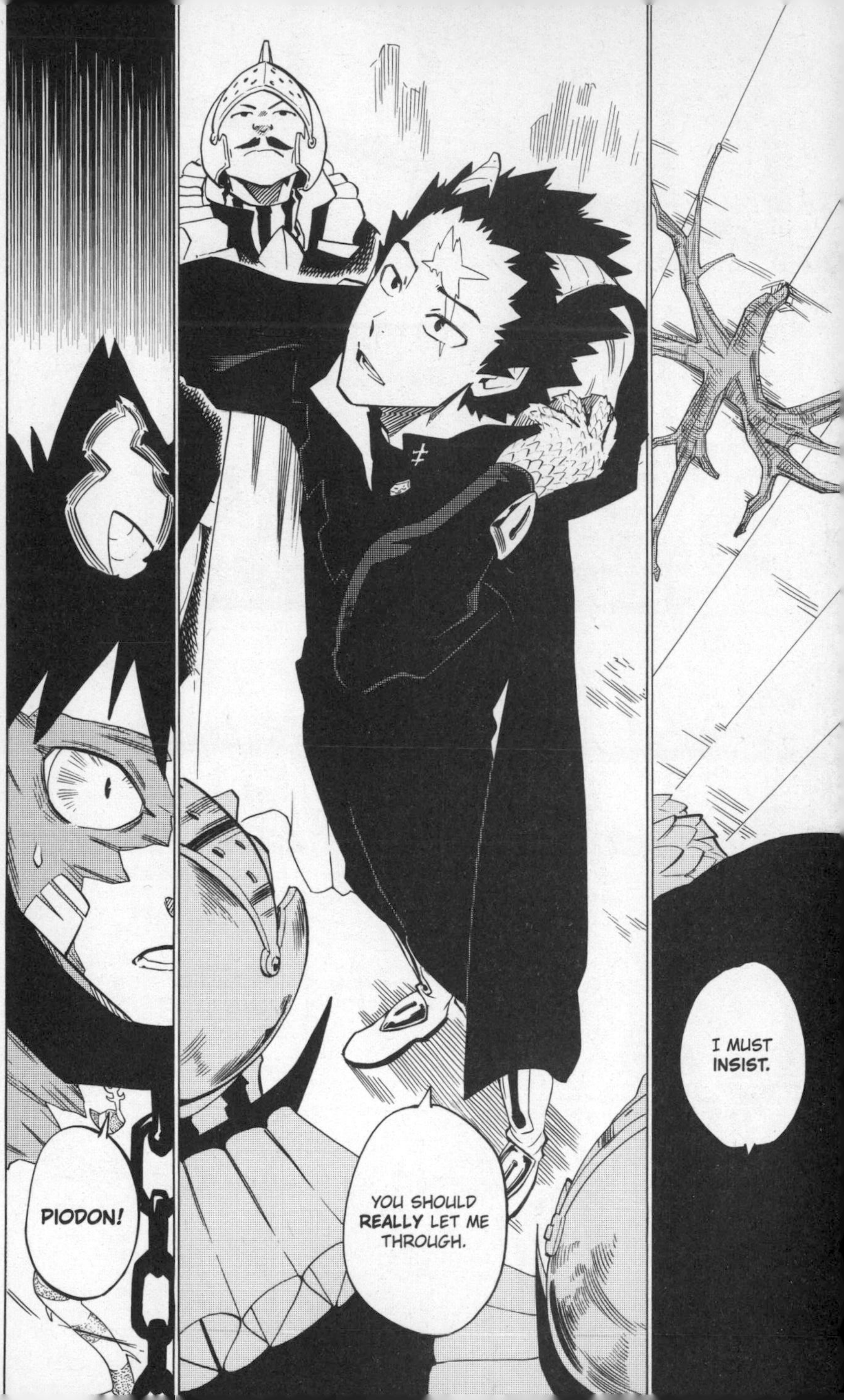
I MUST INSIST.
YOU SHOULD REALLY LET ME THROUGH.
PIODON!

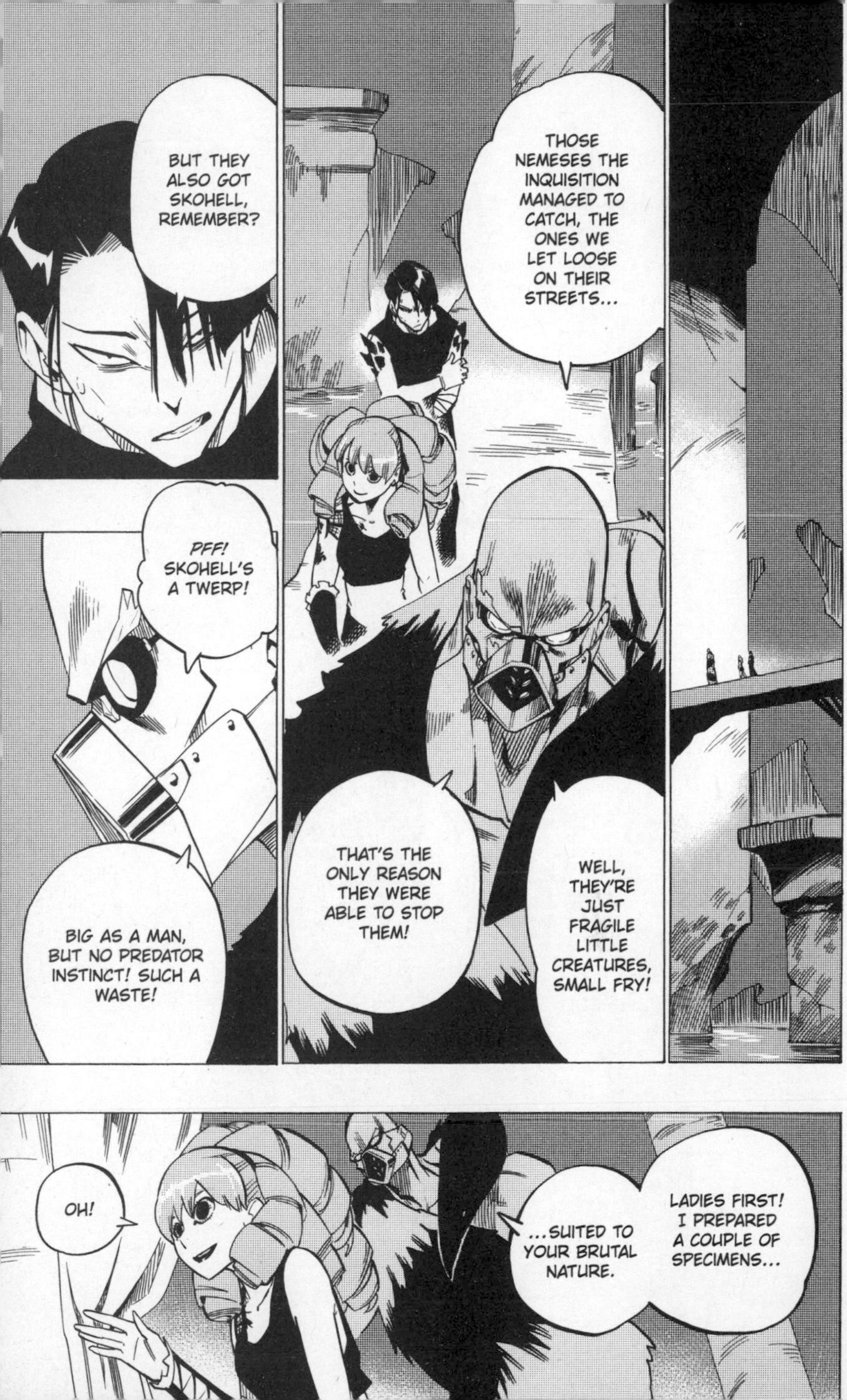
THOSE NEMESES THE INQUISITION MANAGED TO CATCH, THE ONES WE LET LOOSE ON THEIR STREETS...
WELL, THEY'RE JUST FRAGILE LITTLE CREATURES, SMALL FRY!
THAT'S THE ONLY REASON THEY WERE ABLE TO STOP THEM!
BUT THEY ALSO GOT SKOHELL, REMEMBER?
PFF! SKOHELL'S A TWERP!
BIG AS A MAN, BUT NO PREDATOR INSTINCT! SUCH A WASTE!
LADIES FIRST! I PREPARED A COUPLE OF SPECIMENS...
...SUITED TO YOUR BRUTAL NATURE.
OH!

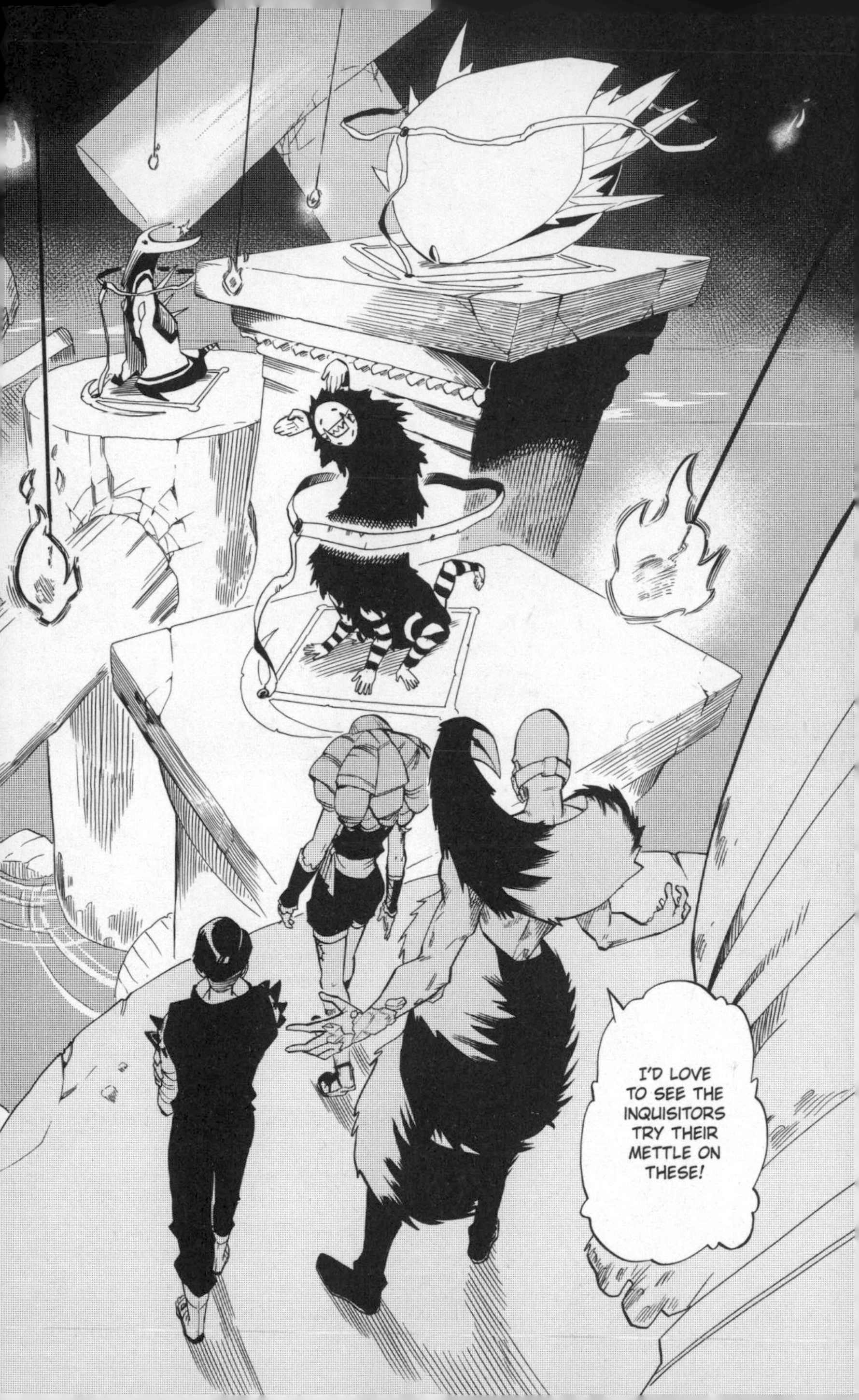
I'D LOVE TO SEE THE INQUISITORS TRY THEIR METTLE ON THESE!

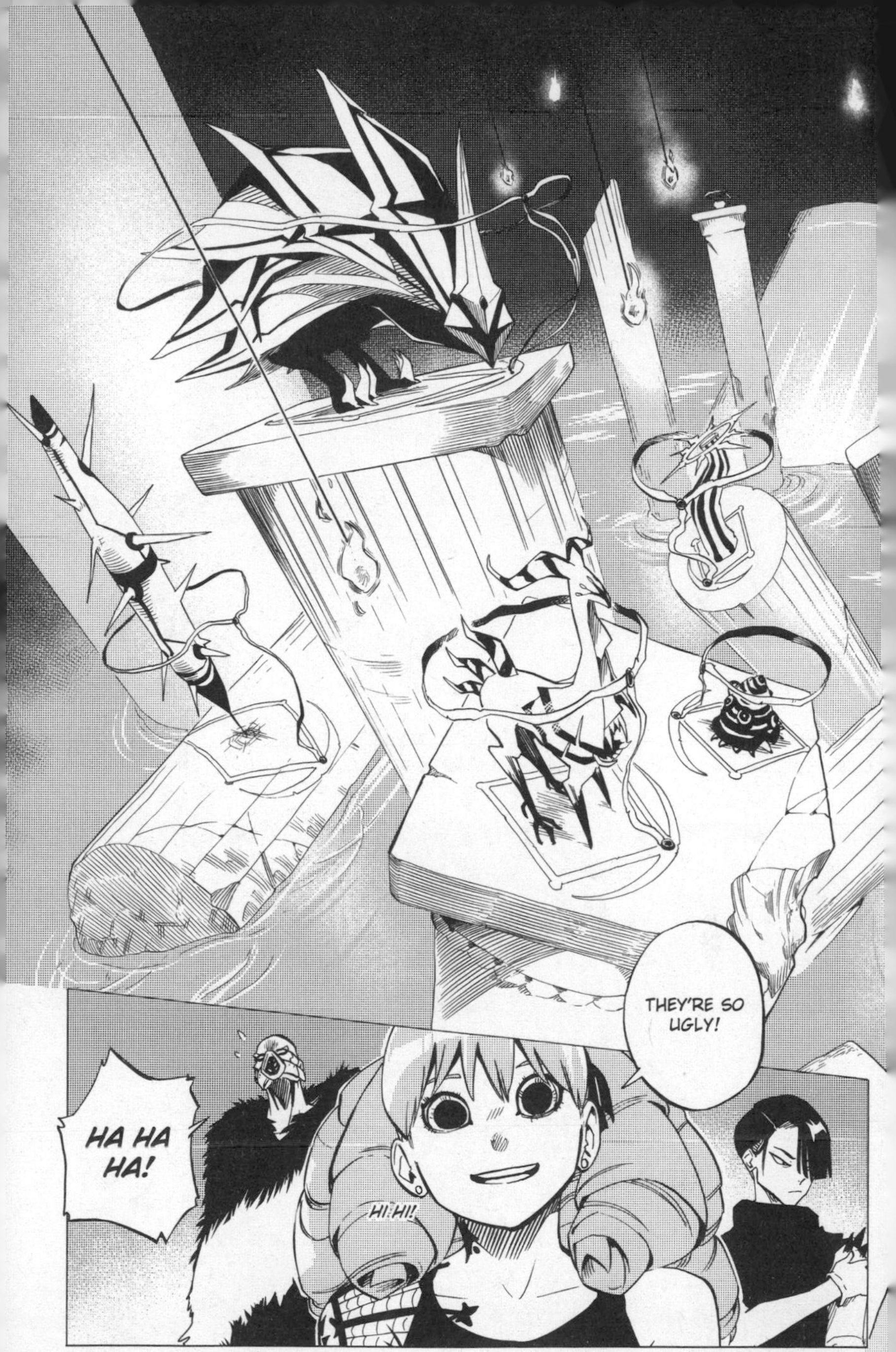
THEY'RE SO UGLY!
HI HI!
HA HA HA!

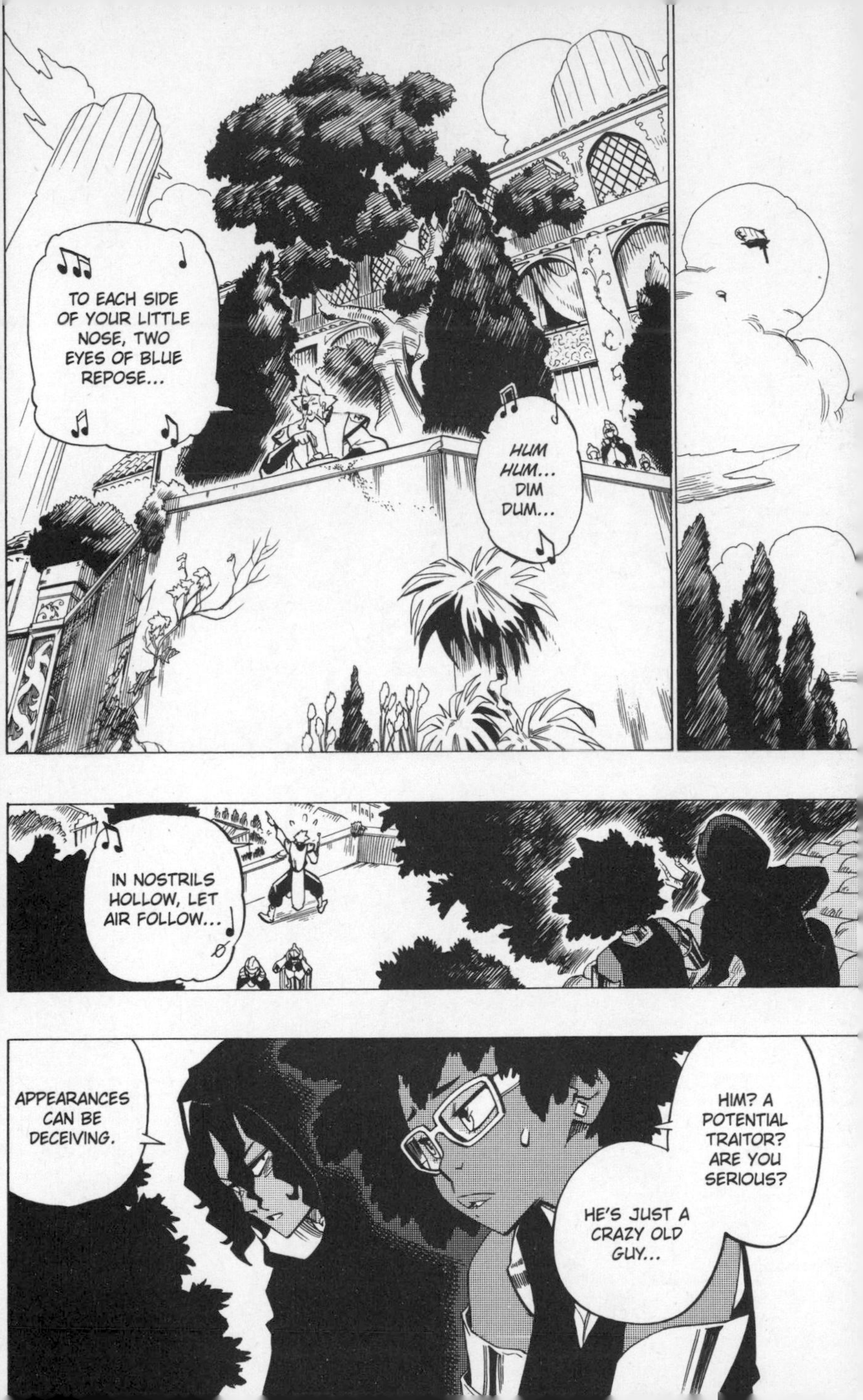
TO EACH SIDE OF YOUR LITTLE NOSE, TWO EYES OF BLUE REPOSE...
HUM HUM... DIM DUM...
IN NOSTRILS HOLLOW, LET AIR FOLLOW...
HIM? A POTENTIAL TRAITOR? ARE YOU SERIOUS?
HE'S JUST A CRAZY OLD GUY...
APPEARANCES CAN BE DECEIVING.

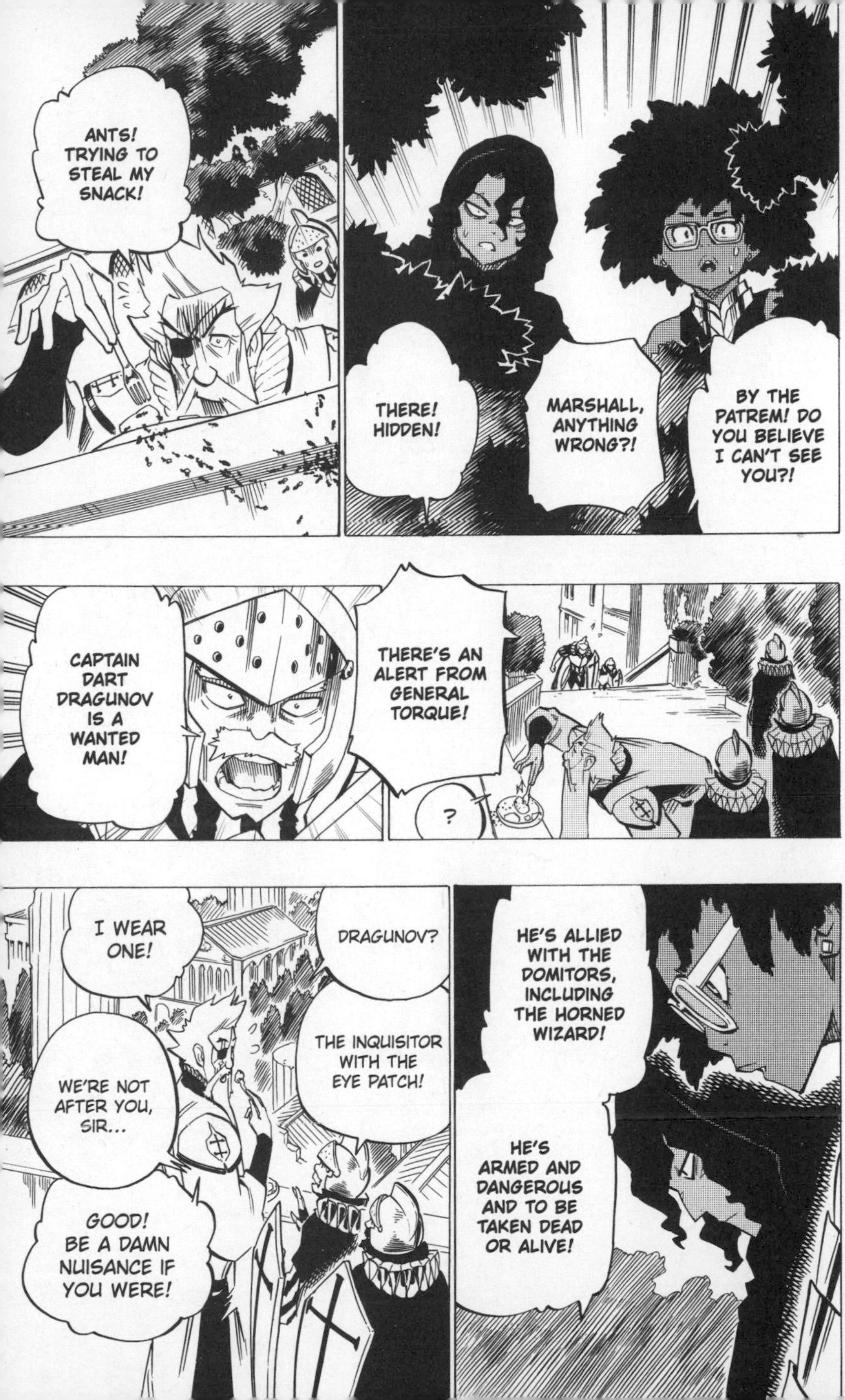
BY THE PATREM! DO YOU BELIEVE I CAN'T SEE YOU?!
MARSHALL, ANYTHING WRONG?!
THERE! HIDDEN!
ANTS! TRYING TO STEAL MY SNACK!
?
THERE'S AN ALERT FROM GENERAL TORQUE!
CAPTAIN DART DRAGUNOV IS A WANTED MAN!
HE'S ALLIED WITH THE DOMITORS, INCLUDING THE HORNED WIZARD!
HE'S ARMED AND DANGEROUS AND TO BE TAKEN DEAD OR ALIVE!
DRAGUNOV?
THE INQUISITOR WITH THE EYE PATCH!
I WEAR ONE!
WE'RE NOT AFTER YOU, SIR...
GOOD! BE A DAMN NUISANCE IF YOU WERE!

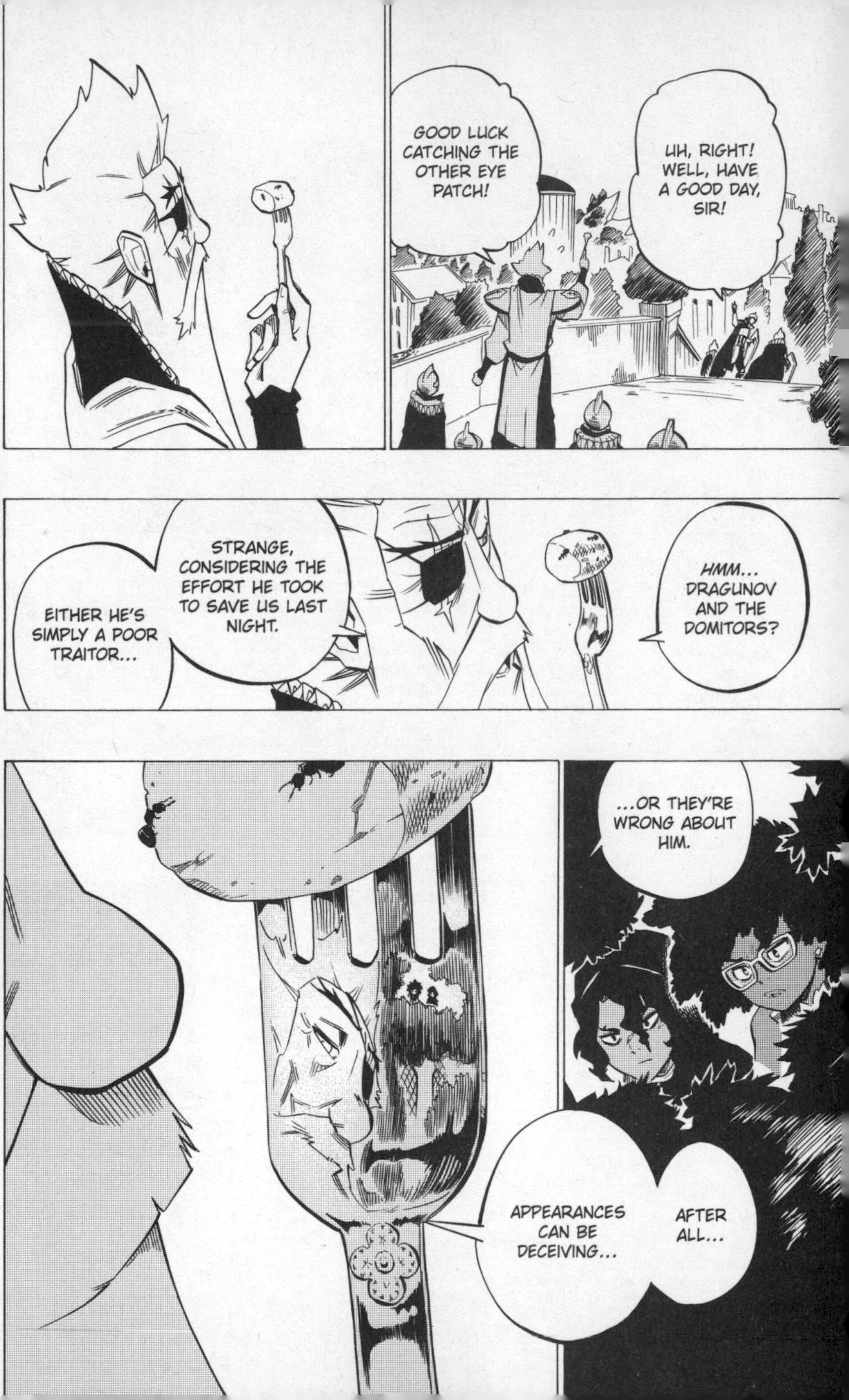
GOOD LUCK CATCHING THE OTHER EYE PATCH!
UH, RIGHT! WELL, HAVE A GOOD DAY, SIR!
HMM... DRAGUNOV AND THE DOMITORS?
STRANGE, CONSIDERING THE EFFORT HE TOOK TO SAVE US LAST NIGHT.
EITHER HE'S SIMPLY A POOR TRAITOR...
...OR THEY'RE WRONG ABOUT HIM.
AFTER ALL...
APPEARANCES CAN BE DECEIVING...

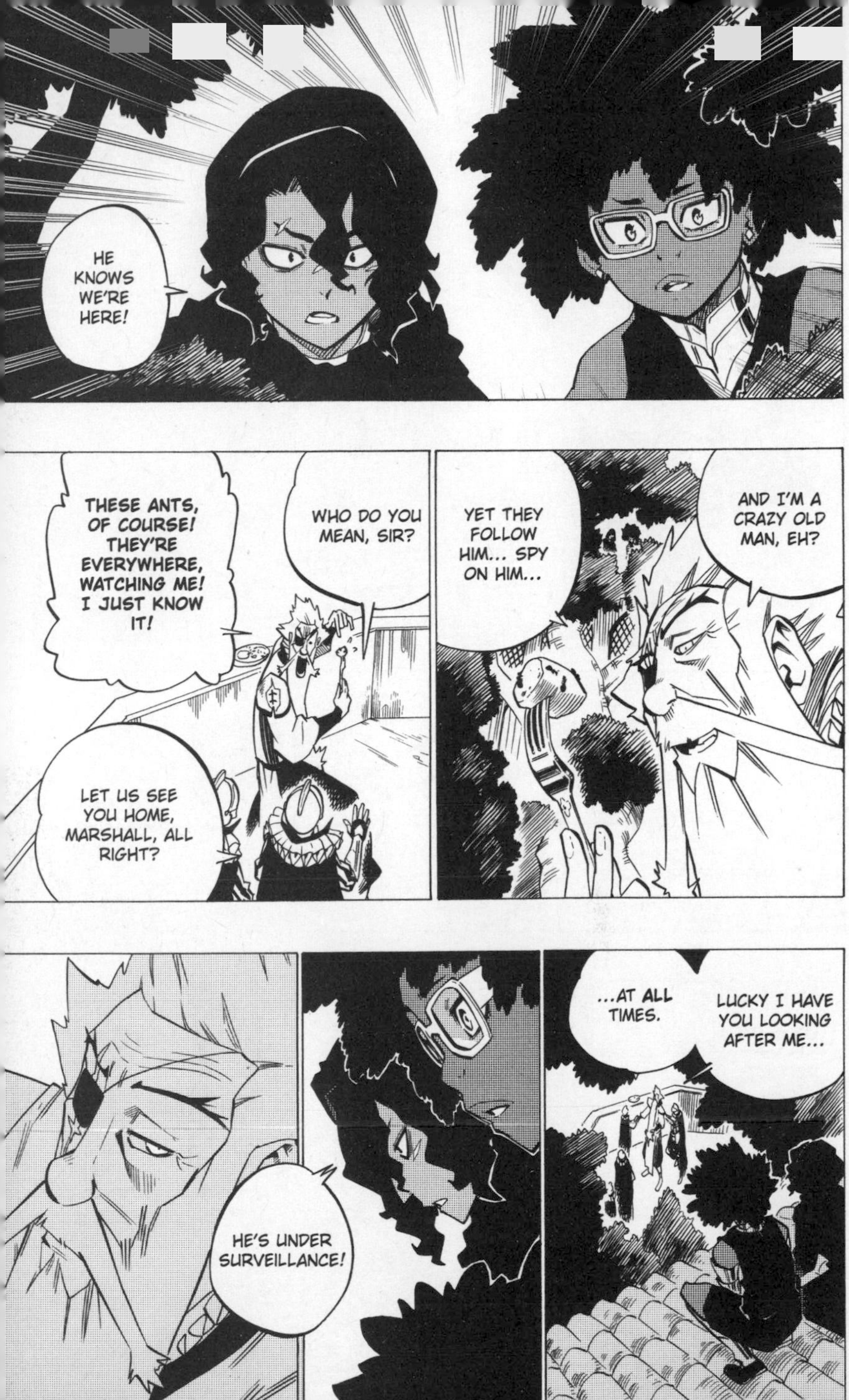
HE KNOWS WE'RE HERE!
AND I'M A CRAZY OLD MAN, EH?
YET THEY FOLLOW HIM... SPY ON HIM...
WHO DO YOU MEAN, SIR?
THESE ANTS, OF COURSE! THEY'RE EVERYWHERE, WATCHING ME! I JUST KNOW IT!
LET US SEE YOU HOME, MARSHALL, ALL RIGHT?
LUCKY I HAVE YOU LOOKING AFTER ME...
...AT ALL TIMES.
HE'S UNDER SURVEILLANCE!

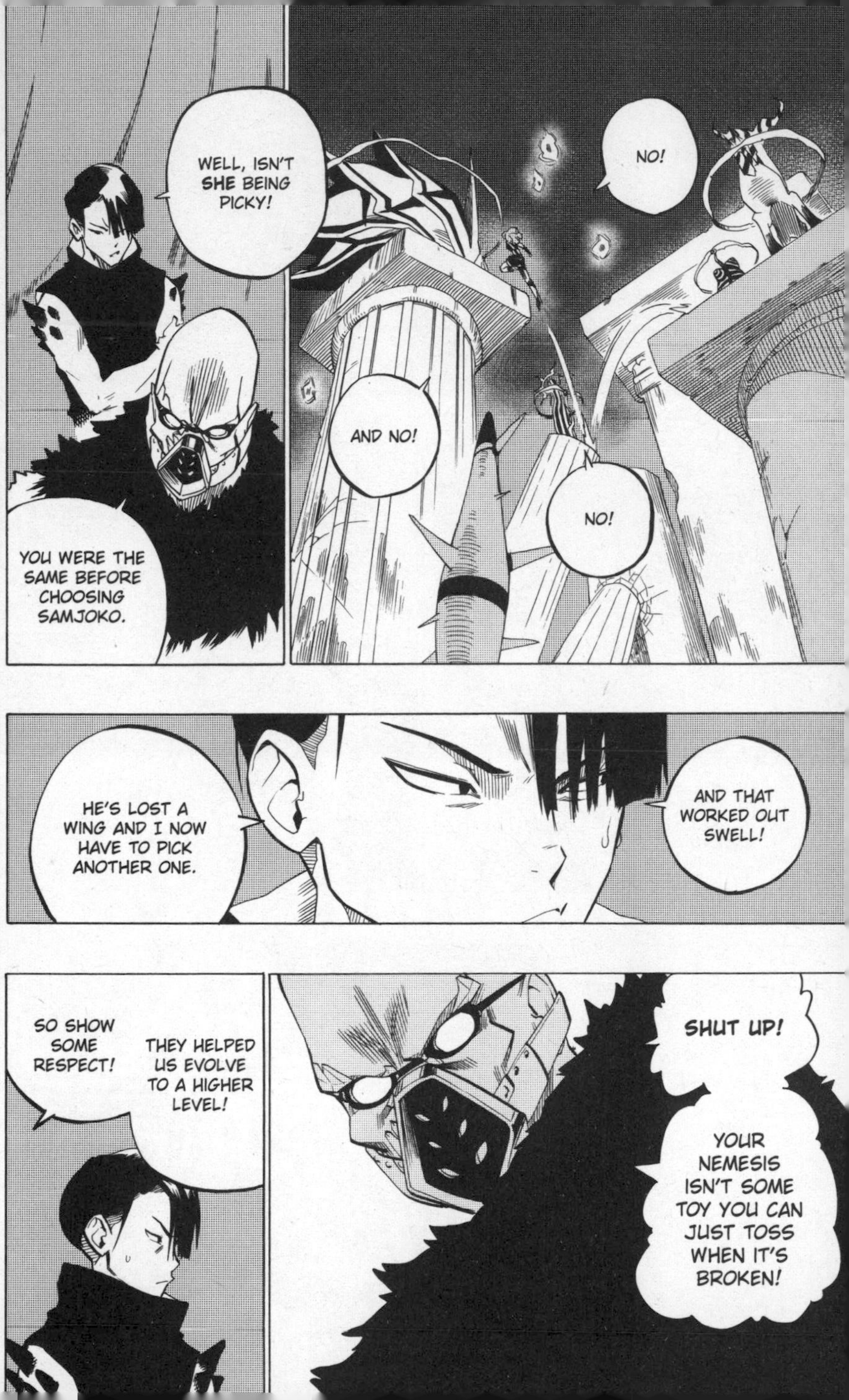
NO!
AND NO!
NO!
WELL, ISN'T SHE BEING PICKY!
YOU WERE THE SAME BEFORE CHOOSING SAMJOKO.
AND THAT WORKED OUT SWELL!
HE'S LOST A WING AND I NOW HAVE TO PICK ANOTHER ONE.
SHUT UP!
YOUR NEMESIS ISN'T SOME TOY YOU CAN JUST TOSS WHEN IT'S BROKEN!
THEY HELPED US EVOLVE TO A HIGHER LEVEL!
SO SHOW SOME RESPECT!

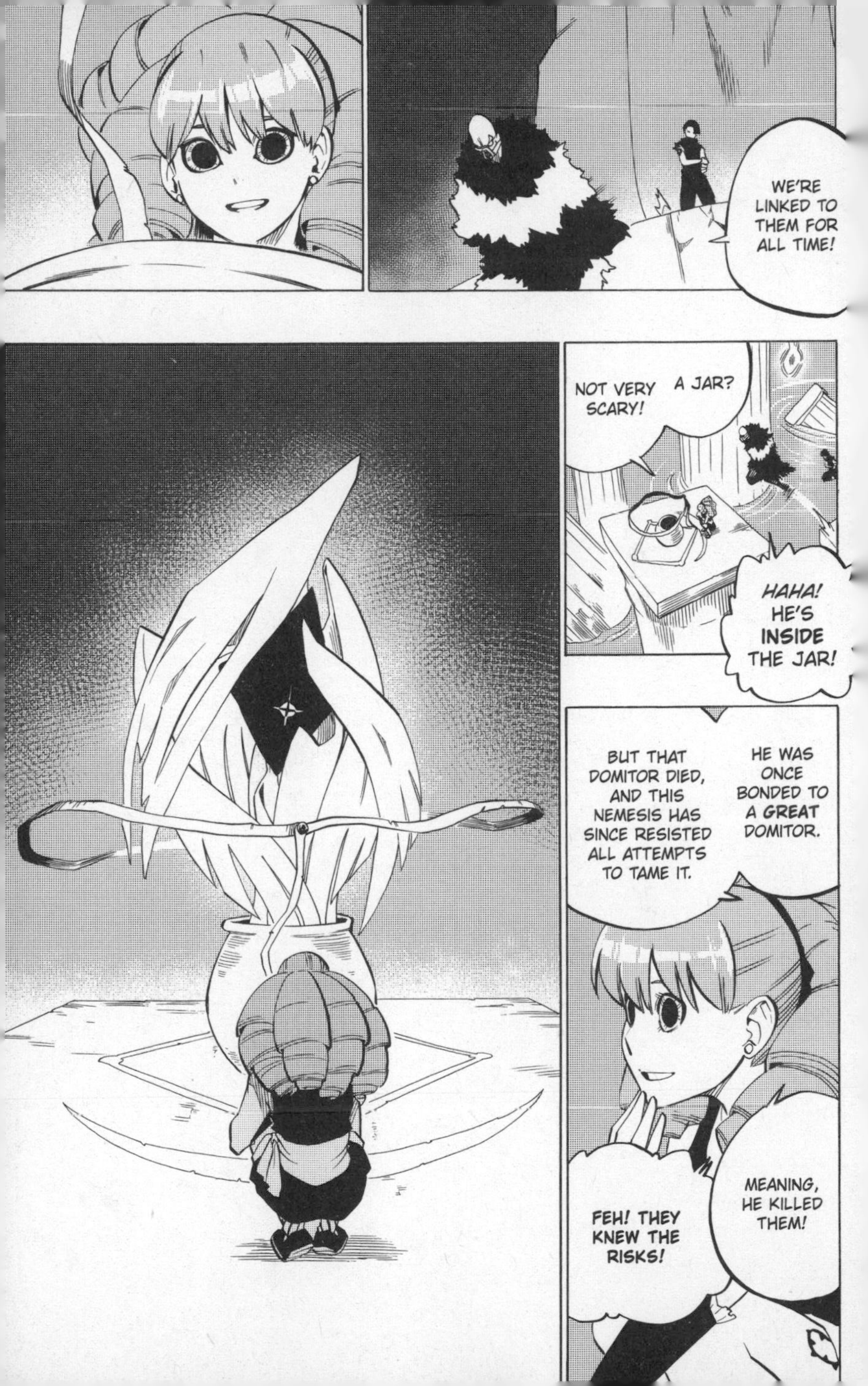
WE'RE LINKED TO THEM FOR ALL TIME!
A JAR?
NOT VERY SCARY!
HAHA! HE'S INSIDE THE JAR!
HE WAS ONCE BONDED TO A GREAT DOMITOR.
BUT THAT DOMITOR DIED, AND THIS NEMESIS HAS SINCE RESISTED ALL ATTEMPTS TO TAME IT.
MEANING, HE KILLED THEM!
FEH! THEY KNEW THE RISKS!

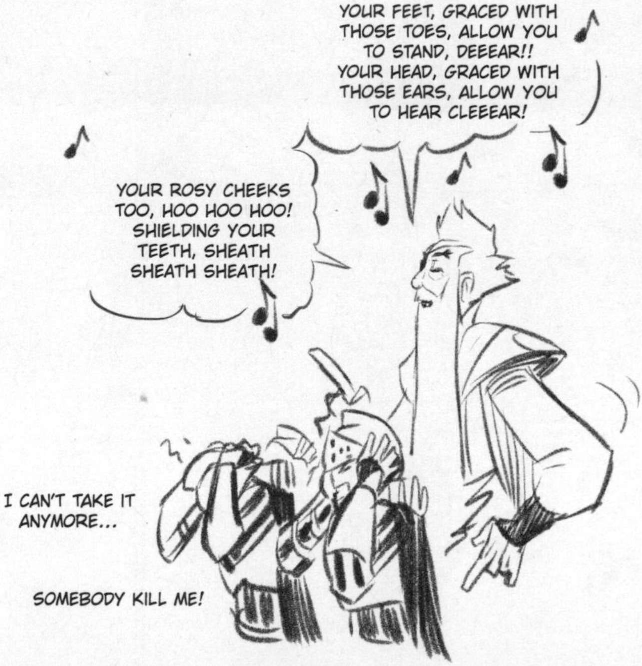
YOUR FEET, GRACED WITH THOSE TOES, ALLOW YOU TO STAND, DEEEAR!! YOUR HEAD, GRACED WITH THOSE EARS, ALLOW YOU TO HEAR CLEEEAR!
YOUR ROSY CHEEKS TOO, HOO HOO HOO! SHIELDING YOUR TEETH, SHEATH SHEATH SHEATH!
I CAN'T TAKE IT ANYMORE...
SOMEBODY KILL ME!

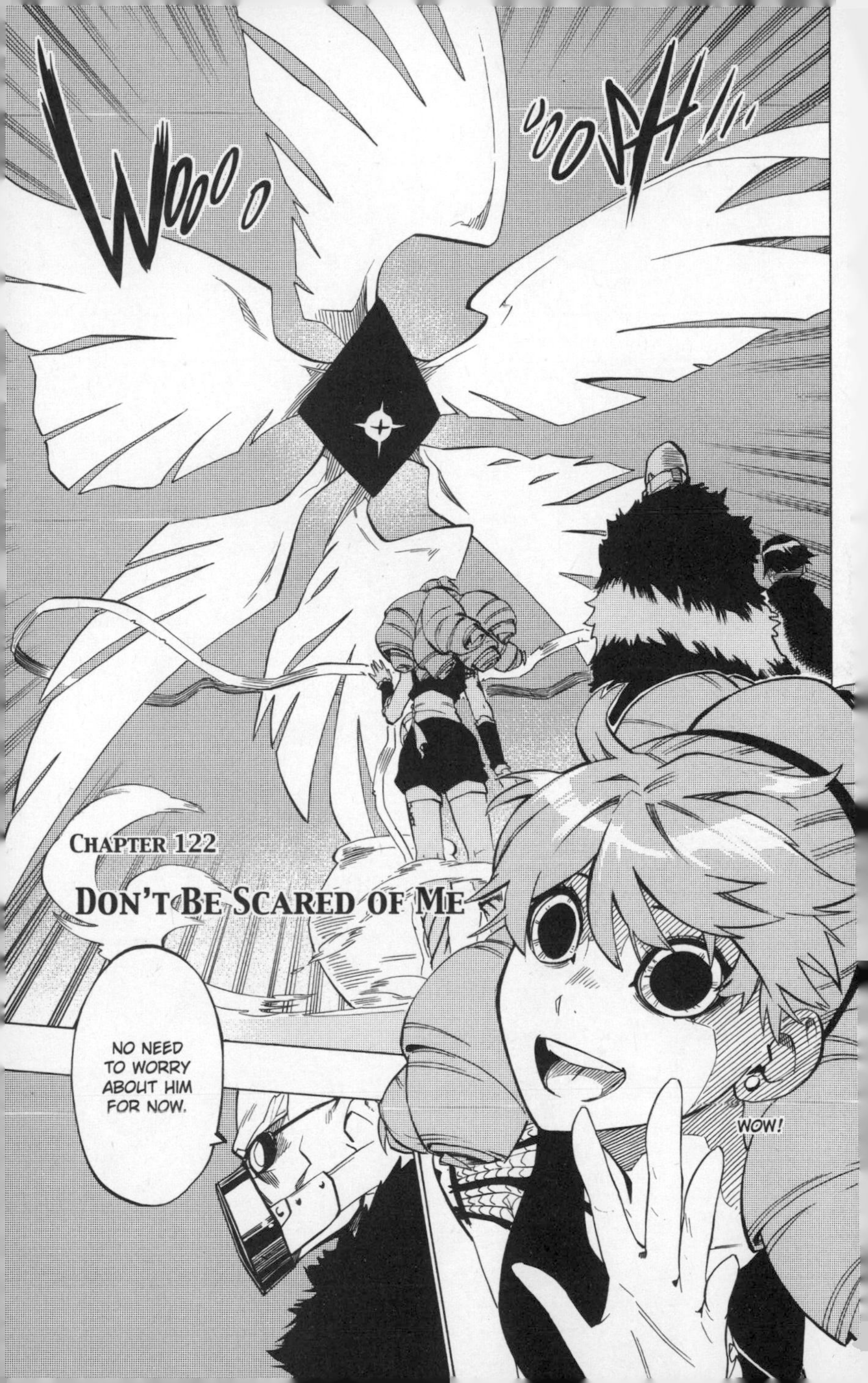
WOOOOOOSH!!
Chapter 122
Don't Be Scared of Me
WOW!
NO NEED TO WORRY ABOUT HIM FOR NOW.

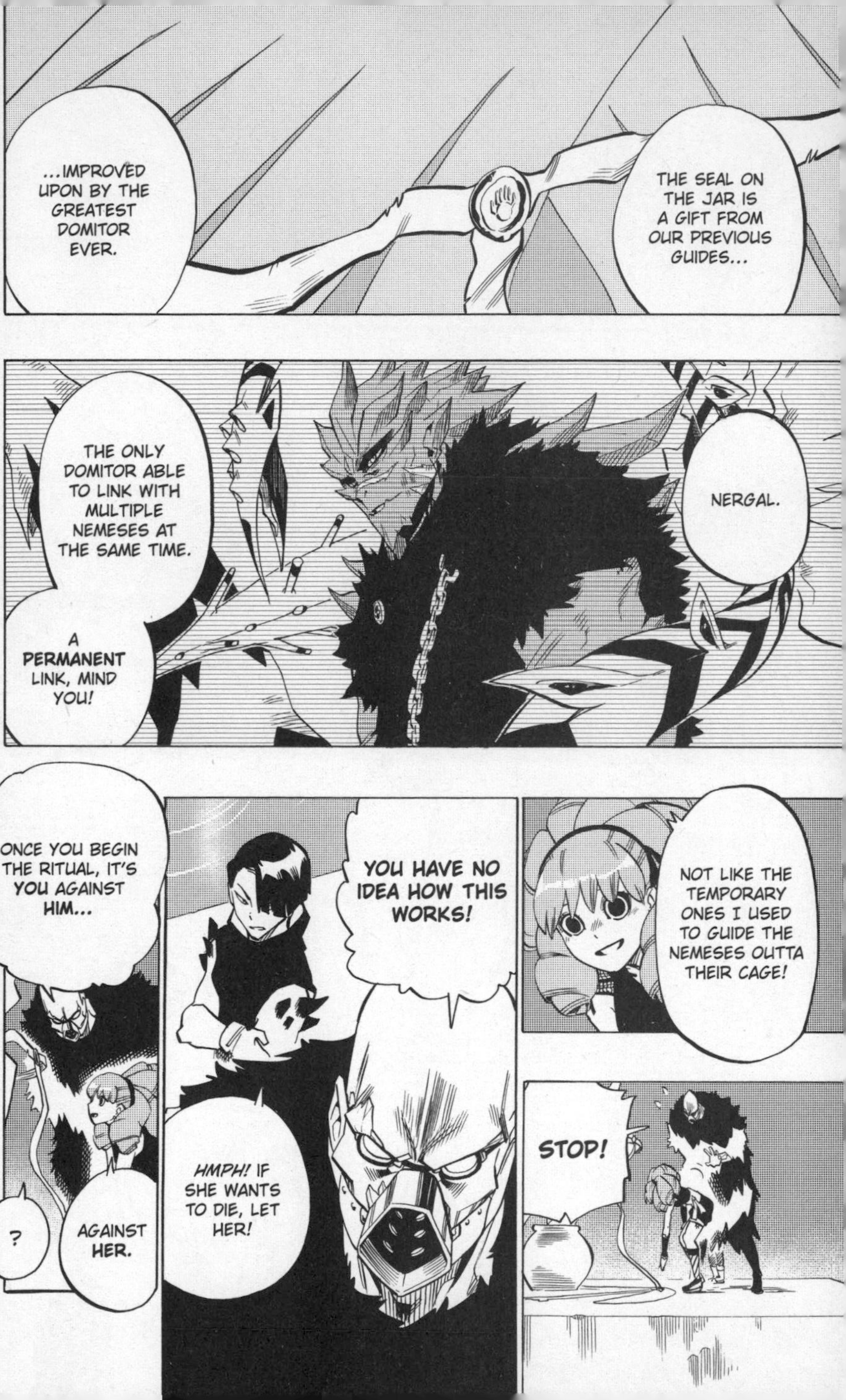
THE SEAL ON THE JAR IS A GIFT FROM OUR PREVIOUS GUIDES...
...IMPROVED UPON BY THE GREATEST DOMITOR EVER.
NERGAL.
THE ONLY DOMITOR ABLE TO LINK WITH MULTIPLE NEMESES AT THE SAME TIME.
A **PERMANENT** LINK, MIND YOU!
NOT LIKE THE TEMPORARY ONES I USED TO GUIDE THE NEMESES OUTTA THEIR CAGE!
STOP!
YOU HAVE NO IDEA HOW THIS WORKS!
HMPH! IF SHE WANTS TO DIE, LET HER!
ONCE YOU BEGIN THE RITUAL, IT'S **YOU** AGAINST **HIM**...
AGAINST **HER.**
?

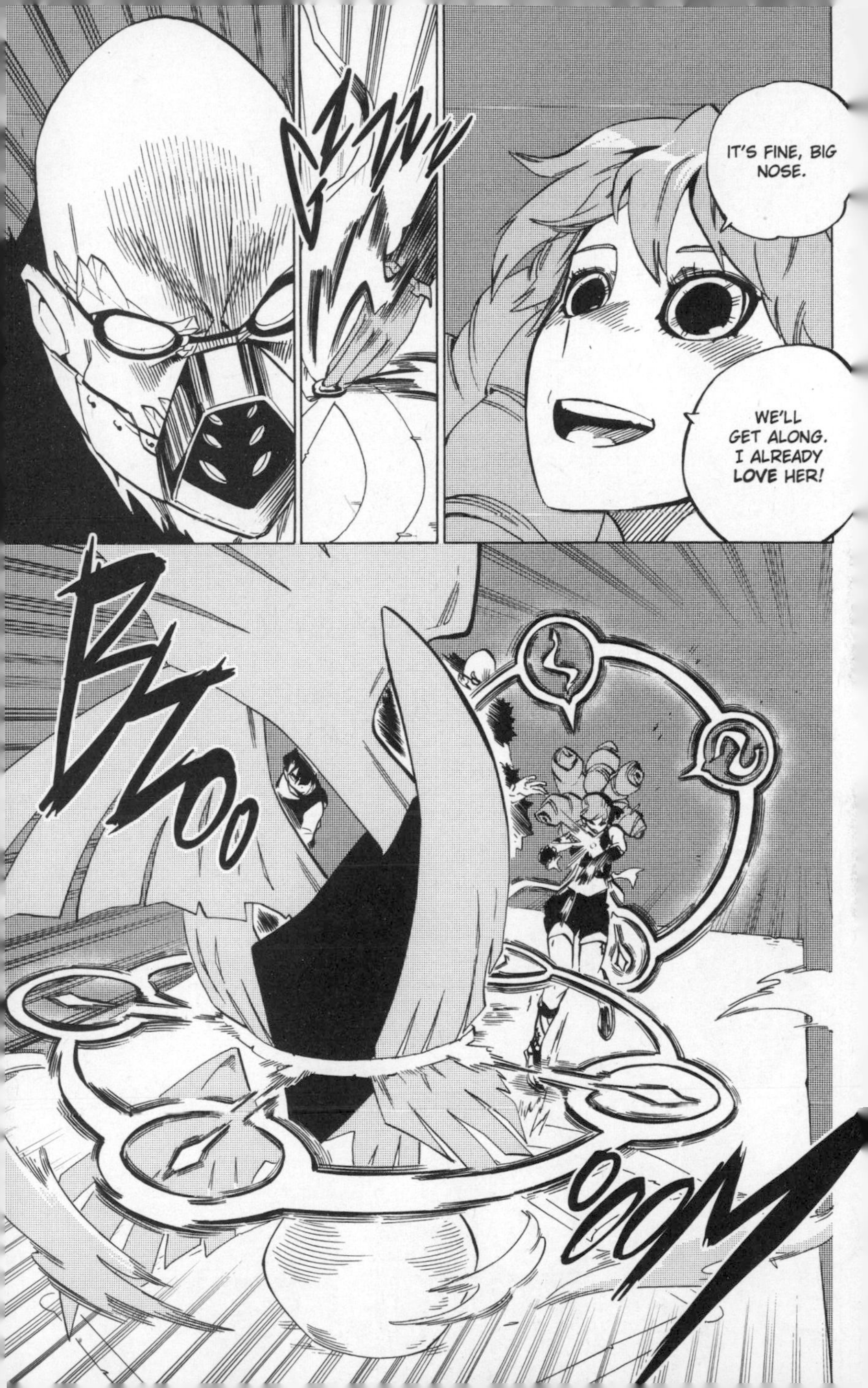
IT'S FINE, BIG NOSE.
WE'LL GET ALONG. I ALREADY LOVE HER!
BZZZZ
BWOOOOM

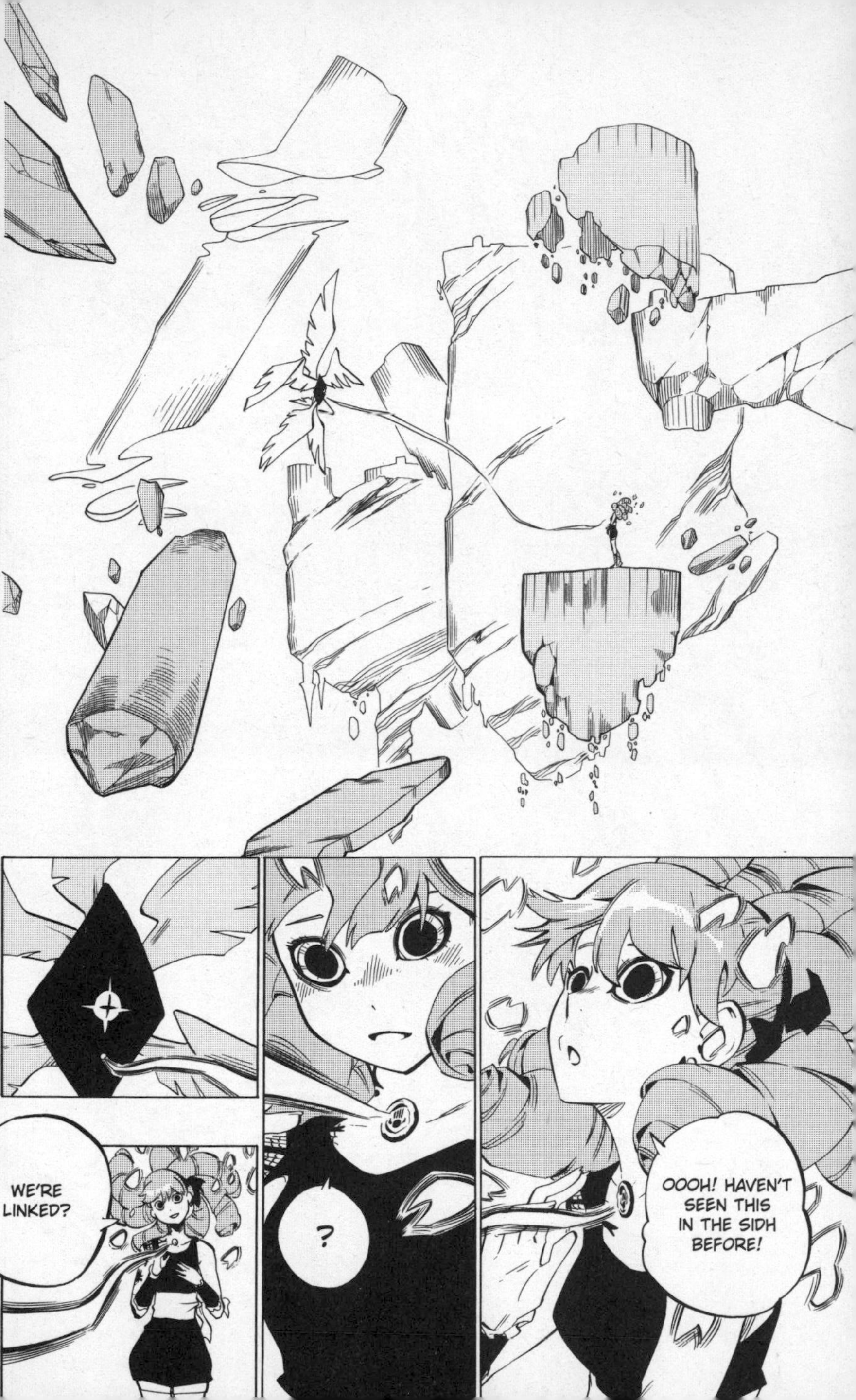
OOOH! HAVEN'T SEEN THIS IN THE SIDH BEFORE!
?
WE'RE LINKED?

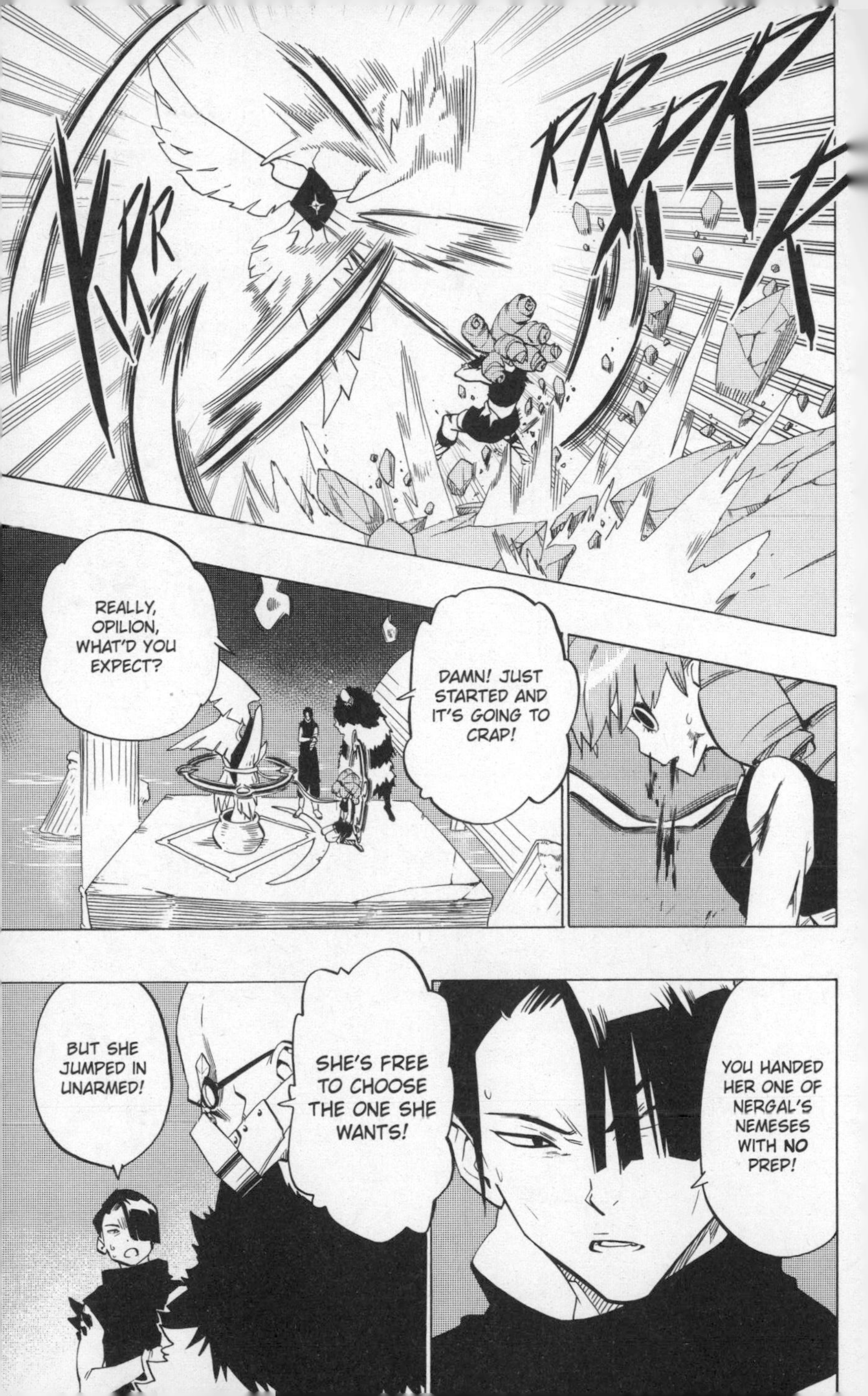
NRR
DAMN! JUST STARTED AND IT'S GOING TO CRAP!
REALLY, OPILION, WHAT'D YOU EXPECT?
YOU HANDED HER ONE OF NERGAL'S NEMESES WITH NO PREP!
SHE'S FREE TO CHOOSE THE ONE SHE WANTS!
BUT SHE JUMPED IN UNARMED!

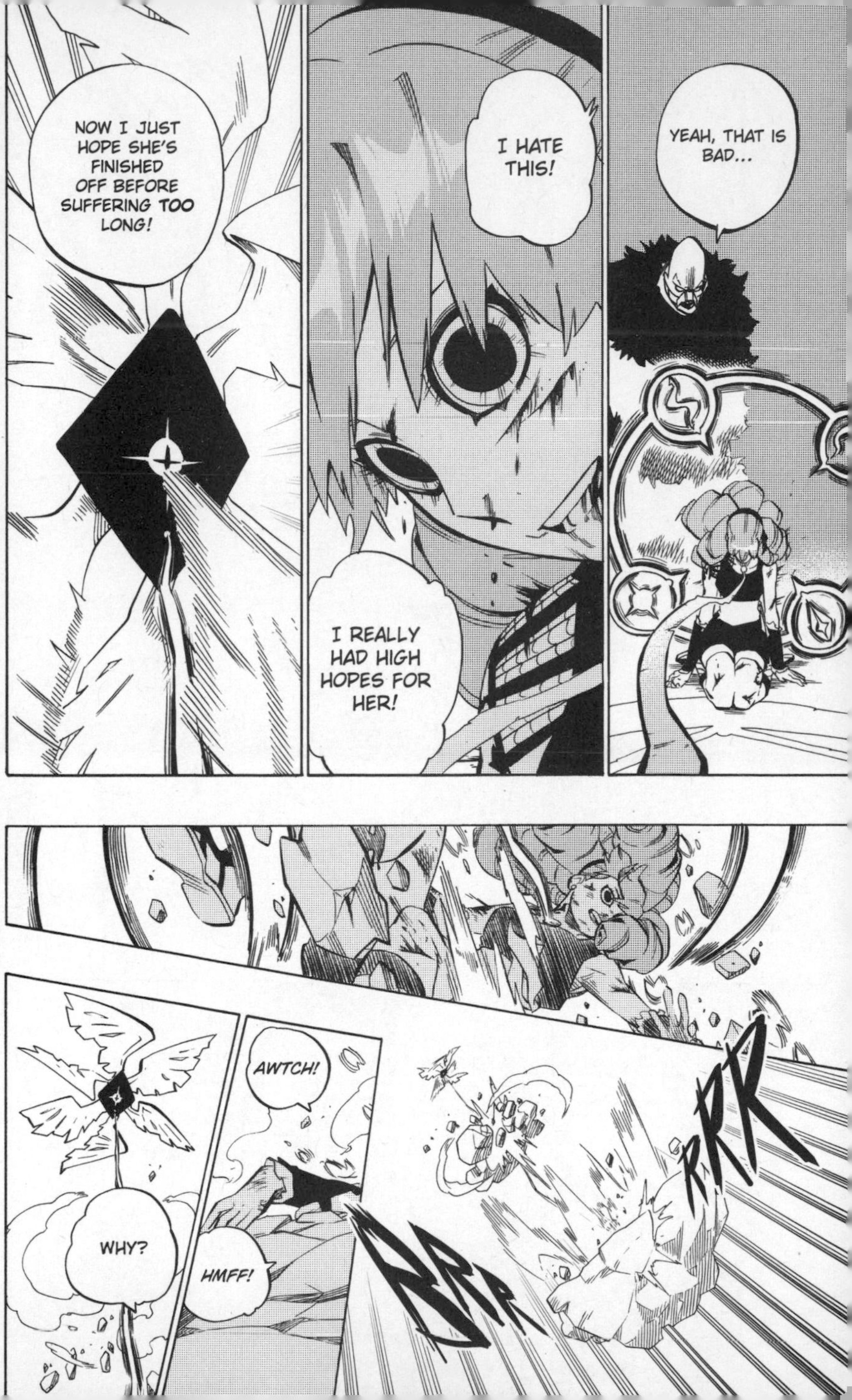
YEAH, THAT IS BAD...
I HATE THIS!
I REALLY HAD HIGH HOPES FOR HER!
NOW I JUST HOPE SHE'S FINISHED OFF BEFORE SUFFERING TOO LONG!
RRR
RRR
AWTCH!
HMFF!
WHY?

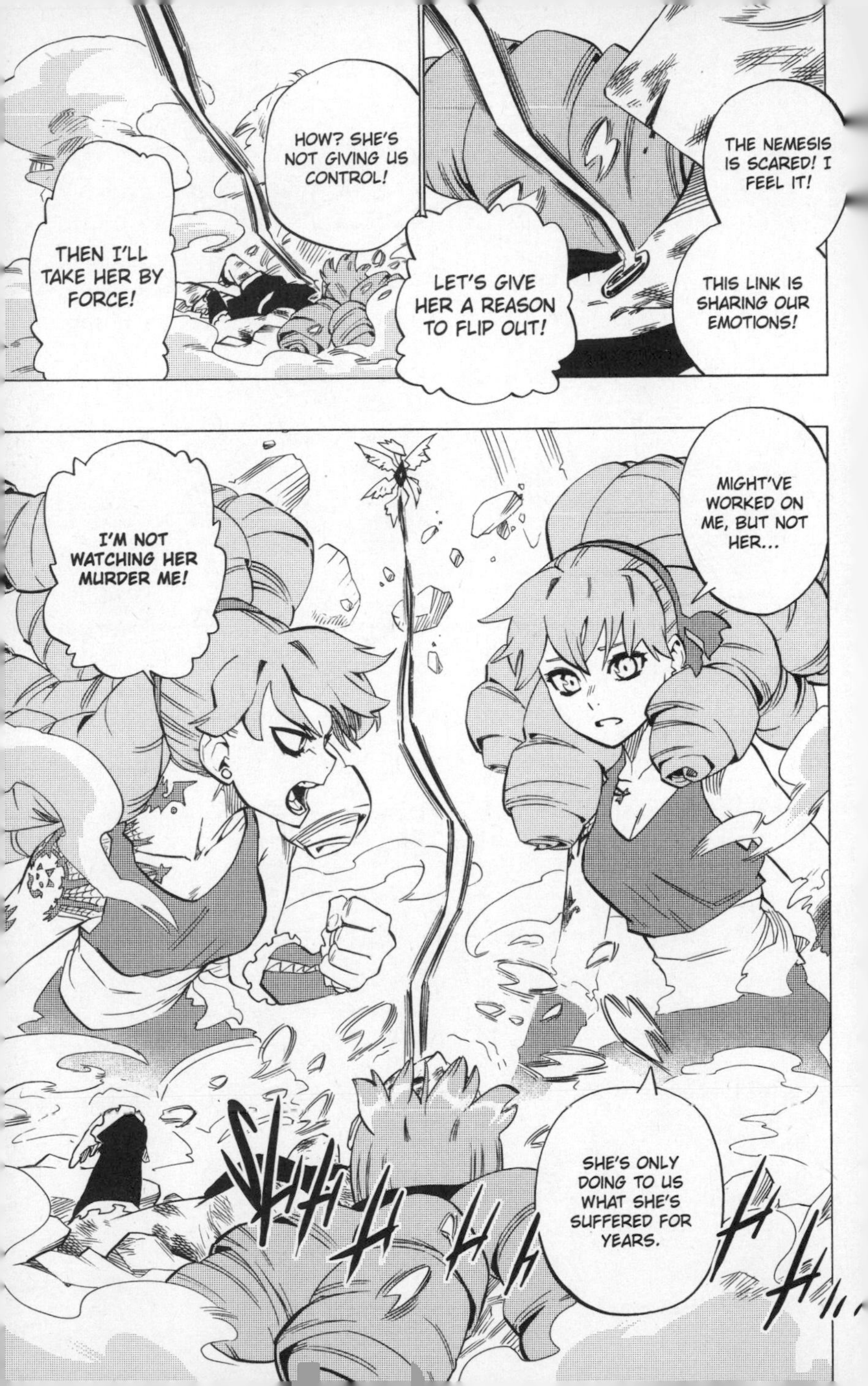
THE NEMESIS IS SCARED! I FEEL IT!
THIS LINK IS SHARING OUR EMOTIONS!
LET'S GIVE HER A REASON TO FLIP OUT!
HOW? SHE'S NOT GIVING US CONTROL!
THEN I'LL TAKE HER BY FORCE!
MIGHT'VE WORKED ON ME, BUT NOT HER...
I'M NOT WATCHING HER MURDER ME!
SHE'S ONLY DOING TO US WHAT SHE'S SUFFERED FOR YEARS.
SHHHHHHH...

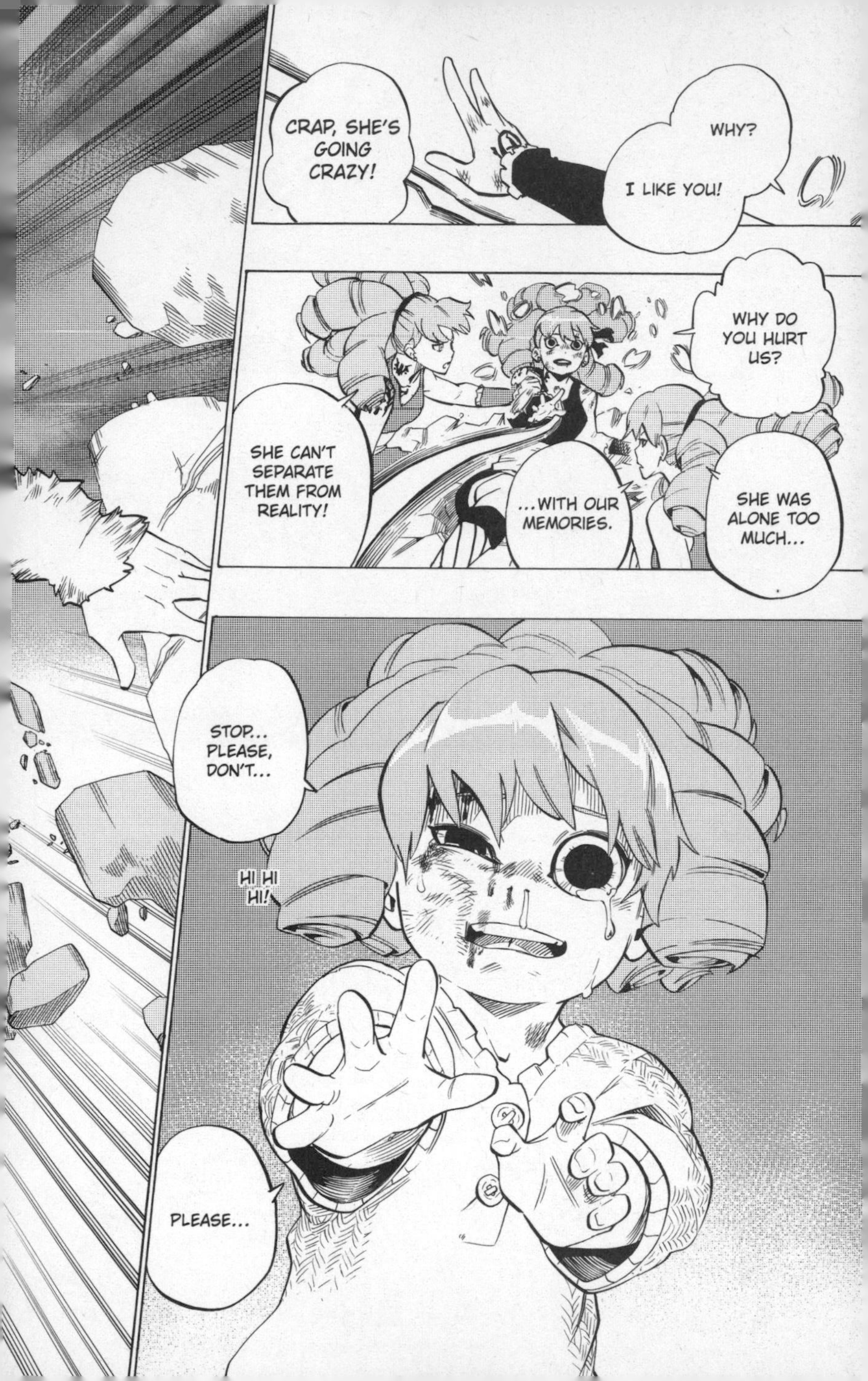
WHY? I LIKE YOU!
CRAP, SHE'S GOING CRAZY!
WHY DO YOU HURT US?
SHE WAS ALONE TOO MUCH...
...WITH OUR MEMORIES.
SHE CAN'T SEPARATE THEM FROM REALITY!
STOP... PLEASE, DON'T...
HI HI HI!
PLEASE...

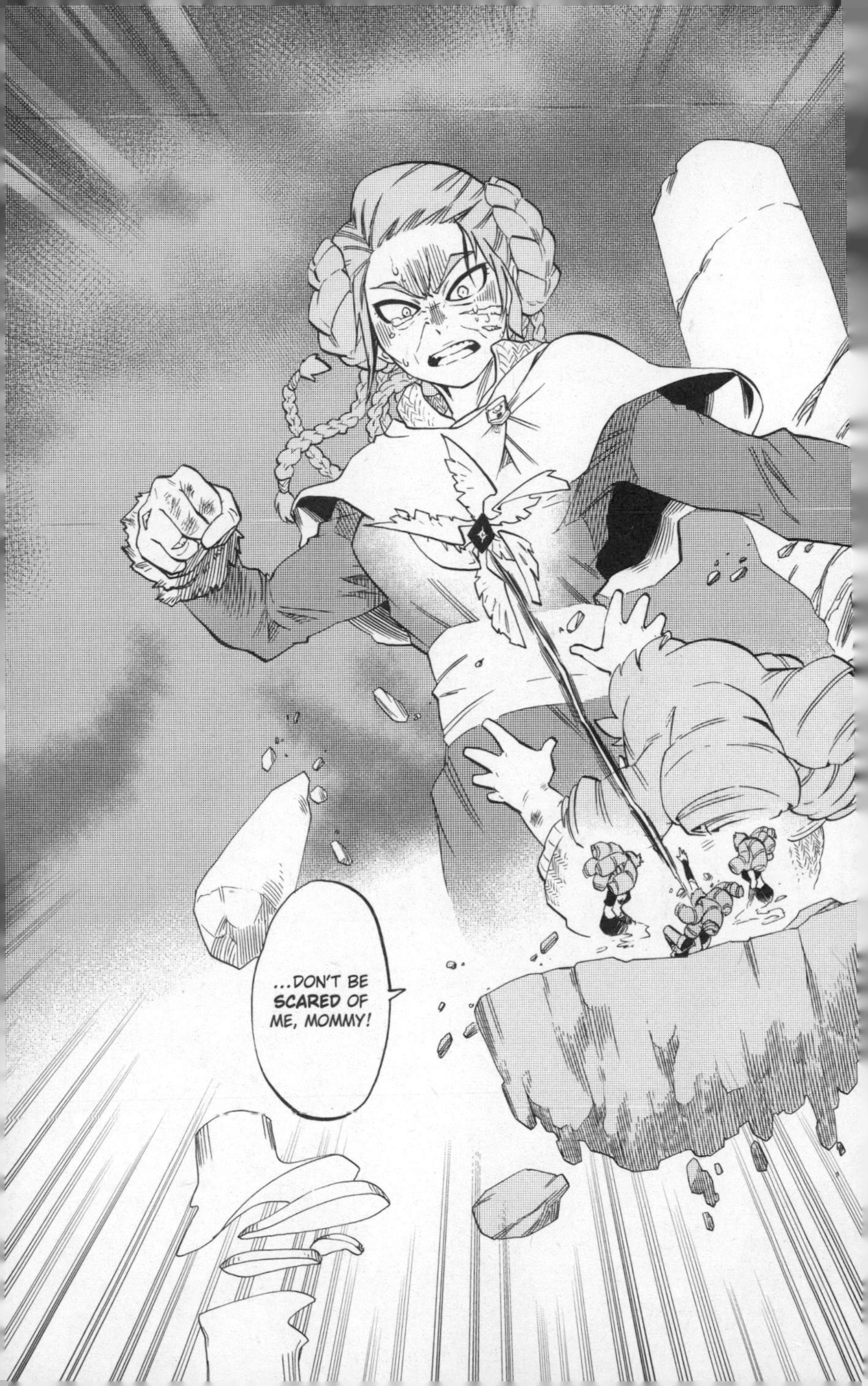
...DON'T BE SCARED OF ME, MOMMY!

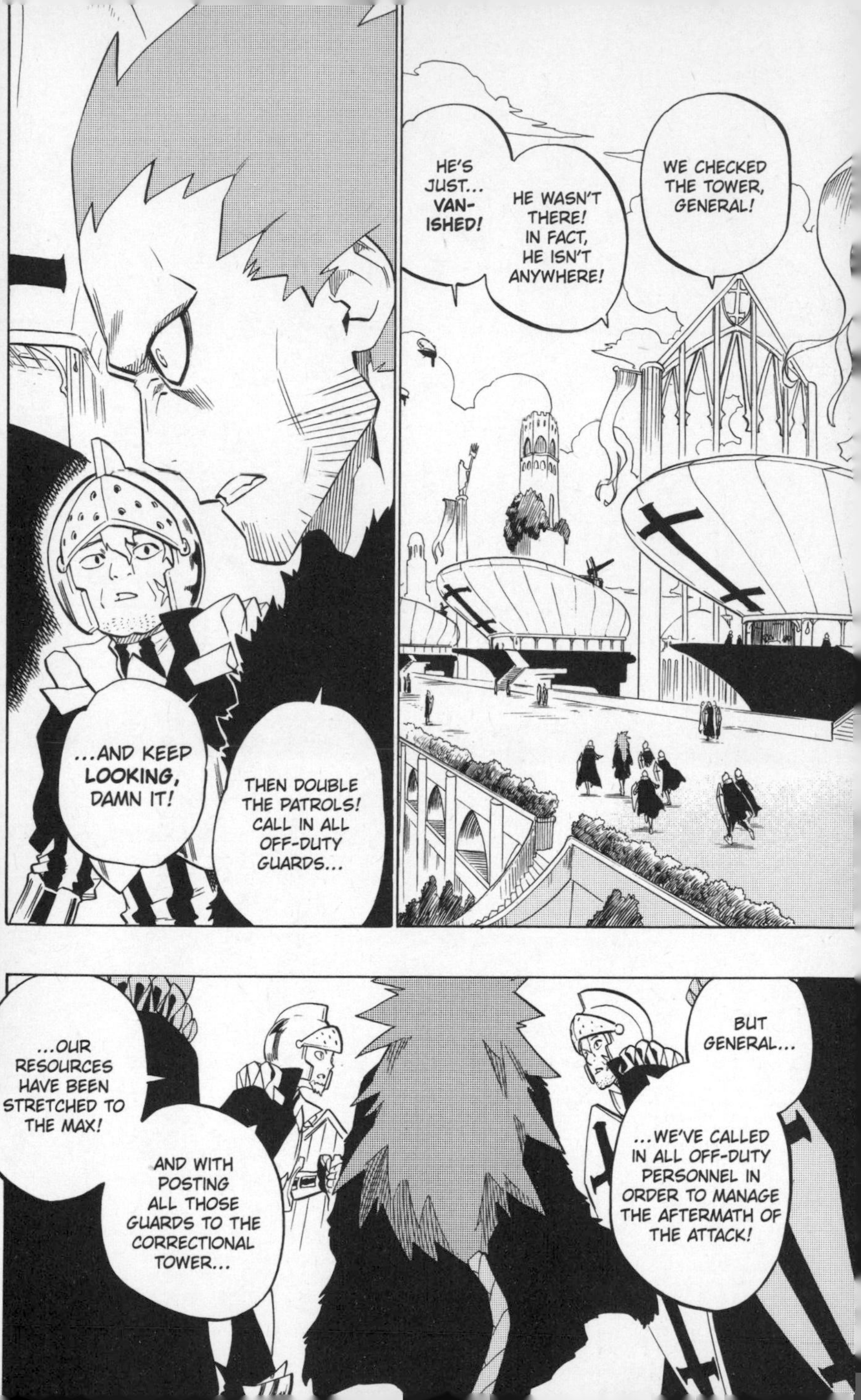
WE CHECKED THE TOWER, GENERAL!
HE WASN'T THERE! IN FACT, HE ISN'T ANYWHERE!
HE'S JUST... VAN-ISHED!
THEN DOUBLE THE PATROLS! CALL IN ALL OFF-DUTY GUARDS...
...AND KEEP LOOKING, DAMN IT!
BUT GENERAL...
...WE'VE CALLED IN ALL OFF-DUTY PERSONNEL IN ORDER TO MANAGE THE AFTERMATH OF THE ATTACK!
AND WITH POSTING ALL THOSE GUARDS TO THE CORRECTIONAL TOWER...
...OUR RESOURCES HAVE BEEN STRETCHED TO THE MAX!

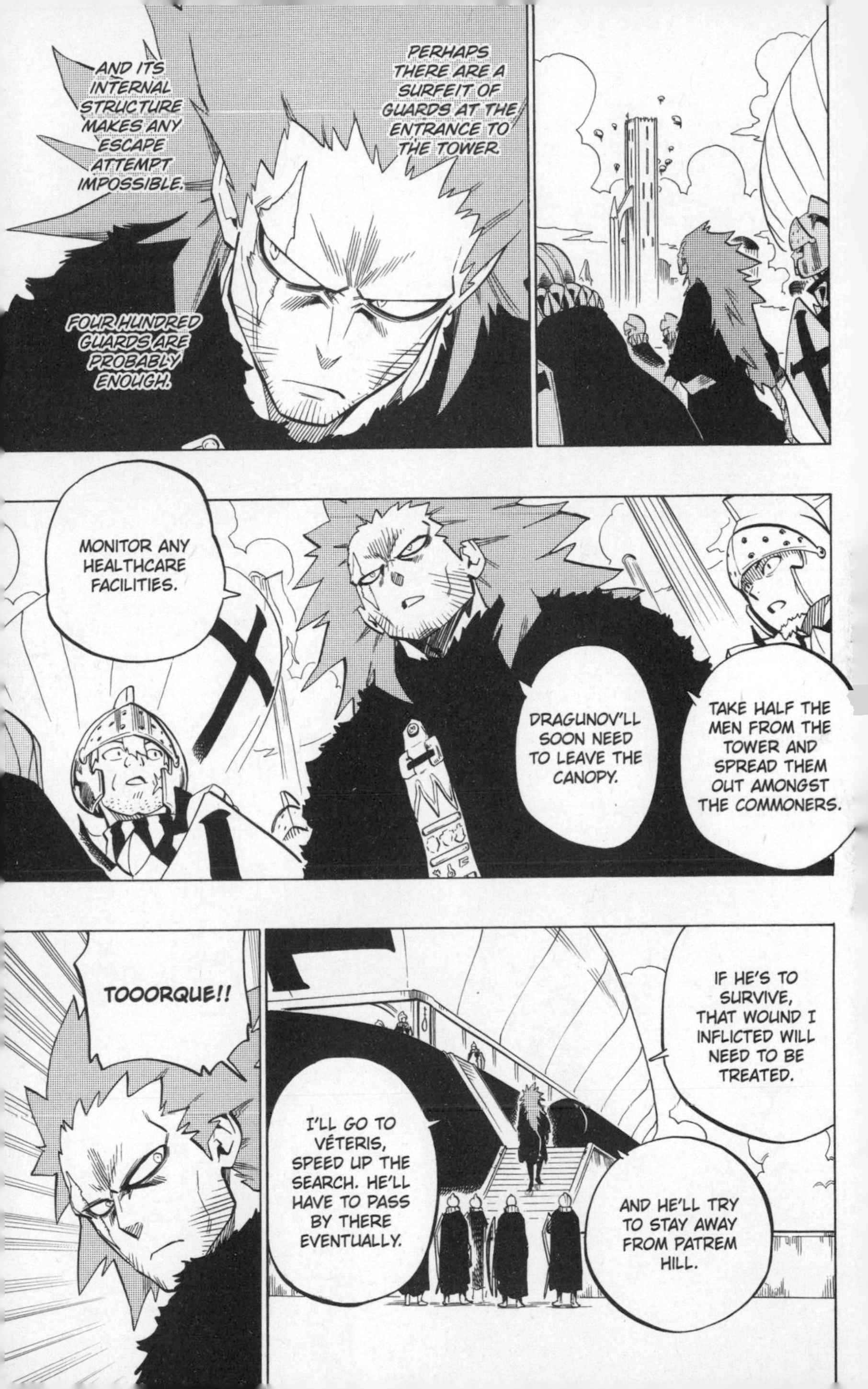
PERHAPS THERE ARE A SURFEIT OF GUARDS AT THE ENTRANCE TO THE TOWER.
AND ITS INTERNAL STRUCTURE MAKES ANY ESCAPE ATTEMPT IMPOSSIBLE.
FOUR HUNDRED GUARDS ARE PROBABLY ENOUGH.
TAKE HALF THE MEN FROM THE TOWER AND SPREAD THEM OUT AMONGST THE COMMONERS.
DRAGUNOV'LL SOON NEED TO LEAVE THE CANOPY.
MONITOR ANY HEALTHCARE FACILITIES.
IF HE'S TO SURVIVE, THAT WOUND I INFLICTED WILL NEED TO BE TREATED.
AND HE'LL TRY TO STAY AWAY FROM PATREM HILL.
I'LL GO TO VÉTERIS, SPEED UP THE SEARCH. HE'LL HAVE TO PASS BY THERE EVENTUALLY.
TOOORQUE!!

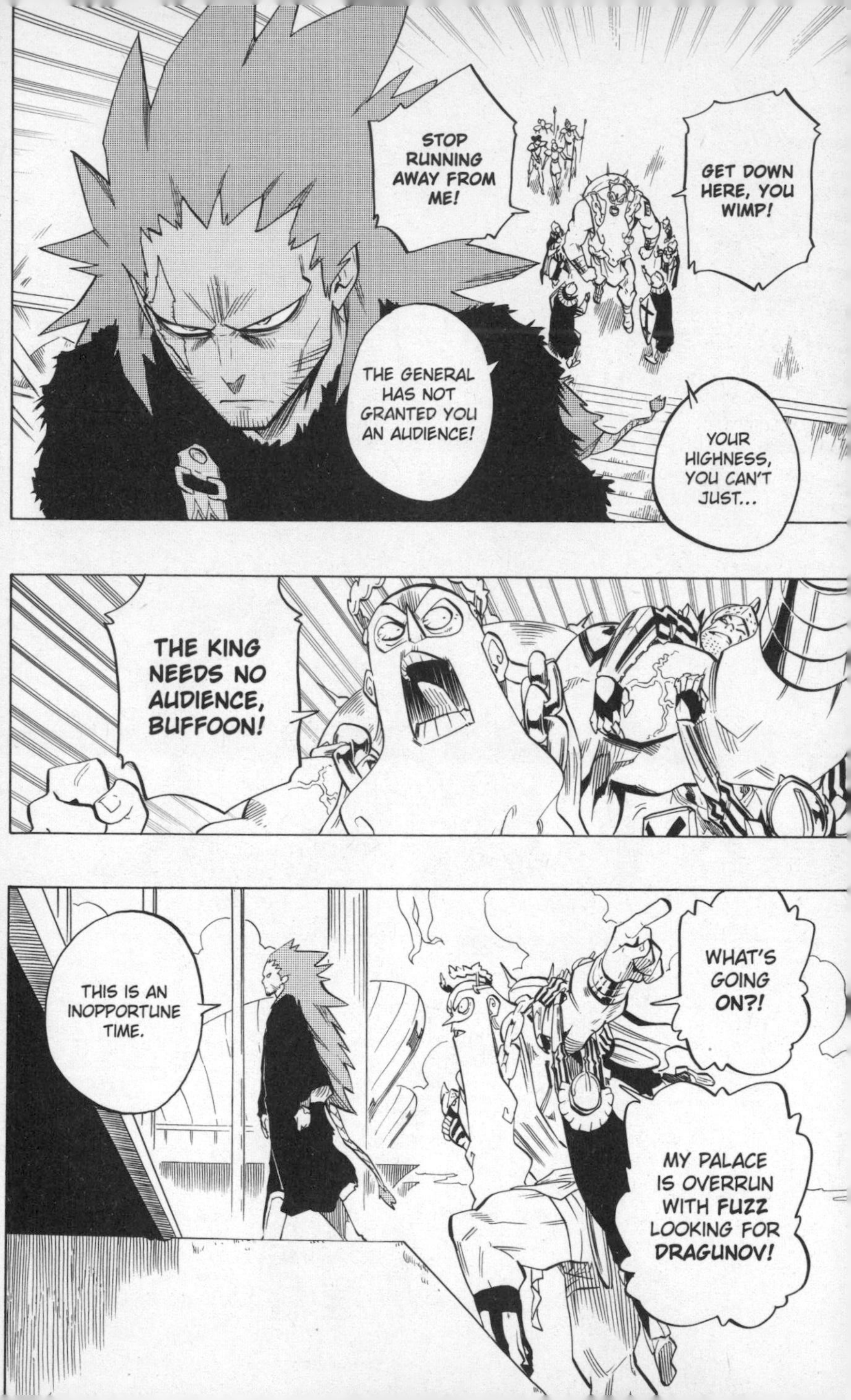
GET DOWN HERE, YOU WIMP!
STOP RUNNING AWAY FROM ME!
YOUR HIGHNESS, YOU CAN'T JUST...
THE GENERAL HAS NOT GRANTED YOU AN AUDIENCE!
THE KING NEEDS NO AUDIENCE, BUFFOON!
WHAT'S GOING ON?!
MY PALACE IS OVERRUN WITH FUZZ LOOKING FOR DRAGUNOV!
THIS IS AN INOPPORTUNE TIME.

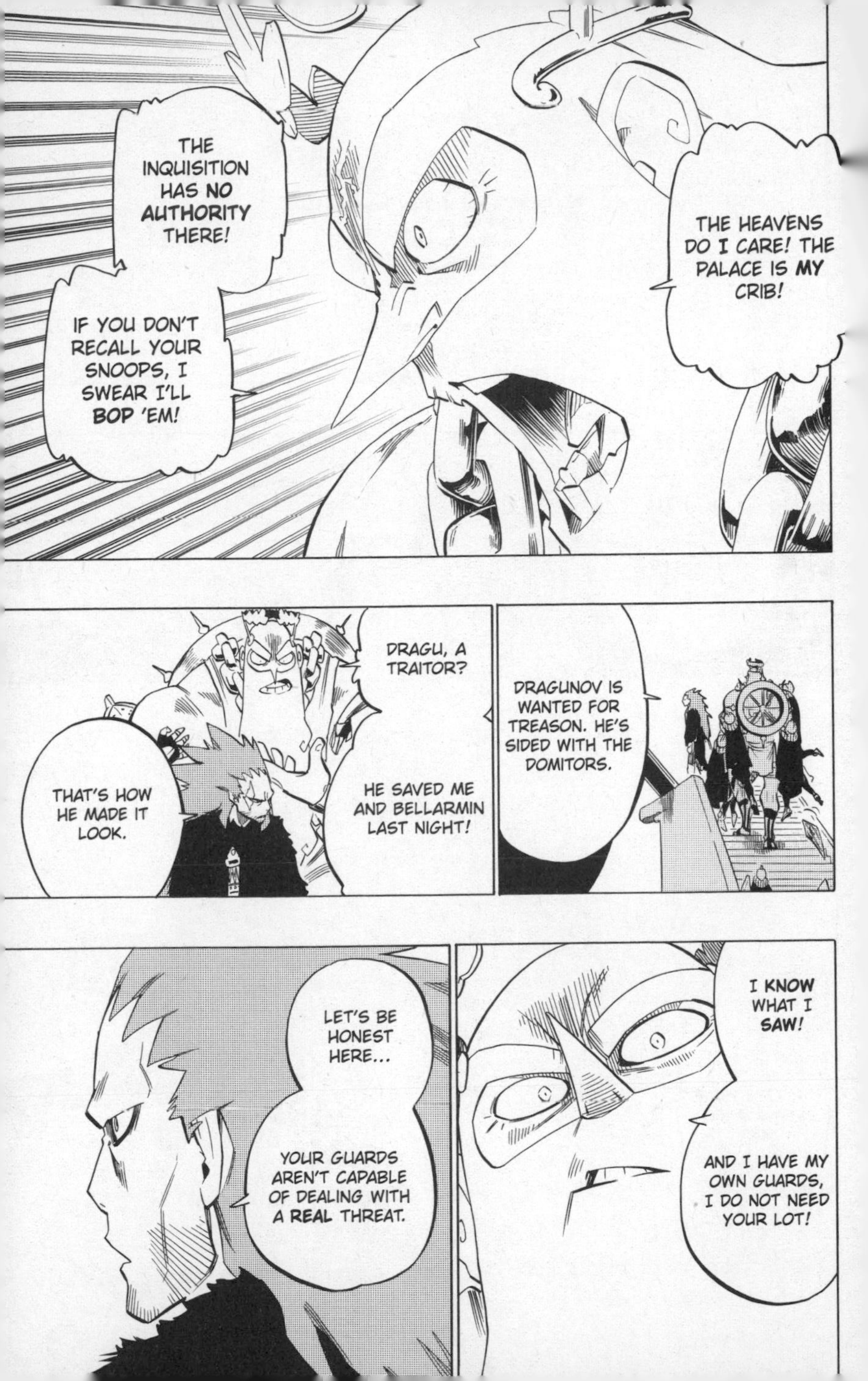
THE HEAVENS DO I CARE! THE PALACE IS MY CRIB!
THE INQUISITION HAS NO AUTHORITY THERE!
IF YOU DON'T RECALL YOUR SNOOPS, I SWEAR I'LL BOP 'EM!
DRAGUNOV IS WANTED FOR TREASON. HE'S SIDED WITH THE DOMITORS.
DRAGU, A TRAITOR?
HE SAVED ME AND BELLARMIN LAST NIGHT!
THAT'S HOW HE MADE IT LOOK.
I KNOW WHAT I SAW!
AND I HAVE MY OWN GUARDS, I DO NOT NEED YOUR LOT!
LET'S BE HONEST HERE...
YOUR GUARDS AREN'T CAPABLE OF DEALING WITH A REAL THREAT.

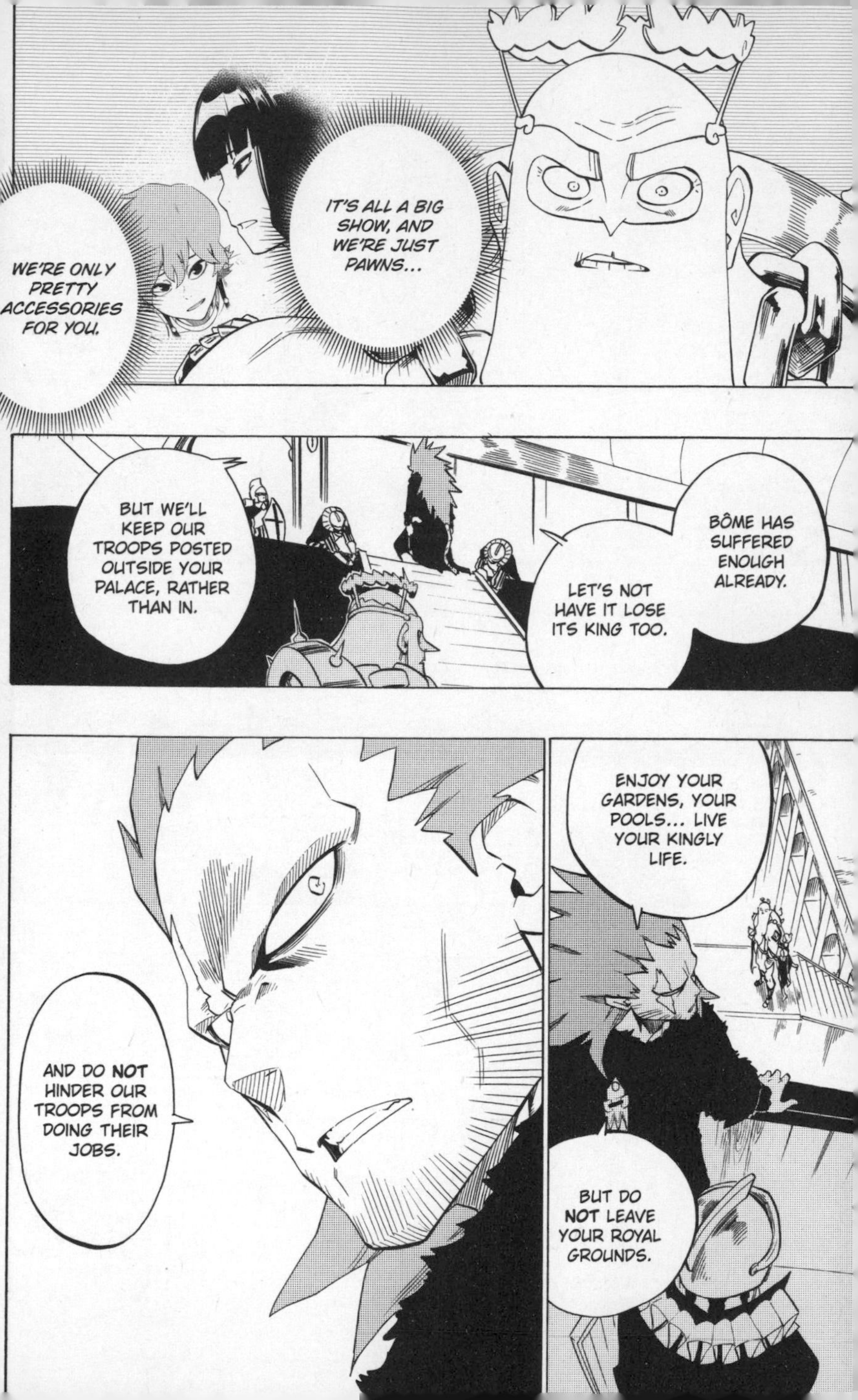
IT'S ALL A BIG SHOW, AND WE'RE JUST PAWNS...
WE'RE ONLY PRETTY ACCESSORIES FOR YOU.
BÔME HAS SUFFERED ENOUGH ALREADY.
LET'S NOT HAVE IT LOSE ITS KING TOO.
BUT WE'LL KEEP OUR TROOPS POSTED OUTSIDE YOUR PALACE, RATHER THAN IN.
ENJOY YOUR GARDENS, YOUR POOLS... LIVE YOUR KINGLY LIFE.
BUT DO NOT LEAVE YOUR ROYAL GROUNDS.
AND DO NOT HINDER OUR TROOPS FROM DOING THEIR JOBS.

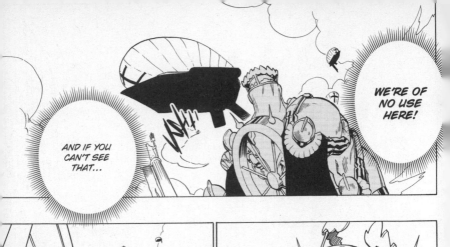

WE'RE OF NO USE HERE!

AND IF YOU CAN'T SEE THAT...

...MAYBE YOU'RE OF NO USE EITHER!

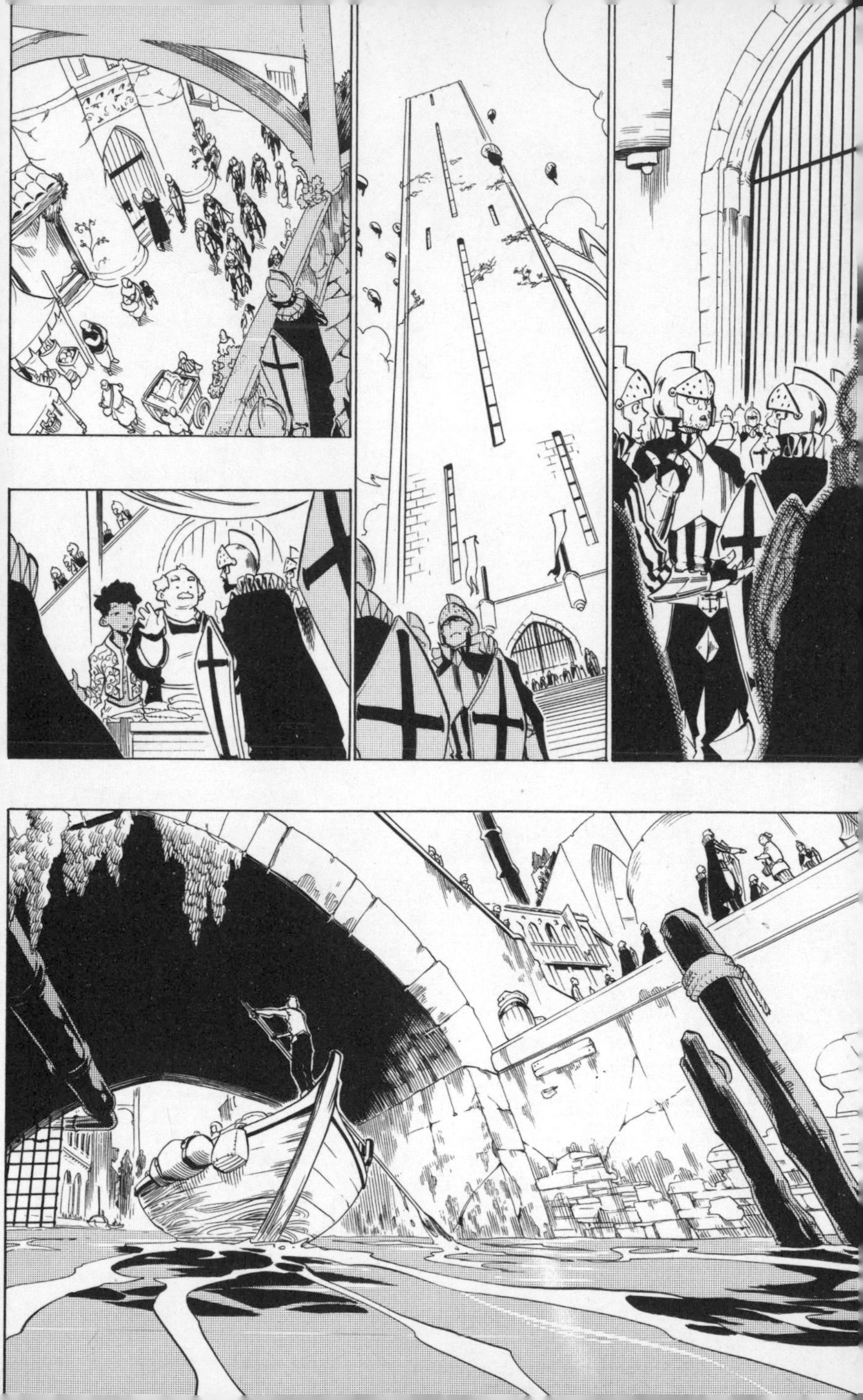

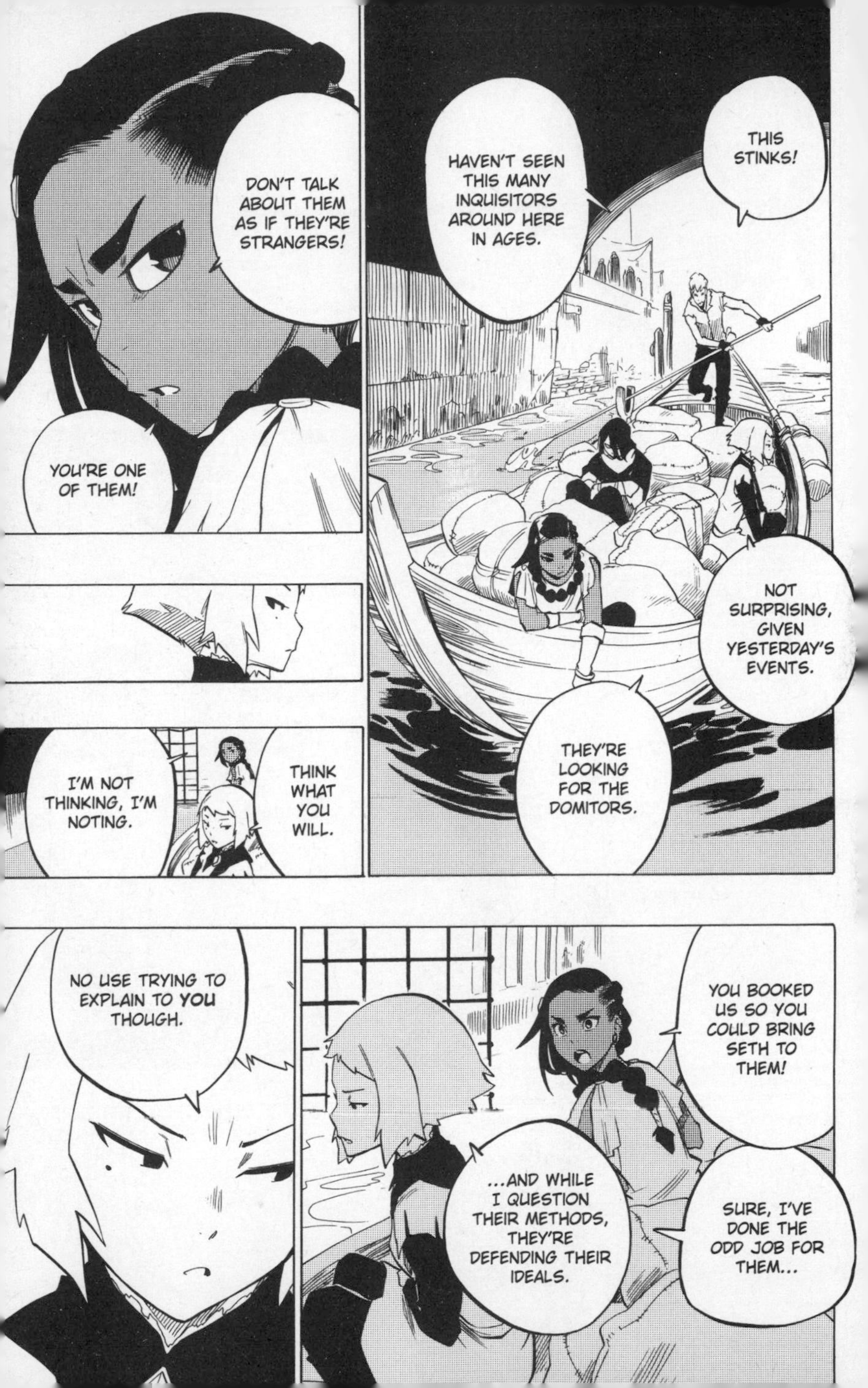
THIS STINKS!
HAVEN'T SEEN THIS MANY INQUISITORS AROUND HERE IN AGES.
NOT SURPRISING, GIVEN YESTERDAY'S EVENTS.
THEY'RE LOOKING FOR THE DOMITORS.
DON'T TALK ABOUT THEM AS IF THEY'RE STRANGERS!
YOU'RE ONE OF THEM!
THINK WHAT YOU WILL.
I'M NOT THINKING, I'M NOTING.
YOU BOOKED US SO YOU COULD BRING SETH TO THEM!
SURE, I'VE DONE THE ODD JOB FOR THEM...
...AND WHILE I QUESTION THEIR METHODS, THEY'RE DEFENDING THEIR IDEALS.
NO USE TRYING TO EXPLAIN TO YOU THOUGH.

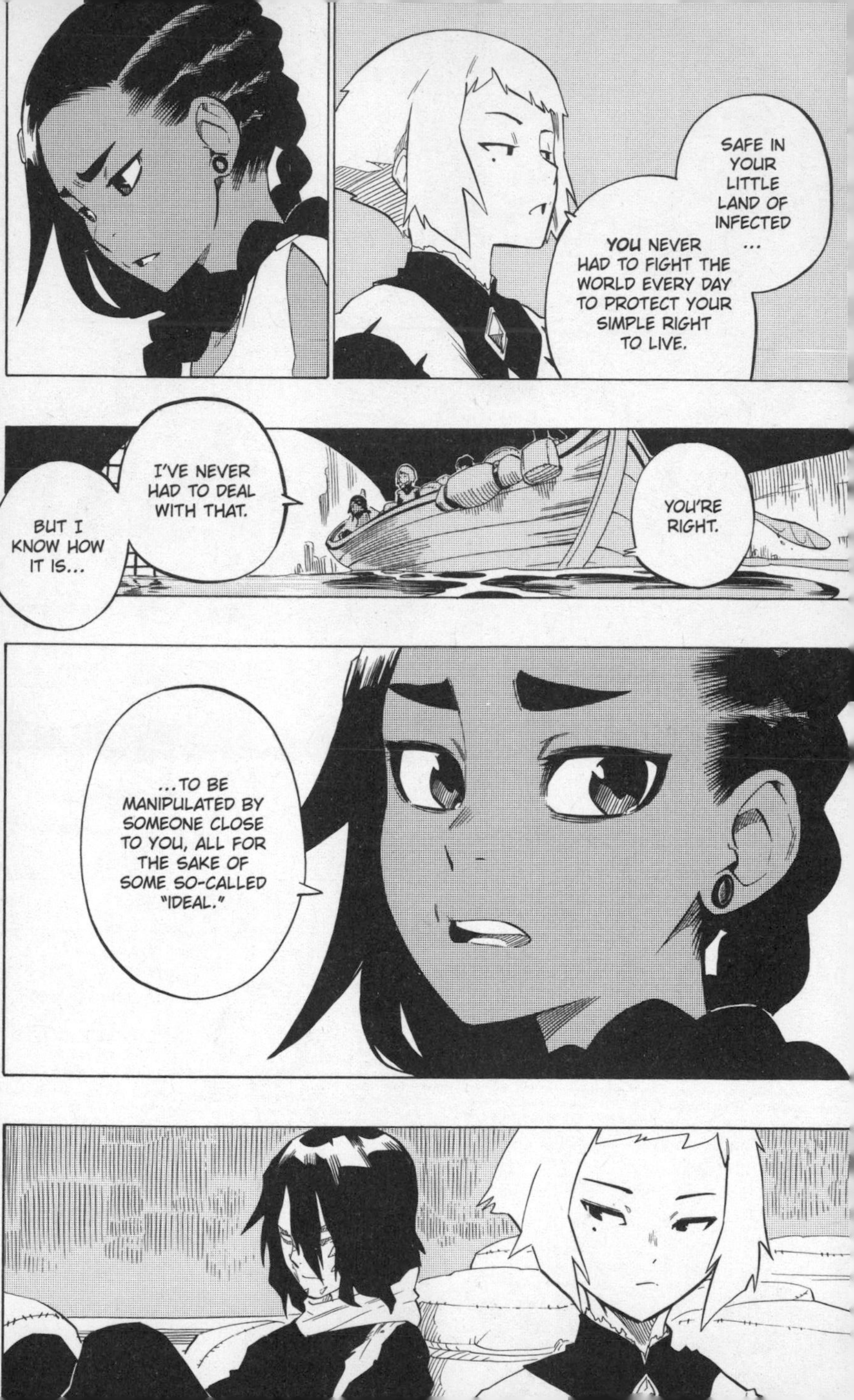
SAFE IN YOUR LITTLE LAND OF INFECTED...
YOU NEVER HAD TO FIGHT THE WORLD EVERY DAY TO PROTECT YOUR SIMPLE RIGHT TO LIVE.
YOU'RE RIGHT.
I'VE NEVER HAD TO DEAL WITH THAT.
BUT I KNOW HOW IT IS...
...TO BE MANIPULATED BY SOMEONE CLOSE TO YOU, ALL FOR THE SAKE OF SOME SO-CALLED "IDEAL."

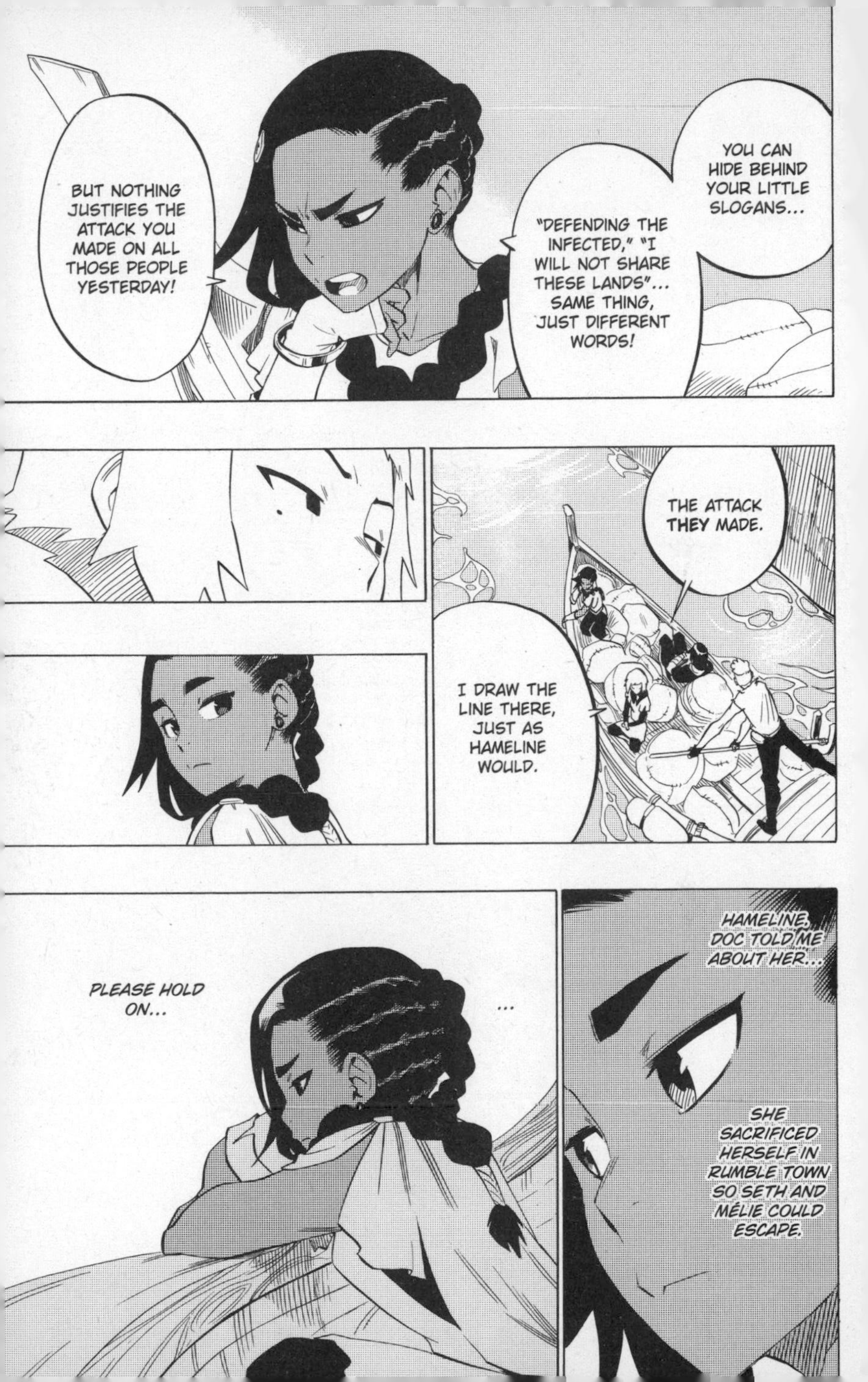
BUT NOTHING JUSTIFIES THE ATTACK YOU MADE ON ALL THOSE PEOPLE YESTERDAY!
"DEFENDING THE INFECTED," "I WILL NOT SHARE THESE LANDS"... SAME THING, JUST DIFFERENT WORDS!
YOU CAN HIDE BEHIND YOUR LITTLE SLOGANS...
THE ATTACK THEY MADE.
I DRAW THE LINE THERE, JUST AS HAMELINE WOULD.
PLEASE HOLD ON...
...
HAMELINE, DOC TOLD ME ABOUT HER...
SHE SACRIFICED HERSELF IN RUMBLE TOWN SO SETH AND MÉLIE COULD ESCAPE.

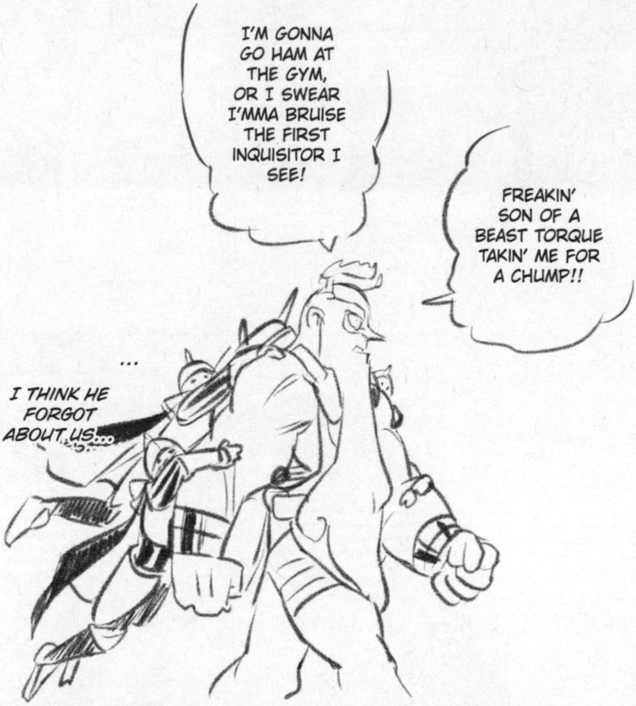
FREAKIN' SON OF A BEAST TORQUE TAKIN' ME FOR A CHUMP!!
I'M GONNA GO HAM AT THE GYM, OR I SWEAR I'MMA BRUISE THE FIRST INQUISITOR I SEE!
...
I THINK HE FORGOT ABOUT US...

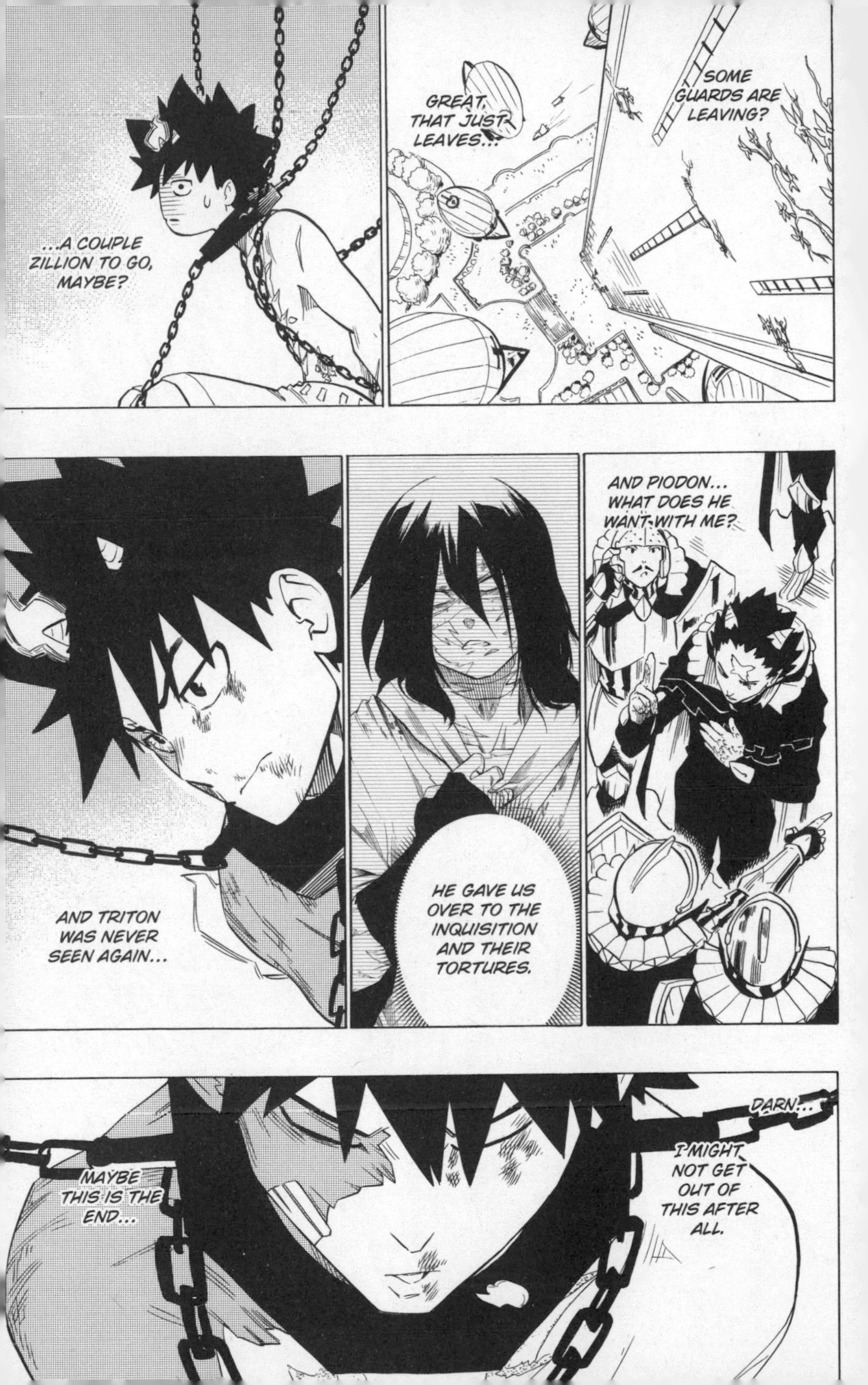
SOME GUARDS ARE LEAVING?
GREAT, THAT JUST LEAVES...
...A COUPLE ZILLION TO GO, MAYBE?
AND PIODON... WHAT DOES HE WANT WITH ME?
HE GAVE US OVER TO THE INQUISITION AND THEIR TORTURES.
AND TRITON WAS NEVER SEEN AGAIN...
DARN...
I MIGHT NOT GET OUT OF THIS AFTER ALL.
MAYBE THIS IS THE END...

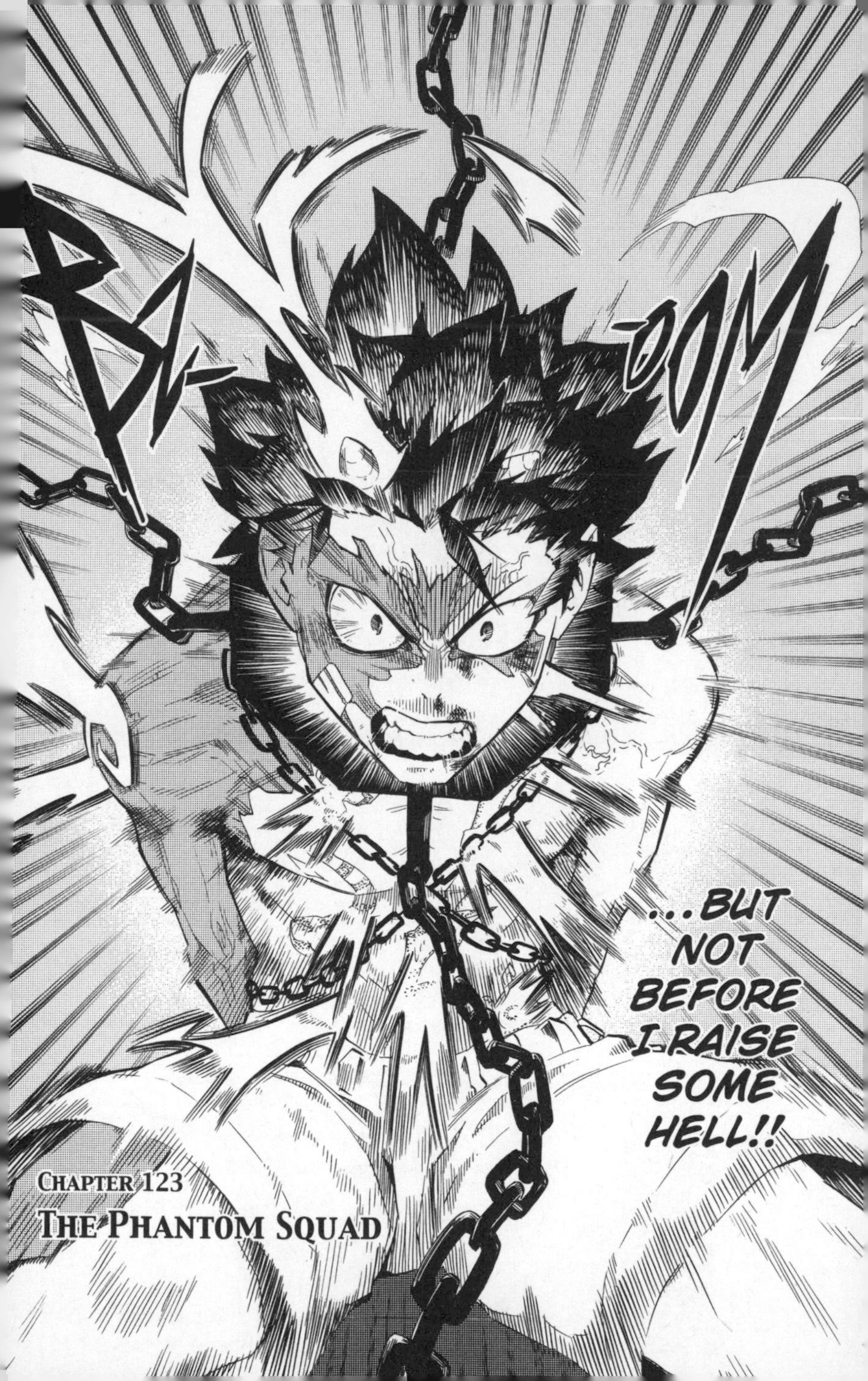
BA-DOOM
...BUT NOT BEFORE I RAISE SOME HELL!!
CHAPTER 123
THE PHANTOM SQUAD

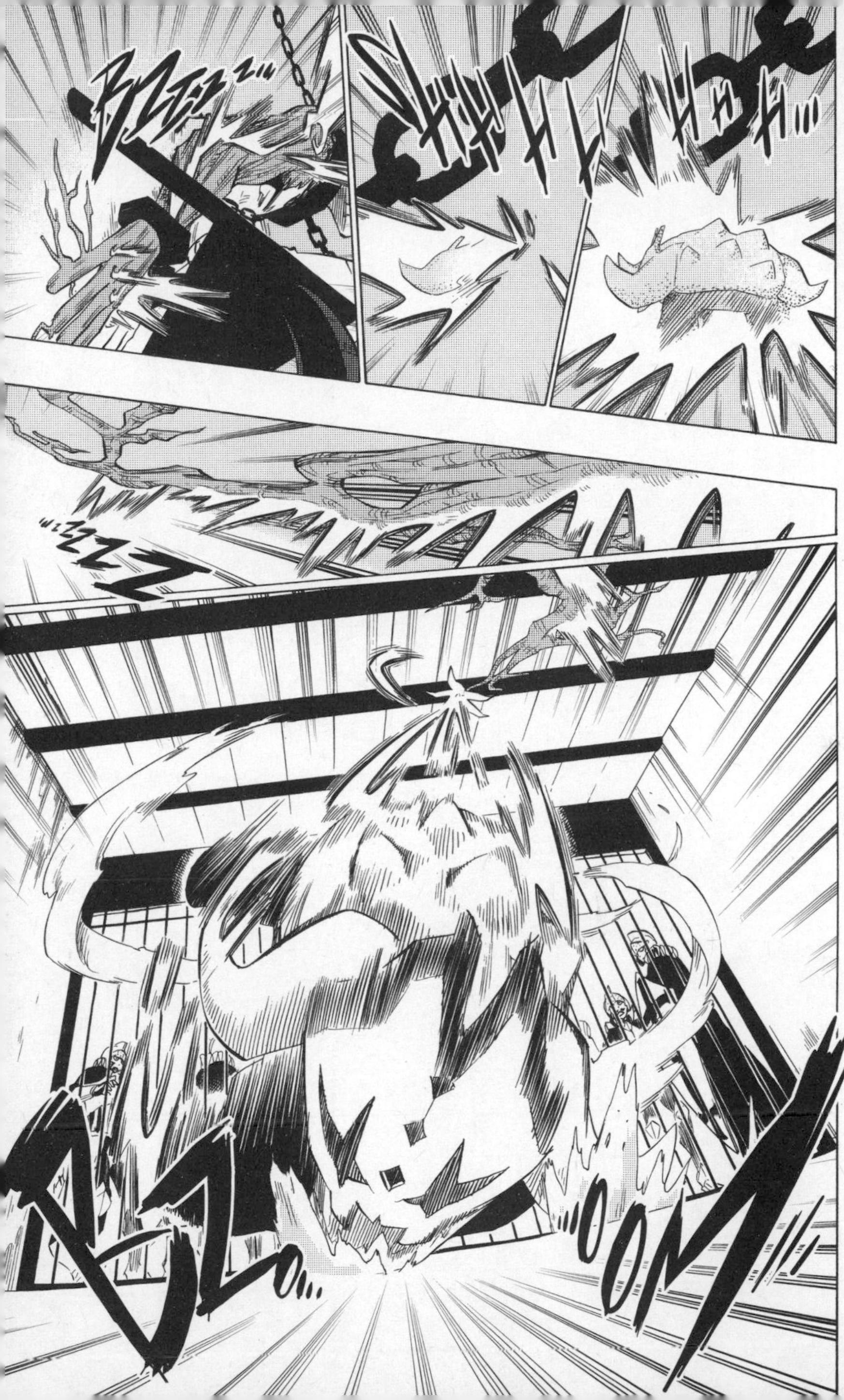
ZZZZZ...
...OOM

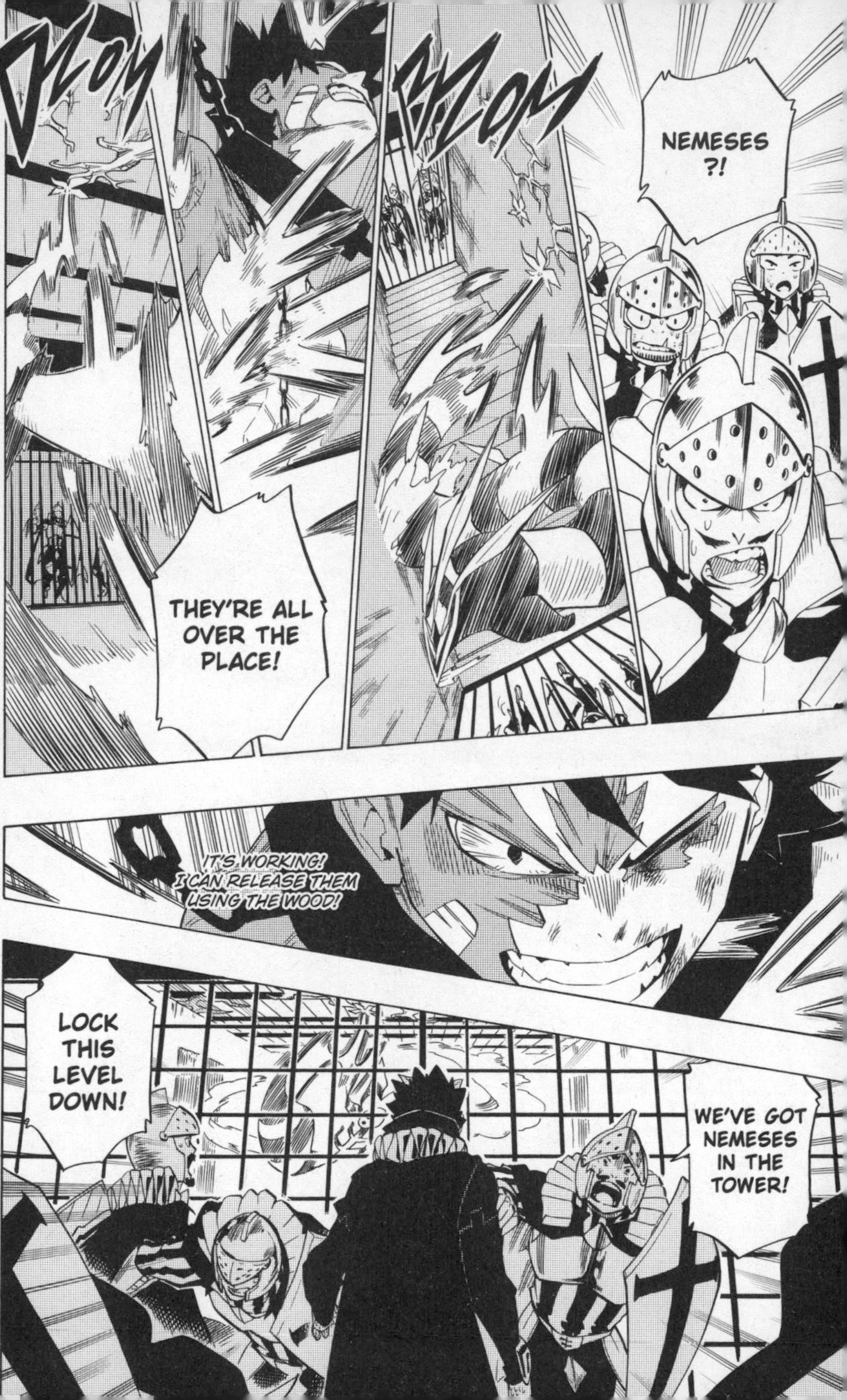
NEMESES ?!
THEY'RE ALL OVER THE PLACE!
IT'S WORKING! I CAN RELEASE THEM USING THE WOOD!
WE'VE GOT NEMESES IN THE TOWER!
LOCK THIS LEVEL DOWN!

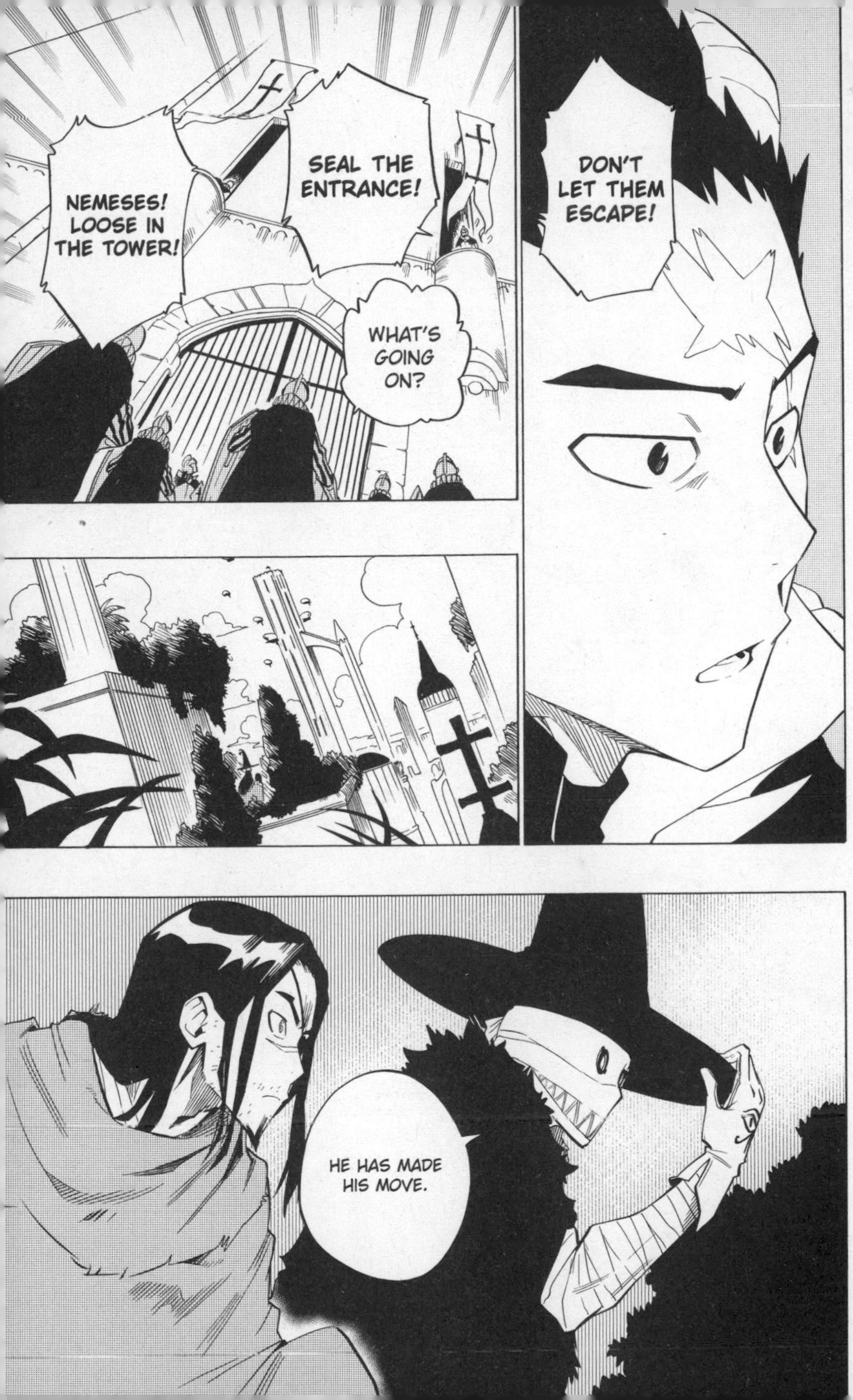
DON'T LET THEM ESCAPE!
SEAL THE ENTRANCE!
NEMESES! LOOSE IN THE TOWER!
WHAT'S GOING ON?
HE HAS MADE HIS MOVE.

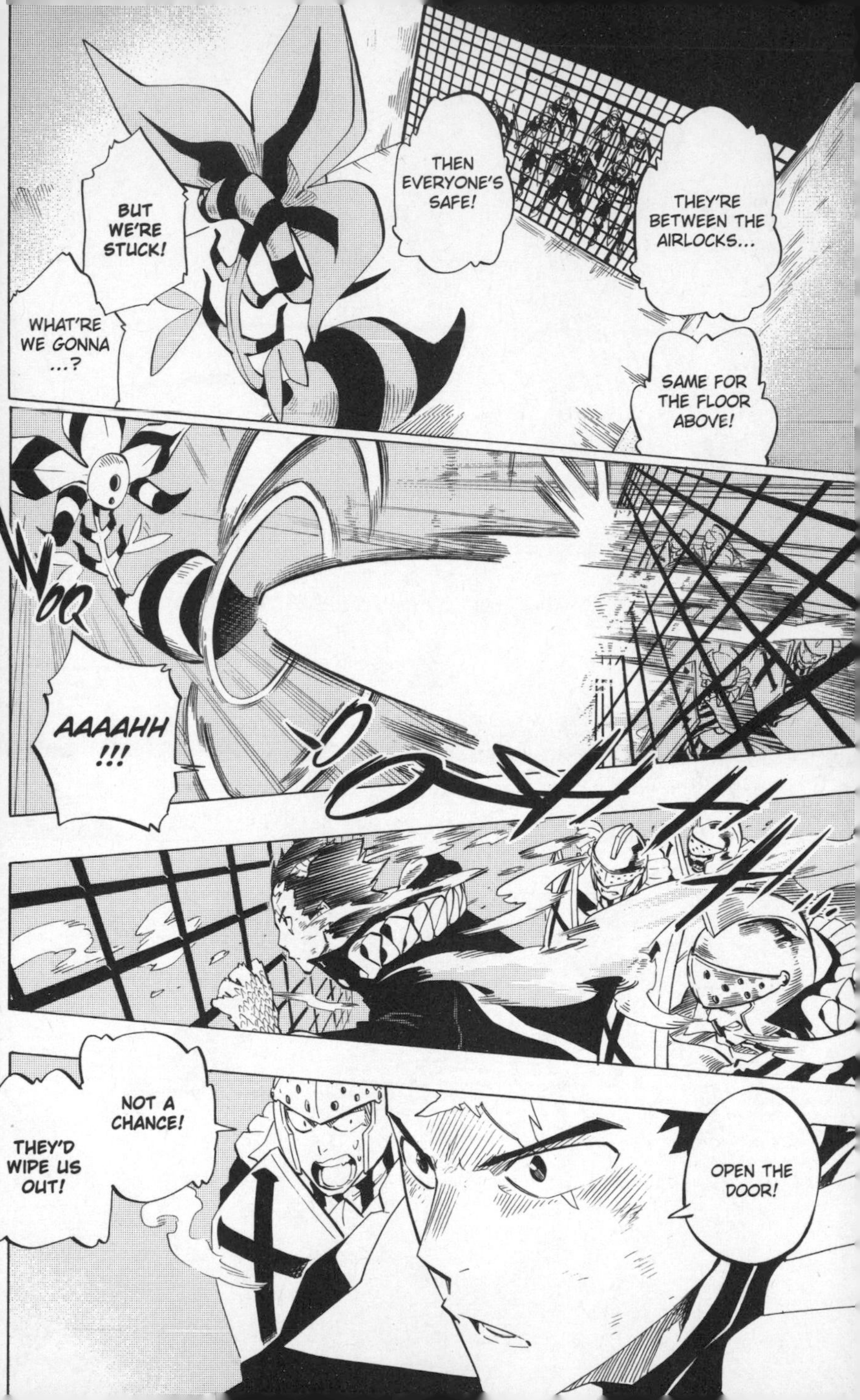
THEY'RE BETWEEN THE AIRLOCKS...
SAME FOR THE FLOOR ABOVE!
THEN EVERYONE'S SAFE!
BUT WE'RE STUCK!
WHAT'RE WE GONNA ...?
WOQ
AAAAHH !!!
OPEN THE DOOR!
NOT A CHANCE!
THEY'D WIPE US OUT!

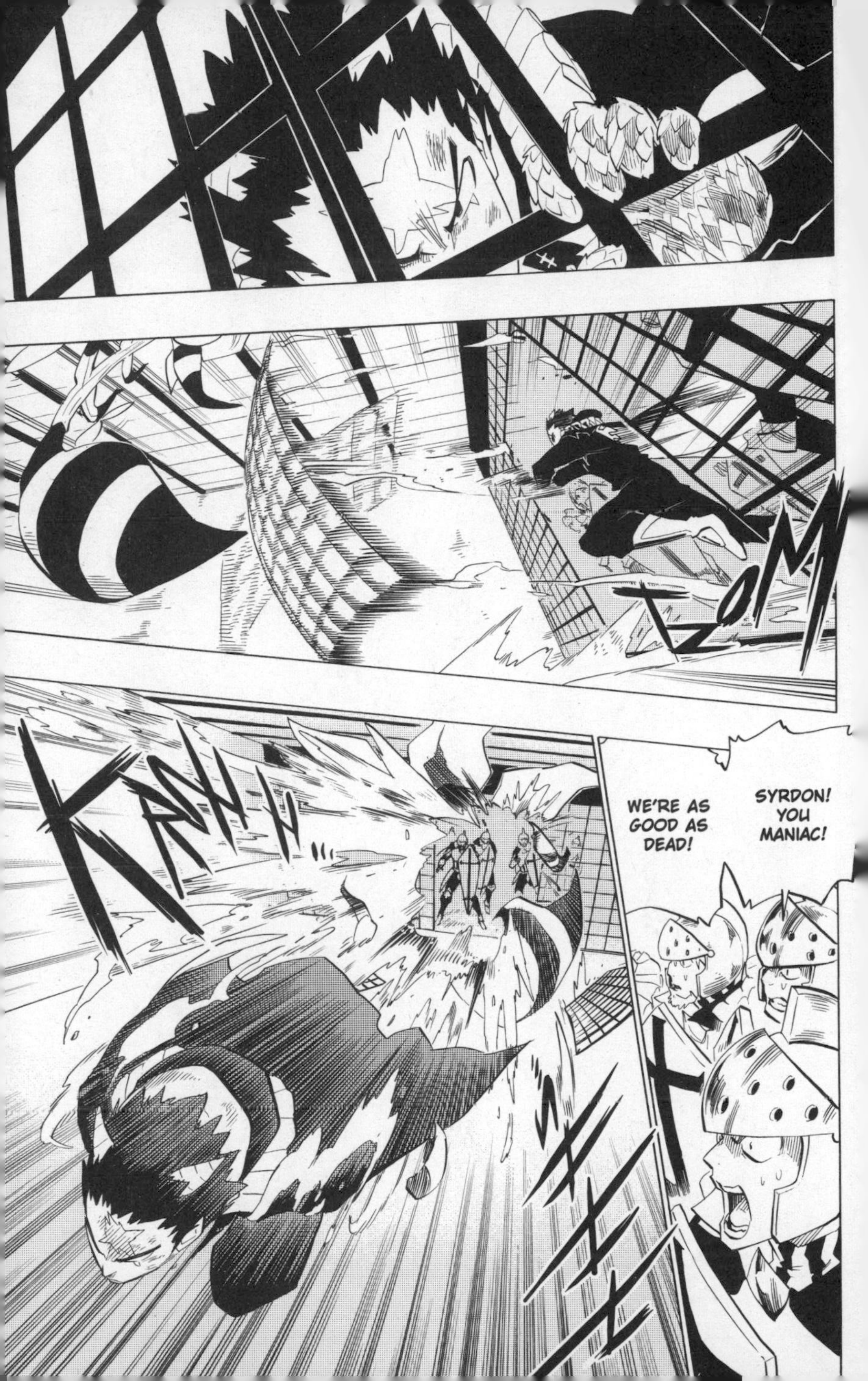
ZOOM
SYRDON! YOU MANIAC!
WE'RE AS GOOD AS DEAD!

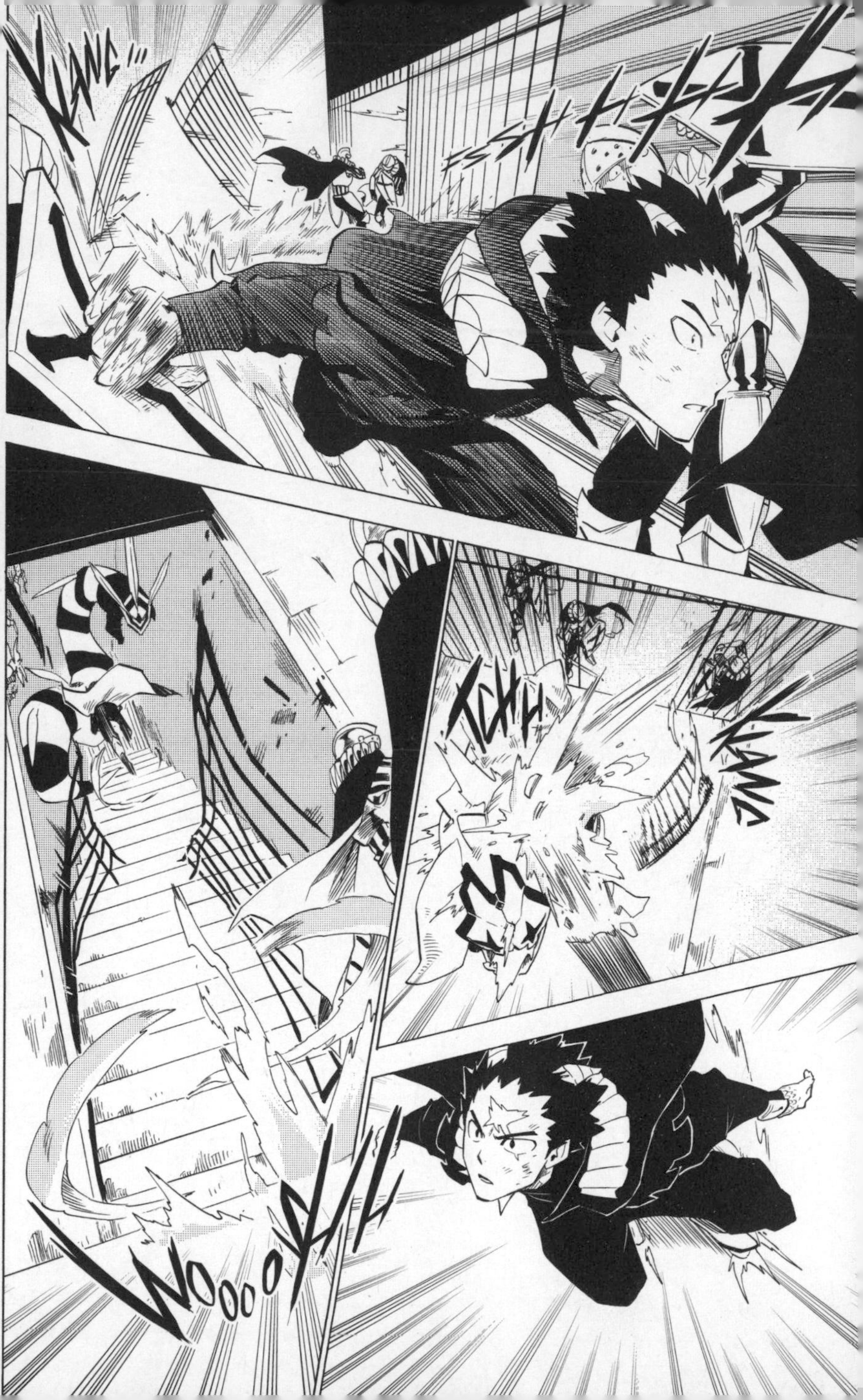
FSSHHHHHHAK
KLANG!!!
KLANG
KCHH
WOOOOSH

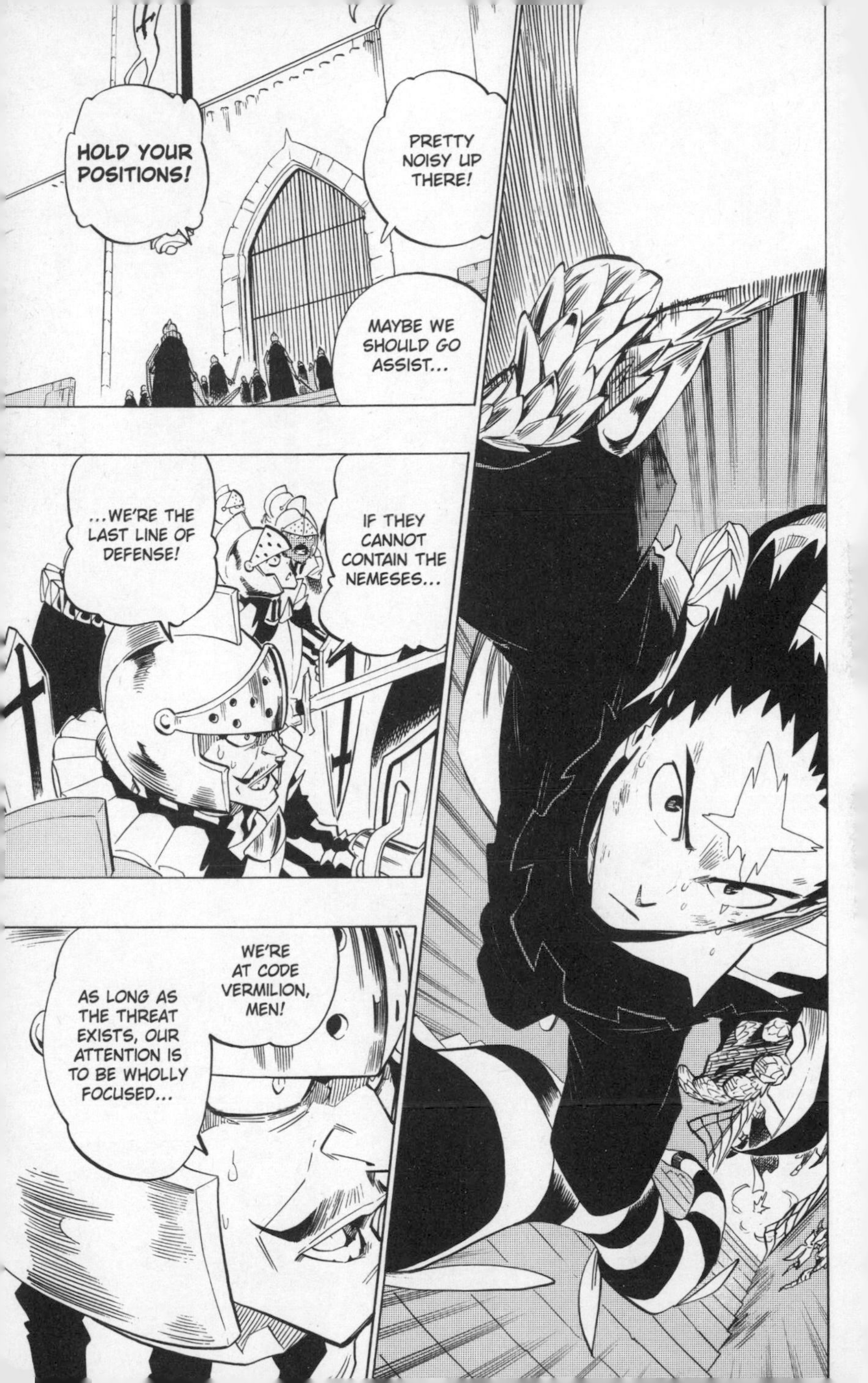
PRETTY NOISY UP THERE!
MAYBE WE SHOULD GO ASSIST...
HOLD YOUR POSITIONS!
IF THEY CANNOT CONTAIN THE NEMESES...
...WE'RE THE LAST LINE OF DEFENSE!
WE'RE AT CODE VERMILION, MEN!
AS LONG AS THE THREAT EXISTS, OUR ATTENTION IS TO BE WHOLLY FOCUSED...

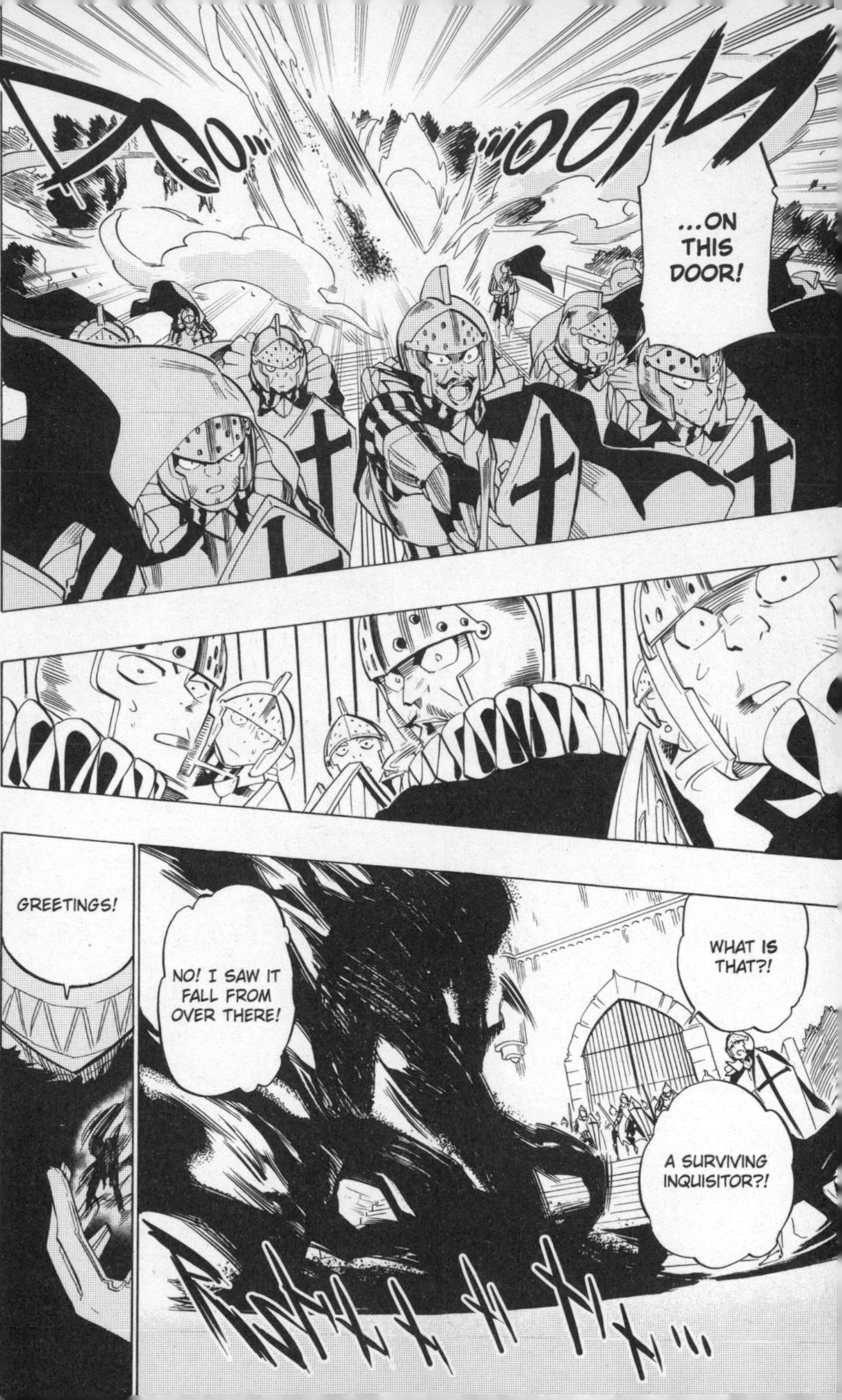
...ON THIS DOOR!
WHAT IS THAT?!
A SURVIVING INQUISITOR?!
NO! I SAW IT FALL FROM OVER THERE!
GREETINGS!

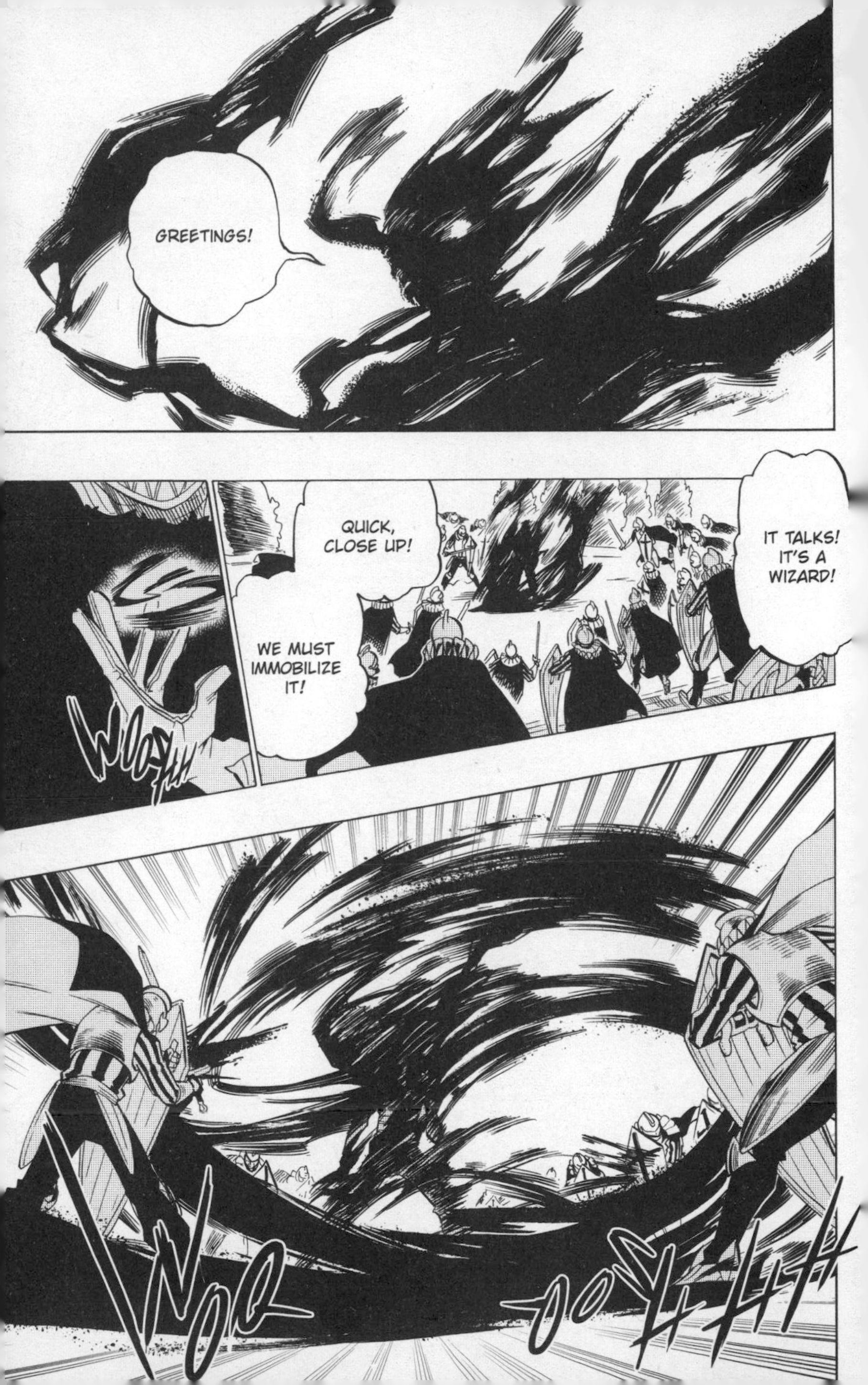
GREETINGS!
IT TALKS! IT'S A WIZARD!
QUICK, CLOSE UP!
WE MUST IMMOBILIZE IT!
WHOOSHH
VROOOOSHHHH

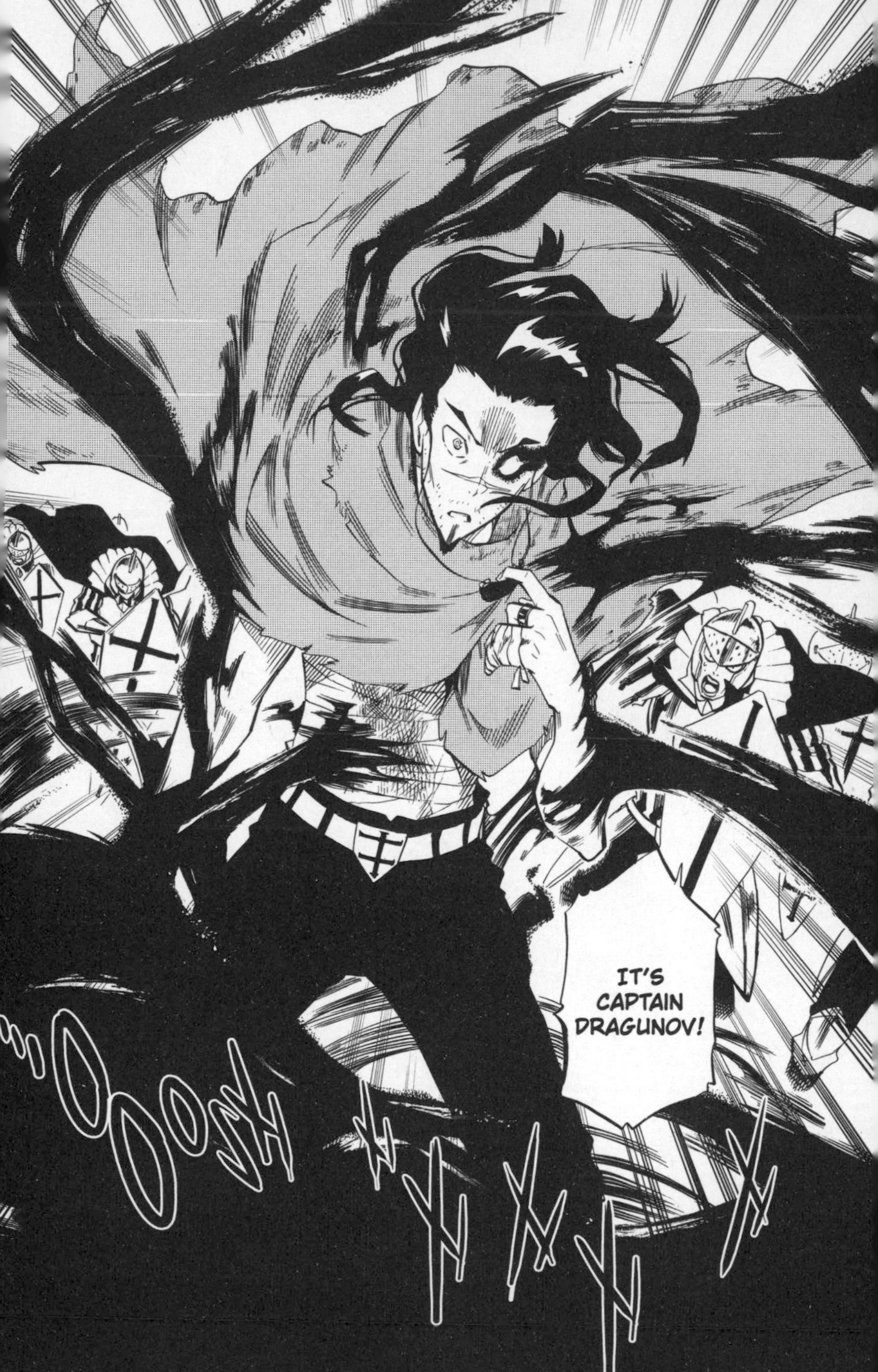
IT'S CAPTAIN DRAGUNOV!

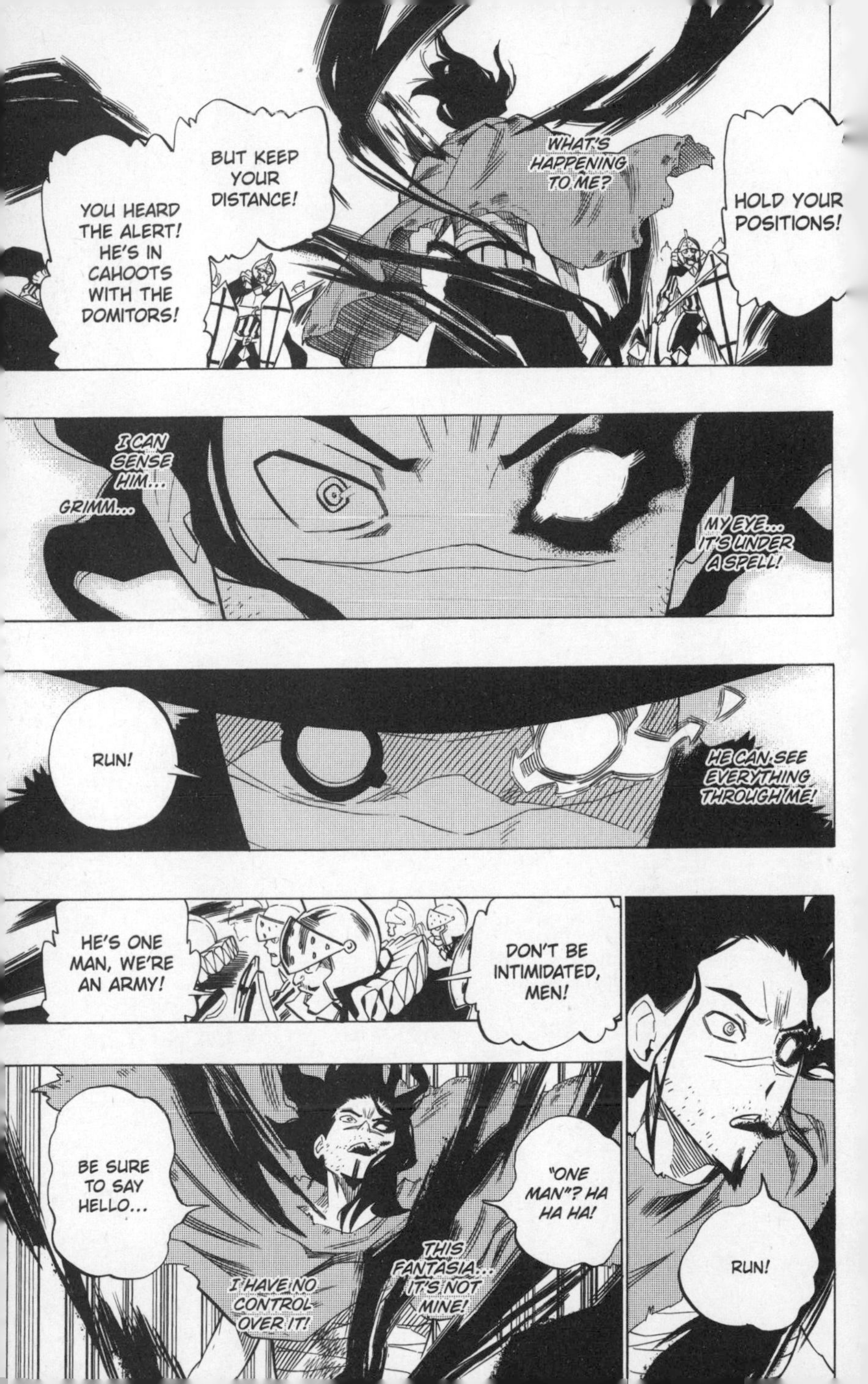
HOLD YOUR POSITIONS!
WHAT'S HAPPENING TO ME?
BUT KEEP YOUR DISTANCE!
YOU HEARD THE ALERT! HE'S IN CAHOOTS WITH THE DOMITORS!
I CAN SENSE HIM...
GRIMM...
MY EYE... IT'S UNDER A SPELL!
HE CAN SEE EVERYTHING THROUGH ME!
RUN!
DON'T BE INTIMIDATED, MEN!
HE'S ONE MAN, WE'RE AN ARMY!
"ONE MAN"? HA HA HA!
THIS FANTASIA... IT'S NOT MINE!
I HAVE NO CONTROL OVER IT!
BE SURE TO SAY HELLO...
RUN!

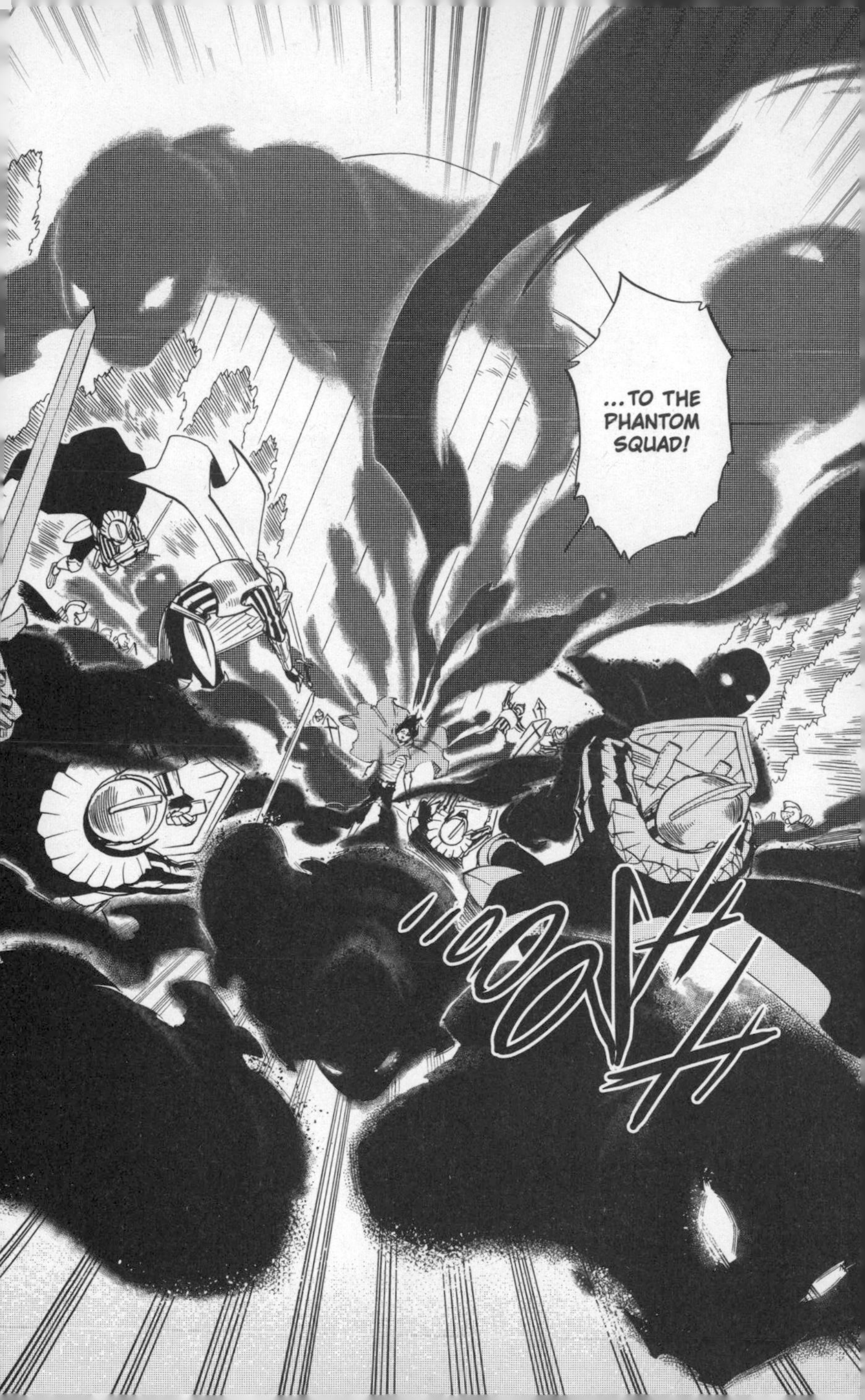
...TO THE PHANTOM SQUAD!
HOOO...

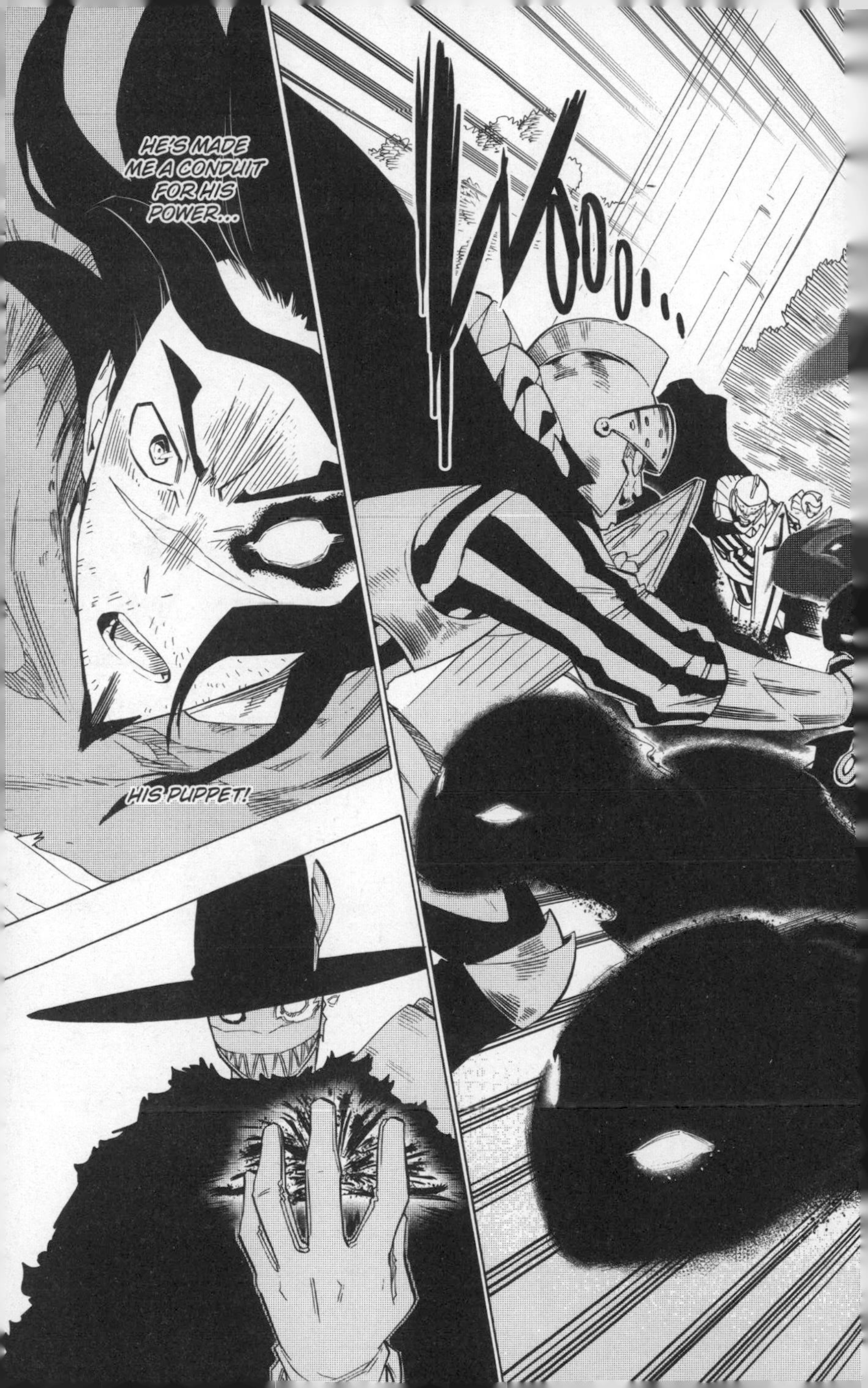
WOOO...
HE'S MADE ME A CONDUIT FOR HIS POWER...
HIS PUPPET!

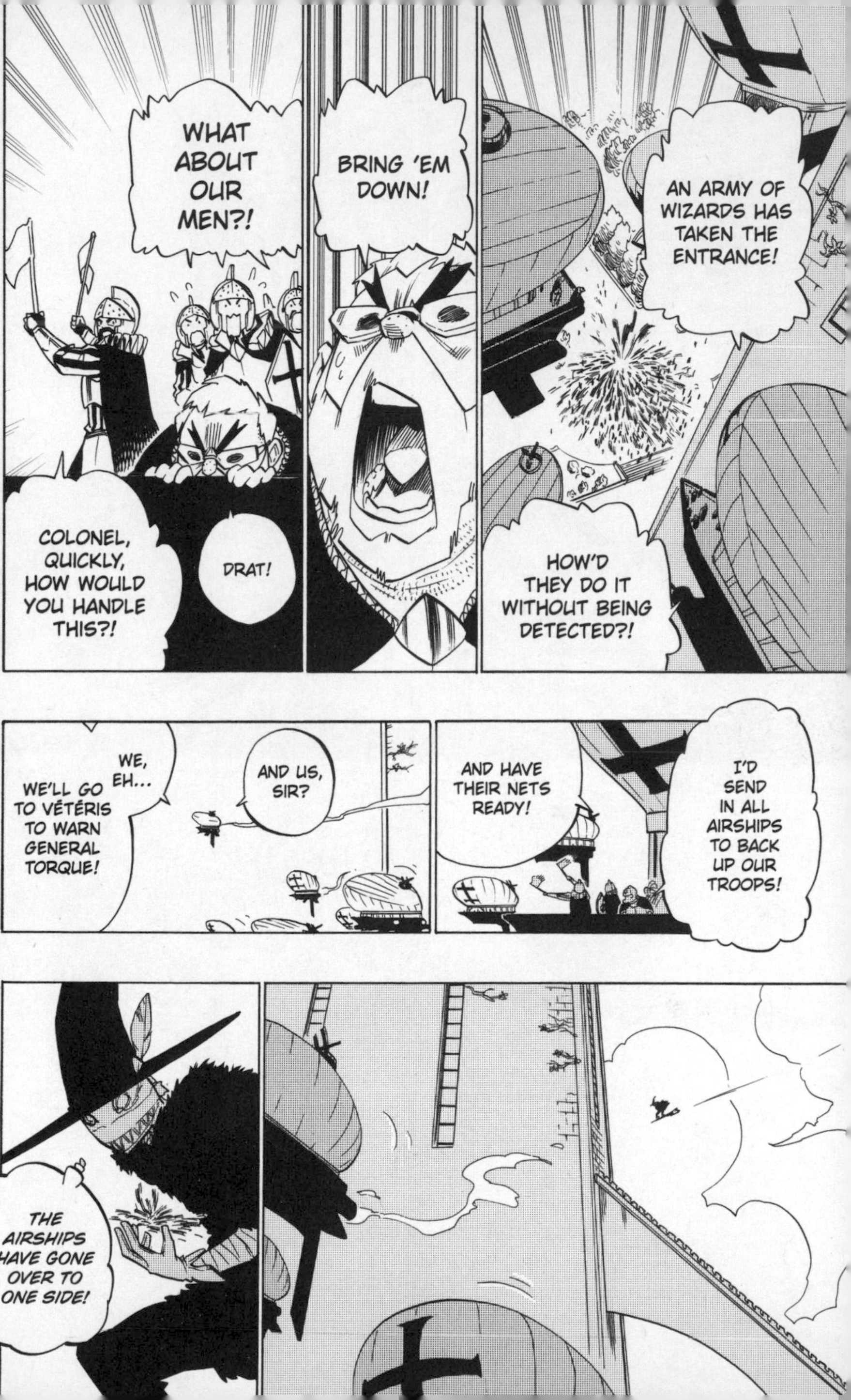
AN ARMY OF WIZARDS HAS TAKEN THE ENTRANCE!
HOW'D THEY DO IT WITHOUT BEING DETECTED?!
BRING 'EM DOWN!
WHAT ABOUT OUR MEN?!
DRAT!
COLONEL, QUICKLY, HOW WOULD YOU HANDLE THIS?!
I'D SEND IN ALL AIRSHIPS TO BACK UP OUR TROOPS!
AND HAVE THEIR NETS READY!
AND US, SIR?
WE, EH...
WE'LL GO TO VÉTÉRIS TO WARN GENERAL TORQUE!
THE AIRSHIPS HAVE GONE OVER TO ONE SIDE!

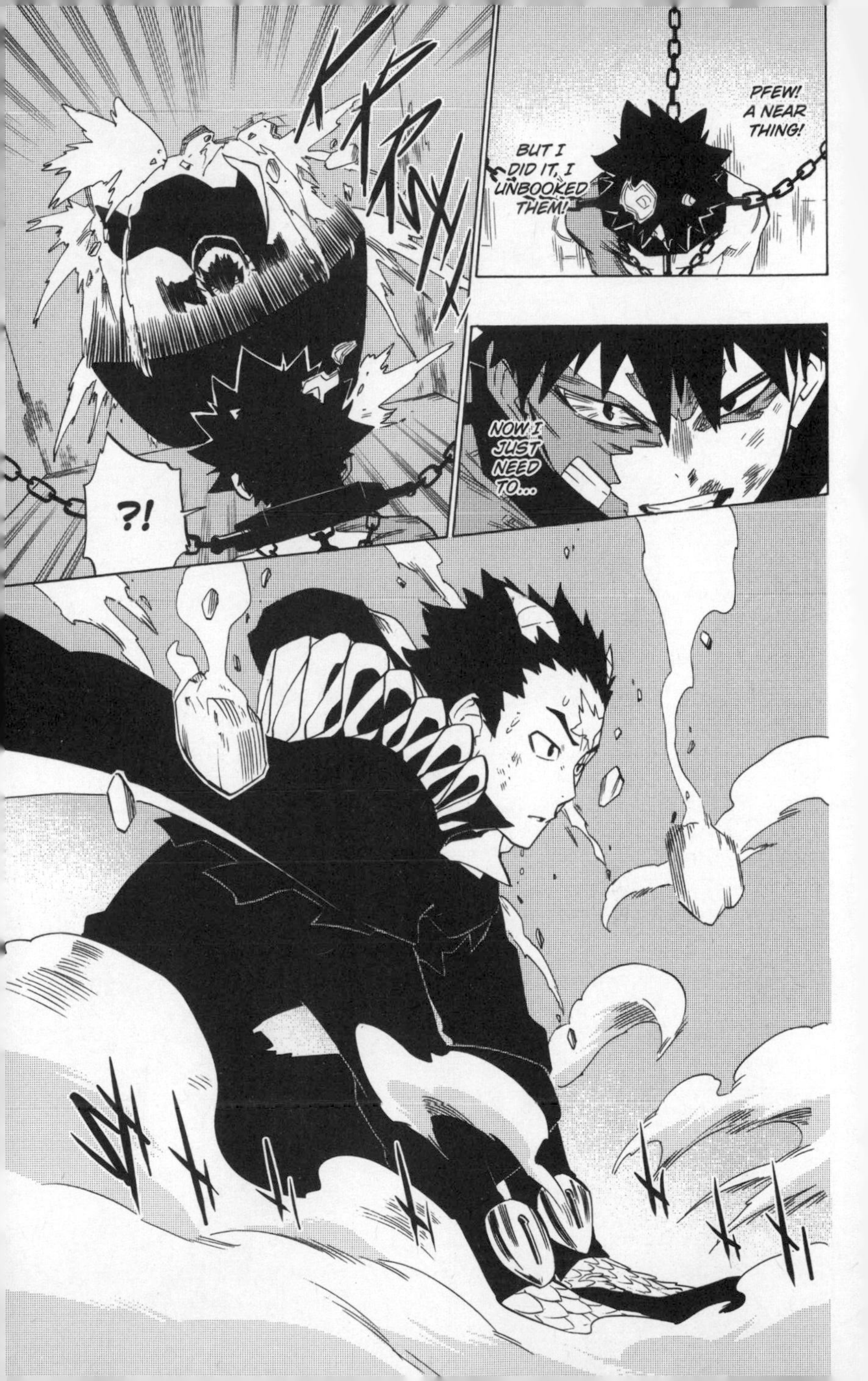
PFEW! A NEAR THING!
BUT I DID IT, I UNBOOKED THEM!
NOW I JUST NEED TO...
?!

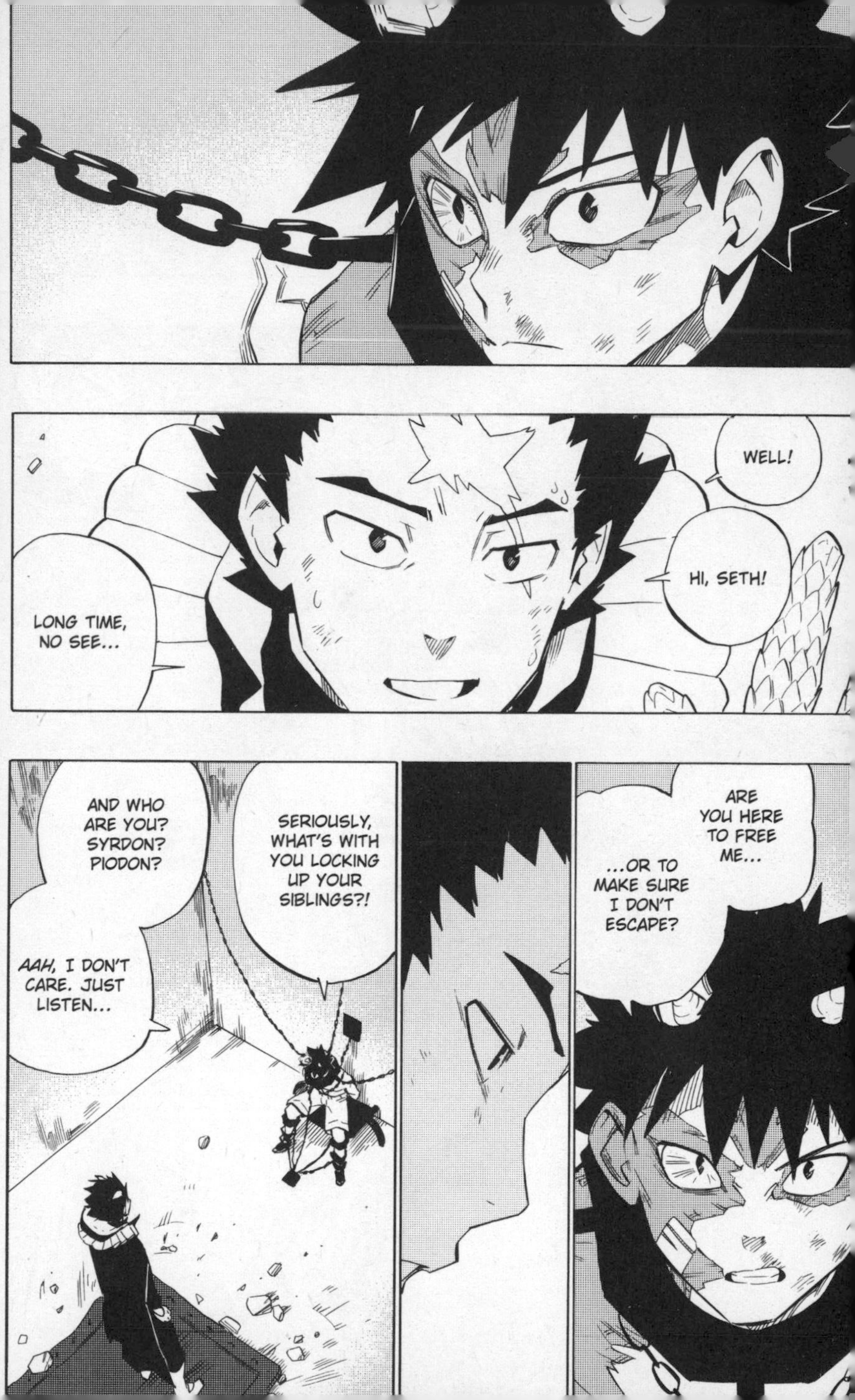
WELL!
HI, SETH!
LONG TIME, NO SEE...
ARE YOU HERE TO FREE ME...
...OR TO MAKE SURE I DON'T ESCAPE?
SERIOUSLY, WHAT'S WITH YOU LOCKING UP YOUR SIBLINGS?!
AND WHO ARE YOU? SYRDON? PIODON?
AAH, I DON'T CARE. JUST LISTEN...

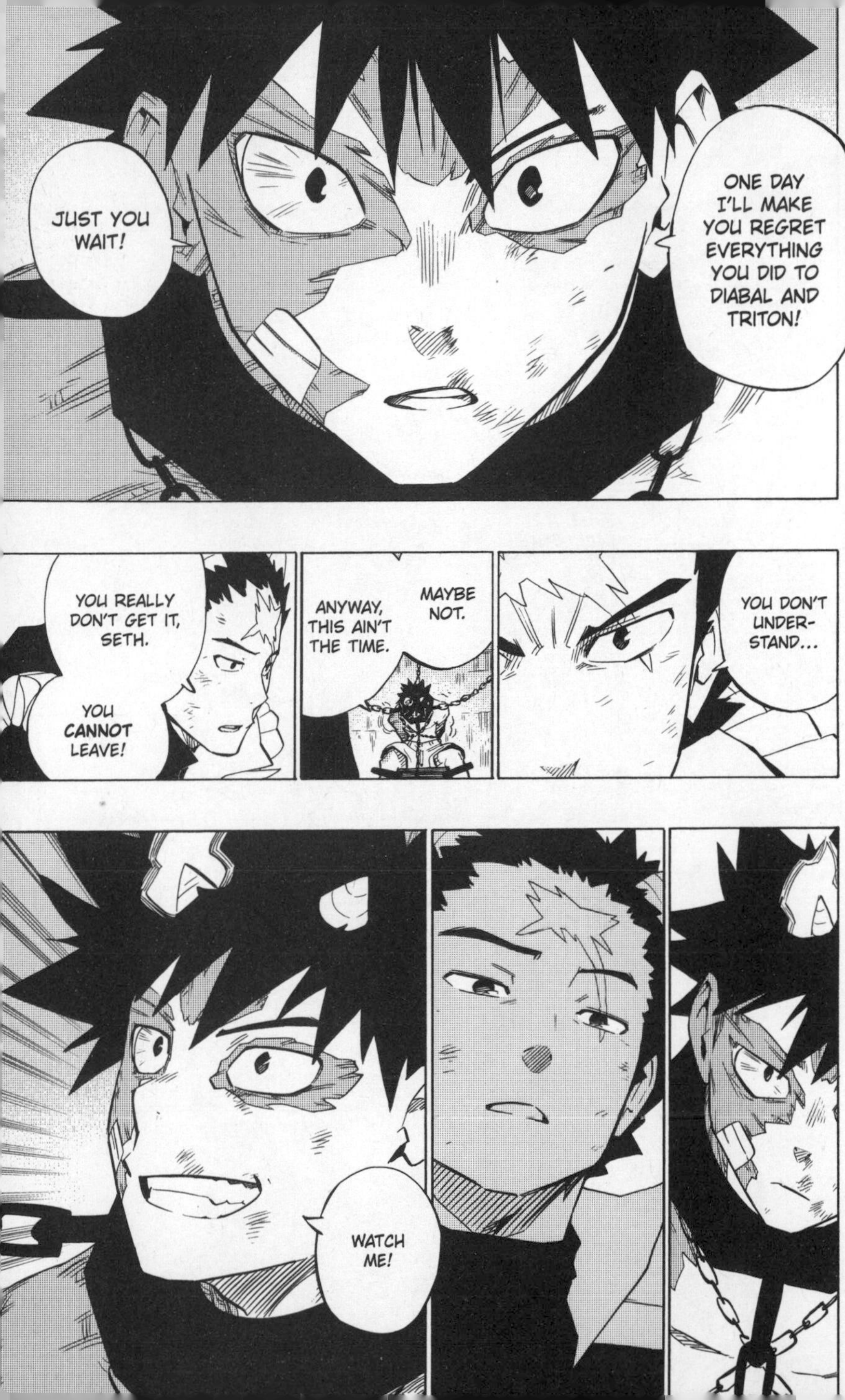
ONE DAY I'LL MAKE YOU REGRET EVERYTHING YOU DID TO DIABAL AND TRITON!
JUST YOU WAIT!
YOU DON'T UNDER-STAND...
MAYBE NOT.
ANYWAY, THIS AIN'T THE TIME.
YOU REALLY DON'T GET IT, SETH.
YOU CANNOT LEAVE!
WATCH ME!

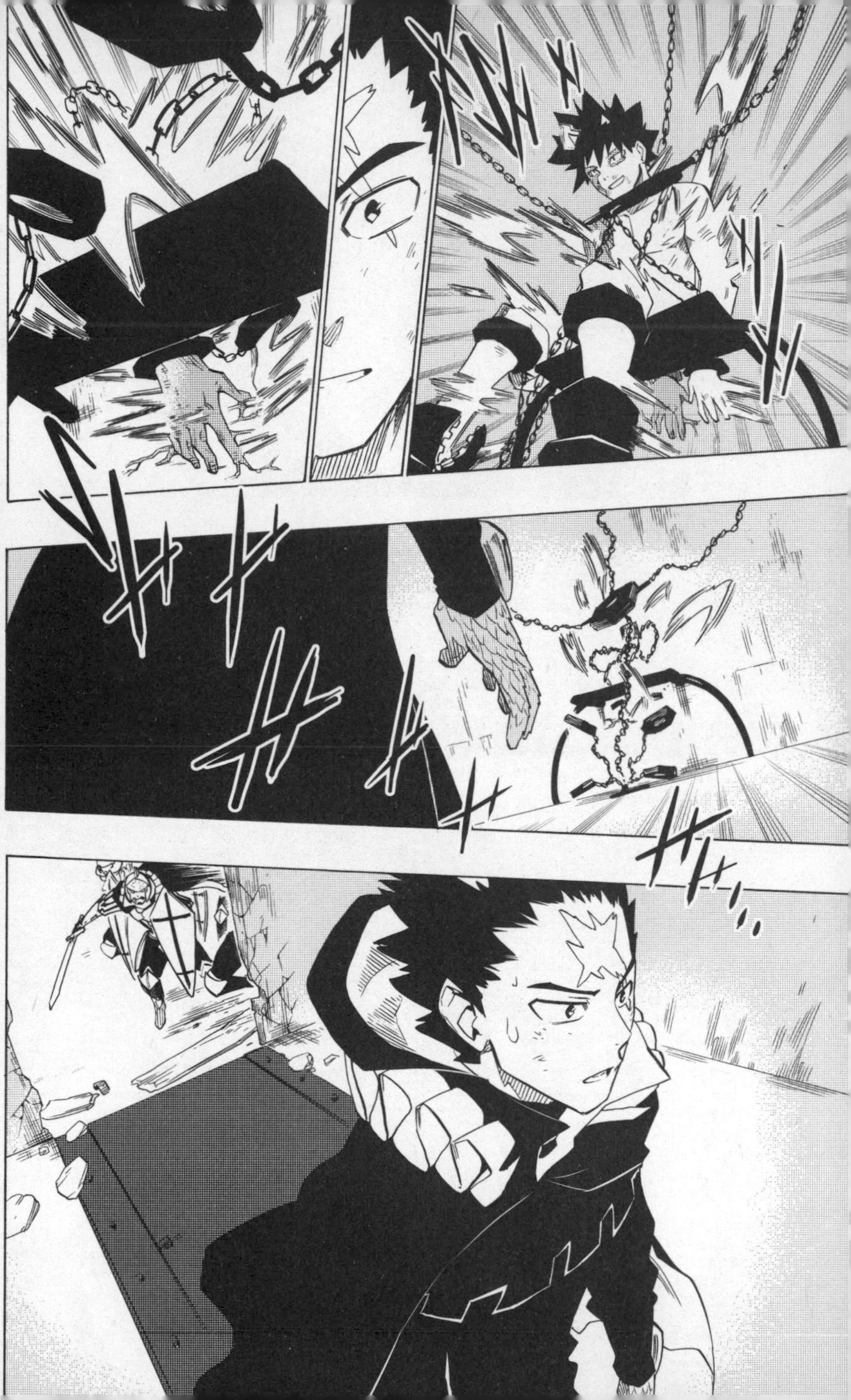

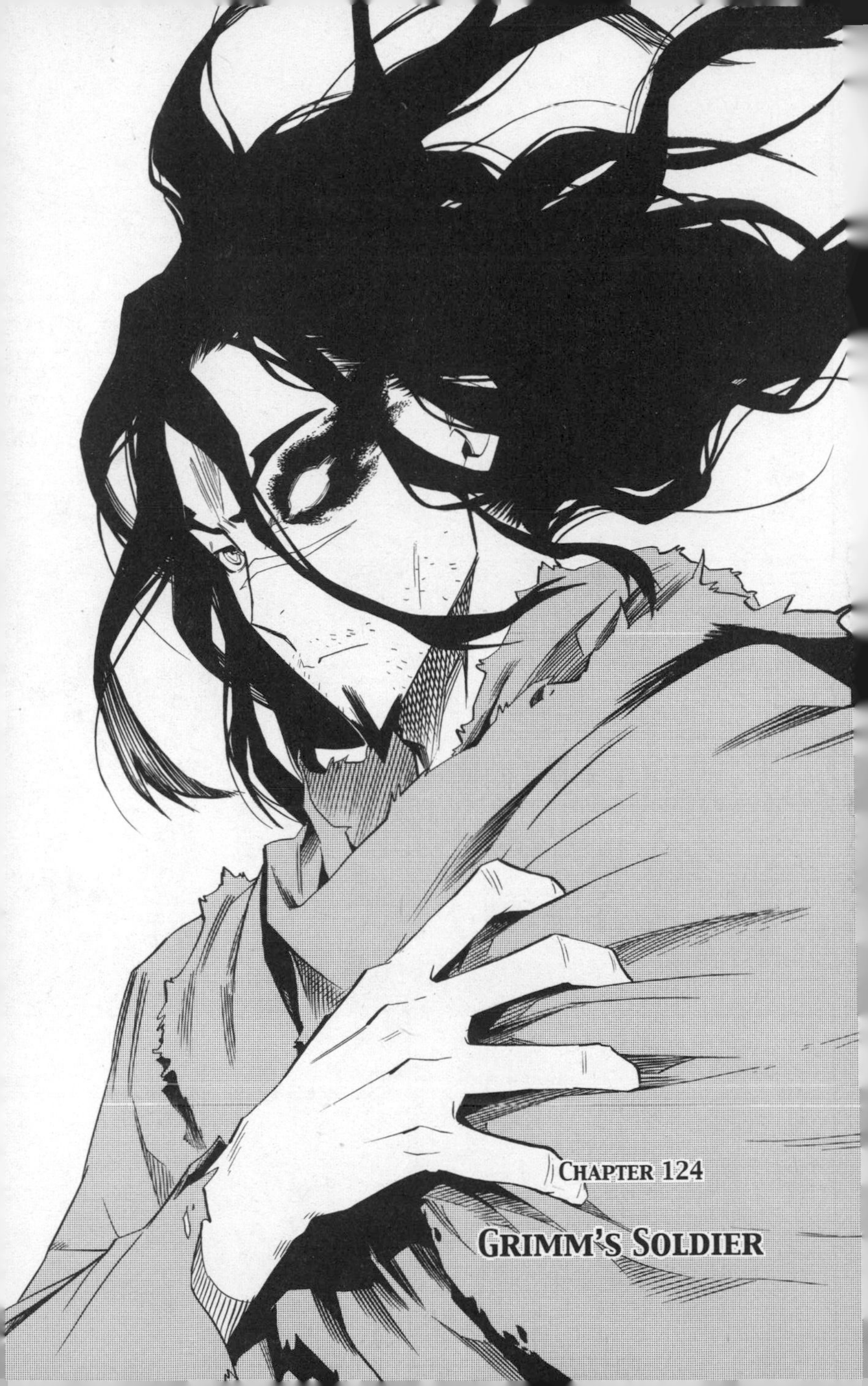
Chapter 124
Grimm's Soldier

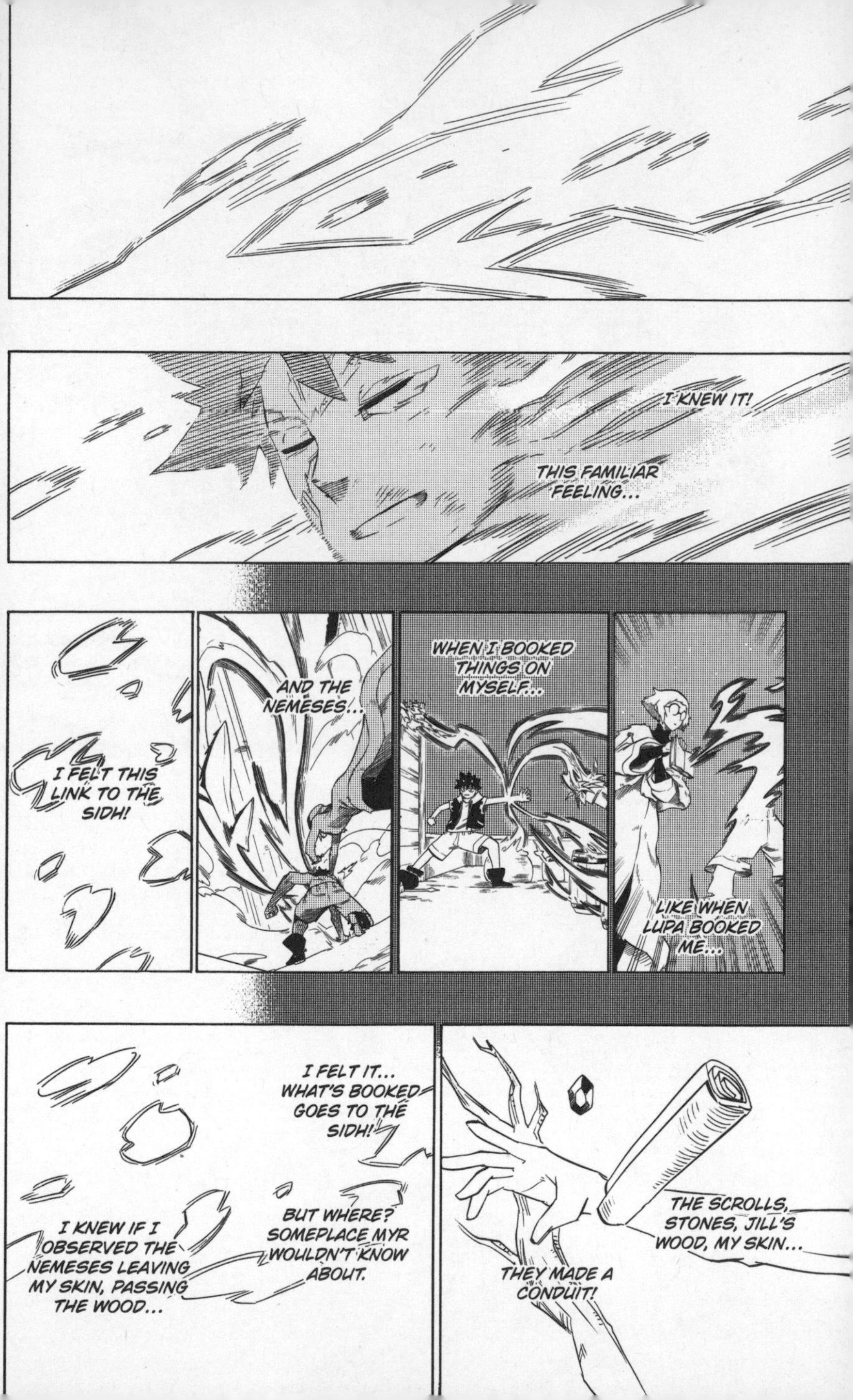
I KNEW IT!
THIS FAMILIAR FEELING...
LIKE WHEN LUPA BOOKED ME...
WHEN I BOOKED THINGS ON MYSELF...
AND THE NEMESES...
I FELT THIS LINK TO THE SIDH!
THE SCROLLS, STONES, JILL'S WOOD, MY SKIN...
THEY MADE A CONDUIT!
I FELT IT... WHAT'S BOOKED GOES TO THE SIDH!
BUT WHERE? SOMEPLACE MYR WOULDN'T KNOW ABOUT.
I KNEW IF I OBSERVED THE NEMESES LEAVING MY SKIN, PASSING THE WOOD...

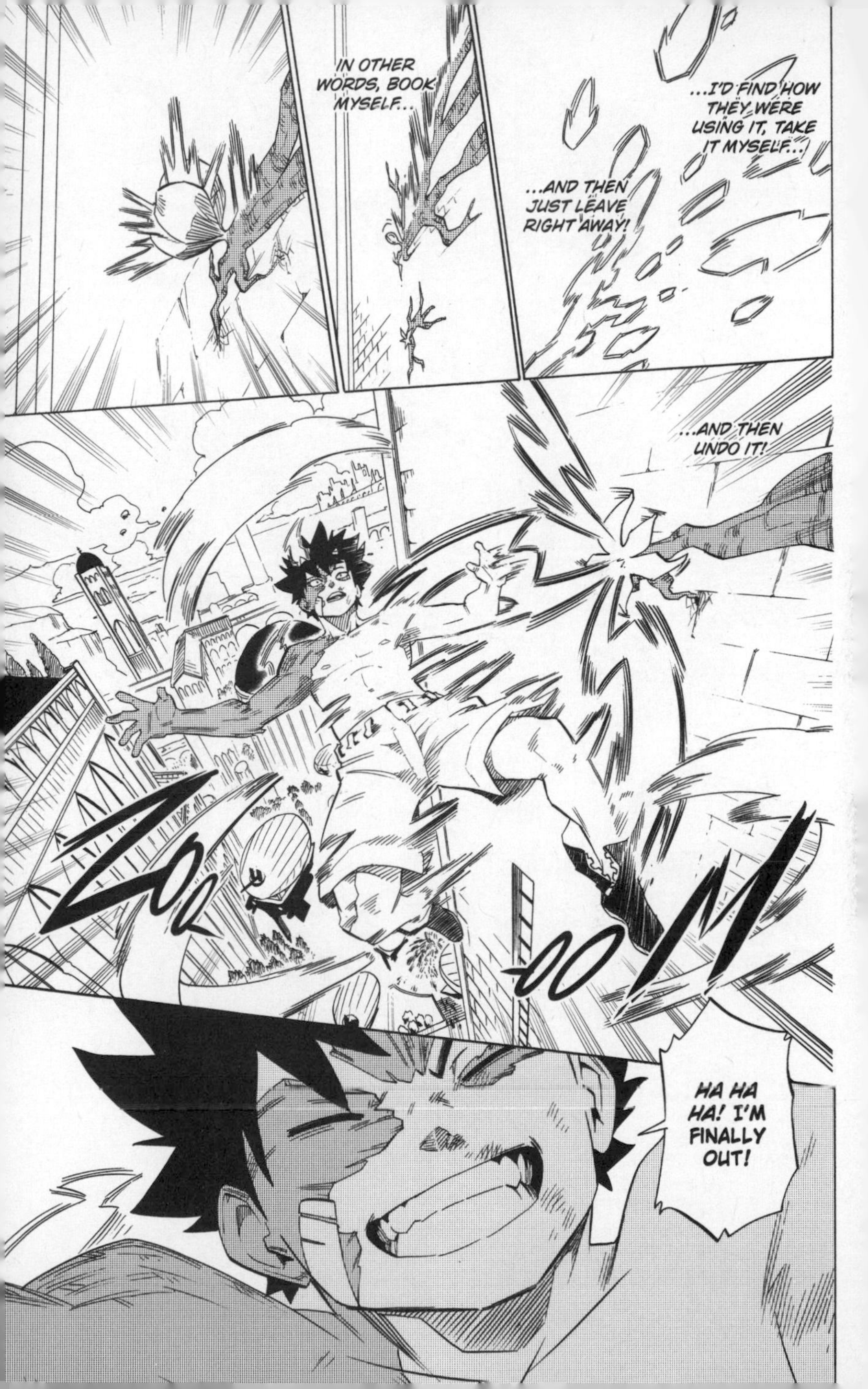
...I'D FIND HOW THEY WERE USING IT, TAKE IT MYSELF...
...AND THEN JUST LEAVE RIGHT AWAY!
IN OTHER WORDS, BOOK MYSELF...
...AND THEN UNDO IT!
ZOOOOOM
HA HA HA! I'M FINALLY OUT!

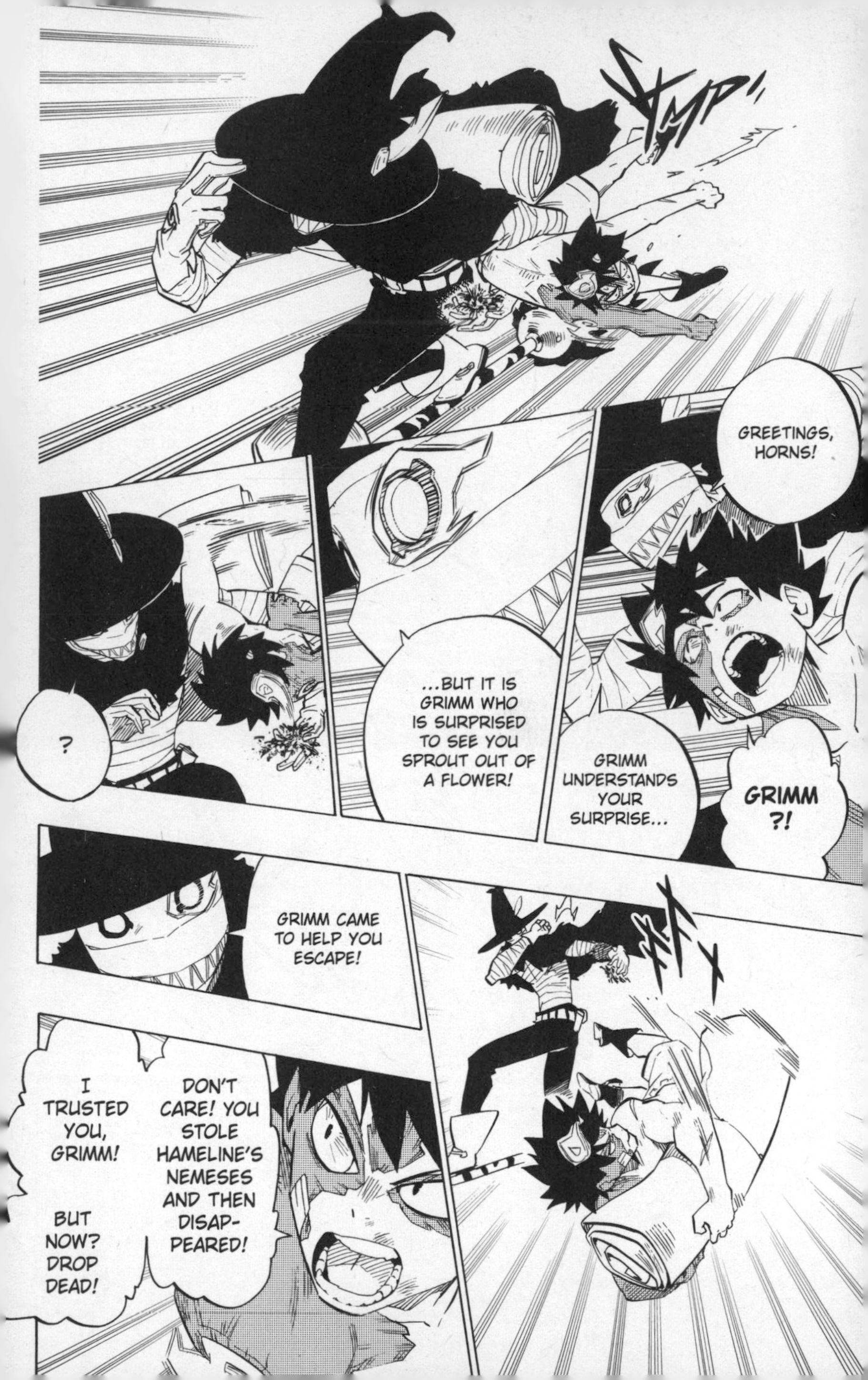
GREETINGS, HORNS!
GRIMM ?!
GRIMM UNDERSTANDS YOUR SURPRISE...
...BUT IT IS GRIMM WHO IS SURPRISED TO SEE YOU SPROUT OUT OF A FLOWER!
?
GRIMM CAME TO HELP YOU ESCAPE!
DON'T CARE! YOU STOLE HAMELINE'S NEMESES AND THEN DISAP-PEARED!
I TRUSTED YOU, GRIMM!
BUT NOW? DROP DEAD!

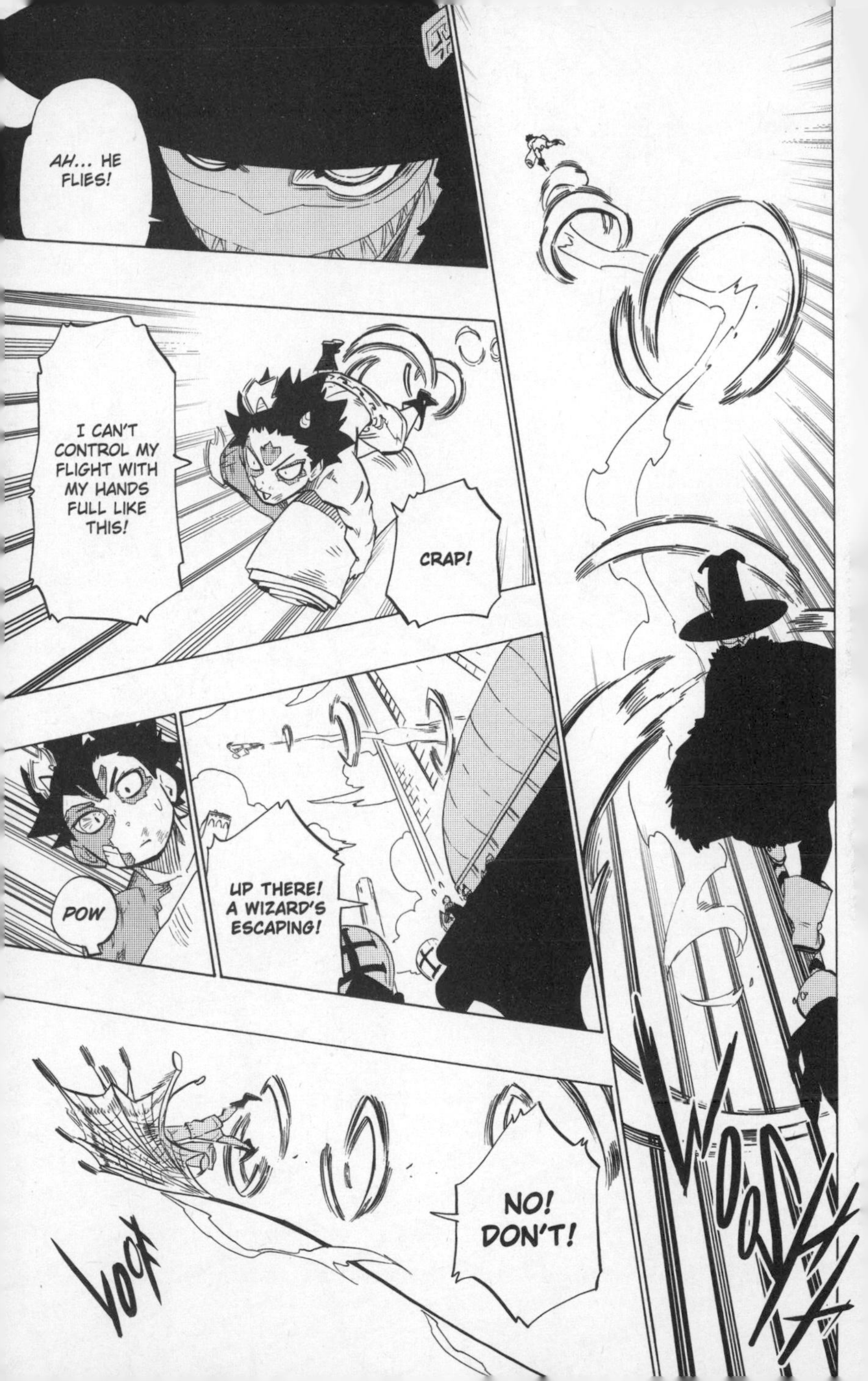
AH... HE FLIES!
I CAN'T CONTROL MY FLIGHT WITH MY HANDS FULL LIKE THIS!
CRAP!
UP THERE! A WIZARD'S ESCAPING!
POW
NO! DON'T!

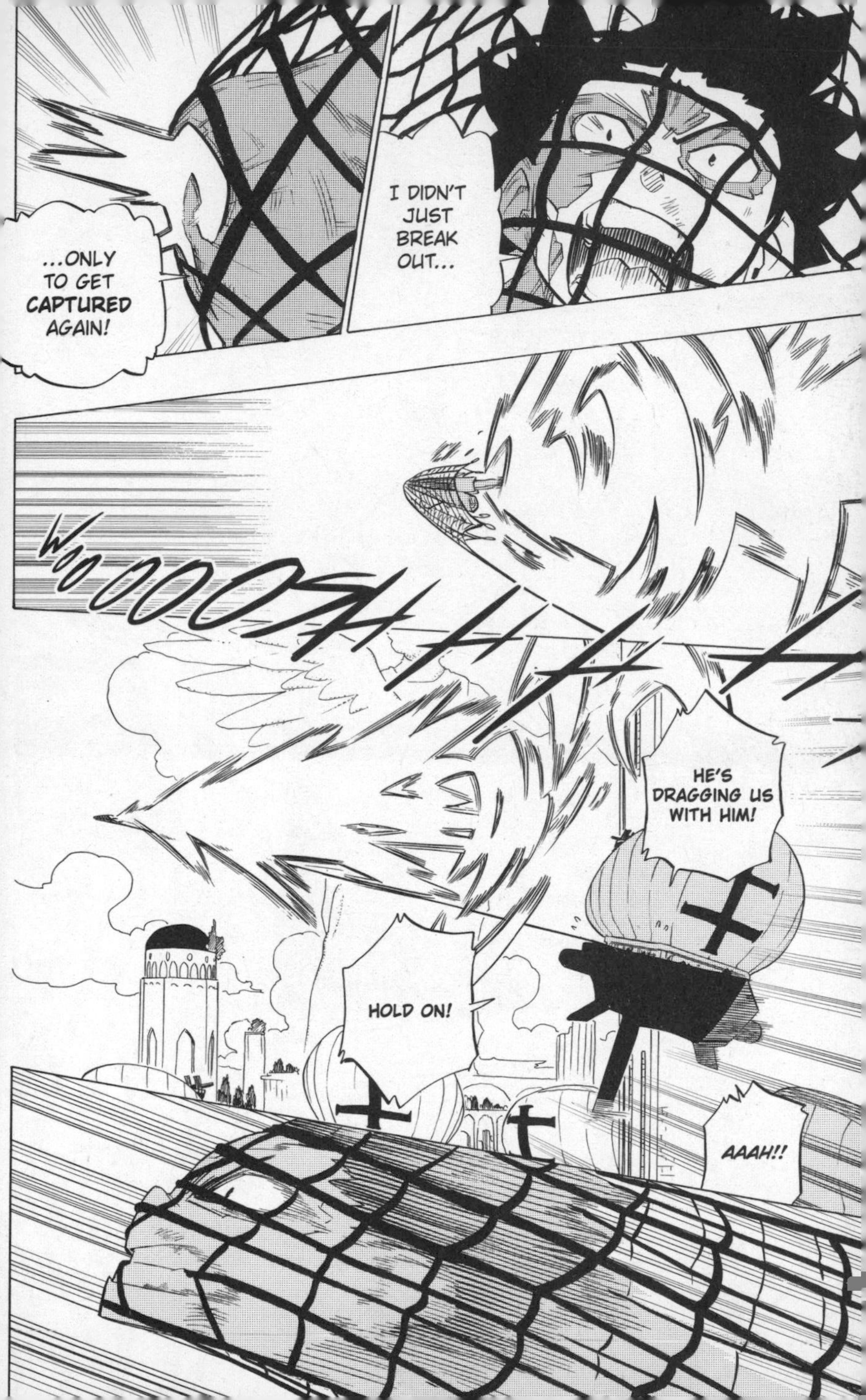
I DIDN'T JUST BREAK OUT...
...ONLY TO GET CAPTURED AGAIN!
WOOOOOSHHHH
HE'S DRAGGING US WITH HIM!
AAAH!!
HOLD ON!

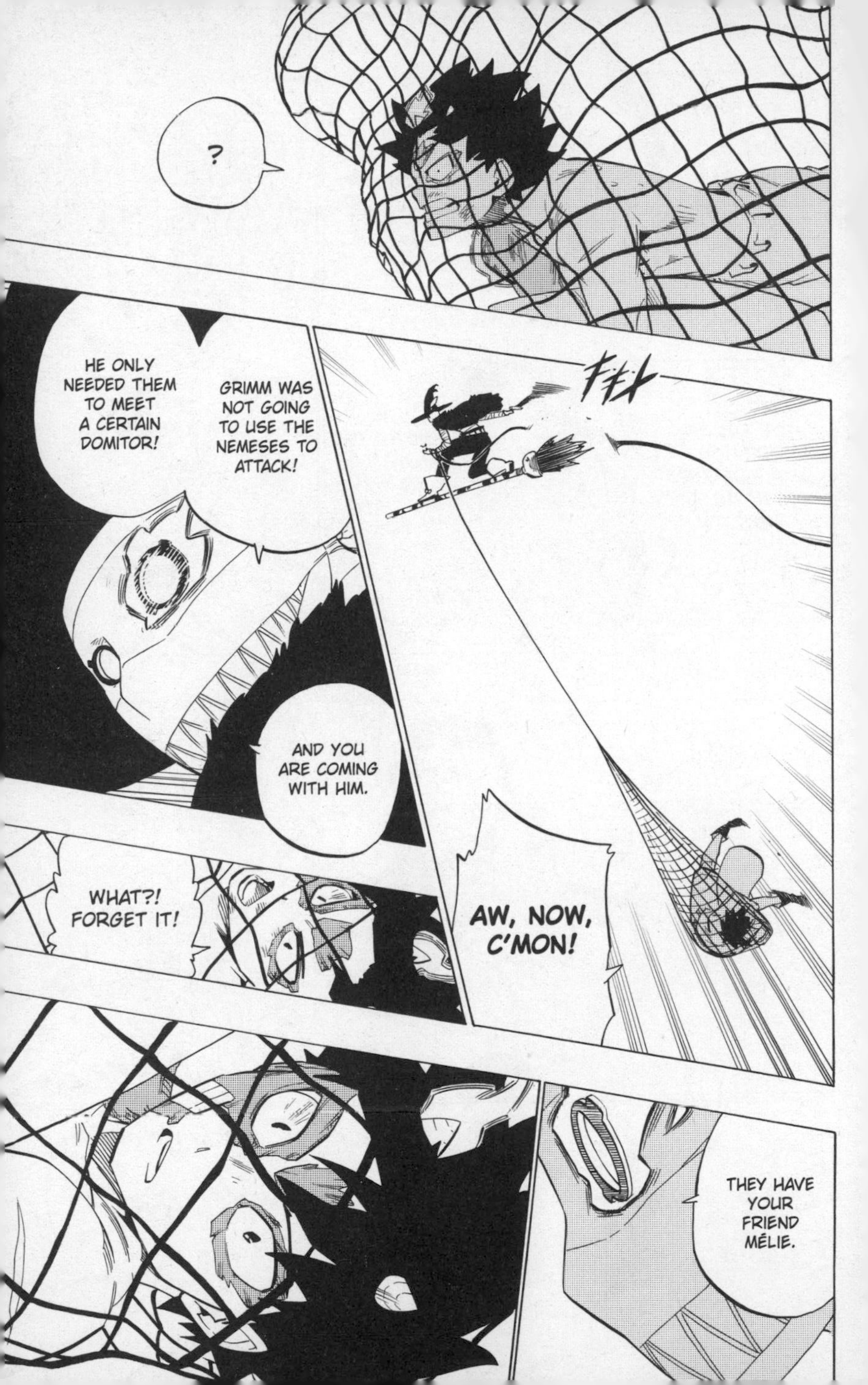
?
GRIMM WAS NOT GOING TO USE THE NEMESES TO ATTACK!
HE ONLY NEEDED THEM TO MEET A CERTAIN DOMITOR!
AND YOU ARE COMING WITH HIM.
WHAT?! FORGET IT!
AW, NOW, C'MON!
THEY HAVE YOUR FRIEND MÉLIE.

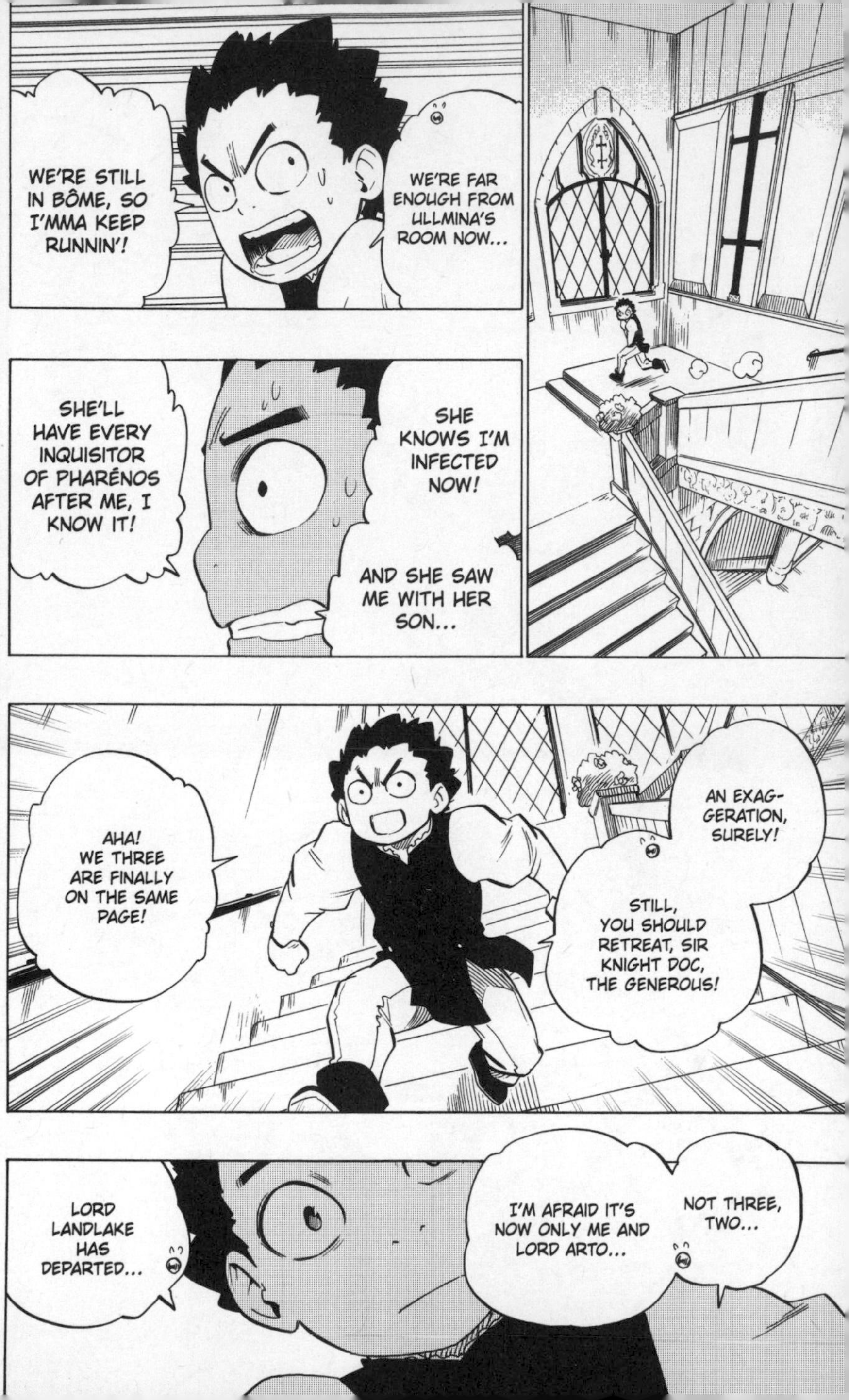
WE'RE FAR ENOUGH FROM ULLMINA'S ROOM NOW...
WE'RE STILL IN BÔME, SO I'MMA KEEP RUNNIN'!
SHE KNOWS I'M INFECTED NOW!
AND SHE SAW ME WITH HER SON...
SHE'LL HAVE EVERY INQUISITOR OF PHARÉNOS AFTER ME, I KNOW IT!
AN EXAG-GERATION, SURELY!
STILL, YOU SHOULD RETREAT, SIR KNIGHT DOC, THE GENEROUS!
AHA! WE THREE ARE FINALLY ON THE SAME PAGE!
NOT THREE, TWO...
I'M AFRAID IT'S NOW ONLY ME AND LORD ARTO...
LORD LANDLAKE HAS DEPARTED...

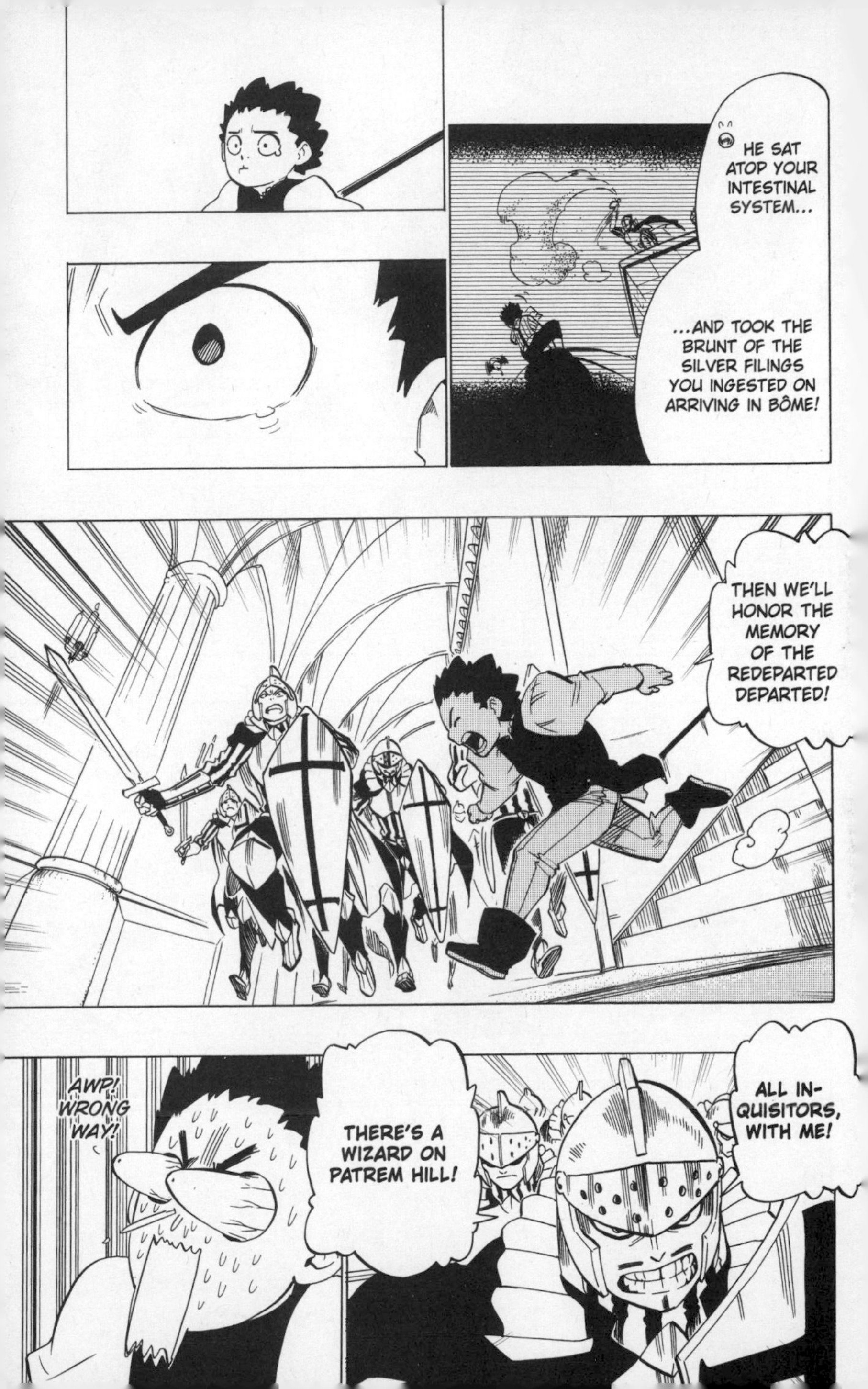
HE SAT ATOP YOUR INTESTINAL SYSTEM...
...AND TOOK THE BRUNT OF THE SILVER FILINGS YOU INGESTED ON ARRIVING IN BÔME!
THEN WE'LL HONOR THE MEMORY OF THE REDEPARTED DEPARTED!
ALL IN-QUISITORS, WITH ME!
THERE'S A WIZARD ON PATREM HILL!
AWP! WRONG WAY!

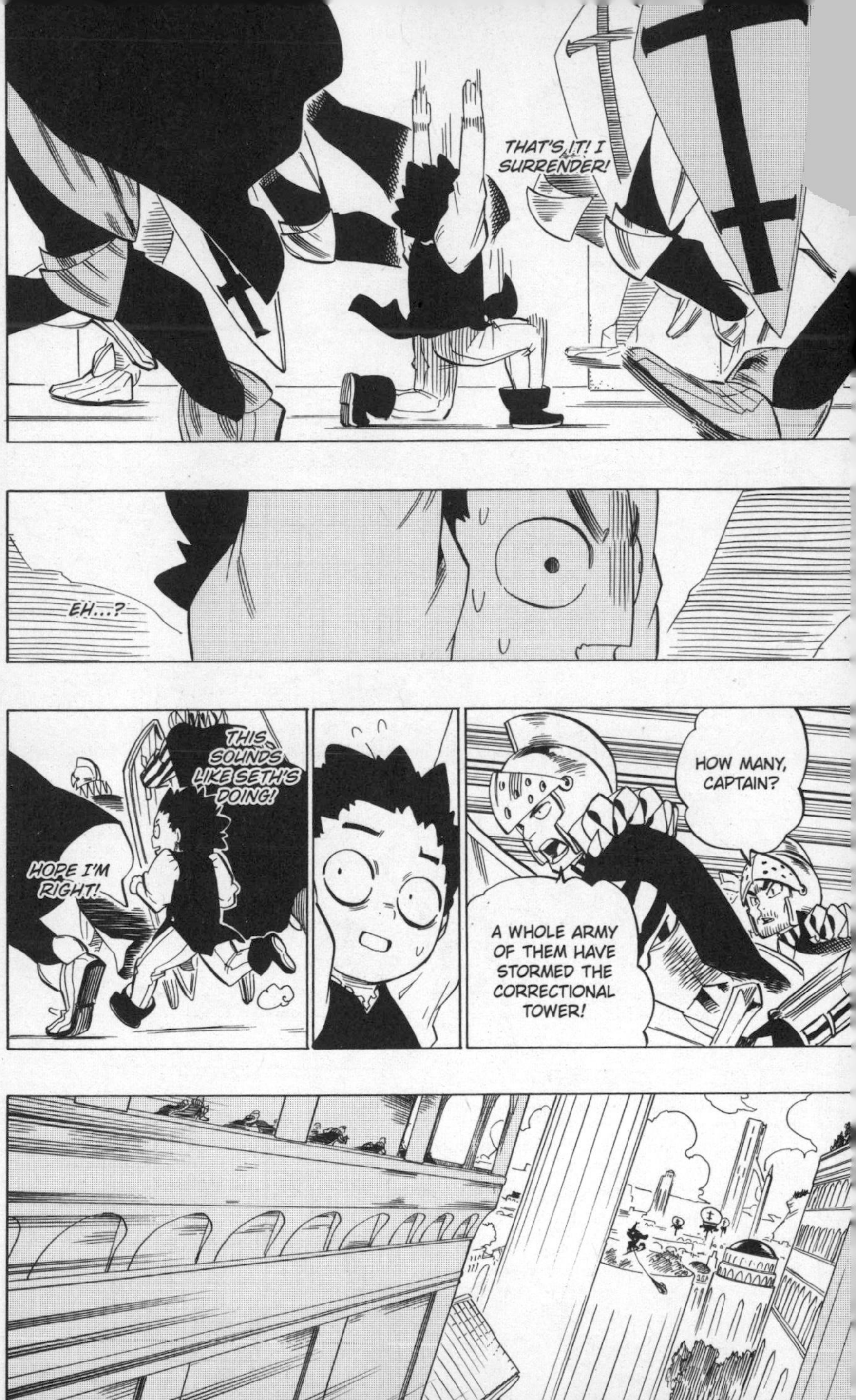
THAT'S IT! I SURRENDER!
EH...?
HOW MANY, CAPTAIN?
A WHOLE ARMY OF THEM HAVE STORMED THE CORRECTIONAL TOWER!
THIS SOUNDS LIKE SETH'S DOING!
HOPE I'M RIGHT!

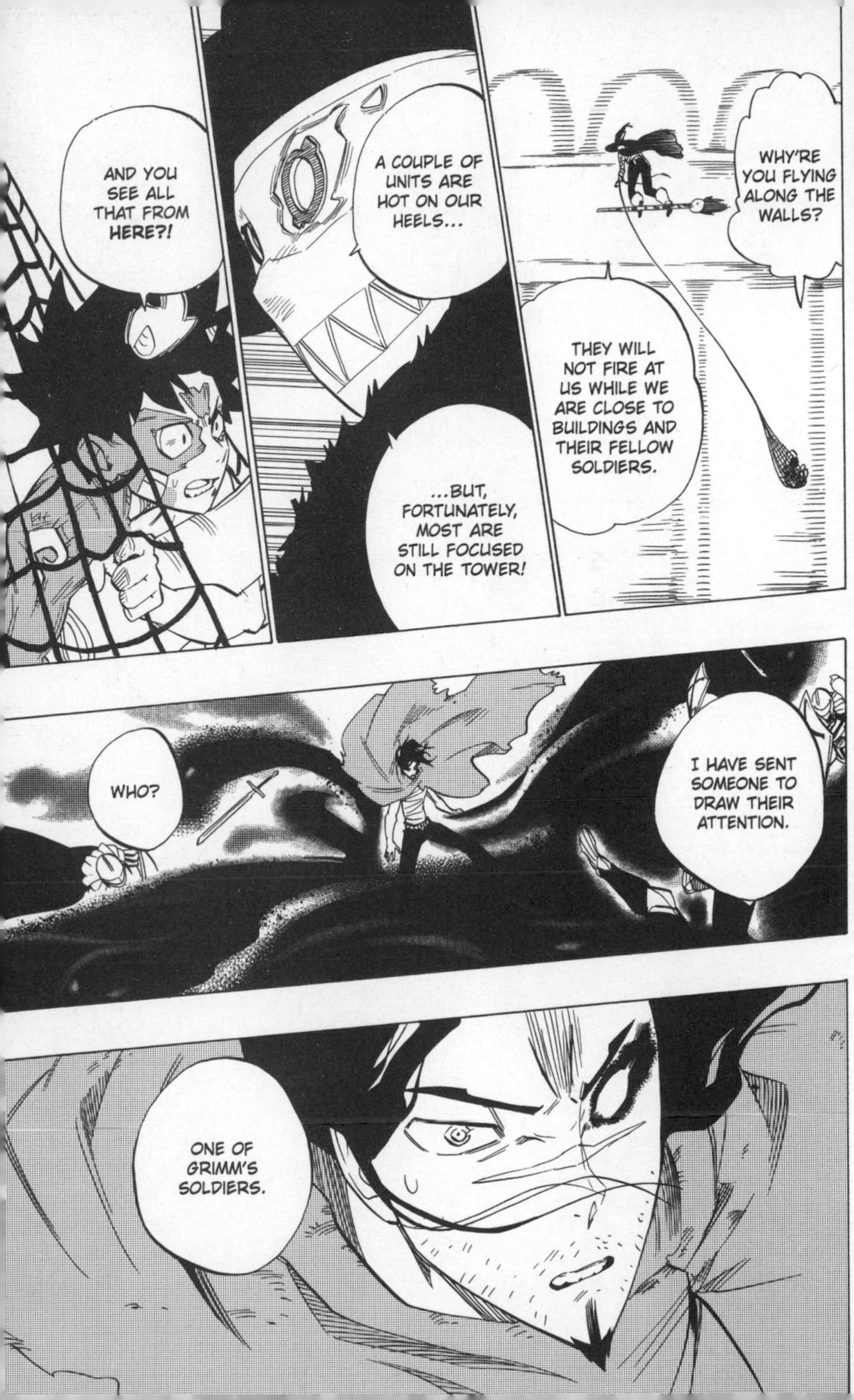
WHY'RE YOU FLYING ALONG THE WALLS?
THEY WILL NOT FIRE AT US WHILE WE ARE CLOSE TO BUILDINGS AND THEIR FELLOW SOLDIERS.
A COUPLE OF UNITS ARE HOT ON OUR HEELS...
...BUT, FORTUNATELY, MOST ARE STILL FOCUSED ON THE TOWER!
AND YOU SEE ALL THAT FROM HERE?!
I HAVE SENT SOMEONE TO DRAW THEIR ATTENTION.
WHO?
ONE OF GRIMM'S SOLDIERS.

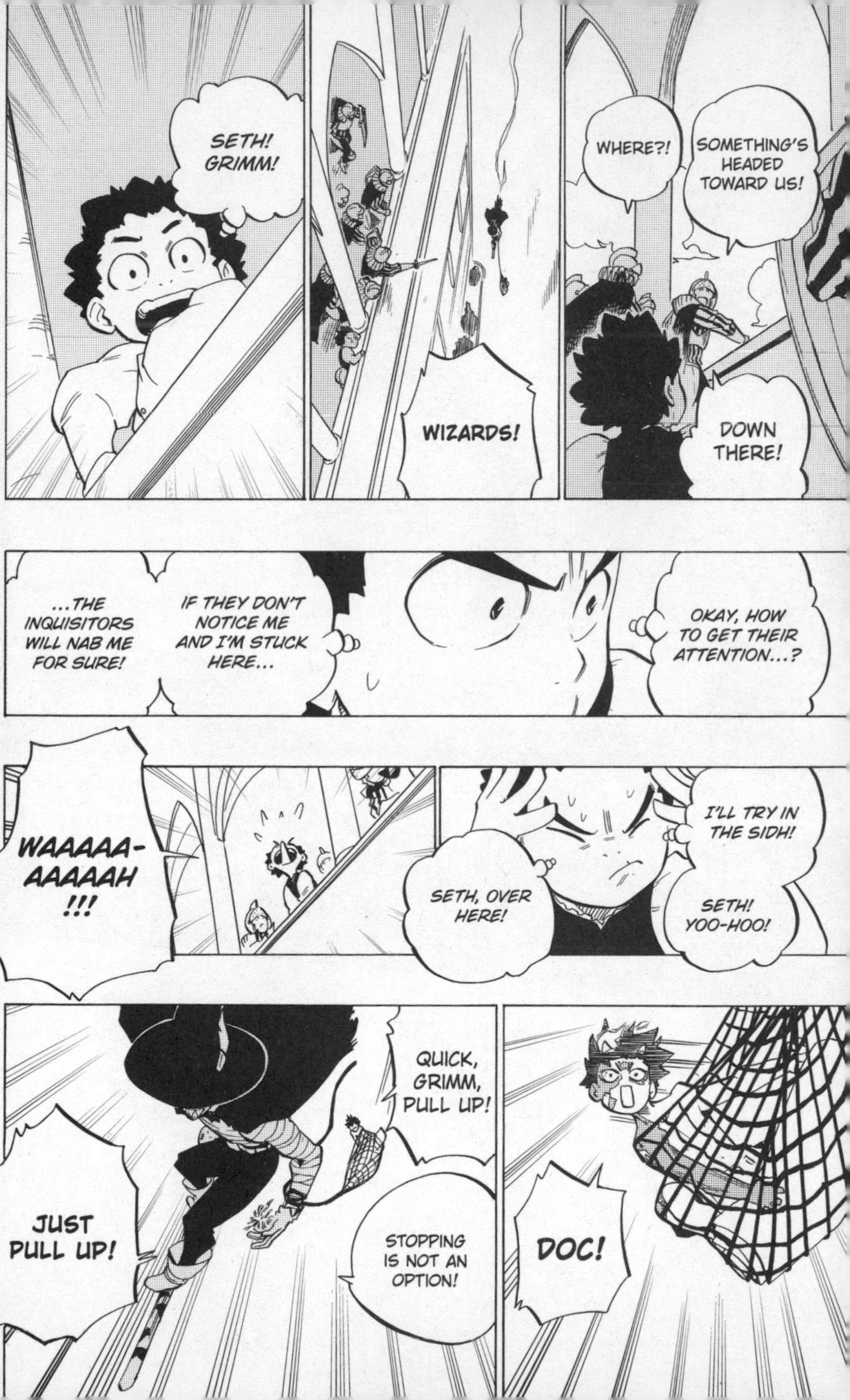
SOMETHING'S HEADED TOWARD US!
WHERE?!
DOWN THERE!
WIZARDS!
SETH! GRIMM!
OKAY, HOW TO GET THEIR ATTENTION...?
IF THEY DON'T NOTICE ME AND I'M STUCK HERE...
...THE INQUISITORS WILL NAB ME FOR SURE!
I'LL TRY IN THE SIDH!
SETH! YOO-HOO!
SETH, OVER HERE!
WAAAAA-AAAAAH!!!
DOC!
QUICK, GRIMM, PULL UP!
STOPPING IS NOT AN OPTION!
JUST PULL UP!

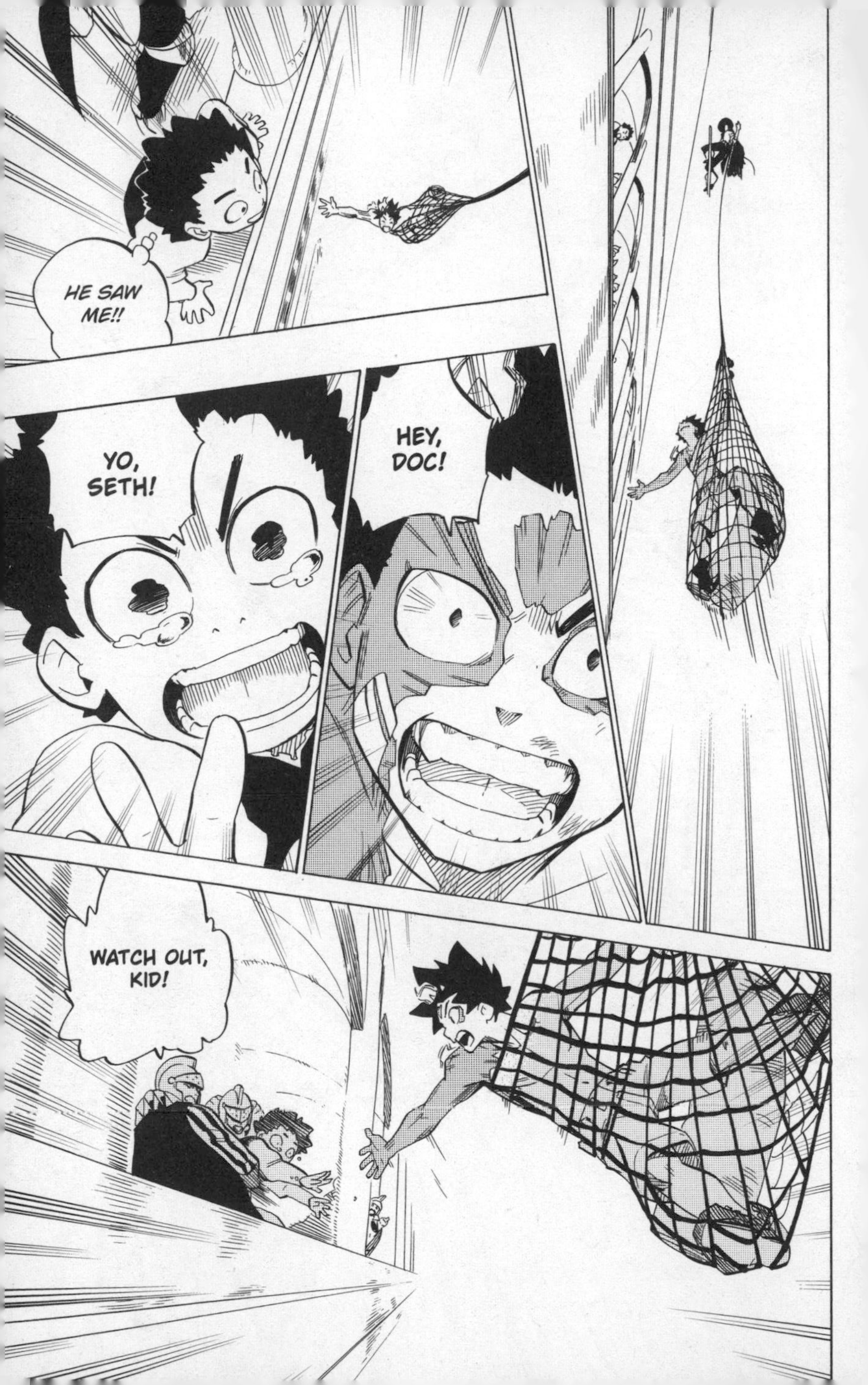
HE SAW ME!!
HEY, DOC!
YO, SETH!
WATCH OUT, KID!

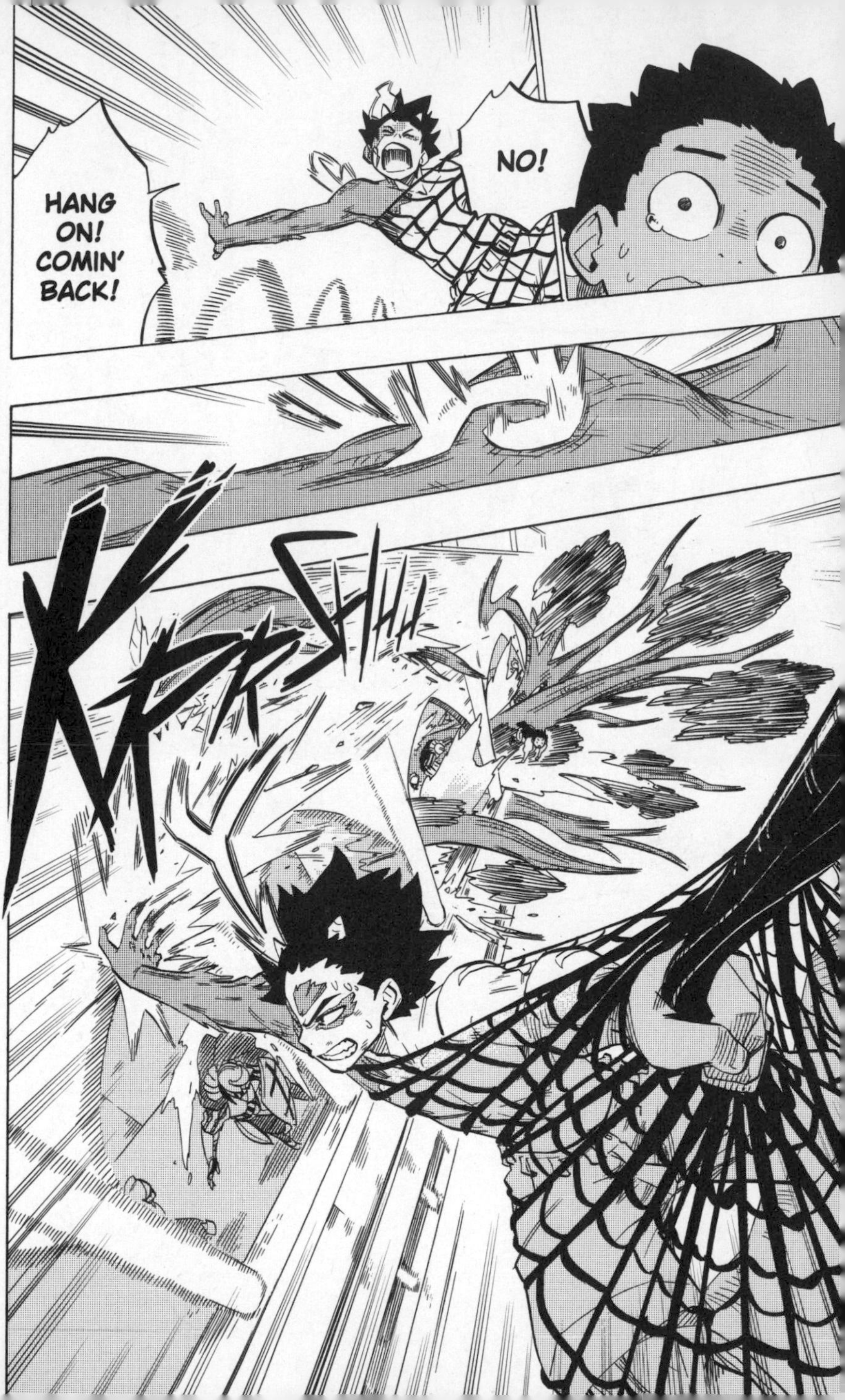
NO!
HANG ON! COMIN' BACK!
KRSSHH

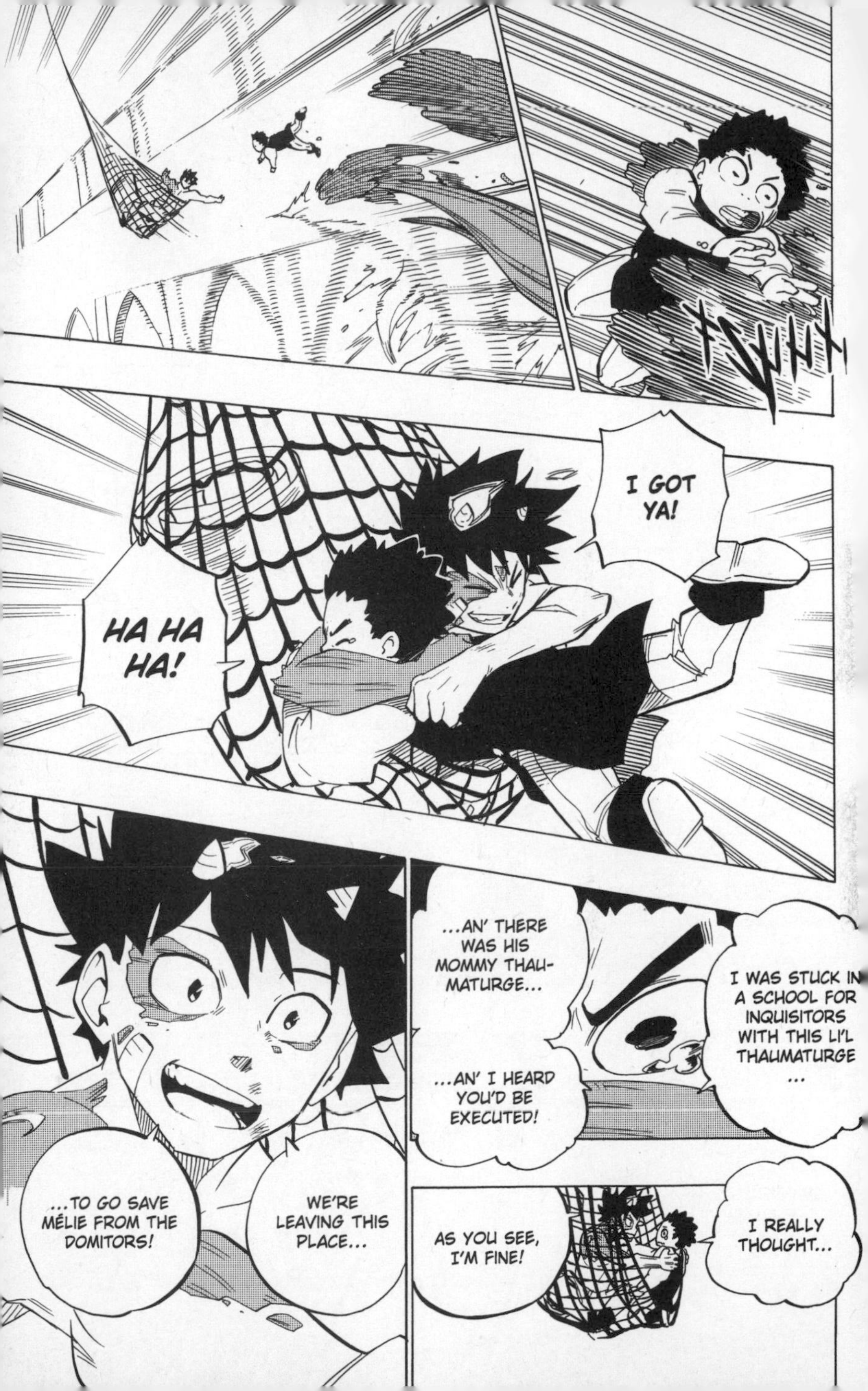
I GOT YA!
HA HA HA!
I WAS STUCK IN A SCHOOL FOR INQUISITORS WITH THIS LI'L THAUMATURGE ...
...AN' THERE WAS HIS MOMMY THAU-MATURGE...
...AN' I HEARD YOU'D BE EXECUTED!
I REALLY THOUGHT...
AS YOU SEE, I'M FINE!
WE'RE LEAVING THIS PLACE...
...TO GO SAVE MÉLIE FROM THE DOMITORS!

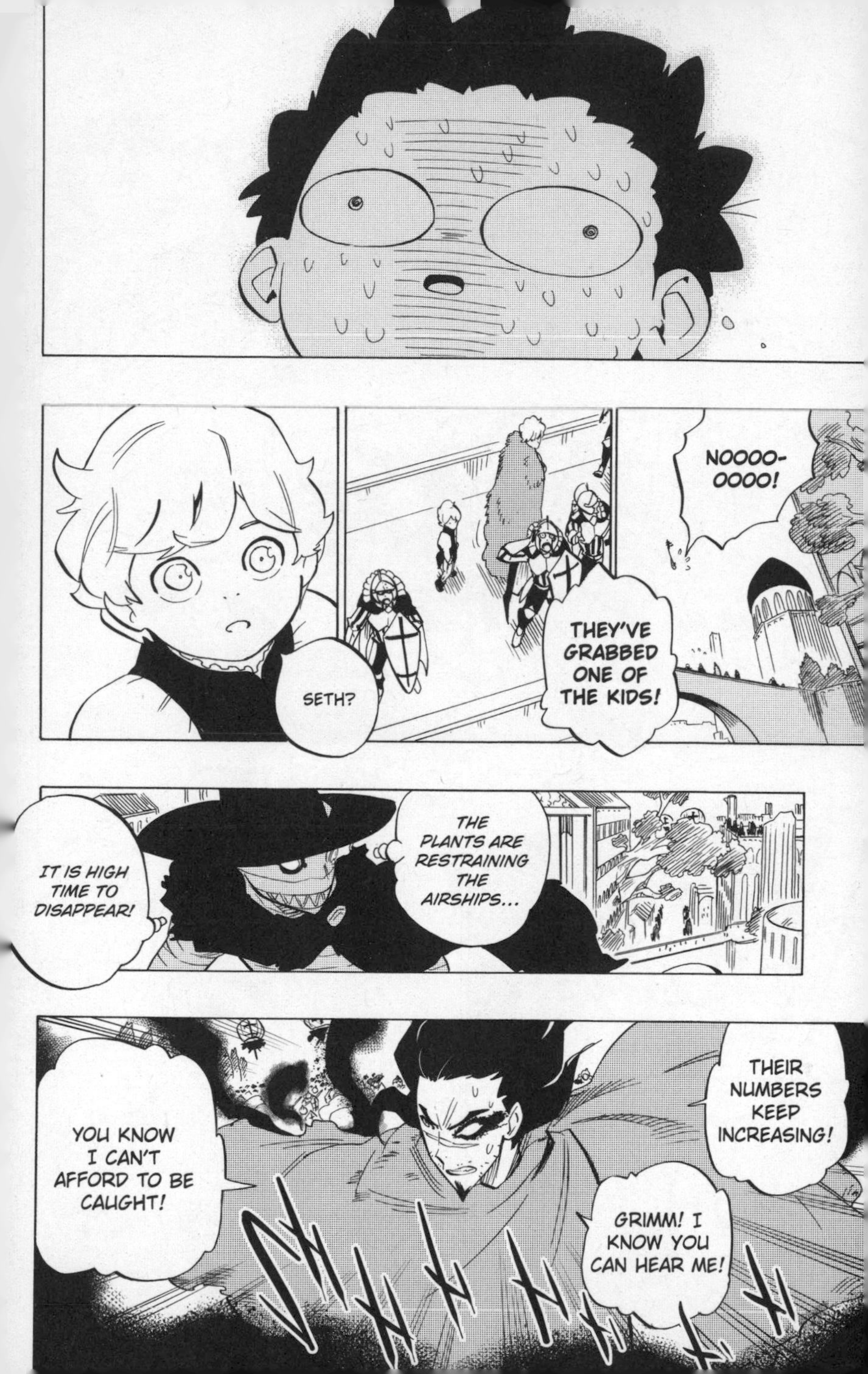
NOOOO-OOOO!
THEY'VE GRABBED ONE OF THE KIDS!
SETH?
THE PLANTS ARE RESTRAINING THE AIRSHIPS...
IT IS HIGH TIME TO DISAPPEAR!
THEIR NUMBERS KEEP INCREASING!
GRIMM! I KNOW YOU CAN HEAR ME!
YOU KNOW I CAN'T AFFORD TO BE CAUGHT!

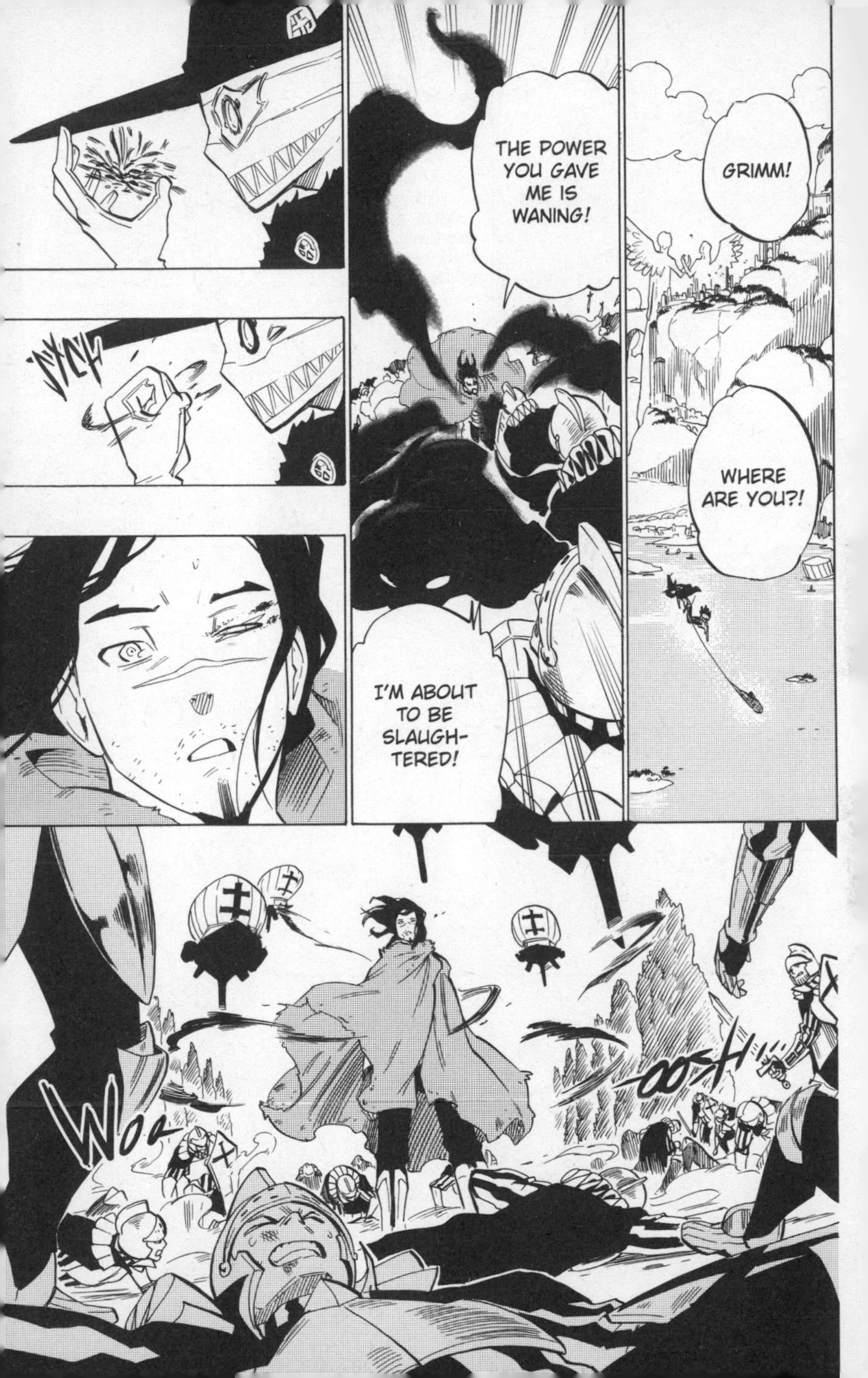
GRIMM!
WHERE ARE YOU?!
THE POWER YOU GAVE ME IS WANING!
I'M ABOUT TO BE SLAUGHTERED!
-OOSH!!
WOA

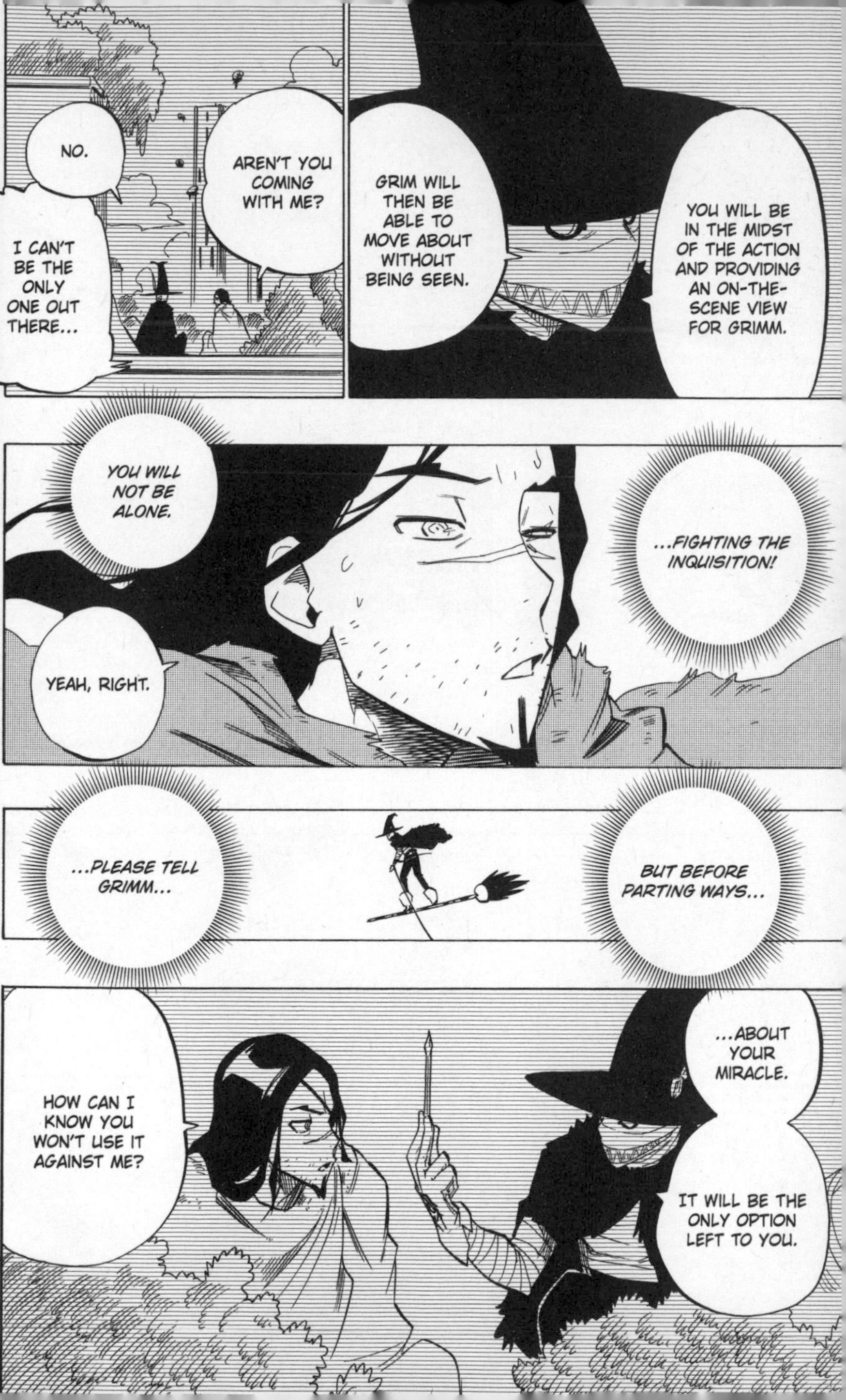
YOU WILL BE IN THE MIDST OF THE ACTION AND PROVIDING AN ON-THE-SCENE VIEW FOR GRIMM.
GRIM WILL THEN BE ABLE TO MOVE ABOUT WITHOUT BEING SEEN.
AREN'T YOU COMING WITH ME?
NO.
I CAN'T BE THE ONLY ONE OUT THERE...
...FIGHTING THE INQUISITION!
YOU WILL NOT BE ALONE.
YEAH, RIGHT.
BUT BEFORE PARTING WAYS...
...PLEASE TELL GRIMM...
...ABOUT YOUR MIRACLE.
IT WILL BE THE ONLY OPTION LEFT TO YOU.
HOW CAN I KNOW YOU WON'T USE IT AGAINST ME?

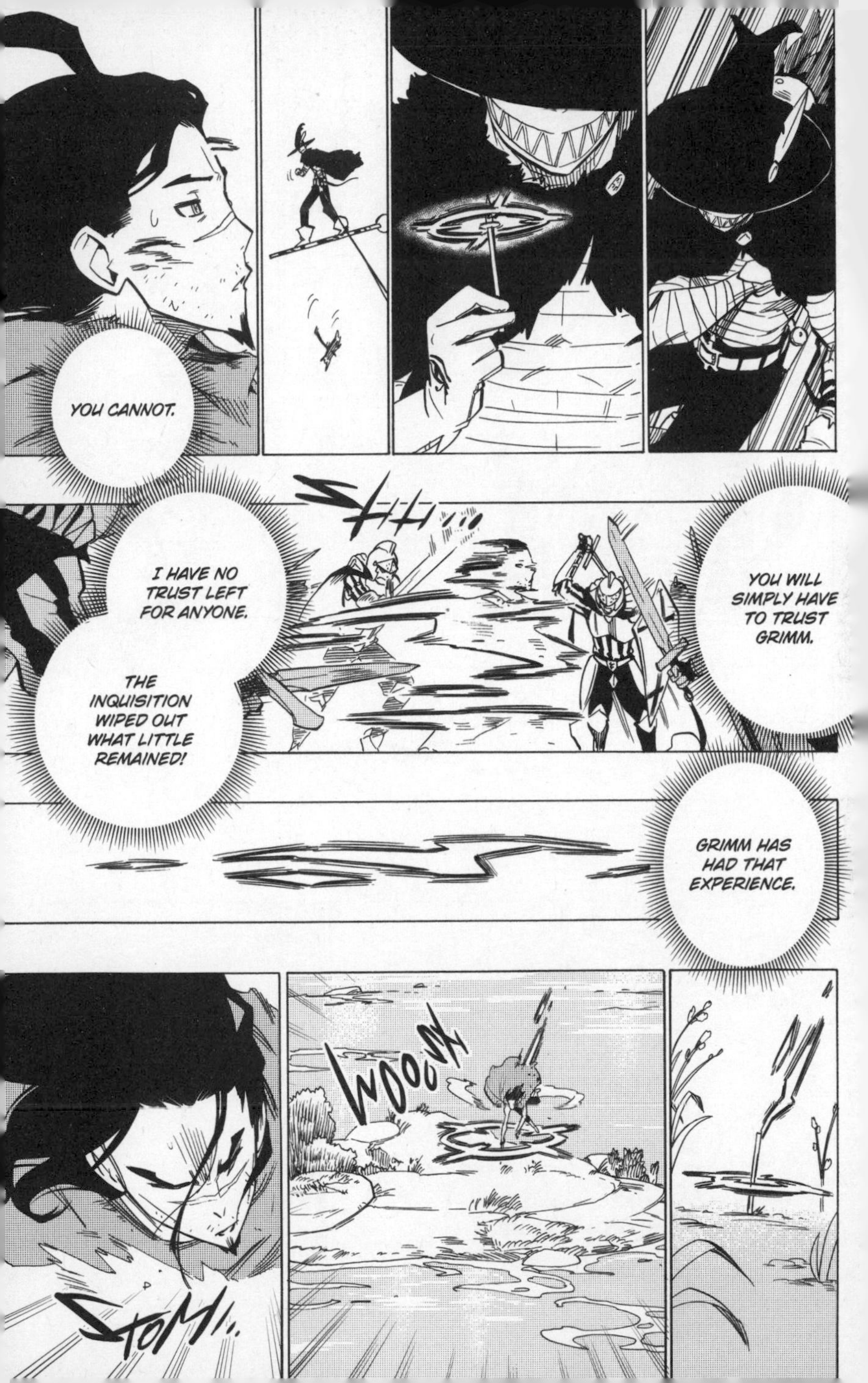
YOU CANNOT.
YOU WILL SIMPLY HAVE TO TRUST GRIMM.
SHHH...
I HAVE NO TRUST LEFT FOR ANYONE.
THE INQUISITION WIPED OUT WHAT LITTLE REMAINED!
GRIMM HAS HAD THAT EXPERIENCE.
WOOSH
STOMP!!

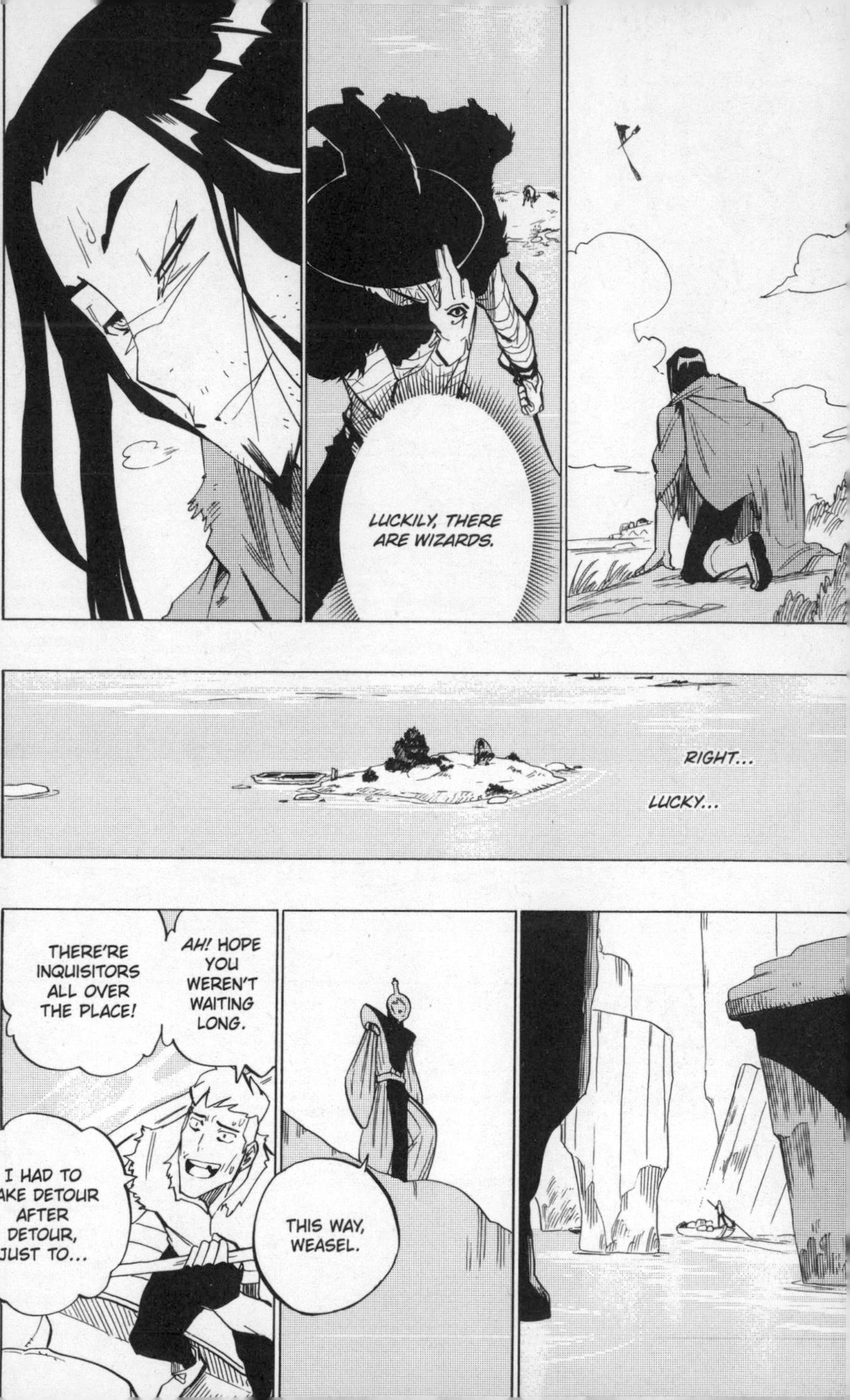
LUCKILY, THERE ARE WIZARDS.
RIGHT...
LUCKY...
THIS WAY, WEASEL.
AH! HOPE YOU WEREN'T WAITING LONG.
THERE'RE INQUISITORS ALL OVER THE PLACE!
I HAD TO TAKE DETOUR AFTER DETOUR, JUST TO...

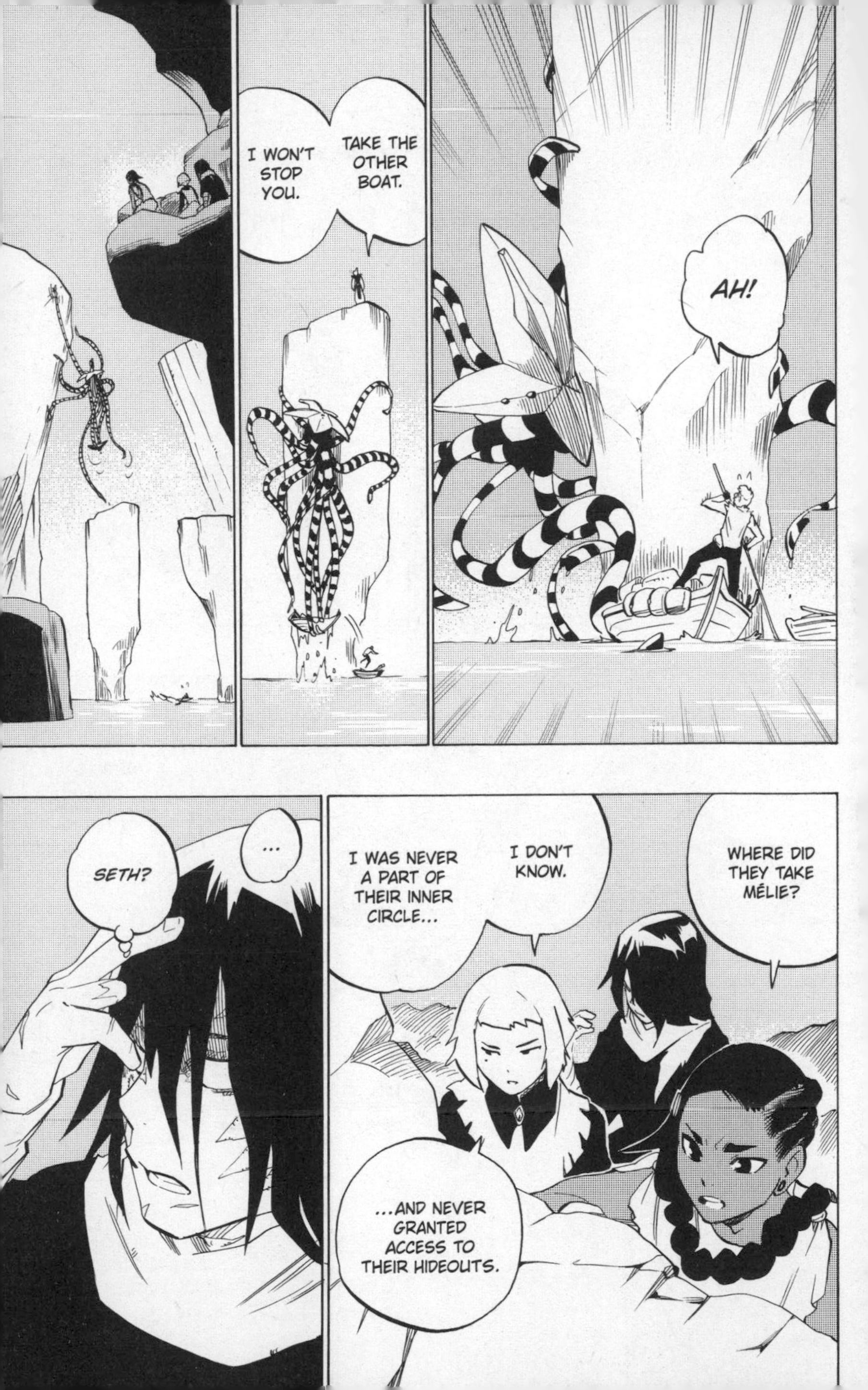
AH!
TAKE THE OTHER BOAT.
I WON'T STOP YOU.
WHERE DID THEY TAKE MÉLIE?
I DON'T KNOW.
I WAS NEVER A PART OF THEIR INNER CIRCLE...
...AND NEVER GRANTED ACCESS TO THEIR HIDEOUTS.
...
SETH?

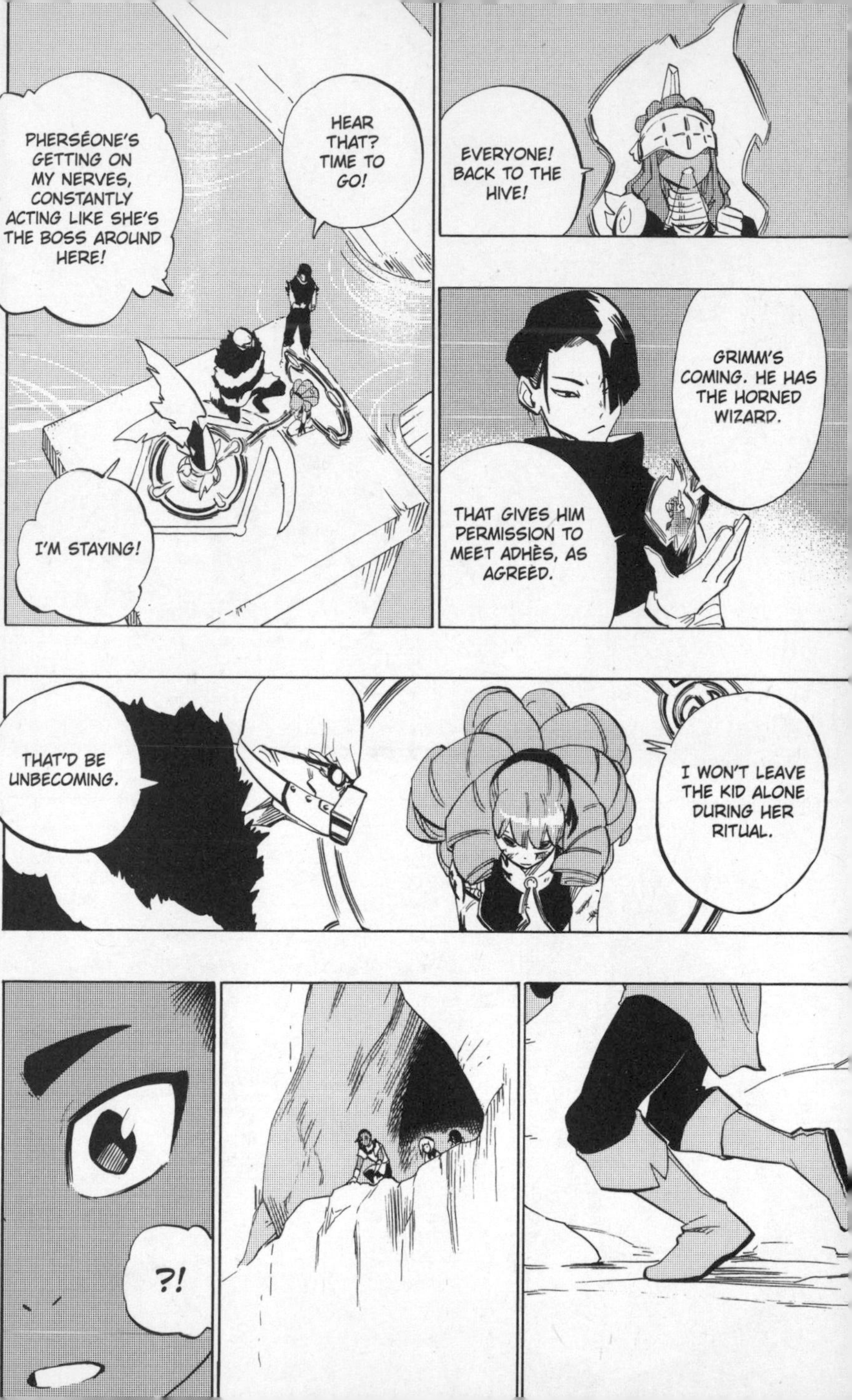
EVERYONE! BACK TO THE HIVE!
GRIMM'S COMING. HE HAS THE HORNED WIZARD.
THAT GIVES HIM PERMISSION TO MEET ADHÈS, AS AGREED.
HEAR THAT? TIME TO GO!
PHERSÉONE'S GETTING ON MY NERVES, CONSTANTLY ACTING LIKE SHE'S THE BOSS AROUND HERE!
I'M STAYING!
I WON'T LEAVE THE KID ALONE DURING HER RITUAL.
THAT'D BE UNBECOMING.
?!

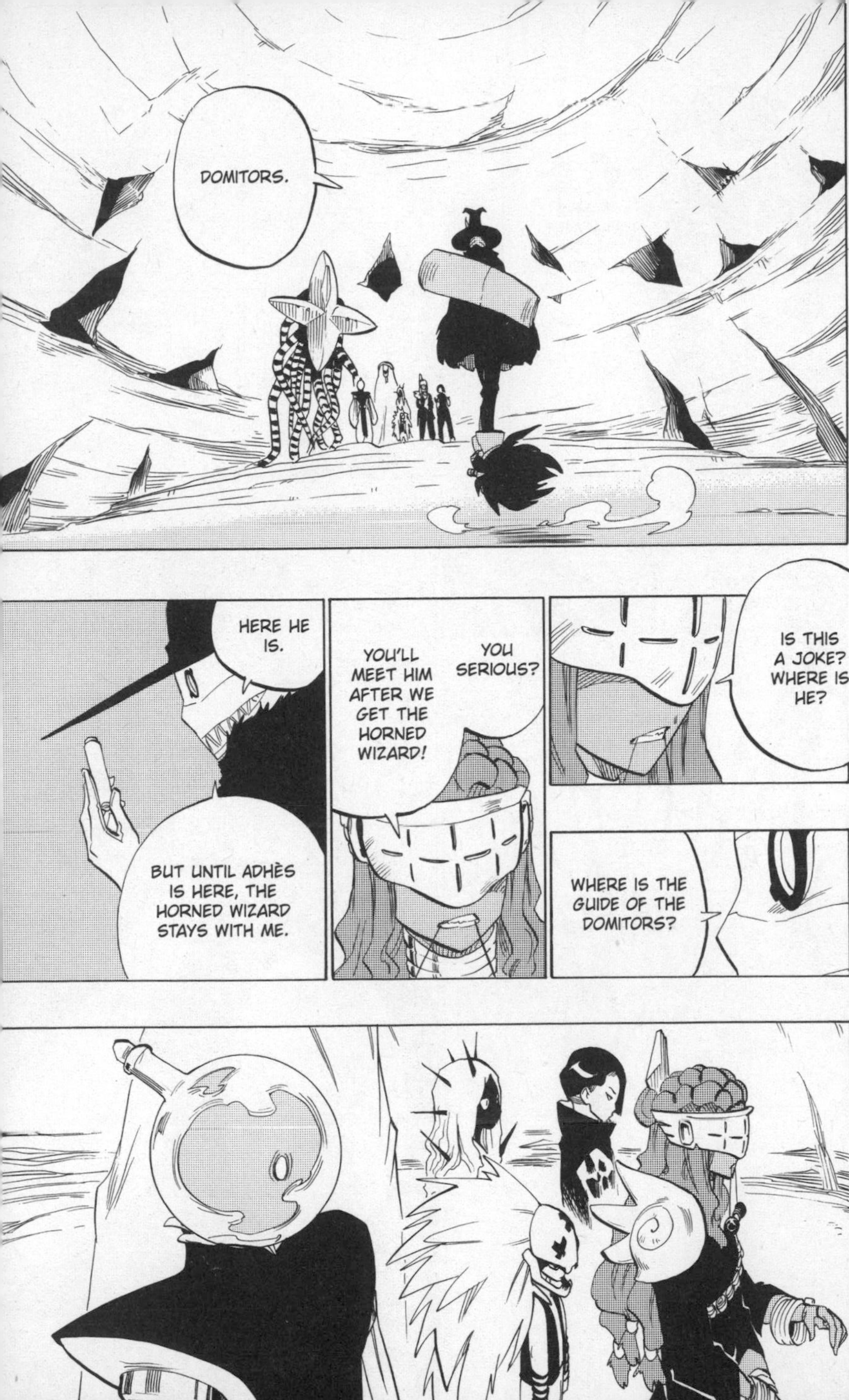
DOMITORS.
IS THIS A JOKE? WHERE IS HE?
WHERE IS THE GUIDE OF THE DOMITORS?
YOU SERIOUS?
YOU'LL MEET HIM AFTER WE GET THE HORNED WIZARD!
HERE HE IS.
BUT UNTIL ADHÈS IS HERE, THE HORNED WIZARD STAYS WITH ME.

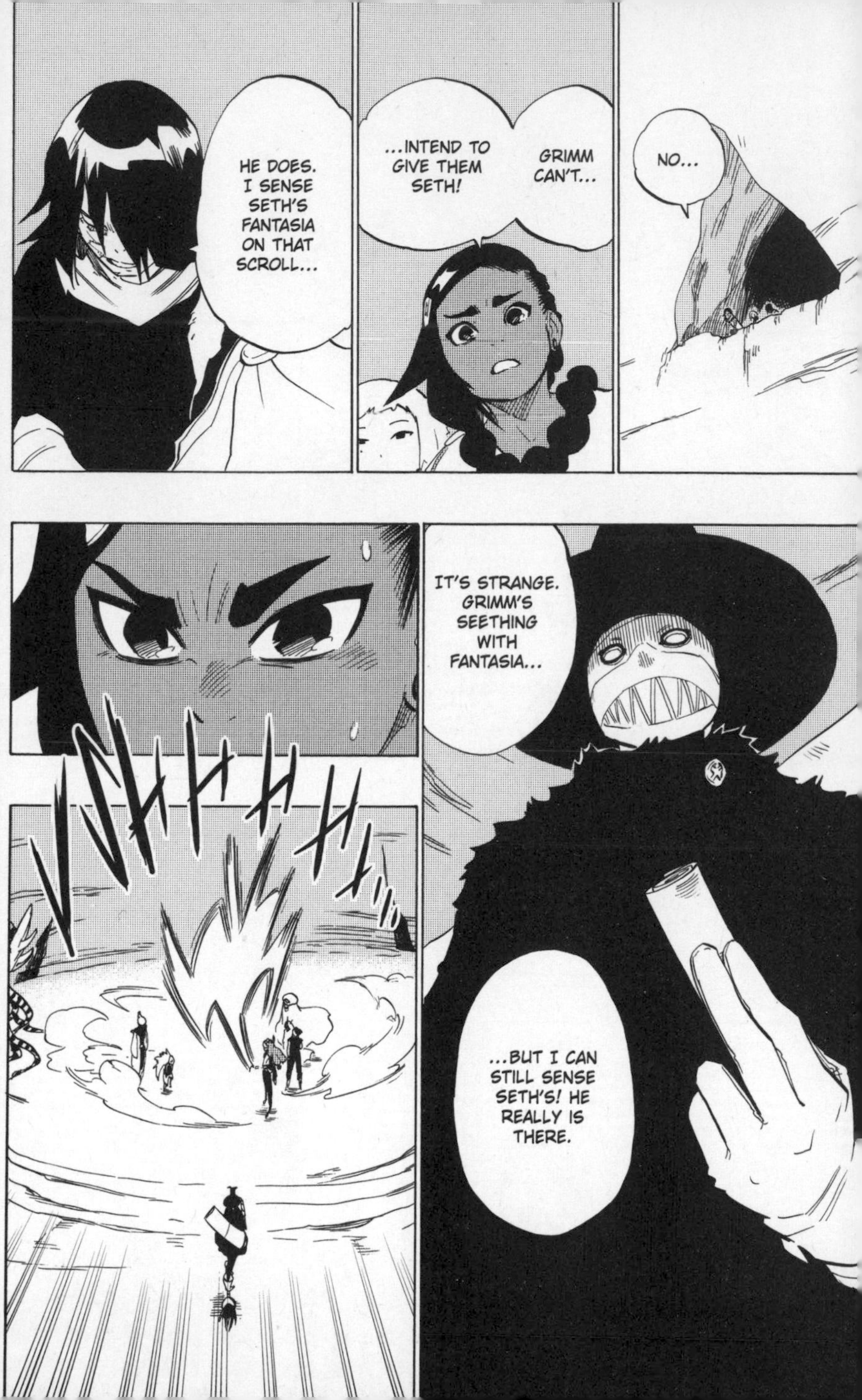
NO...
GRIMM CAN'T...
...INTEND TO GIVE THEM SETH!
HE DOES. I SENSE SETH'S FANTASIA ON THAT SCROLL...
IT'S STRANGE. GRIMM'S SEETHING WITH FANTASIA...
...BUT I CAN STILL SENSE SETH'S! HE REALLY IS THERE.

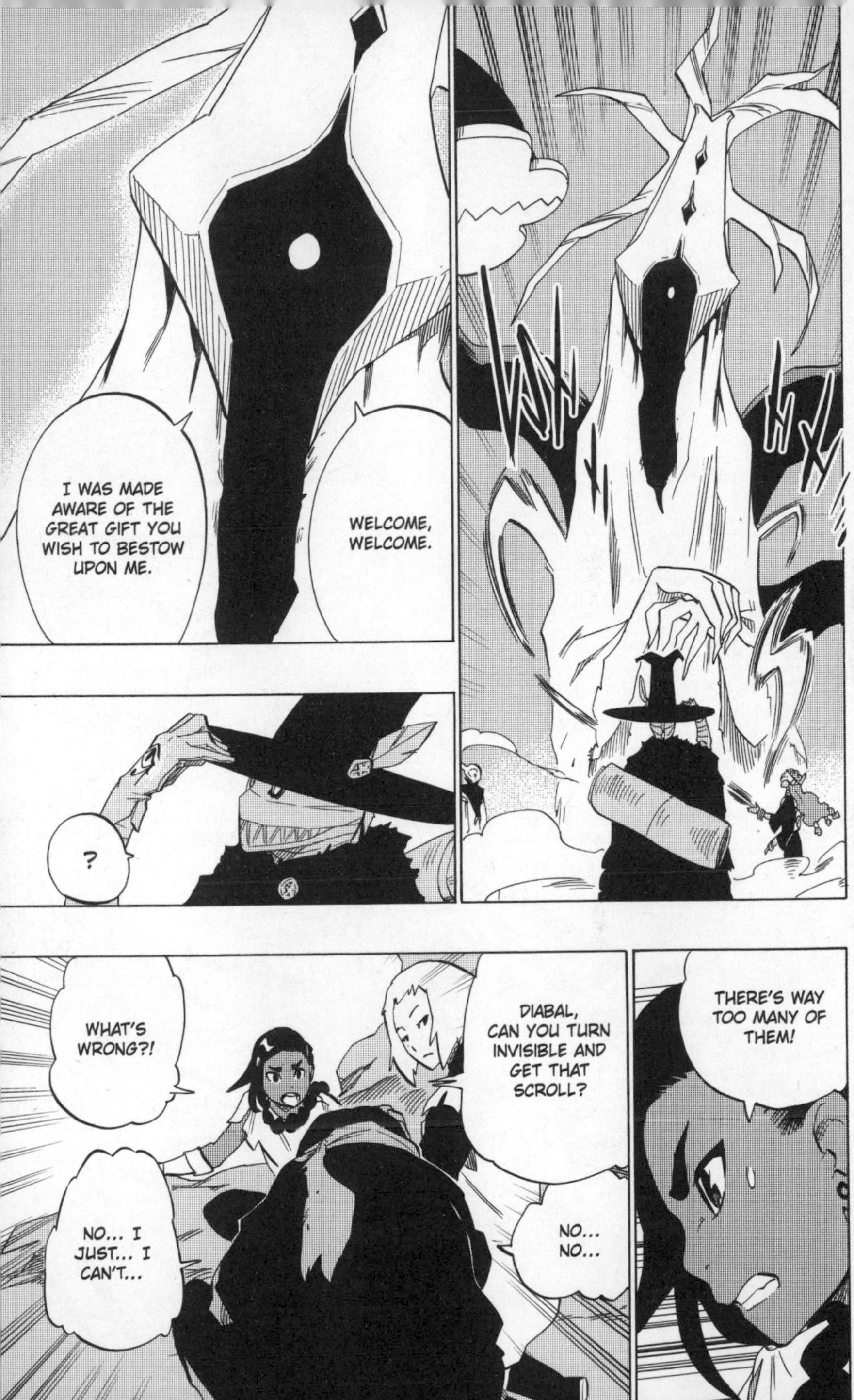
WELCOME, WELCOME.
I WAS MADE AWARE OF THE GREAT GIFT YOU WISH TO BESTOW UPON ME.
?
THERE'S WAY TOO MANY OF THEM!
DIABAL, CAN YOU TURN INVISIBLE AND GET THAT SCROLL?
WHAT'S WRONG?!
NO... NO...
NO... I JUST... I CAN'T...

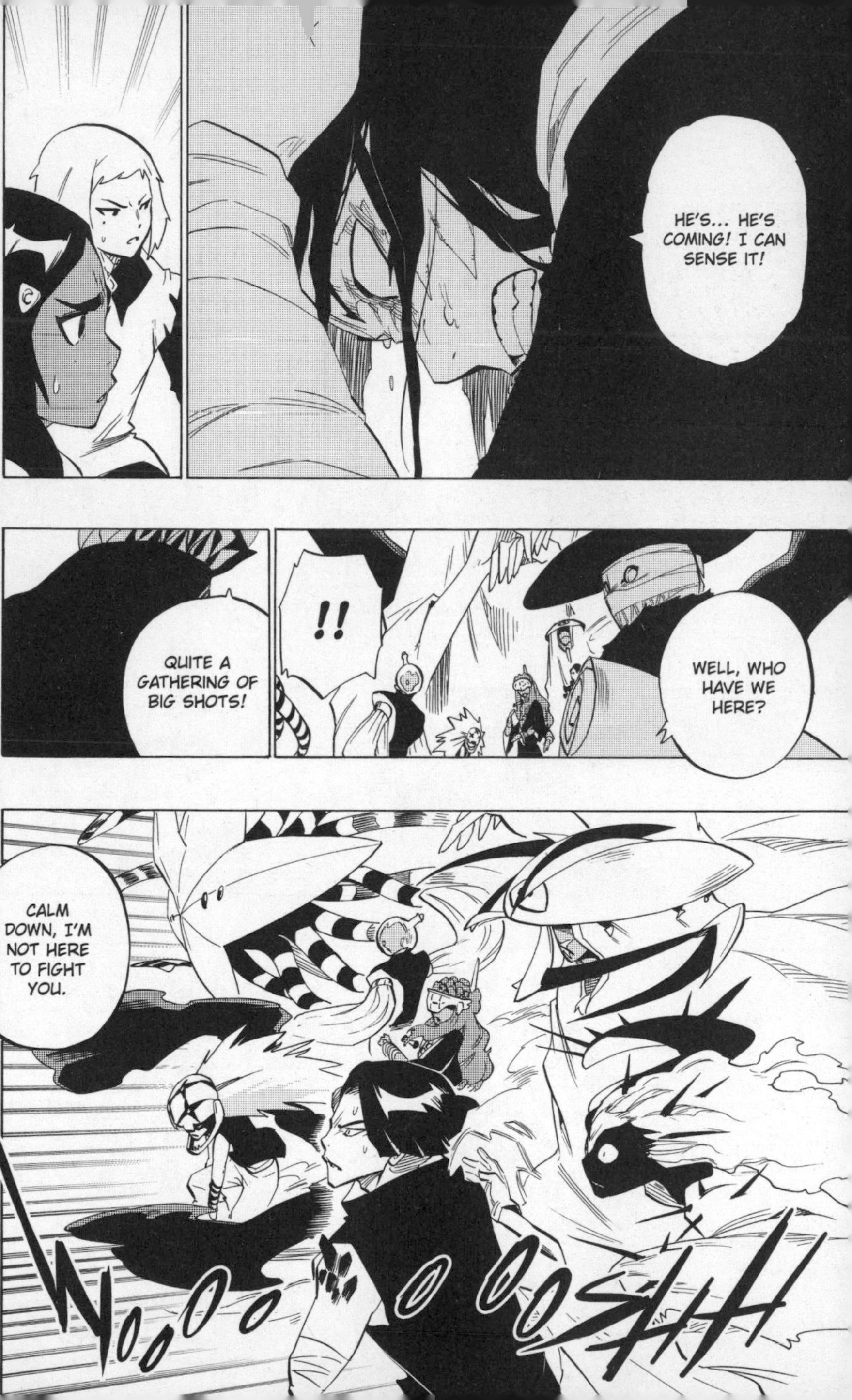
HE'S... HE'S COMING! I CAN SENSE IT!
WELL, WHO HAVE WE HERE?
!!
QUITE A GATHERING OF BIG SHOTS!
CALM DOWN, I'M NOT HERE TO FIGHT YOU.
WHOOOOOOOSHH

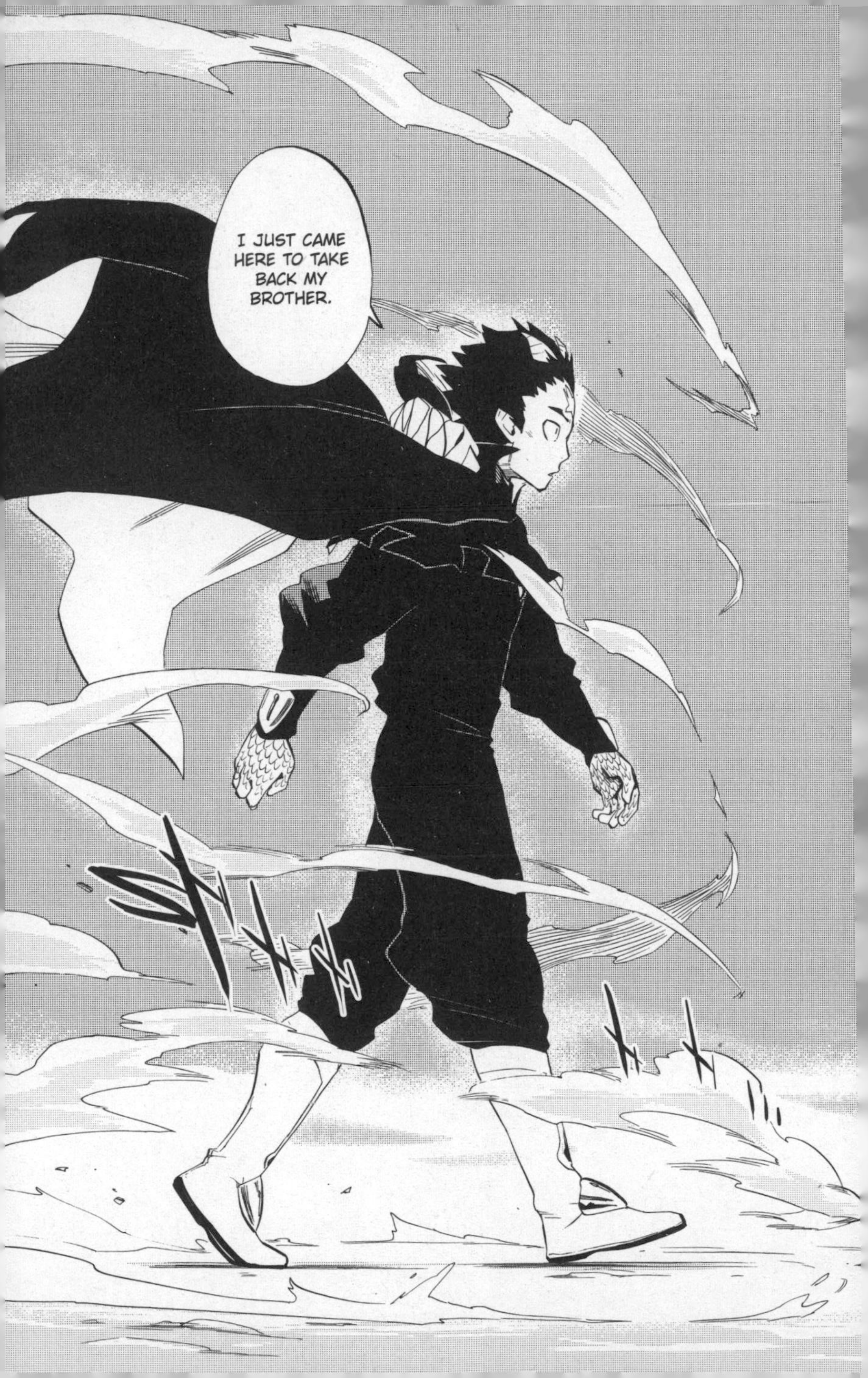
I JUST CAME HERE TO TAKE BACK MY BROTHER.

TO BE CONTINUED...

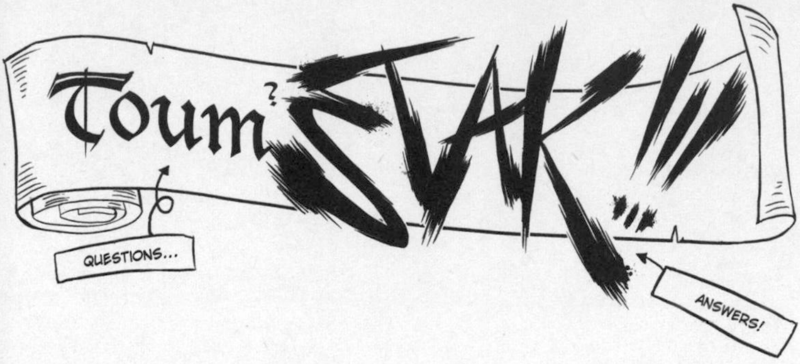
Toum?
STAK!!!
QUESTIONS...
ANSWERS!

<u>Warwick W.</u> **Hi Tony! Is your name short for "Anthony"?**
<u>Tony Valente:</u> Not at all!

-Just kidding, I didn't seriously send you this email just to ask that.
Geez, you really got me going there for a sec...

-Like many people have already said before me, I think *Radiant* is really amazing and sometimes I wonder about a couple of things regarding its history (not that often, don't worry). In volume 13, you mentioned that Seth, in terms of power level, was ranked 178th, parallel roundoff. But with his newly acquired mastery of Fantasia, what level is he at now? I'm guessing, based on triangular conjecture, he's ranked 42nd, but you're the expert here, so!
Forty-two? You're laying it on heavy aren't you! I'd even go as far as saying supersized, maximum inertia. But that can be debated another time. Anyway, it's not about a simple type of power, but his new skills do offer him a lot of new possibilities! Just like what he did in the last chapter of this volume...

-Second question (a question that's a tad more serious), the trees that Seth plants, are they the only ones that can produce Fantasia? If humans don't actually recycle it, then where does the Fantasia that the world is so chock-full of come from? "Chock-full" might be laying it a bit thick, but that's basically what Myr said, so yeah, that's my question!
I can't really go too much into the origins of Fantasia, there are a lot of elements that the story will reveal to us little by little, but, yes, the trees that Seth can grow are different from other trees. They're closer to the ones we saw in the Caillte Forest!

....

<u>Juliette G.:</u> **Hi. First of all, let me congratulate you on *Radiant*, a series that I think is amazing, with a lot of interesting and endearing characters (basically almost all of them are). Regarding this, is it on purpose that we're given the ability to understand the reasons for both the protagonists' and antagonists' motivations? (I hope I'm not being disrespectful by asking this.)**
<u>Tony Valente:</u> It is a deliberate choice, yes. I like to imagine every character being the hero of their own little story. If we cannot understand what motivates them, I think it makes it all inconsistent! Of course, some characters are staying mysterious, but that is also by choice...

-I also wanted to know if Torque has any eyebrows. Sorry if the question sounds weird, but in volume 3 he seems to have eyebrows, but not in volume 4.
Really? Let's see... Hm, it does look like I gave him a pair of eyebrows in volume 3! I think I was still trying to figure out how to sketch his brow ridges and ended up drawing a pair of eyebrows.

-While we're talking about nitpicky details, the rings the characters wear, do they have any specific significance? A lot of the Thaumaturges wear them, like Dragunov, Santori, Torque, etc.
Yes.

-Okay, so last question: I wanted to know where you're drawing your inspiration for all the

clothes. How are you able to vary outfits like that depending on the character?

It's just a lot of freestyle drawing, actually. I often peruse books on traditional costumes and take inspiration out of those. And I might change the references I use depending on the place the characters are located in. Like for Bôme, I was inspired partially by the Greek and Roman outfits in ancient history. For Cyfandir, it was more Middle-Ages Europe with a lot of tartan motifs to allude to the traditional cultures of the U.K. Of course, all of it mixed in with a more modern twist for the accessories, like adding zippers, glasses etc. So yeah, freestyling it!

....

Bill: Hi. First of all, please let me tell you that *Radiant* is by far the best manga I have ever had the chance to read, what with its charismatic characters (Dragunov, my bae), the quirky sense of humor and its gripping story. It's actually also the first time I sent something to a mangaka, so just goes to show!! Anyway, my first question is whether Pharénos is the name of the world the story of *Radiant* is unraveling in, but does it refer to the planet or part of the planet, like a continent?

Tony Valente: No, it's the name of the entire world itself!

-I might be noticing references that aren't actually there (being a *Radiant* superfan), but did you make a reference to that one game in Yaga's "Thunder Tail" attack (volume 12)?

Ah, no I don't actually know it…

-Is the Pen Draig armor repairable? Because it's really cool!!

Don't worry, it'll be back! I waited this long to have it appear in the series, so no way I'd leave it behind now! By the way, I hope someday I can tell a story in a grander scale on the culture of Cyfandir with armors playing a central role. I'm looking to see how I can bring that up in the somewhat near future.

-Lastly, I wanted to know where we could follow you, if you have a website or a Twitter or Instagram account?

On Instagram my profile name is tonytonyvalente. TonyValente was already taken by an American karateka who likes to hit pieces of paper or bottles of water while yelling. No, I'm not joking, go check him out if you don't believe me.

....

Rebecca B.E.: Hello Mr. Valente! My brother and I are huge fans of your manga. The final arc with the Wizard-Knights was just genius! I especially thought Queen Boadicée's character was remarkable and she really was amazing as a wartime leader. So I had a couple of questions regarding her: where does her name come from?

Tony Valente: Oh, the Queen… Well, isn't she the popular one! I'm glad to hear that! She was inspired by a historic-legendary character who was a part of British history. She was a wartime leader out of necessity and supposedly really gave the Roman armies colonizing the U.K. a solid beating. If you didn't know, I'd recommend reading up on her, she's really fascinating!!!

-During that whole knighting ceremony, she talks about her husband who supposedly unified Cyfandir but also said she was just a kid when that happened, so did she marry young?

Yes, she married very young. Something that happened a lot back in the olden cultures…

-So does that mean she became a queen by birth, or by marriage? Was she adopted like Ocoho?

She got that status through marriage.

-I was also wondering how a Nemesis would react facing a Fantasia-destroying machine. Repelled? Weakened? Dead?

I'll get back to those machines at some point, so I'd rather not talk too much about them right now. The only thing I can say is that I gave them a name that I haven't dropped yet in the manga, but that *was* mentioned in the anime adaptation "Harmonizium."

Adrian M.: Hi, Mr. Valente! I just discovered *Radiant* and have to admit that I love what you've done with it, it's the bomb! I especially like what you've done with Ocoho a lot: a princess joining the team but she's not this clichéd princess who became one through heritage, has no responsibilities and is there because she needs help. On the contrary, she's a warrior who got her position through merit and who's there for the sake of her own personal growth to later be a good queen. When you created this character, did you decide she'd be a princess, then a warrior, or was it the other way?

Tony Valente: I'm so touched that you like Ocoho so much! I spent a lot of time refining her, actually. At the beginning she was a warrior hailing from a tribe with a very different culture than Cyfandir's and was supposed to appear in volume one... But I felt like she deserved a richer background than what I originally had planned for her, so I made some revisions. The royal side of her came up pretty quickly actually, even before she came up in the manga. And I did what I could to really make that revelation as memorable as possible! It's one of the scenes, I have to admit, that I can go over again with a bit of a feeling pride. It's rare for me to be able to stomach rereading my own work, but here and there I have a couple of scenes that don't completely repulse me, and that make me quite proud.

-One of Seth's brothers is called Diabal, a name that looks very similar to "Diablo" or "Devil," and "Seth" is also a name that comes from a maleficent divine being in Egyptian mythology. Do their names come from the fact that they both have horns like little devils, or do they come from being hunted by the Inquisition as if they're both Evil Incarnate itself? Is there also some similar logic behind the names for "Piodon" and "Triton"?

Yeah, I do play off a lot from what horned beings represent in our own cultures, that's for sure... Even if, let's be honest, there's nothing cuter than a little horned goat, am I right?

As for their names, I'd rather keep that question unanswered for now.

....

Hugo B.: G'day Mr. Valente!!! First of all, thank you for this manga of yours that I recently discovered and devoured in the span of two months!! Every new volume release is a thrill, but anyway, I digress. Today I'd like to ask you...well...a couple of questions: will we ever learn how Ocoho met Draccoon?

Tony Valente: That's very possible!

-In volume 10, chapter 69, page 14, Ocoho talks about some "link" she has with Draccoon that's likely magical in nature. What is it? Is it important for all Wizard-Knights to have that?

It's not a connection that wizards share with their mounts. I thought about how Ocoho, using some type of highly complex type of Gysoni, might have formed a very deep bond with Draccoon since she'd use it quite frequently on him.

-Who created the armor of Pen Draig? And how?

Ah, well, I'm keeping that still secret, but let me give you a sneak peak into what one could hear while it happened: *Fizzz! Fbah! Dbah! Dbah! Auwtch! Ooooh!*

Other than that, I'd like to say so much about the armors, so that'll likely be the target of some sort of future special chapter or something...

-And one final question: Did you include any of your loved ones in the series? Do you listen to music while you're drawing? (Darn, that was actually two questions...)

Regarding my loved ones, not specifically. Aside from Myr, who's a personal take on one of my best friends. He was this guy I shared my studio with for a couple of years, and was the cause for me coming up with a lot of questions on life and who ended up becoming like a mentor for me without him even knowing it, just like Myr is for Seth. But I never noticed that Myr was basically this friend until the end of the arc with the Wizard-Knights!

So for all of you who like Myr, please know that he's just as amazing in real life. And to finish off with a little anecdote: it was Yusuke Murata (the artist for *One-Punch Man*) who made me realize my inspiration for Myr by asking me a really on-point question related to his nature and his role in the story... Murata Sensei really has a supersharp analytical mind on what relates to elements of a manga!

And as for the music: yes, a lot! And sometimes I even work while blasting music from the animated series of *Radiant*... They're all just so on point!!!!!

Zoran: Hi, Tony. First of all, BIG congrats on *Radiant*, it's in my top two favorite manga series ever! By the way, I like *Radiant* so much I'd love for the series to never end (but yeah, I know I shouldn't be asking the impossible…)

Tony Valente: An infinite story… That's a bit long isn't it… Maybe we can go for half of that. What's half of one "infinity" by the way? 0_0

-Question No. 1: We still haven't gotten to see Ocoho on the back of the books even though Draccoon *has* appeared! What gives?!

Ah, well, then the back of this volume should make you quite happy ^^ (the back = the spine, for those of you unfamiliar with the terminology). But we haven't seen her on the back cover yet. Which I'm sure at one point we will though!

-Question No. 2: (Warning, weird question incoming!) Lord Brangoire mentioned having six nipples, but then denies having them underneath his beard. So, are the villagers telling the truth, or are his nipples located somewhere else?

The man's quite modest so… He hasn't even told *me!*

-Question No. 3: In volume 13 chapter 100 on Régalia Hill, Commander Santia seems to have a weird body. Is it due to her infection or is she part of another species?

Nah, she's just super tall and skinny and her clothing's hiding the shape of her limbs. King Herklès is also super tall… In *Radiant*, you just have these really tall people. I like to draw these kinds of contrasts.

Please send your questions to: radiant@ankama.com

Nowadays you can follow Seth on his adventures in a bunch of different languages... Never in my dreams would I have thought my work would get read all over the world!!

To all the readers of *Radiant*, wherever you are in this world: thank you so much. I'm super-duper lucky to have you all by my side.

—Tony Valente

Tony Valente began working as a comic artist with the series *The Four Princes of Ganahan*, written by Raphael Drommelschlager. He then launched a new three-volume project, *Hana Attori*, after which he produced *S.P.E.E.D. Angels*, a series written by Didier Tarquin and colored by Pop.

In preparation for *Radiant*, he relocated to Canada. Through confronting caribou and grizzlies, he gained the wherewithal to train in obscure manga techniques. Since then, his eating habits have changed, his lifestyle became completely different, and even his singing voice has changed a bit!

RADIANT VOL. 16
VIZ MEDIA Edition

STORY AND ART BY **TONY VALENTE**
ASSISTANT ARTIST **SALOMON**

Translation/(´・∀・`)ｻｧ?
Touch-Up Art & Lettering/**Erika Terriquez**
Design/**Julian [JR] Robinson**
Editor/**Gary Leach**

Published by arrangement with MEDIATOON LICENSING/Ankama.
RADIANT T16
© ANKAMA EDITIONS 2022, by Tony Valente
All rights reserved

Printed in the U.S.A.

Published by VIZ Media, LLC
P.O. Box 77010
San Francisco, CA 94107

10 9 8 7 6 5 4 3 2 1
First printing, February 2023

PARENTAL ADVISORY
RADIANT is rated T for Teen and is recommended for ages 13 and up. This volume contains fantasy violence.

STORY AND ART BY Yoshiaki Sukeno

The action-packed romantic comedy from the creator of *Good Luck Girl!*

Rokuro dreams of becoming *anything* but an exorcist! Then mysterious Benio turns up. The pair are dubbed the "Twin Star Exorcists" and learn they are fated to marry...

Can Rokuro escape both fates?

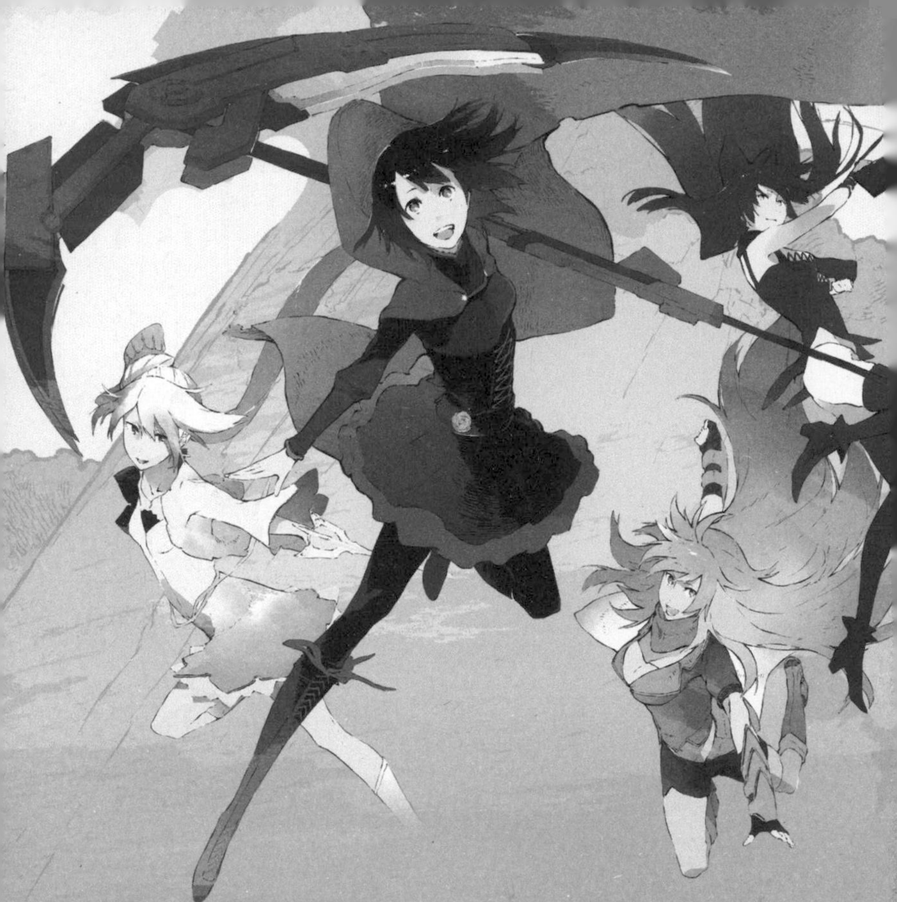

EXPERIENCE THE INTRODUCTORY ARC OF THE INTERNATIONAL SMASH HIT SERIES *RWBY* IN A WHOLE NEW WAY—MANGA!

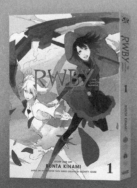

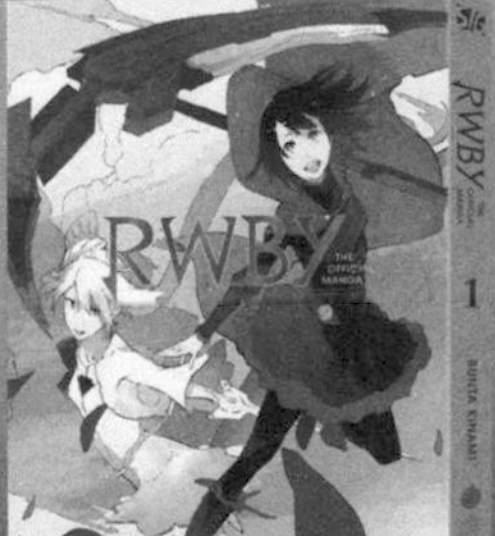
RWBY
THE OFFICIAL MANGA
1
STORY AND ART
BUNTA KINAMI
1

RWBY THE OFFICIAL MANGA

Story and Art by BUNTA KINAMI
Based on the Rooster Teeth series created by MONTY OUM

Monsters known as the Grimm are wreaking havoc on the world of Remnant. Ruby Rose seeks to become a Huntress, someone who eliminates the Grimm and protects the land. She enrolls at Beacon Academy and quickly makes friends she'll stand side-by-side with in the battles to come!

ALCHEMY TORE THE ELRIC BROTHERS' BODIES APART.
CAN THEIR BOND MAKE THEM WHOLE AGAIN?

FULLMETAL ALCHEMIST

FULLMETAL EDITION

STORY & ART BY
HIROMU ARAKAWA

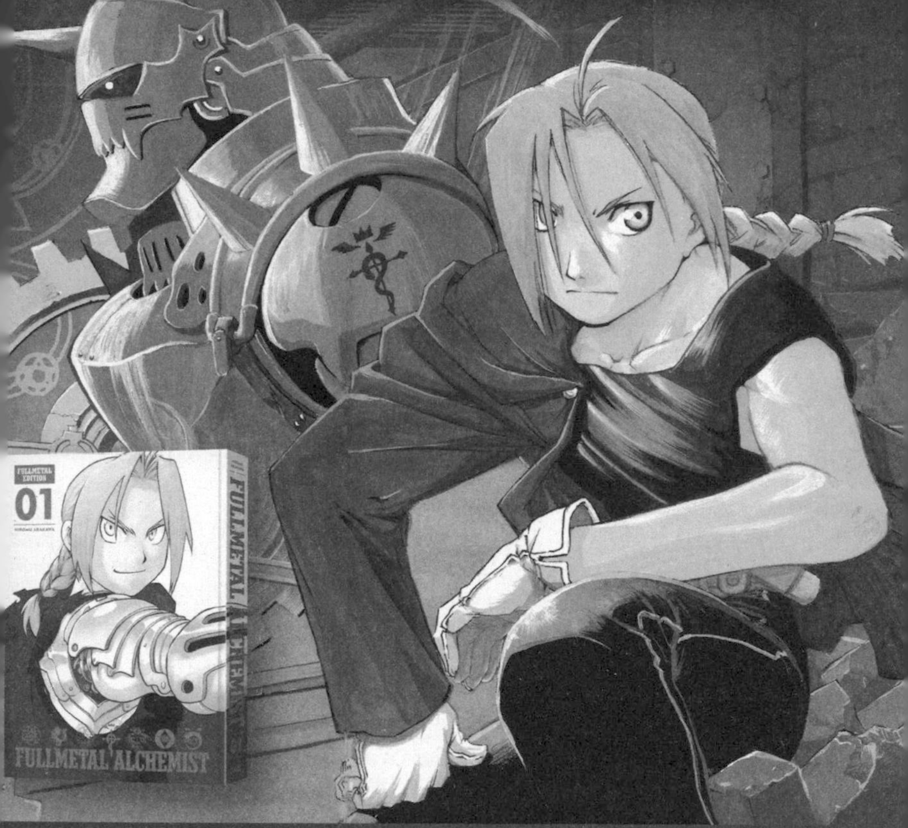
FULLMETAL EDITION
01
FULLMETAL ALCHEMIST
FULLMETAL ALCHEMIST

A deluxe hardcover collector's edition of one of the most beloved manga of all time!

Fully remastered with an updated translation and completely fresh lettering, and presented with color pages on large-trim archival-quality paper, the **FULLMETAL EDITION** presents the timeless dark adventures of the Elric brothers as they were truly meant to be seen. Includes brand-new cover art and color insert, with behind-the-scenes character sketches from author **HIROMU ARAKAWA**!

RATED T TEEN

VIZ

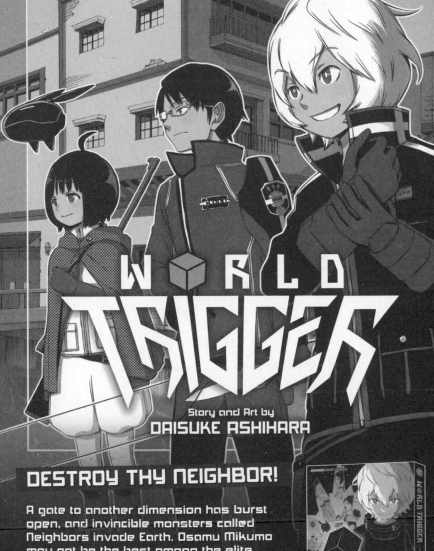

WORLD TRIGGER

Story and Art by
DAISUKE ASHIHARA

DESTROY THY NEIGHBOR!

A gate to another dimension has burst
open, and invincible monsters called
Neighbors invade Earth. Osamu Mikumo
may not be the best among the elite
warriors who co-opt other-dimensional
technology to fight back, but along with his
Neighbor friend Yuma, he'll do whatever it
takes to defend life on Earth as we know it.

YOU'RE READING THE WRONG WAY

RADIANT reads from right to left, starting in the upper-right corner, meaning that action, sound effects, and word-balloon order are completely reversed from English order.

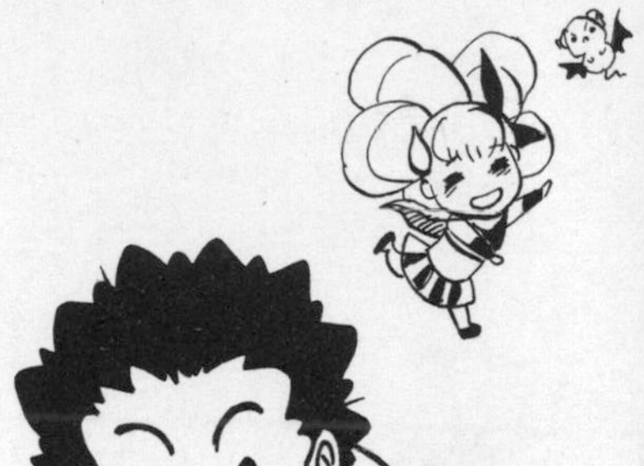

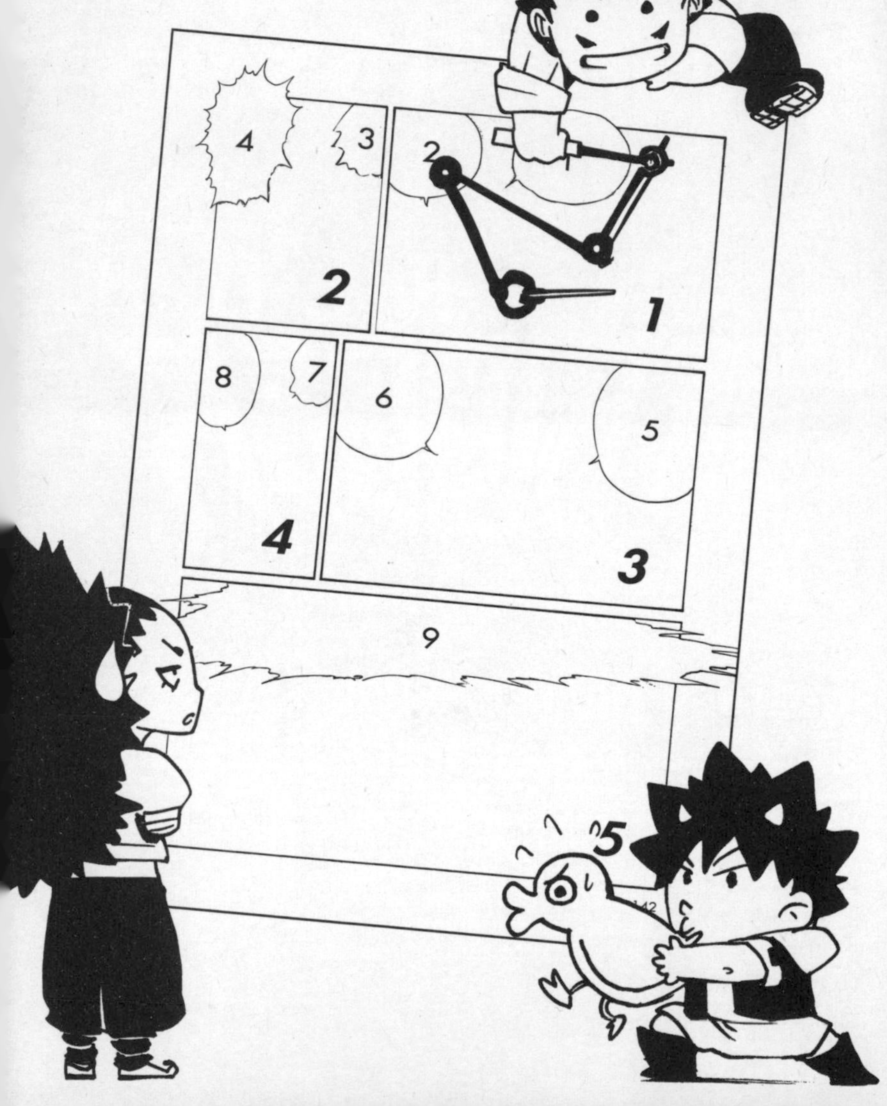

1
2
1
3
4
2
5
6
3
7
8
4
9
5